WENDY ELLIOTT

grít
AND
Grace
IN A
WORLD
GONE
MAD

HUMANITARIANISM
IN TALAS, TURKEY
1908 - 1923

Gomidas Institute
London

About the Author: Wendy Elliott, MEd, is a writer, designer and instructor. She is the author of a young adult novel, *The Dark Triumph of Daniel Sarkisyan*, won an award for her radio play, *Millennium Madness*, and has a passion for education, history and genealogy. Her interest in Armenia stems from four volunteer assignments she completed there in 2006-2009 for a Canadian international development organization. Wendy lives near Toronto and can be reached at *wendyelliott.ca*.

Cover Design: Wendy Elliott. Front cover photo: Susan Wealthy Orvis Papers; Back cover photo: Armenian Refugee Tents, Aintab, 24 June 1909, Bain News Service, US Library of Congress. Fonts: Bank Gothic, American UncD, Zurich Black, Vivaldi, Arial Narrow, Boycott (by Ryoichi Tsunekawa, Flat-it), and Adobe Garamond Pro.

ISBN 978-1-909382-44-2

For further details please contact:
Gomidas Institute
42 Blythe Rd.
London, W14 0HA
England
Email: *info@gomidas.org*
Web: *www.gomidas.org*

To all the front line humanitarian workers whose courageous actions help survivors survive, and to their financial, political and emotional supporters, who help keep them going.

CONTENTS

Part IV: A Time To Uproot

List of Maps

Foreword

I first met Wendy Elliott in 2009 in my native country of Armenia. I was working in Yerevan at the American organization, National Democratic Institute, when a colleague said, "Today's guest speaker for the Young Political Leaders' school is Wendy Elliott from Canada. Will you interpret for her?" I was happy to do so. I remember we introduced ourselves, exchanged smiles, and she handed me a small Canadian flag pin. Little did I know that only a few years later, I would end up in Canada as an immigrant with my wife Meri and our one-year-old daughter Mariam, and that Wendy and I would collaborate to make public the remarkable story of a small group of humanitarians who displayed true grit and amazing grace under fire.

In 2012, as I was trying to adapt to my new life, working and studying hard to become a part of Canadian society, I never stopped being connected with Armenia. I continued writing articles for *168 Hours*, an Armenian newspaper, and kept up to date on the issues affecting my homeland. In 2014 I attended the Genocide and Human Rights University Program offered jointly by Zoryan Institute and the University of Toronto. It gave me more knowledge and understanding of not only the Armenian genocide, but all genocides of the twentieth century and the phases leading up to them. One day I met a young woman from the Armenian community of Toronto who had read one of my articles. She told me she had met a couple at a local church whose great aunt had been a missionary in the Ottoman Empire and had saved 3,000 orphans. I was immediately interested, and visited Nancy and Eric Moore, who showed old pictures and told me about their aunt, Susan Wealthy Orvis. I wrote an article about this missionary and her heroic actions, and as I had become friends with Wendy after arriving in Canada, I asked her to help me to polish it. She did some extra research and considerable editing, so I offered her co-authorship. That article turned out to be the impetus for this book.

After the article was published in the Boston-based *Armenian Weekly*, I was contacted by Julia Ann Orvis, a great niece of Susan Wealthy Orvis. Julie had original archival material of the missionary in an old trunk, and asked if I would like to see it. Of course, my answer was yes! I was astounded to learn that Julie had contacted several scholars over the years, but no one had expressed any interest in these original documents. When I shared the news with Vahan Kololian, a successful Armenian-Canadian business man who was sponsoring a project for positive change in Armenia which I was working on, he was as excited by this news as I was, and graciously offered to share the travel costs to Wisconsin with me.

When I saw the trunk in Julie's house, I had goose bumps. What a treasure it was! It contained more than 450 letters, photographs and other documents, including an account of the orphans and how they ended up in orphanages. For me, an Armenian, it was like discovering a very important missing piece of my own history. On the outside of one of the envelopes Susan had written: "Very valuable. A record of the sufferings and faith and loyalty of Christians in Talas, Turkey during the World War 1914-1918. Keep this, S.W.O." For the next hundred years, Susan Wealthy Orvis' family had honoured her request. But now was the time to do something important with the material.

I spent the whole day and night photographing the archive, thinking about what to do with it. By the time I got home, I decided that Wendy would be the perfect person to turn it into a book. She had already written a book set in Armenia, a young adult novel about survivors of the Armenian genocide. She had self-published *The Dark Triumph of Daniel Sarkisyan*, and had done such thorough research for it that even I learned new things about Armenia from it, including many old names of streets in my own city of Yerevan! Most importantly, and above all, Wendy had the heart and soul to do it. In many ways, she reminded me of Susan Wealthy Orvis. Wendy had been an international development volunteer in Armenia, and one of her assignments was in Gyumri (formerly Alexandropol), Armenia's second largest city, where Susan had helped establish an orphanage and relief centre. Both Wendy and Susan had gone back to school in mid-career to earn a master's degree in education, Susan in religious education and Wendy in distance education. Susan taught elementary and high school pupils in Talas, and Wendy taught college students in Ontario. Both were strong, independent, caring women with an interest in making the world a better place. They even shared the same birthday!

Unfortunately, not even my relentless insistence that people should know this story could persuade Wendy to write it. She said she didn't have the same amount of passion as I, which would be necessary for the time and effort the project would require. But I had an ace up my sleeve. I had gone to Boston to obtain from Harvard's Houghton Library a copy of Susan's handwritten journal about her harrowing journey across Siberia during the Russian Revolution and her courageous work in Alexandropol. I urged Wendy to read "Through Russia 1917", convinced it would change her mind. It did. She was hooked by Susan's quirky personality, positive, down-to-earth attitude and amazing adventure. After four years of intensive research and writing, Wendy has woven the story of Susan and her brave Talas colleagues into the events of the last destructive years of the Ottoman Empire to produce this captivating book.

Grit and Grace in a World Gone Mad is the perfect title for a book about the highest values shown during the darkest times. Within a span of 15 years, a small group of American and Canadian missionaries and relief workers, part of a massive international humanitarian effort, saved thousands of Armenian, Greek and Turkish lives while the despotic leaders of the empire were dragging its people through two coups d'état, four regional wars, three genocides and a world war. It's a story that needed to be told to acknowledge and thank these brave people. It's also a story that needs to be read to understand how indifference to corruption, callousness to suffering, acceptance of fake news as fact, and demonization and fear of "the other" can lead to violence and ultimately to genocide. It's happening in our world today, and it will happen tomorrow unless we learn the lessons of history. *Grit and Grace in a World Gone Mad* is an important step towards that goal.

Kamo Mayilyan
Toronto and Yerevan, 2018

Grit and Grace in a World Gone Mad

An Important Word About the Words

This book is written in Canadian English, which is a hybrid of British (*labour* not *labor*) and American (*organization* not *organisation*). Additionally, quotations from Americans will contain American spelling, and British quotations British spelling. Since most place names were changed after 1923, I have chosen the most common name and spelling among the missionaries and relief workers for a place during the time period. For example, present-day Elâzığ was known variously as Kharpert, Harput, Harpout, and Harpoot; I use Harpoot for ease of pronunciation. Please refer to the Glossary for other seeming abnormalities or for finding present-day location names. I also use common spellings of the period, e.g., Talat for Tâlat.

Almost every paragraph contains small endnote numbers. If you are a scholar, you'll be delighted to find the source of the information in the Notes section. If you aren't, ignore them—unless you're one of those people who likes to read the occasional note that has more information. I ask strict scholars to kindly ignore long passages of dialogue not indented in the proper academic style, and any minor word or punctuation change I have used in dialogue that is sprinkled throughout the book. It has been done sparingly, and only in the interest of flow and readability. All the dialogue has been taken directly from the letters, journals and memoirs of the person "speaking."

Dates are written as Month Day, e.g., December 25, according to the Gregorian calendar, which we use today. This explains the change in dates by 13 days of some Russian or Ottoman events, which were recorded in the old Julian calendar. For instance, the Bolshevik Revolution is called the October Revolution, though it took place in November according to today's calendar.

In English the courtesy title of "Mister" comes before a name; in Turkish, titles such as Agha, Bey, Effendi and Pasha follow a name (or sometimes are in the middle, e.g., Dr. Nazim Bey Selanikli). Not all Turks used a surname back then.

The missionaries tended to use "Ottoman Empire" and "Turkey" interchangeably. When I refer to the Empire I mean the larger territory (see Map 3), of which Turkey is one part. The government of the day was the government of the Ottoman Empire. Missionaries also used the names "Turkey," "Asiatic Turkey," "Asia Minor" and "Anatolia" interchangeably. In fact, Anatolia is defined by geographers as the area roughly equivalent to the American Board's Western Turkey Mission (see Map 1). This geographical difference was understood at the time because the area east of Anatolia was often referred to as "eastern Anatolia." Though today the region is eastern Turkey, Armenians know it as "western Armenia" because it was the location of the six mostly-Armenian occupied vilayets of the Ottoman Empire, and is part of their traditional homeland. Similarly when they referred to the Caucasus they usually meant the Transcaucasus, roughly equivalent to today's Georgia, Armenia, and Azerbaijan.

Regarding the different Christian denominations, most missionaries and relief workers were Protestant (Congregationalists, Presbyterian, Anglican, etc.), though there were Roman Catholics and Friends (Quakers) among them. Most Greeks were Greek Orthodox, most Russians were Russian Orthodox, and most Armenians were members of the Eastern Apostolic Church, but were called Gregorians. However, it is important to know there were also Protestant and Roman Catholic Armenians and Greeks. Except for reference to the Dervishes, I do not distinguish between the various Muslim sects.

grít
AND
Grace
IN A
WORLD
GONE
MAD

Part I: A Time to Plant

Grit and Grace in a World Gone Mad

1

A New Breed

As revolutions go, the Young Turks' was short, sweet, and relatively bloodless. It lasted twenty-two days in July 1908. Only a few dozen officials and army officers died. Its purpose was not to overthrow the sultan, but to force him to restore the constitution of 1876, which guaranteed justice for all subjects of the Ottoman Empire, freedom of religion, and freedom of the press.[1] When news spread of the abolition of the sultan's vast espionage network, release of political prisoners, amnesty for political exiles, and most importantly, a restored constitution, a "carnival of joy" erupted throughout the Empire. "We are all brothers!" declared Ismail Enver, one of the revolutionaries. "Under the same blue sky, we are all proud to be Ottomans!"[2]

A young missionary in Constantinople wrote to her friends back home in the United States, "Last Sunday Turks, Christians and Jews in one wagon were seen embracing and congratulating one another. People can scarcely take time to sleep for their joy!"[3]

In Brousa a man who had been falsely accused of being a spy "made an impassioned speech, among other things, denouncing the spies and the spy system, in words of fire! Oh, the joy of uncurbed speech at last! As he stepped down into the crowd again, he exclaimed, 'I have lived for this hour!'"[4]

Susan Wealthy Orvis, an American missionary stationed in Talas, was on vacation when she heard the news. It was midnight as her boat approached Beirut. Fireworks lit up the sky. "The city was beautiful," she said. "The many lights in the houses, which are in terraces, reaching up from the shore and in a curve around the harbor, were more brilliant than usual that evening, for the city was celebrating the new constitution." She was surprised when she reached Jerusalem that there had been no celebration. The reason became clear two weeks later, when they started "putting up their flags. They have had to wait till the governor of the city would give permission,"[5] she added wryly.

The Young Turk revolutionaries proclaimed "Liberty, Justice, Equality and Fraternity, for all the races and religions of the empire, with equal rights and equal duties for all." George Washburn, American-born president of Constantinople's Robert College, had "no reason to doubt the honesty and sincerity" of the Young Turks, but he cautioned that lofty goals were one thing, and implementation quite another: "As we in

America proclaimed these principles in 1776, and have not yet been able to put them in force in all parts of our country, we may expect to wait some time before they can be fully carried out" in the Ottoman Empire.[6]

No one had to wait long before they saw which way the wind blew.

~ ~ ~

Susan Wealthy Orvis loved her name. She loved it almost as much as she loved God and her family. Sometimes she had to use her middle initial, but whenever possible, she used her full name. Even letters to her siblings were signed, "Your loving sister, Susan Wealthy Orvis." The love of her name was an extension of the love she felt for her grandmother, for whom she was named. She was very proud of her grandmother, Susan Wealthy White Orvis, who had graduated from Oberlin College in 1844.[7] At that time less than one percent of Americans were college graduates, and even fewer were women.[8] When Susan-the-younger left Dubuque, Iowa for Talas, a town in the middle of Turkey, in 1902 to become a missionary, she brought with her all her worldly goods. They included her grandmother's college diploma, as well as her own from Iowa State College (later Grinnell College). After all, it was expected that, except for returning home to the States every seven years for a one-year furlough,[9] she would remain in Turkey until she retired—or died, whichever came first.

Susan had thought seriously about becoming a missionary during her last year at college. She had joined the Student Volunteer Movement for Foreign Missions (SVM) and learned about missionary work conducted by the American Board of Commissioners for Foreign Missions (known as ABCFM, or simply, the American Board) in Africa, India, China, Japan and Turkey. ABCFM had been founded by Congregationalists, though now its missionaries belonged to various Protestant denominations, and was the largest Christian mission society in the Ottoman Empire. The once-mighty Empire was still fairly big, encompassing parts of northern Africa, Mesopotamia, the Balkans, Egypt (though Egypt was a *de facto* British protectorate), Lebanon, most of Syria, and all of Turkey (see Map 3). The land where St. Paul was born, where Noah's Ark landed, and where St. Basil lived, held enormous attraction for Susan.

ABCFM had four divisions in Turkey: Eastern, Central, Western (see Map 1) and "European" (the latter in the Balkans). Trying to convert Jews had proved to be a losing battle, so the mission in Jerusalem would soon close. Trying to convert Muslims was not advised. One could convert to Islam, but one could never leave. There was actually a death penalty for Muslim apostates, though by 1900 it was generally accepted that they would no longer be put to death.[10] That left as possible converts

Christians of other denominations: Roman Catholic, Greek Orthodox, Russian Orthodox, Armenian Gregorian (Apostolic), and Protestants of various ethnicities. There were an estimated 16 million Christians in Turkey,[11] certainly enough for the ABCFM to invest time, money and effort. And they had invested a considerable amount since 1819. In 1902, when Susan attended the annual SVM convention in Toronto, and made the decision to go to Turkey,[12] there were 172 missionaries in 18 stations responsible for 312 outstations, with 14,901 communicants in the four divisions.[13]

Though the common perception of a missionary was a "somber-garbed, psalm-singing, nasal-voiced, narrow-minded proselytizer,"[14] that was not true of Susan and her colleagues. She was part of a new breed. First, she was college-educated. In her case, she had had to work as a rural school teacher from age 16 to 25 before she could earn enough money to attend college, but she had graduated with the highest honours. She was also the daughter, niece and granddaughter of ministers, and a great granddaughter of deacons—all Congregationalists. In fact, she could trace all the branches of her family back to the Puritans who settled the Massachusetts Colony in the 1630s.[15] One group of Puritans were "strict Calvinists, who believed in predestination and a God who was an active participant in the daily life of earthly matters."[16] They were known as Congregationalists because of their conviction that the congregation should not answer to a central ecclesiastical authority, but rather govern itself.[17] They believed in the "priesthood of all believers,"[18] that is, that each person had the right to a personal interpretation of the principles of Christianity. Of course, to acquire a personal conviction, it was necessary to be able to read, and especially to be able to read the Bible in one's own language—an impossibility for most Greeks, Armenians, Assyrians or Catholics of the time. Catholic bibles were printed in Latin, which few lay people could read, and in most other denominations it was uncommon for anyone other than a priest to possess a bible.

Susan was unmarried. She was not conventionally pretty, but she was a handsome woman with a lovely smile. However, at 28 years old, it was statistically unlikely that she ever would become a wife, making her options as a woman in 1902 America very limited: live off the charity of relatives, or support herself as a teacher, nurse, office clerk or factory worker. Women could not vote, could not borrow money without the written consent of a male relative, and in most areas could not own property. The lure of living an independent life, travelling to foreign lands, and being somewhat of a celebrity—as missionaries were when they came home on furlough—was an attractive proposition. The American Board preferred to hire professional women in their late 20s-early 30s: mature enough to be responsible with a few years of occupational experience, but still young enough to be able to learn a new language.[19] If there were a checklist for candidates, Susan would have earned a perfect score.

She signed up, packed up, and went to New York to begin her journey. There she met Adelaide Dwight, who was also heading to Talas to teach at the Girls' School. Adelaide was five years younger and had a similar background, with a few minor exceptions: She had been born in Constantinople to missionary parents and had only two years' teaching experience after graduating from Smith College. They were joined by Rev. Henry and Jane Wingate, both 37, their two children, John and Dorothy, and Rev. Henry Harrison Riggs, known as Harry to his friends and family. The Wingate family had been on furlough in Wisconsin and were looking forward to returning to Talas. Henry had met Jane in 121890 when they were both teaching at the Marsovan station,[20] 200 miles north of Talas, and it had been a true Congregational-style romance. They had moved to Talas in 1893, and within five years, Henry had established the Boys' School with 70 pupils, 46 of whom were boarders.[21] Henry and Harry were both graduates of Carleton College, '96 and '97 respectively, though Henry had gone on to Yale Divinity, whereas Harry had just graduated from Auburn Seminary. Harry had been born in Sivas, also to missionary parents, and was about to begin his own mission work in Talas.

The group sailed on the *von Moltber* steamship to Hamburg in early September, and arrived in Talas a month later, via train from Berlin, Vienna and Budapest to Constantinople. They then proceeded via ship to Samsoun, and then in wagons to Marsovan and Cesarea.[22] Susan and Adelaide were delighted with the reception they received. "A hearty Oriental welcome," as Henry described it. "Nearly five hours before arriving at Cesarea, people began to meet us, and by the time we rode into the city there was a great cavalcade of horses, donkeys, wagons and people on foot."[23] Five miles away, and 4,500 feet above sea level was the mountain town of Talas. More and more people gathered along their path as they got closer. At Talas, "we passed through rows and rows of school children, marshaled out in double file," said Adelaide. "The boys clapped as we passed through their ranks, while the girls sang a song which they had learned for the occasion."[24]

"Every member of our station turned out," said Stella Loughridge, principal of the Talas Girls' Boarding School. "It was not an ordinary occasion, for were not *two* American ladies coming to the school?"[25]

School children gathered to welcome Adelaide Dwight on her return to Talas in 1909. SOURCE: Susan Wealthy Orvis Papers.

~ ~ ~

The Young Turks were a new breed then, too. But they were not a cohesive group. In fact, they were not even a political party. They were likely named after the Young Ottomans, the secret society of intellectuals who were instrumental in creating the first constitutional government three decades earlier.[26] After Sultan Abdul Aziz had been "suicided" in June 1876, and his nephew and successor, Murad V, proved mentally unstable a month later, Murad's brother, Abdul Hamid II, was proclaimed Sultan—but only after agreeing to accept the constitution and its parliament. In 1877, when the Russian Empire declared war on the Ottoman Empire, Hamid suspended parliament. The following year the Ottomans lost both the war and large portions of the empire, as determined by the Treaty of Berlin, with enormous input from Great Britain, France, Austria-Hungary, Italy, Germany and Russia. The result was independence for Romania, Serbia, and Montenegro; autonomy for Bulgaria; reforms for Bosnia and Herzegovina; and a considerable part of the Transcaucasus for Russia. Hamid immediately suspended the constitution. He ruled with an oppressive fist and a vast network of 100,000 spies for the next thirty years.[27] Not surprisingly, most of his subjects grew very unhappy.

From middle clockwise, Susan Wealthy Orvis (c1902), and (c1916-1918) Stella Nelson Loughridge, Jane Wingate (with two youngest sons), Henry K. Wingate, and Adelaide Susan Dwight. SOURCE: SWO, Susan Wealthy Orvis Papers. Other four missionaries: US Passport Applications.

In 1889 a group of students of the Imperial Medical School in Constantinople plotted to overthrow him. They were soon joined by students from the Veterinary, Artillery, and Engineering schools, and the Naval Academy. Despite the group's secrecy, the Sultan's spies managed to identify the culprits, who were arrested and expelled. The exiles, still committed to their cause, eventually regrouped in Paris to form the secret Society of Progress and Union.

Meanwhile in Constantinople another secret group was formed. There were not many career options for young, upper-class Ottomans except to join the military or civil service. Given the perpetual unrest in the Balkans, a large portion of the military was stationed in the European *vilayets* (provinces). They had a great deal of interaction with their European counterparts. The contrast was palpable in every way: pay, uniforms, equipment, authority, and regard. Many army officers appealed for reforms, but there were few improvements. A similar situation arose within the civil service. Constantinople straddles the Bosporus—the strait that separates Europe and Asia—and is the gateway for trade between the Black and Mediterranean Seas. Senior civil servants had considerable contact with international personnel and ideas. Their calls to bring the Empire into the 20th century were more or less ignored by the Sultan. As a consequence, a group of army officers and civil servants created the secret Ottoman Freedom Society.

Through a chance encounter in 1907, the Ottoman Freedom Society and the Society of Progress and Union became known to each other. Deciding they had a common goal, and would be more effective if they worked together, they merged to form the Committee of Union and Progress (CUP). Even so, it was clear from the start there were two distinct factions. Their seven-article declaration of intent outlined the structure of the new society: two headquarters and two chiefs ("internal" in Salonica, Macedonia, and "external" in Paris, France). Each was "empowered to modify one and another's operations only through persuasion." However, for the time being, they were all working together for a common purpose—to reinstate the constitution of 1876.[28]

There was one other significant group that supported the revolution: the Hay Heghapokhakan Dashnaktsutyun (Armenian Revolutionary Federation), or Dashnaks, for short. This political party was created in the Transcaucasus after the war with Russia. One of the conditions of the Treaty of Berlin was reformation of the provincial administration of the Ottoman Empire. For Armenians living in their traditional homeland east of Anatolia, this was an especially important issue. The Sultan had always viewed the Armenians who lived there as Russian allies, and therefore a threat to his territory. He had allowed, if not sanctioned, raids on them by their Kurdish and Circassian neighbours. Consequently, there was a vital need for Armenians to be protected by law, and to have legal equality for their language and customs. After the Treaty, this became known as "the Armenian question." In 1890, with no reforms in sight, the Dashnaks formed a socialist party from the merger of many small groups.[29] Between 1894 and 1897 Sultan Abdul Hamid stepped up his repression of Armenians, with impunity. More than 100,000 were killed during the Hamidian massacres,[30] including 25,000 Assyrians.[31] Though there was international outrage, there was no international interference. Thus, the bloody "Red Sultan,"[32] as he came to be known, suffered no serious consequences. Ten years later, there were still no reforms. It is no wonder that, when the Dashnaks caught wind of the Young Turks' plan, they whole-heartedly supported them. It was time for a revolution.

~ ~ ~

"All the windows have heavy iron bars, just like a prison," Susan wrote to her brother, John, about her new home in Talas. "We have a massive stone building that has been adapted to the needs of the school, though originally built for a private residence by a rich Armenian family." She described the large iron gates which opened onto the street and were "kept closed, night and day, only being opened to admit those who have answered the question, 'Who is it?' At first I could not enjoy living in such a fortress, but after I heard how all the missionaries and native [*yerli*][33]friends had spent the time in the building during the dreadful massacre times [eight years before], I appreciated the security of it."[34]

Talas was located in the *sanjak* (county/district) of Kaisarieh (see Map 2) in the middle of the ancient region of Cappadocia. It was a mountain town of 15,000 Armenians, Greeks and Turks,[35] nestled in the shadow of 10,000-foot Mt. Argæus, some fifteen miles away. Residents could not see the great mountain from their homes because there was a lesser one in-between. Or as one traveller of the time noted, "Ali Dagh intervenes, a hump of mountain like a vast pit-head heap, rising three thousand feet above the town."[36] An hour's walk down the hill and to the northwest was Cesarea, the bustling capital city of the sanjak.* The American Board had established a station in Cesarea in 1854 because it was the centre of commerce and society. Though picturesque with its flat roofed houses, tall minarets, round-domed mosques, baths, thirteen-acre market, imposing castle, and beautiful mountain view, it was also considerably larger (40,000), dirtier, and not as safe as Talas.[37] The missionaries preferred the clean mountain air and clean streets of Talas, and it soon became their base of operation. The Talas-Cesarea station was responsible for the largest of all ABCFM territories: 32 outstations scattered over the 35,000 square miles of the 800,000-strong sanjak.[38]

The station was a "fertile field to be cultivated,"[39] and they had toiled hard. The Boys' School was an excellent example. Situated atop a large

---

* The city and the sanjak had the same name, pronounced *kay-saria*, but spelled in various ways. (The Latin pronunciation of the Roman emperor Caesar is *kai-sar*, which is where the confusion lies.) To keep things simple, I will refer to the city as Cesarea, and the sanjak as Kaisarieh, which was used on local maps circa 1920. The ABCFM station was officially known as Cesarea, but informally as Talas. Again, for simplification, I will use Talas as the station's name.

The view of Talas from the Boys' School, with Ali Dagh rising on the left.
SOURCE: American Research Institute in Turkey and SALT Research.

hill, overlooking terraced gardens with "Ali Dagh's peak as a backdrop," this grand four-storey building was years in the making. When Henry Wingate started the school in 1898, it was little more than several dozen students in a couple of rented houses. Since then he had raised money in the United States, bought the property in Talas, obtained the necessary permits, and oversaw the construction of the majestic school. When it opened officially in 1908, it was "a visible testament to Henry's dedication and resolve."[40]

By then, Susan had settled into Talas very nicely. She had become fluent in Turkish, the official and common language of all Ottomans. She had seen much of the surrounding countryside while "touring" the outstations, and was acting principal of the Girls' Boarding School, now that Principal Stella Loughridge was away on a one-year furlough in Lincoln, Nebraska. Adelaide Dwight, who had accompanied Susan to Talas, proved to be quite fragile physically, but was a well loved teacher. Henry Wingate and Herbert Irwin, principal and teacher respectively of the Boys' Boarding School, were also ordained ministers and did much of the evangelical work. Their wives, Jane Wingate and Genevieve Irwin, conducted "women's work," which was just about anything else that needed doing. The Irwins were Canadian, as were ten percent of the ABCFM missionaries. Herbert was born in Port Hope, Ontario, and had graduated from the University of Toronto and Manitoba College. In 1903 he married Genevieve Du Val, also a graduate of Manitoba, and within a

(Top) The Talas Boys' School high on the hill, overlooking its terraced gardens and the town. *(Below)* The Boys' School with its long stone wall protecting part of the Mission's compound. SOURCE: American Research Institute in Turkey and SALT Research.

month they had joined the Talas mission. Genevieve was born in Wilmington, Delaware but had moved to Winnipeg at the age of twelve when her father, Rev. Frederic Du Val, a proponent of the Social Gospel movement, became the minister of Knox Presbyterian Church there.

Rev. James Fowle, from Woburn, Massachusetts, had been in Talas since 1878 when he met and married Caroline, daughter of Rev. Wilson A. Farnsworth of the Talas station. James was in charge of touring— driving his old wagon, often on a month's journey, from outstation to outstation, to administer to his flock. The hospital was run by two doctors, William Dodd, who had established it in 1893, and Wilfred Post, with their wives Mary Dodd and Annie Post, and two nurses, Rachel B. North and Emma Cushman. The kindergarten in Cesarea was usually operated by Fanny Burrage, but she was currently on furlough in her hometown of Arlington, Massachusetts.[41]

When news of the 1908 Young Turk revolution reached the Talas mission, everyone was happy to hear that the constitution had been restored with "little shedding of blood." The American Board rejoiced. As the commissioners saw it, "mission work, which has struggled on in the face of tireless opposition, will now be, in large measure, *free*."[42]

~ ~ ~

In July the revolution brought joy to the Empire. By August, the euphoria began to dissolve. The harvest failure—a repeat of the previous year—reduced grain supplies yet again. Recent harsh winters and dry summers had reduced livestock, resulting in a sharp rise in meat prices. A financial crisis in 1907, caused by American banks, negatively affected the global economy. Real income had steadily eroded while the cost of living steadily rose.

The port workers in Constantinople were the first to take action. They held a massive strike, which threatened to disrupt waterfront commerce,[43] especially for the British- and French-owned Quay Company.[44] It was a test for the Young Turk government. "Their movement had been represented by their enemies as anarchical; their cause would be lost were they to fail to preserve order among the populace." Their solution was to send in the cavalry. One officer told the strikers they were conducting themselves as "friends of the old regime" would have. He warned that if they were not back at work the next day, just like the police of the previous era, "I will, with my own hand, shoot down the first man who refuses to do so, and the rest of you will be swept into the sea or into prison." They went back to work, though some were later arrested.[45]

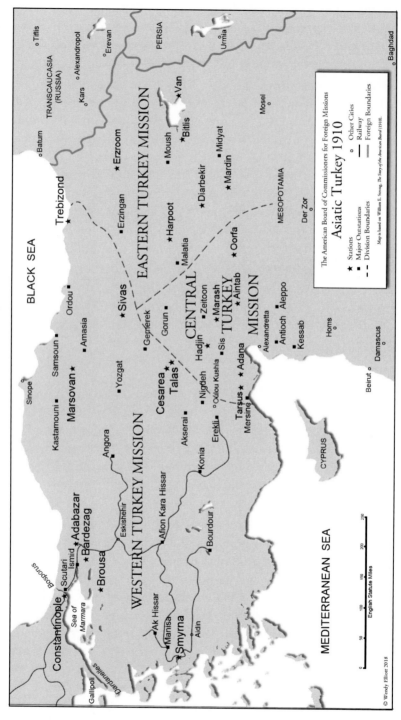

Map 1

The busy port of Constantinople in the Sea of Marmora and the Bosporus strait.
SOURCE: US Library of Congress.

In September rail workers went on strike. They had formed a loose union in August, and sent a telegram to the Grand Vizier (prime minister), demanding the dismissal of the director-general of the German-owned Anatolian Railway Company "to end the deplorable, despotic, tyrannical, humiliating and arbitrary doings which have gone on for nineteen years." Even though many Young Turks sympathized with the workers' grievances, they could not afford the disruption to the vital transportation and communication systems of the Empire. There was also considerable pressure from Deutsche Bank, an investor in both the railway and the Ottoman economy, to end the strike. The government's attorney made a back-to-work deal with the union's president. One of the unfortunate consequences was "the Muslim Turkish workers . . . considered that the Ottoman Christian union leadership had abandoned them in favor of their European and Christian employers."[46] Cracks in the "we are all Ottomans" claim began to expand.

The end of joy came definitively in October. The Empire shrank once again. Austria-Hungary annexed Bosnia-Herzegovina, Bulgaria declared its independence, and Crete announced its union with Greece. Rising nationalism and unrest had been evident in the Balkans for many years, but the new Ottoman government was reluctant to go to war. The public was furious over the loss of territory, reacting with spontaneous demonstrations, marches, and "a new form of protest: the boycott." The Committee of Union and Progress supported this boycott against Austrian and Bulgarian goods and services, largely because it kept the focus away from the government.[47] Only three months old, CUP faced serious problems. The internal squabbles were mainly over how to govern, since most of the Committee members had little experience. The external ones were obvious: a failing economy, a possible famine, a probable war.

What had started out so promising seemed to be rapidly spiralling downward. In Talas, Susan and her colleagues were committed to saving souls; if war were to occur, they just might end up having to save lives.

2

In Sickness and in Health

The goal of ABCFM missionaries was nothing less than to change the world. Their chief officer, Corresponding Secretary Dr. James Levi Barton, explained how they would do it: "Correct thinking and right beliefs are the dominant forces that rule men and nations. These constitute the only realm in which great and fundamental conquests can be won. They are the only realm to which we may appeal in our endeavor to change the life of the world."[1] For the missionaries, correct thinking and right beliefs were based on Protestantism, science, and good old American know-how.

The slogan of the Student Volunteer Movement was "Evangelization of the world in this generation."[2] But evangelism had changed considerably since the days of "a man in civilized garb preaching to savages, at least half naked, from an open Bible." The modern missionary engaged in a variety of work. For example, Rev. Fredrick W. MacCallum of Warwick, Ontario, lately of the Marash station, was an ordained minister, but he also acted as a fundraiser and a superintendent in the construction of a bridge between Zeitoon and Alabash. For five months each year, local residents were unable to cross the swollen, swift-moving River Gureddin to conduct their business. Fred saw an opportunity to relieve their extreme poverty. He appealed to Lady Cavendish, President of the English society Friends of Armenia, for funds. The society sent $1,144. He bought materials and, much to their gratitude, used $880 to hire local workers to build a bridge.[3]

Modern missionaries had been heavily influenced by the Social Gospel movement, which applied Christian ethics to social justice issues. Late nineteenth-early twentieth century industrialization, immigration, and migration to urban centres had produced great wealth in North America, but had also caused a great deal of poverty, inadequate housing and slums, alcoholism, unsafe working conditions in factories, and a faltering education system. Social Gospel reforms were based on the belief "that people were not inherently evil or depraved but were conditioned by their surrounding environment. Improve the environment, and you improve the person, which in turn would open the way to Christ."[4] After Darwin there had also been a shift in Protestantism in Western society from a literal interpretation of the Bible to one of ethical guidance. The result of these influences was a firm belief that the best way to evangelize the world

A girls' gymnastics class in Talas. SOURCE: Susan Wealthy Orvis Papers.

was through education, health care, and leading by example. For the young, single women missionaries, who were directly employed by the ABCFM-affiliated Woman's Board of Missions, the objective included ending the oppression of women. They saw the education of women and girls as the most efficient way to improve the home and community environment, daily hygiene as the prerequisite to good health, and both as the gateway to living a more spiritual life.[5]

Following this ethos, by 1908-09 the Talas station consisted of the boys' boarding school (76 boys, including 37 boarders), the girls' boarding school (134 girls, 51 as boarders), a kindergarten with 30 children, and a 40-bed hospital and dispensary. There was also a kindergarten in Cesarea with another 50 children. The classrooms were modelled after American schools of the day, with blackboards, desks, and rows of busy students, all quiet and orderly. The curriculum was fashioned after the standard American version, including gymnastics and music, but with a few exceptions: There were daily Bible lessons, most of the subjects were taught in Turkish, and the other languages taught were Greek, Armenian and English.[6] In the early years (1901-1904) when Stella, Susan, Adelaide and Herbert arrived and began to study Turkish, much of the early teaching was left to the relatively untrained native teachers. This was problematic, so the American Board instigated language examinations for missionaries starting in 1904. Though they acknowledged their importance, as Stella noted, studying for the exams made them nervous "companions in misery."[7]

In both Talas and Cesarea there were Young Men's Christian Association (YMCA) clubs with a total membership of 300. In the reading rooms, the boys and young men participated in gymnastics, study, and Bible instruction. Most of the regular attendees in Cesarea were Muslims, a fact that surprised and delighted the missionaries who were waiting for the day when these young men would "see the light." The schools, hospital and church also had a Christian Endeavor Society,[8] a youth-led group with weekly devotional meetings.

Because the territory of the Talas mission was twice the size of Switzerland (see Map 2), Rev. James Fowle spent many days in his old wagon visiting the 32 outstations. In 1909 he toured for 1,634 miles in 111 days. One of the most important aspects of the touring program was the Bible woman, a term given to a native employee of a mission who was a travelling evangelist. She would go door-to-door, visiting women in their homes, "repeating portions of Scripture, or reading the Bible, singing hymns, praying, telling her own personal experience of God's goodness." The Bible women received a few weeks or months of training in Bible reading and church history and geography, but were also given lessons in physiology, health and hygiene, homemaking, sewing, and even astronomy to help dispel any superstitions the residents might have.[9] These women were indispensable to the work of the mission. They were also cheap, with a salary of "less than one seventh of that of an American woman missionary,"[10] which in Talas was $93 per year.[11]

One of the guiding principles of the mission was that the recipients of education and health care should pay for the benefits. The reasoning was that payment would reinforce the value of the service. Mission hospitals in the Ottoman Empire were established only with great bureaucratic difficulty, and on the understanding they were charitable institutions. Certainly wealthy people could pay fees for visits and operations, but accepting only wealthy patients was contrary to the mission's purpose. Therefore, it was common practice to treat all patients, and charge them based on their ability to pay. For example, in 1906 of the 342 patients in the Talas Hospital, 95 received free treatment, 104 made partial payment, and 143 paid in full.[12] A Turkish official who was restored to health after a knee re-section said, "It is not what I have paid that makes them care for me this way. This man beside me paid nothing and is cared for just as well. In any other place I would have been put out long ago. There is love here, and such love as I never heard of elsewhere."[13]

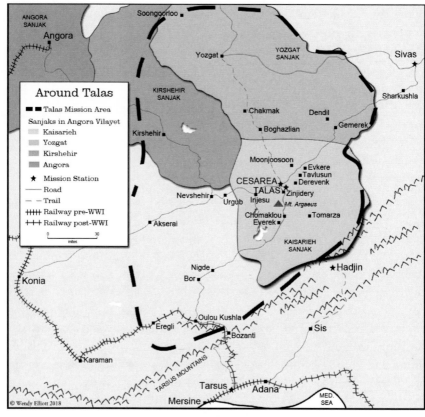

Map 2

Similarly, parents were expected to pay their children's tuition, though some students were accepted on scholarship. Stella had refused admittance to a very desirable girl because her father refused to pay what the school "felt sure he could pay. He kept his daughter away for three weeks but finally succumbed." The process was not easy for her. "It is a principle in this country to pay always less for a thing than is asked," she said. "We often say that if it were not for the wrong principle involved, we would do well to ask a lira or two above what we expect to receive. We would get the proper amount then without half the wear and tear of bargaining. . . . Sometimes I fear I am getting to think too much of money, but I know that giving help where it is not needed never does any good, but often harms, and at the same time deprives other girls of help, which they sadly need. When I feel like weakening, I always think of that."[14]

～ ～ ～

Money was also a major concern for the Young Turks. In fact, the Empire's dismal economic situation was one of the reasons many of the younger members of the elite had supported the revolution.[15] They were intent on moving into the 20th century. Wars and the lavish lifestyle of previous sultans had been expensive. Sultan Abdul Aziz, in particular, was "wildly extravagant" in his construction of palaces.[16] Though the sultan owned all the land in the empire and the peasants rented it by paying taxes, the income was not enough to cover his costs. Further complicating matters, foreigners who lived and conducted business there operated under treaties, from the 16th century onward, called "capitulations." Initially designed to promote free trade, they ended up restricting industrial expansion, impeding resource development, and preventing the government from setting appropriate customs duties. Ottoman businesses paid a 10% custom tax for foreign trade and 2.5% for internal trade; in contrast, resident foreigners paid a flat 5% for exports and imports. Naturally, these foreigners, including the American Board, benefitted financially from the capitulations and did not want to see them gone.

In the late 19th century, the government had exhausted its domestic sources for borrowing, and had borrowed from European banks fifteen times in twenty years. It had defaulted on its loans at least once. By 1881, not trusting the Imperial Ottoman Bank to honour the Empire's foreign debt, European creditors forced the creation of the Ottoman Public Debt Administration (OPDA). Thereafter, certain revenues (e.g., tobacco, salt, silk, fisheries, fiscal stamps, spirits and wines) were automatically ceded to the OPDA to pay down the debt.[17] In 1910-11 the total foreign debt was approximately £T 112 million.* The gross revenue collected by the OPDA was £T 4.7 million, and the amount required for the payment of the debt's interest was £T 5.2 million. In other words, there was a shortfall of almost half a million £T.[18]

Although Turkey was rich in resources, it was also a land of extreme poverty evidenced by hillsides denuded of timber, undeveloped government-owned mines, crops raised by primitive irrigation methods, and antiquated farming techniques commonly used in the time of Abraham. Though there was a good telegraph system, there were only a few small telephone systems, such as within the missionary compound in Marsovan or connecting a few government offices in Constantinople. The post office was so badly run that foreign governments operated their own postal systems within the country.[19] Modern transportation was limited to

---

* Turkish lira (as written on a typewriter of the time)

a few decent roads along the coasts, and main railway lines in the western and coastal areas. Most roads were in terrible shape. A visitor to Talas described the route from Sivas as an ancient sunken highway: "Each hollow way is roughly an inverted semicircle in section. In the bottom are always two deep, narrow, parallel channels, formed by the wheels of vehicles. Between them is a blunt ridge with a shallow depression along the middle—beaten out by the feet of men and animals. Because wheels cut faster than feet, the wheel tracks sink in time till axles strike the central ridge, and the road becomes impassable to vehicles."[20] Every few seasons, bridges would be washed away, making the crossing of a river almost impossible. ABCFM Secretary Barton remarked that the poor conditions in the interior required "the transportation of all freight by horse or camel, thus discouraging commerce and trade, increasing the price of imports, and making export practically impossible." It also explained "why a famine may prevail in one part of the country when at the same time, less than three hundred miles away, the crops are abundant." Consequently, the Ottoman Empire was seen by foreigners as backward and financially inept. In fact, the Empire was widely known for the last few decades as the Sick Man of Europe.[21]

The boycott against Austrian goods, which had begun after the annexation of Bosnia-Herzegovina, was still strong in the winter of 1908-09, but the Ottoman press condemned any sort of aggression towards customers, such as obstructing people from entering shops, or booing and shouting at them as they left. It was fine to write anti-Austrian articles or hang posters, but aggressive acts were "meaningless, unnecessary and excessive and 'charlatanry'." How much better it would be, they said, to concentrate on an "economic awakening" for the Ottoman Empire—to construct a native industry, abolish the capitulations, and develop the economy for Ottoman subjects.[22] Reformers were calling for a comprehensive program to make this happen.

Heading into the spring of 1909, the economic outlook was not encouraging. "Wheat is five times what it was five years ago," said Rev. Ernest Partridge, on returning to his post in Sivas from the Black Sea. On the way he had passed countless carcasses of horses which had died because of the high price of grain. "The day laborer's wage in Sivas is one-third what is paid in Constantinople, while the price of bread is higher, and work hard to find."[23]

~ ~ ~

Every year the four ABCFM divisions of Turkey held their own annual general meetings (AGMs). As was the custom, representatives from each station, and native preachers and teachers from their outstations who spoke English, all travelled to a central location for the meeting. Central Turkey's AGM was usually held in April, and in 1909 its location was Adana. In early April, 9 pastors, 12 unordained preachers and six other delegates set out to Adana from 20 towns and villages in the Cilicia region.[24] They never made it. Circumstances in far off Constantinople set off a chain of events that had a profound effect on the rest of Turkey.

On April 3 a group of religious extremists formed the Muhammadan Union, and produced propaganda materials against the policies and secularism of the Young Turks. On April 6 Hasan Fehmi, editor of *Serbesti*, a newspaper that frequently expressed negative views of the Young Turks, was murdered. It was rumoured that a faction of the Committee of Union and Progress was behind it.[25] The next day, anger against the ruling party turned his funeral into a mass demonstration.[26] On April 10, Ali Kemal, a journalist and liberal reformer,[27] wrote a column in *İkdam* against the government. He and seven others were rounded up. Ali Kemal escaped, and fled to England; the others were hanged.[28] On April 12 a Macedonian battalion brought to the city the previous week "to replace the supposedly less reliable Arab and Albanian contingents, mutinied, taking their officers prisoner. The next morning, together with a large number of *softas* (students from the religious schools), they marched to the parliament building," where they were joined by more dissatisfied troops. Among their demands were the dismissal of the Grand Vizier and other government officials, amnesty for the rebels, and the restoration of the *sheriat* (Islamic law). The latter demand was strange because sheriat "had never been abolished and continued to hold sway in the field of family law." Fearing for their safety, the Young Turks, who held the majority in the Chamber of Deputies, either left the city or went underground.[29] On the same day, three *hodjas* (Muslim teachers or scholars) arrived at Konia, and began preaching in the mosques, urging people to make a *jihad* (holy war) against Christians.[30] There were calls for a jihad in Cilicia and other areas of Turkey, too.

On April 14 Christians were attacked en masse in Cilicia. It was totally unexpected. When British Vice-Consul Major Charles Doughty-Wylie heard of attacks against Armenians in Adana, the region's largest city, he took the next train from his station in Mersine. "So little had I expected that any massacre was imminent that I took my wife with me," he said. "I saw several men killed on the way, and the town was full of a howling mob looting the shops." Gunfire was everywhere.[31]

The panoramic skyline of Adana in 1903, showing (*l to r*) the Mission residence, the steeple of the Gregorian Church, the Armenian Catholic School, and the steeple of the Protestant Church—all destroyed in April 1909. SOURCE: American Research Institute in Turkey and SALT Research.

Four bullets ripped through the house of Rev. W. Nesbitt Chambers, the 55-year-old Canadian who headed the Adana station. They just missed his wife, Cornelia, and his nephew, Lawson. A visiting Armenian was badly wounded. Nesbitt saw almost 2,000 refugees crowd into the local Armenian boys' school before it was fired on, and then set ablaze. People fled for their lives. For more than two weeks the scene was repeated for every large building that was used as a refuge: the Jesuit college, the Gregorian and Protestant churches, the American Mission House, the American Seminary for Girls, and the French Catholic School for Girls. All burned to the ground.[32]

In the midst of the massacres Nesbitt and Lawson appealed to the *vali* (governor), Djevad Bey, to contain the violence, but he "sat still and allowed the populace to shoot and burn as they pleased." It took several days before Vice-Consul Doughty-Wylie was finally able to force the vali and the commandant, Remzi Pasha, to order troops to restore order. Even then they were so passive he had to lead the detachment himself. When he was wounded, Lawson temporarily took his place.[33] Once he was patched up, "with arm in sling and coat buttoned across his breast," Doughty-Wylie continued to lead until at last the massacres ended.[34] By April 24 the Young Turks had managed to organize an armed resistance in Constantinople and re-take the capital.[35] The next day they sent a contingent to Adana.[36] By month's end, the region was finally calm, though martial law had been instituted throughout the entire country.[37]

While 3,000 to 5,000 Christians and almost 2,000 Muslims lost their lives in Adana, an estimated 25,000 Christians died in the Cilicia region, including the 27 Armenian delegates who were on their way to the AGM.[38] Nesbitt Chambers had tried to help Armenian preacher Hovagim Effendi cross the street, but he was attacked and died in his arms.[39] Two

The "smoldering heap of ruins" of Adana, 1909. SOURCE: Bain News Service, Adana, Turkey, 1909, US Library of Congress.

missionaries in Hadjin, D. Miner Rogers of the American Board, and Henry Maurer of the Mennonite Mission, were also killed.[40] Whole villages were wiped out. Some Christians were forced to convert to Islam on pain of death, and "in many cases, women and children were carried off for slaves."[41]

What followed was an enormous need for relief and food rations. In one day an estimated 22,000 people were fed in Adana alone.[42] Nesbitt felt overwhelmed. "A weary procession of thousands of people, men, women, and children. Some carrying a few articles they had been able to seize; men hunting for wives and children; women, knowing that their men had been killed, looking for children, children looking for parents— the saddest sight I have ever seen," he said. "The city lies before us a smoldering heap of ruins. A sad, sad sight."[43]

˜ ˜ ˜

Herbert Irwin and the other Talas missionaries were confused by the incoming reports. "We knew something serious was happening in Adana and district, but we were ignorant of what it was."[44] Another thing they did not know was that riots and massacres had been planned for Talas and Cesarea, too. Murderous attempts in Kaisarieh had been quickly put down by "the decided and energetic action of the *mutesarrif* (governor of the sanjak)," said Sir William Ramsay. Ramsay was working in the region at the time, collaborating with fellow archeologist Gertrude Bell on a book about the ancient ruins near Konia. "But that an organised scheme of massacre had been planned at some centre, and systematically preached by agents, who either had or pretended to have a religious character as hodjas and dressed accordingly, is beyond dispute. Whether it was with or without the cognisance of the old Sultan no proof can be discovered."[45]

Despite the call for a jihad in Konia, Christians had been saved there, not by the vali, who had "shut himself up in his house for six days, pleading illness," but by three level-headed men: an Armenian dragoman (professional interpreter), an Albanian soldier, and the Sheikh of the Mevlevi (an order of Sunni Muslims, known then as the Whirling Dervishes). The dragoman was in constant touch by telegraph with his employer, the British Consul, who happened to be in Mersine at the time, and who instructed him to "receive every refugee" who wanted to enter the British compound. The young Armenian opened the gates. The Albanian, who had been an exile of Abdul Hamid before the revolution, and Sheikh Abdulhalim Celebi, one of the most respected persons in Turkey and known for his broadminded views, calmed the excited crowds, and advised them "not to attack their Christian brothers." These three helped to avoid a major catastrophe.[46]

In Aintab Rev. Fred F. Goodsell reported that the bloody head of a Muslim had been thrown into the Armenian quarter, and for several hours, "the city was on the brink of a massacre." Agha Ahmed, a local Muslim leader, worked tirelessly with the *kaimakam* (district governor) to uncover the facts. They soon discovered that a Turk "had killed a brother Muslim, evidently with the intention of creating difficulty between the races." Once they made their findings public, the tension abated.[47]

In the weeks that followed the government voted to provide $150,000 in relief funds, but that money would be "slow in reaching its destination, whereas the American Board treasury could forward from [the United States] to the centers of need" $50,000 almost immediately.[48] Missionaries from all over Turkey, including Herbert and Genevieve Irwin, trekked to Cilicia to help. Even though they were glad to provide assistance, they were well aware of the dangers.[49]

The relief effort required intensive weeks of work to establish orphanages for fatherless children, and what they called "industries," such as weaving and sewing shops, to provide employment for the (mainly) women who had survived. They also tried to rescue women and girls who had been captured by mountain nomads—about 400 from Adana alone— though it was considered a losing endeavour. Local authorities had no power to inspect women or interfere in the family life of Muslims. Ramsay

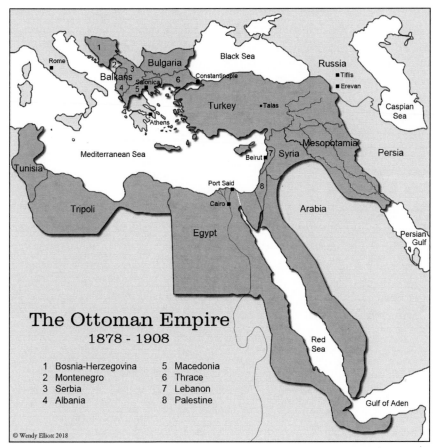

The Ottoman Empire
1878 - 1908

1 Bosnia-Herzegovina   5 Macedonia
2 Montenegro   6 Thrace
3 Serbia   7 Lebanon
4 Albania   8 Palestine

© Wendy Elliott 2018

Map 3

found complaints against their inaction unjustified. "The nomads would have killed their prisoners rather than admit their fault," he said. "And it was impossible to detect a girl here and there among the tents, dressed like others, and terrorised into silence."[50]

In the weeks and months that followed, the Young Turks made many changes. Though it was never proven that the sultan had been behind the coup and the massacres, Abdul Hamid was deposed and transported to Salonica. His brother, Mahomet V, was proclaimed his successor.[51] Courts-martial and local trials resulted in the execution of 124 Muslims for the events in Adana. Seven Armenians were also executed in an apparent attempt to appease angry local Muslims.[52] The Turk who had tried to start a massacre in Aintab was publicly hanged.[53] Djevad Bey, now the ex-vali of Adana, was sentenced to six years' exclusion from public service, and Remzi Pasha, the military commandant, to three years' imprisonment.[54] None of the decisions felt like justice to anyone, including the new Minister of the Interior, Mehmet Talat, who bluntly told American diplomat Lewis Einstein that he had wanted Djevad to hang "for allowing the murder" of all those people.[55]

As is common after an internal attack in a country, the government reacted by imposing restrictions on public conduct. There was a new law on "vagrants and suspicious persons" which restricted individual freedoms, a law making all male Ottoman subjects—Muslims, Christians and Jews—eligible for military service, a law restricting the freedom of the press, a law on public gatherings to limit meetings and demonstrations, and a law of associations, making political organizations "that bore the names of national groups" illegal.[56] Within the loose coalition of Young Turks, the Committee of Union and Progress began to gain more power, and Talat began to emerge as one of its leaders.

3

Squabbles, Rifts and Splits

Talat Bey, the new Minister of the Interior, was very proud of his humble beginnings in Adrianople in European Turkey. Gossip suggested he was a Pomak—a man of Bulgarian ancestry whose family had long ago converted to Islam—but he was not in any way religious. "I hate all priests, rabbis, and hodjas," he once proclaimed.[1] As a young man, Talat had been a letter carrier, and then a telegrapher. He had worked his way up to Chief Secretary of Posts and Telegraphs in Salonica.[2] It was in this position that he had been introduced to what eventually became the Committee of Union and Progress. Even though he was now a politician, he liked to keep up his skill. "His most cherished possession was the telegraph instrument with which he had once earned his living."[3] He even "had a special private telegraphic line run to his house from which he ran his communications."[4] He was powerfully built, rather like a boxer with a "huge sweeping back, . . . rocky biceps, . . . and wrists twice the size of an ordinary man's."[5] His frame matched his forceful personality, quick mental agility, and large appetite. He was known to "devour a pound of caviar at a sitting, washed down by two glasses of brandy and two bottles of champagne."[6]

In some ways, Talat enjoyed a good measure of popularity. He was very genial, with a mercurial sense of humour, a refreshingly frank manner of speaking, and "a certain willingness to oblige in personal matters."[7] But he also possessed a fierce determination to achieve his goals, and "an almost superhuman insight into men's motives."[8] Diplomat Lewis Einstein, who quite liked him in the early days, noted that Talat's "lack of education and real ignorance are concealed under a cloak of cynicism, and he has fine Oriental contempt for those who seek to propitiate him."[9]

Before the revolution Talat had believed in the possibility of creating a democracy in the Ottoman Empire, and the first cabinet of the Young Turks reflected that. It had consisted of "an Arab-Christian, a Deunme (a Jew by race, but a Muslim by religion), a Circassian, an Armenian, and an Egyptian."[10] But as opposition mounted from the army, softas, foreign governments, debt collectors, fellow politicians, boycotters, and various other factions, he and his fellow party members were finding it difficult to govern. The ABCFM's description of the new constitutional government was succinct and accurate: "beset by enemies within and without, plagued by their own mistakes, and hampered on every hand by distrust or deceit."[11] From late 1910 onward the situation was so often critical that one editorial said, "A crisis seems to be almost the normal condition in that seething empire."[12]

As an example, in 1908 Crete had declared its union with Greece, though it had been part of the Ottoman Empire for centuries. Many port workers and low-ranking bureaucrats were irate over this news, and proposed an anti-Greek boycott. Fortunately for the Young Turks, who "did not want to risk the newly created atmosphere of fraternity," Greece vetoed the union. A boycott did not occur. However, by 1910, the boycott movement was revived. This time it was organized against Greek merchants doing business in port cities, such as Constantinople and Trebizond. The problem was that it negatively affected Ottoman Greeks, too, "since both groups had profound and intimate relationships. The debates on the definition of Greekness bred tension between the Muslim and Orthodox communities, and harmed their relationship," by the time the boycott ended in November 1911.[13]

Even the famous 50,000 street dogs of Constantinople were problematic. Mary Mason Poynter, a ten-year resident of the city, described "walking gingerly around them, especially if it be summer, as they lie at full length on the pavements. . . [They had] a pleasant wag, and never a bite or bark." But when the Young Turks decided to get rid of them in 1910, Poynter said with blunt irony, "To tell the truth, it hardly seems that this great canine population in the streets is up to date enough for a Turkey whose ruling Committee stands for union and progress."[14] At night, police and assistants, "armed with lassoes and wooden tongs, and followed by a train of dustcarts,"[15] scooped up the unsuspecting beasts and deported them to the Isle of Oxias in the Sea of Marmora. There was an international outrage over their treatment. "Dog lovers who have visited the island allege that the animals are being gradually starved to death," read one newspaper. "A number have already died. If this state of things is allowed to continue, the process of extermination will be accelerated by the dogs eating one another. . . The authorities in Constantinople must be either ignorant of the inferno to which they have consigned the animals, or callous to the suffering they are causing."[16] The general consensus was callousness.

Most nationalists within the Empire wanted autonomy, not separation, but hardliners in the Young Turk government were deeply disturbed by the uprisings and demonstrations in Yemen, Arabia, and the Balkans. Fearing their loss of control, they were against any kind of decentralization, and any local change that might signal autonomy, even to the extent of "the introduction of the Latin script in Albanian schools."[17] They also began to embrace the idea of "Turkification" of Ottomans as the best way "to liberate the Ottoman Empire from European dominance," and regain its once-glorious past, though the height of the Empire was beyond living memory. Journals with names like *Türk Yurdu* (Turkish Homeland) and *Yeni Hayat* (New Life) sprang up to promote the need for a national economy and a national consciousness. Writers such as Alexander Helphand, and Ziya Gokalp[18] believed that a prosperous nation was not possible when there were different cultural, religious and ethnic groups within it. By "national," they meant Turkish. Therefore the concept of developing a national consciousness really meant the need for the Turkification of all Ottomans.

Street dogs in Constantinople. SOURCE: Underwood & Underwood, July 17, 1911, US Library of Congress.

After the annexation of Bosnia-Herzegovina, the Young Turks negotiated with Austria-Hungary to end the capitulations, and voted in favour of granting £T 200,000 to help resettle 400,000 Muslim Bosnians in Turkey. An editorial in the *Tasviri Efkiar* questioned what was to be gained by this re-colonization. "We must concentrate our efforts on caring for the millions of inhabitants we already have," it stated emphatically. "The Arab looks with suspicion on the Turk, the Turk on the Kurd, the Kurd on the Armenian, the Greek on the Bulgarian. We must try to establish love and harmony between these races, and the only way to do this is by the application of justice for all."[19] The large influx of migrants was a signal for many Ottomans who did not like the direction the Empire was heading. They themselves immigrated to the United States in "alarming proportions": 300,000 from Syria and 80,000 mainly Armenians from Anatolia, and "several thousands of Albanians, Greeks, Bulgarians and others."[20] The government applied to France for yet another loan to pay for the migrants' resettlement, but this time France declined. However, the government did manage to secure £T 11 million from a group of Austrian and German capitalists at 4% interest, thus increasing the national debt yet again.[21]

Religious zealots decried the secularism and the lack of adherence to Islamic values of the Young Turks. "They do not keep the fast in the blessed month of Ramadan, but eat and get drunken and neglect their prayers."[22]

The revolution, which had started out so promisingly, was rapidly deteriorating into a political quagmire. Enemies of the government included fellow politicians who disagreed with its centralizing policies and dubious governing methods, ethnic nationalists who desired autonomy, religious zealots who abhorred its secularism, foreign governments which deplored its "scandalous, crumbling, decrepit, penniless"[23] state, and journalists who reported on it all. It was certainly not safe reporting negatively on the government: Ahmet Samimi Bey, editor of *Sada-yi Millet*, was murdered in 1910, and Zeki Bey, editor of *Sehran*, was murdered in 1911.[24]

There was one bright spot, however. The extension of the Berlin-Baghdad Railway recommenced, and by 1911 had reached as far as Oulou Kushla, 125 miles southeast of Talas.[25] Other than that, the outlook for the Young Turks' survival was poor. Serious disagreements within the party over the concepts of unity and progress threatened to tear it apart.

~ ~ ~

Another serious rift that had been brewing for years was about to come to a head. It was between the medical and teaching missionaries of Talas. At its root was a difference of opinion about how the mission was run, and about religion. Dr. William S. Dodd had arrived in Talas in 1886 with his wife, Mary Carter Dodd. He had been born in Smyrna, the son of a missionary, and had been educated at Princeton and Union Seminary. By 1887 he had established a small hospital and dispensary at the Talas station.[26] Such facilities were becoming more popular for three reasons: They provided much-needed modern medicine to the region; they were "outposts for scientific research" that contributed much to the collective medical knowledge,[27] and, as the American Board realized, the power of healing aided their evangelical work. Given the element of trust between a doctor and his patient, and by extension the patient's visiting family, relationships developed much faster with medical missionaries than with other missionaries. Personal care included daily prayers, scripture readings, and private interviews. Upon being discharged, every patient received a Bible.[28] As a Board secretary explained it, "These create in the wards a restful, wholesome Christian atmosphere and in the heart of the patient a

The Talas hospital. Unseen from this view is an attached wing, half the size of this building. SOURCE: American Research Institute in Turkey and SALT Research.

desire to respond to the love of God."[29] William recorded in 1889 that 98 new members joined the Protestant church in Talas, a large increase in membership compared to previous years. For this reason, "medical services fell under the general mission strategy of the organization and were used as a tool to appeal to the masses in a systematic way."[30]

He had been joined in 1899 by Emma Cushman from Paterson, New Jersey, a stout woman who was described as "an efficient trained nurse," with a "forceful personality."[31] She and William worked well together, but as the reputation of the little hospital grew, so did the need for a larger, American-style hospital, with the latest equipment, more beds, and more staff. The Dodds appealed to their friends at home to help raise funds for the construction of such a facility. The American Christian Hospital was incorporated in New York in 1901, officially governed by a board of trustees (which included names such as Dodd and Carter) but run by William in Talas.[32] In 1901 nurse Lillian Cole arrived from Montclair, New Jersey. Dr. Wilfred M. Post, born in Beirut and educated at Princeton, and his wife Annie Stabb Post, joined the mission in 1904. The staff grew with native assistants, such as Dr. Krikor Tekyan, who were either graduates of the Syrian Protestant Medical College in Beirut or who

Later photographs (c1918-1922): Emma Cushman, Lillian Cole (later Sewny),
Wilfred Post and William Dodd. SOURCE: US Passport Applications.

were being trained by the missionaries; some short-term American and British nurses; and young trainees from the mission's school.[33]

By 1905 nurses Lillian and Emma had developed a serious personality clash, which created "a good deal of unpleasantness in the hospital."[34] To compound the problem, Emma had accompanied a new nurse, Belfast-born Rachel North, from Constantinople to Talas, a journey of more than a week. By the time they reached the hospital, Rachel was thoroughly biased against Lillian. Within six weeks of her arrival she had written to the trustees in New York, describing Emma as "very unselfish" with "a well balanced character," Wilfred and Annie Post as "charming people," and herself as being "heartily in sympathy" with the ideals and methods of William and Mary Dodd. Lillian, however, while "anxious to make her work in the field count and to live in friendly relations with her fellow workers," did "not always show good judgment" and was "quick tempered" and "at a disadvantage in her earlier training."[35]

Lillian was not shy about discussing her views with—as William pointedly noted—"her special friends" among the teachers at the Girls' Boarding School, that is, Stella, Susan, and Adelaide. He damned her with faint praise, calling her "a first-class private nurse" and excellent in the operating room, but ill-suited for hospital nursing.[36] No one ever questioned the medical work or the quality of health care administered by the doctors and nurses of Talas. The real problem began in 1904 soon after Lillian had been appointed a missionary by the American Board, which entitled her to do evangelical work. William, her supervisor, directed her work, but without consulting the rest of the mission. It was her religious views he found lacking. So did the rest of the medical staff. "I hesitate to speak for fear of seeming uncharitable," Wilfred said in a letter to a hospital trustee, *but* "she has been much influenced by the popular speculation theology of the day and inclined to abandon what are generally accepted as evangelical views, especially as regards the personality and regenerating power of the Holy Spirit, the inspiration and authority of Scripture, the lost condition of these out of Christ and their only hope in Him, the doctrine of eternal death, etc." He added, "Miss Cole has taken up with the broad view of the day, more because they are attractive and appeal to her, I am sure, than from any careful study or deep conviction."[37]

Because the station had always operated as a democracy, with open and transparent consensus among the missionaries, and given this was a non-medical issue, Lillian bristled at William's direction. By the end of January 1906, she and the medical staff had all had enough of the conflict. "As I am unwilling to be under the sole control of Dr. Dodd acting independently of the Station," she wrote to the hospital trustees, "I beg to present my resignation to take effect July 1st."[38] The trustees and the regular missionaries accepted her resignation with sadness; the medical missionaries were relieved to see her go.[39] After a year's furlough in the United States, Lillian moved to nearby Sivas, where she helped build a hospital, trained local girls to be nurses, and married the mission's Armenian doctor, Levon Sewny. But her departure did not solve the problem.

For the next two years the mood at the Talas station was tense. There were two hostile camps: the hospital staff with its strict biblical doctrine and adherence to a literal interpretation of the scriptures, versus the non-medical missionaries, who tended to support the ideas expressed through the Social Gospel movement. On Christmas Eve 1908, William, Mary, Wilfred and Annie sent a joint letter of resignation to ABCFM Secretary James Barton. For them, it had come down to a matter of standing by their colleagues in the Talas mission who were "taking a wrong course," or standing by those in Kaisarieh who were "right," thus further antagonizing their colleagues. They chose to leave Talas entirely.[40]

In a last-ditch attempt to resolve the problem Rev. Joseph Greene, the ABCFM Secretary in Constantinople, sent James P. McNaughton from Smyrna, Henry T. Perry from Sivas, and George E. White from Marsovan to Talas to try to help.[41] After three days of private and collective probing, and lots of praying by all, this small committee of three summed up the conflict into three issues: administrative, religious, and personalities. William's view on administration, they concluded, was that the hospital was an independent entity because of its separate incorporation, thus entitling him to make unilateral decisions regarding the activities of the hospital staff. The missionaries saw the incorporation as a "trap" that had been set to fool them, and "the station 'got caught' in it."[42] They were angry that the hospital staff acted "like a club," with "aggressive independence" and arrogance in telling them they had "no right to question" the hospital's decisions.[43]

The religious conflict was clear cut. It involved the "New Life" movement that had taken hold in several outstations during the previous five or six years. New Life called "for the complete submission to the will of God, recognition of the Divine Power to save from a life of sin, [and] a very literal acceptance of the Bible," among other things.[44] The investigating committee found a degree of "perfectionism and . . . a spirit of pride and self conceit" included in "their own peculiar tenets." The hospital staff regarded the movement "as a spiritual revival, lifting people to a higher plane, bringing them to forsake sin and bow before God," whereas the other missionaries saw it "as lowering the spiritual tone, dividing communities into factions, and, in the main, harmful."[45]

The committee did not mince words about the personality conflicts. Everyone had "allowed themselves to entertain and express misgivings, mistrust and misrepresentations concerning the other party." The result was "an atmosphere of suspicion, and want of confidence as would tend to stifle personal piety, and render spiritual effort sterile." William Dodd and Henry Wingate were particularly conflicted. William had previously called Henry a "dominating factor in the station counsels,"[46] and there certainly was some truth to that. In 1906 Caroline Fowle had written to her father that Henry had "changed a good deal the past year. . . . He is far more ready to consult with the others than he used to be. I feel that he is a better Christian than he was."[47]

William was in complete disagreement with this assessment. "Henry," he said, "is known throughout the field as 'irreligious,' and people have little respect for him as a Christian." In fact, he accused Henry of being "practically a Unitarian," because "when a man says he does not believe in the pre-existence of Christ, doubts his miraculous birth, says that on earth he was certainly nothing but a man, that he received some sort of divinity after his resurrection . . . I cannot see any practical difference between this and Unitarianism." William was worried about Henry's influence on the Girls' School, and saw a "danger of Mr. Irwin going in the same way, though he is now thoroughly orthodox."[48] Of course, Herbert Irwin's father-in-law was a strong proponent of the Social Gospel in Winnipeg, so it was more likely that he would have been influenced by his wife and her father than by the wayward Henry. Students of the Boys' School where

Henry was principal refuted William's charges, and perhaps fearing his expulsion, requested their document in support of him be forwarded to the American Board for consideration, which it was.[49]

The investigating committee also found that all the personnel in Talas "were wearied and ashamed of a condition of strife, and longed to end it." The hospital staff agreed to consult the missionaries and be governed by a local committee as an experiment. Likewise, the missionaries agreed "to grant public toleration to the New Life people in the field, to admit [to] differing theological views among the members of the re-united station, and to work together in mutual sympathy and support in the building up of Christ's Kingdom in this wide and needy region."[50]

It was all for nought. By the summer of 1910 communication had broken down irrevocably, and the Dodds and Posts, together with the ever faithful Emma Cushman, resigned from the American Board and left Talas forever. They later started a hospital in Konia. The stress had taken its toll on 65-year-old James Fowle; he and Caroline retired to the United States. Rachel North returned to the United States, too. After attending the Moody Institute in Chicago,[51] she was appointed a missionary in Mardin.

Because its legal status was in limbo, the Talas hospital closed down. There had been 460 patients served in 1910,[52] so its closure was inconvenient, to say the least.

~ ~ ~

On September 28, 1911 without warning Italy demanded the Ottoman Empire immediately evacuate Tripolitania and Benghazi, the last remaining Ottoman territory in Africa. When the Young Turks refused, Italy declared war. The area was not particularly valuable to the empire, but the loss of the vilayet would send a negative signal to Arabian Ottomans further east. When the government was slow to act, Ottoman army Major Enver, one of the 1908 revolutionaries, took 50 officers to Tripolitania "to galvanize the Arab resistance, which had already started under the leadership of the militant Sanusiya religious order. During the next year the Bedouin troops led by these officers successfully harassed the Italians and prevented them from making much headway inland."[53]

While struggling to fight enemies abroad, the government continued to fight its internal opposition. The most significant group was within its own precarious coalition. By November, those who opposed the leaders' authoritarianism and commitment to centralization broke away to form the Entente Libérale party.[54] The Young Turks were no more. From then on, the hardliners were known as the Committee of Union and Progress, CUP, or simply, the Committee.

It had been a messy, acrimonious divorce. The campaign in early 1912 bore that out. Several journals were suppressed, and rumours floated around that CUP was going to arrest Entente deputies to prevent their re-election.[55] An open letter from Kiamil Pasha, the ex-Grand Vizier and current Entente member, to the sultan was widely-circulated. Kiamil accused the Committee of having a "despotic attitude," which made them unable to govern within a constitution, thus resorting to martial law. They had replaced competent officials in Constantinople and the vilayets with "inexperienced and incompetent Committee followers," and their "maladministration" had caused Italy to declare war, European powers to decline friendship, and the problems in Crete, Yemen, Arabia, and the Balkans. Kiamil warned of the threat against the very existence of the caliphate and the empire. "Unless the Committee relinquishes its control," he said, "another revolution will take place, aided by the army, against their despotism."[56]

The message of the Entente's election campaign to non-Muslim Ottomans was the threat of a repeat in their own communities of CUP's attempt to Turkify Albania. Its message for Muslim Ottomans was that CUP's leaders did not personally adhere to Islamic values (this despite Entente members not being particularly "good" Muslims themselves). The direction of the Entente's campaign forced CUP to champion Islam even further.[57] CUP also launched "a campaign of violence and intimidation" against the Entente and its supporters. The result was a huge election victory in April 1912 for the Committee.[58]

Unfortunately for the empire, a parliamentary majority was not an indication of stability. Within months, the minister of war, Shevket Pasha had "resigned in disgust over the unreliability of the army. Desertions of soldiers and alienation of civilians spread."[59] Then, just as Kiamil predicted, there was a military revolt in July. The power shifted from the Committee to the Entente.[60] There were two important results: Martial law was lifted, and investigations into election fraud by CUP proved to be true. Many of the leading members of the Committee were persecuted, forcing them underground or into exile—at least, temporarily.[61]

4

The Empire Shrinks

By 1911 the situation in Talas had settled into an amicable routine, and the station began to expand. The American Board had purchased the hospital from the New York trustees for $12,000, and had convinced Dr. Alden R. Hoover to transfer from Marsovan to become its new director. Alden and his wife, Esther, agreed to stay for a year, but fit in so nicely they were later convinced to stay longer. Their life at the mission was made even more agreeable when Alden's sister, Edith, a nurse, and her husband, Rev. Arthur C. Ryan, arrived for a year's language study.[1] Being with family made a huge difference in their daily lives. The mission had also gained two other members. Rev. Charles Henry Holbrook, a minister from Salem, Massachusetts, was in Talas for language study, too. Theda Phelps, born in Greenville, Michigan and a graduate of the Illinois Training School for Nurses, had been nursing for the last seven years, most recently in Cheyenne, Wyoming.[2] Much to their delight, Theda and Susan Wealthy Orvis soon discovered they were distant cousins on Susan's mother's side, going all the way back to the Connecticut Colony in 1653.[3]

In 1909 the station had acquired another teacher. Clara Childs Richmond was a recent graduate of Miss Wheelock's Kindergarten Training School in Boston, which was on the cutting edge of early childhood education.[4] She was effervescent, enthusiastic, and perhaps due to the pins perpetually falling from her hair, she always had a wild appearance, as if she had just come in from a wind storm. It was exactly the kind of exuberance that made a teacher appealing to young children. She was quite a breath of fresh air for Fanny Burrage in the new kindergarten building in Cesarea.

After receiving official permission from the local authorities, construction began on a new building for the Girls' School, too. From a religious standpoint, things were looking up when three Circassian boys became the first Muslim boarders in the Boys' School's history. Still more good news arrived when the Catholicos of nearby Sis visited Talas and advised his Armenian parishioners to "avail themselves of the educational advantages" the missionaries offered. The Talas station was overjoyed. To them, these endorsements signalled confidence in their evangelical work. Still, after a four-week tour of eleven villages and two cities within the sanjak, Arthur and Susan came to the conclusion that they could be doing

(Top) Theda Phelps, Clara Richmond, and Arthur Ryan (c 1922). *(Below)* Edith Ryan with the two Ryan children, Alden Hoover, and Esther Hoover with their two daughters. It was common c 1920s for family photographs to be accepted by the US Passport Office. SOURCE: US Passport Applications.

a better job in training local teachers. What was really needed, they decided, was a school of pedagogy.[5]

Luckily for the older boys, the mission schools were ranked by the government as *idadieh* (preparatory), therefore the boys were exempt from military service.[6] But there were other negative forces to deal with. A heavy frost killed the fruit crops and injured the beautiful, productive walnut trees, a loss of £T 50,000 to Cesarea alone.[7] A measles epidemic swept through the area, making many adults and children seriously ill. "The hospital is full to overflowing," Adelaide said in her mission report. "In the slackest time there were eighteen patients, while now the average is forty or more." The disease was often followed by pneumonia, leaving an "appalling" death rate in its wake. However, she concluded on an up-beat note: "The prospect for the spring is most promising."[8] Prospects, however, are not guarantees. By fall the Empire had plunged into "the long-expected Balkan war."[9]

~ ~ ~

No sooner had the conflict with Italy ended in October 1912, with the loss for the Ottomans of its African territory, than Montenegro declared war by invading Ottoman Albania. Its allies, Bulgaria, Greece and Serbia, quickly joined in. They were fed up with the unfulfilled promised reforms, and wanted real independence. Mobilization in the empire was immediate. "The government is commandeering all the horses it can for its cavalry and artillery, seizing in many cases the wagons, . . . and paying about 40% of the value to the poor drivers," said Rev. Charles T. Riggs. From his vantage point in Constantinople, he witnessed the mostly-inexperienced troops pass through on their way to the Balkans. "Of course, trade is seriously hampered by this sudden loss of clerks, *hamals* (porters), workmen, etc., as well as by the scarcity of horses and carriages. The railway service is suspended—the entire rolling stock being needed for the transport of troops."[10]

Fighting on land and sea was fierce, but war was not the only strife in the region. There was a "quarrel for supremacy" between the Entente and the Committee, one that so rattled newly arrived missionary Jessie Holeman, she told her friends back home in Washington, DC, "Just now there is more danger from civil war than there is of violence from the lower element and fanatics. If you can imagine yourself sitting upon the top of a volcano with the feeling that at any moment an eruption may occur, you will know our condition here."[11]

She had good reason for anxiety. In November 1912 the Entente Libérales "got wind of a plot to bring off a coup d'état in Constantinople, and by prompt and vigorous action" arrested the culprits. Talat Bey, the former Minister of the Interior, was one of them, though a court-martial a few weeks later released many of the plotters.[12] On January 13, 1913 CUP supporters organized a massive anti-government demonstration at the Sublime Porte (the seat of government). *The Orient* reported that "the recent lenience of Kiamil Pasha's Cabinet toward the arrested Unionists seems to have been interpreted by the latter as a mark of weakness." The editorial contained a gloomy warning: "Former experiences have shown that the Committee leaders are capable of almost anything for the sake of gaining the upper hand."[13]

Less than two weeks later, government leaders met at the Porte to contemplate the surrender of Adrianople to Bulgaria. The issue was emotionally charged because the town was mostly Muslim and had once been the capital of the Ottoman Empire. Talat, Major Enver and about two hundred CUP supporters rushed to the Porte to stage a coup d'état "for patriotic reasons."[14] The commotion drew Nazim Pasha, the Entente

Leaders of the Committee of Union and Progress: Talat and Enver. SOURCES: Talat (Bain News Service, US Library of Congress), Enver (US Library of Congress).

war minister, outside to investigate. He was shot dead. So were five or six others. A dozen men were wounded. After Talat and Enver entered the council chamber and forced Kiamil to resign, Enver drove off to the Palace to see the sultan. He returned shortly and announced "to the waiting crowd the news that Mahmut Shevket Pasha had been appointed Grand Vizier."[15] In June, the Committee of Union and Progress gained full control of the government after Shevket Pasha was assassinated by an Entente Libérale supporter. Within days an Egyptian prince, Said Halim Pasha, became the new Grand Vizier, Enver's uncle, Halil Bey, became President of the Council of State, and Talat was once again appointed Minister of the Interior.[16]

"An administration founded on violence and murder is seldom a success," said *The Orient* ominously.

~ ~ ~

Within days of the start of the Balkan War, the Talas hospital's assistant doctor and druggist were drafted into the army. "They rode away in their lieutenant's uniforms leaving a sad gap behind them," said Adelaide. Alden Hoover found a replacement for the doctor, but there were not many druggists in the region. The dispensary had to struggle on without him.[17] In the early days of the war the mission was only aware of the fighting because of the daily bulletins issued by the local newspaper, *Argæus*. By December, Adelaide reported that "only two wagon-loads of wounded soldiers have come back as yet; no refugees have appeared."[18]

So life and work rolled on. They celebrated Christmas with a few small trees, "obtained with great difficulty by the American families."[19] The Ryans completed their language studies and moved to their permanent station in Constantinople. The Wingates returned from their year-long furlough, and brought with them Elsey Bristol. She was a graduate of the University of Wisconsin, and had taught for ten years at Madison Central High School, had gone back to school herself to earn a master's degree, and then taught for another six years. Henry had convinced her to come to Talas to take on two jobs at the Boys' School (secretary and English teacher), and to tutor to his own children. She was looking forward to becoming part of the community.[20]

Meanwhile Susan had agreed to a request by the local Protestant church to supervise its girls' school. Stella and her colleagues were very pleased. "This is something we have long hoped for, as the school has not fitted its pupils for our boarding school," said Adelaide. "Time has been wasted when their graduates came out here hoping to enter our high school, and had to enter the seventh grade!"[21]

But as the months passed, even though they carried on their teaching, medical and evangelical work, life in Kaisarieh got harder for everyone. The hospital operated regularly at full capacity, now with 55 beds, coping with cholera, typhus, and "the usual amount" of tuberculosis. There were four nurses in training, which helped considerably, but Genevieve Irwin was worried, because "hundreds of children died from measles, largely through ignorance of proper care" at home.[22]

In February *The Orient* reported that "the severest weather of the whole winter struck all parts of the country . . . with ten feet of snow at Bitlis, the coldest spell for several years in Sivas, and deep snows throughout the whole of the Anatolia plateau." There had been heavy casualties during the recent victory of Bulgaria near Gallipoli, followed by urgent appeals from mission stations all over Turkey for financial aid, especially for the soldiers' families.[23] William Peet, ABCFM Treasurer for the Turkey Missions, sent Red Cross money to Talas to help the needy among its 2,700 households (1,500 Greek, 900 Armenian, 280 Turkish, and 20 Protestant).[24] Stella, Adelaide, Herbert and Henry volunteered to be on the distribution committee. They decided to buy flour, and give tickets to those who applied for aid, based on half a batman* per person per week.

They visited homes in pairs twice a week to ensure the need was still there, first asking permission to enter the premises and look through the

---

* One batman was "nearly seventeen pounds."

James Barton, Elsey Bristol, and William Peet (c.1918). SOURCE: US Passport Applications.

occupants' possessions. Henry accompanied Adelaide, who described the typical household as "a room with an earthen floor, with a cellar dug down under a raised platform that takes up about two-thirds of the space. On this wooden platform is an earthenware dish of hot ashes, and over it a small table, covered with quilts that come down far enough on all sides to cover the knees of the people who sit there. One or two wooden chests, and a few shelves with two or three quilts and a few dishes make up the furnishings of the room, except for a few minders or square cushions that take the place of the sedir we find in better houses. Perhaps there is one square window in the room, possibly two. There may be another room with a fireplace and another chest or two in it; usually there is, and possibly an empty stable. In such a place we would find a family of from three to six—mother-in-law, wife, and anywhere from one to four children."[25]

While Adelaide talked to the women about their clothing and bed linens, Henry would "go down the rickety ladder into the dark cellar, with a smoky wick in a tin lamp for light." They would often find "a few bits of wood—sometimes charcoal—and dried weeds for fuel; a handful of native macaroni or perhaps beans, and a few scrapings of flour in the bottom of the chest."

One woman was reluctant to open a locked chest, saying she could not find the key even though it was visibly lying on the shelf. When Henry crossed the room, the woman quietly unlocked it, and opened it, whispering to Adelaide, "It is my daughter's trousseau." The chest contained an apron, an old shawl, and a couple of cotton dresses. "I hadn't the heart to tell her she ought to have sold them before she applied for help," Adelaide said sadly.

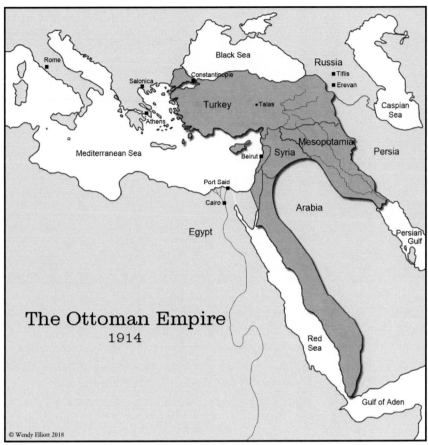

Map 4

In another house they found a young mother, about twenty years old, shaking with malaria. She had had nothing to eat but onions. They gave her bread and quinine. One old lady had sold everything she possibly could, and was terribly embarrassed to be seen in such a needy state. She looked dazed when Adelaide suggested she could repay the aid by helping others once she was financially comfortable again—as if the thought of a brighter future was simply inconceivable. But she blessed the missionaries when they left, saying, "May your time of want never come." Blessings like this became a common occurrence as they toured the town. Rather than having stones thrown at them, which used to happen frequently in the "unfriendly quarters," they now heard murmurs of "They are helping the soldiers' families."[26]

Everyone in the mission was aware of the danger their colleagues in the Balkans' missions faced, and that it was possible the war could arrive at

The missionaries' children singing "gladly in praise of the Star-Spangled Banner."
SOURCE: Susan Wealthy Orvis Papers.

their own doorstep. However, they downplayed the worry in their letters home. "We have all our plans, what to do in case of a disturbance," said Stella, "but we have no reason to expect one, and are hoping and praying that the change, if it does come, will be made quietly and peacefully."[27]

"The suspense and strain are wearing on us all," said Susan, "but we have not suffered any special difficulty here in Talas and Cesarea. We hope for better days and more opportunities. Surely all this suffering and bloodshed is not in vain. It comes at great cost, but liberty is worth even this."[28]

In a letter to the women in the congregation at home who sponsored her, Susan wrote, "The worst feature of it for us, far away in the interior, is that the different classes are all in mortal fear, each of the other, lest a general massacre take place. The women of Talas spend their nights watching and listening in fear and trembling." She assured her readers that the missionaries themselves were "not inclined to fear any danger. The government is taking measures to maintain order and prevent trouble. Until the war is ended, the time is critical however, and we can only wait and pray for this land, which is already burdened so heavily."[29]

Her own land, the United States of America, was never far from her mind, nor the minds of most of her colleagues. On July 4, 1913 the Western Turkey Division held its AGM in Talas. "Patriotism in the centre of Asia Minor is so strong that even Canadians and Germans are irresistibly drawn into the celebration of America's great day," *The Orient* reported gleefully. Present were thirty adults from the Talas station, and Charles Holbrook, now residing in Sivas, seven children, and the newest Hoover baby. "First the children gave a carefully prepared program of speeches, songs, and exercises with the Stars and Stripes, all of which were heartily applauded. The two Canadian children [Hugh and Corinne Irwin] among them laid aside all national prejudice for the time, and joined gladly in praise of the Star-Spangled Banner." After they ate "a bounteous supper" on the lawn, complete with ice cream and lemonade, the revellers participated in sack and obstacle races, and "repaired once more to the decorated plot in front of the new Girls' School building, gay with its flags, bunting, and portraits of Washington, Lincoln and [the new American President, Woodrow] Wilson."[30] No doubt a good time was had by all.

~ ~ ~

Eight hundred miles to the west, the Balkan War had been bitter, bloody, and blood-thirsty—like "something out of Dante's Inferno," said one journalist. "Only his dark genius could recreate all the horrors of the cold swamps out of which stick the twisted and mutilated bodies of the fallen." Another reporter described a scene as a "ghastly theater of blood: Everywhere bodies reduced to mere bones, blue hands ripped from forearms, the bizarre gestures, empty eye-sockets, open mouths as if calling in desperation, the shattered teeth behind the torn and blackened lips."[31] After the war ended in the spring of 1913, there was a two-month Second Balkan War between June and August for Bulgaria and the other Balkan states to finish arguing. But from mid-spring to the summer, detailed, horrific descriptions were commonplace in newspapers around the world. *The Orient* reported, "In a single issue of a most reputable and trustworthy English daily, we find these statements from persons on the spot: 'The Bulgarians are more cynical.' A lieutenant said, 'I kill Turks as I would rats.' 'In Montenegro I met some Serbs shortly after the Serb army arrived at Durazzo. They boasted at the dinner table that the Serb army had completely exterminated the Muslim Albanian tribe of Lyuma.' ... Later a Montenegrin official assured me very earnestly that 'we have completely exterminated the Rugova tribe. I assure you not one remains.'" The editorial stated, "There has been a most humiliating amount of proof from various points during this war that the instincts of the brute still exist in men of all nationalities and all creeds."[32]

"Atrocities" is defined as shocking, brutal injuries to "combatants in action or *hors de combat*, non-combatants in a theatre of military operations, non-combatants behind the front, or soldiers and civilians in time of peace."[33] There were tales of atrocities committed by Christians, and just as many stories about atrocities committed by Muslims, although not many of the latter were printed in the Turkish press. Susan wrote to her mother that the assistant doctor and the druggist from Talas had finally returned home after thirteen months of service. They had been drafted for their professional skills, and were therefore not on the firing lines. But they had witnessed the ugliness of war. "Terrible things were done by Muslims and Christians alike," said Susan. "The tales they tell are not pleasant to hear. And through all the months, their own side was not the one they wished to have win. Think of such a situation!"[34] In the end, the army was reduced to recruiting "boys not yet out of their teens."[35] It had been a sad, sorry, ugly war.

Afterwards, the Carnegie Endowment for International Peace conducted an extensive inquiry into the "long list of executions, assassinations, drownings, burnings, massacres and atrocities." It concluded that "there is no clause in international law applicable to land war and to the treatment of the wounded, which was not violated, to a greater or less extent, by *all the belligerents*." It found that the worst atrocities were not conducted by soldiers, but by civilians. However, "the true culprits are those who mislead public opinion and take advantage of the people's ignorance to raise disquieting rumors and sound the alarm bell, inciting their country and consequently other countries into enmity."[36]

There were many groups with vested interests that tried to either mislead or influence public opinion in their favour, starting with the CUP government. Gloating over the fact that it was civilian bands, not regular soldiers, who committed the worst atrocities, Dr. Mehmed Nazim, a high Committee official, described in a letter to his colleague, Dr. Bahaeddin Shakir, the goal of a band member named Hasan the Sailor. He was "to slay ten Bulgarians for each murdered Muslim. He does not differentiate in order to fulfill his goal. No Bulgarian, man, woman, old or young, can escape alive from the axe of Hasan the Sailor until he reaches the number of ten. Hasan the Sailor has become the god of a few districts, and Bulgarians tremble when they hear his name. . . The impact of these bands on the Bulgarians is greater than the impact of one hundred thousand troops dispatched by the administration."[37]

It was common for a Muslim band that had killed Bulgarian Christians to leave a letter on a corpse, addressed to the local district governor, indicating that the person had "been killed to avenge the Muslim killed at such and such [a] place."[38] However, the Turkish press downplayed atrocities committed by Muslims, and recounted in gory detail those committed by Christian Bulgarians. The tales were reminiscent of the Crusades of the Middle Ages. Indeed, Enver wrote to his wife about "the savagery the enemy has inflicted," and said, "Everywhere there are signs of the wretchedness brought by the most recent Crusade."[39] More than 200,000 soldiers—of all ethnicities—had been killed, and countless civilians died.

In 1913 the Interior Ministry created the Office for the Settlement of Tribes and Immigrants.[40] By mid-year, a quarter of a million refugees, mostly Muslims from the Balkans, were resettling in Turkey. Tens of thousands more had yet to arrive.[41] They were understandably angry over the loss of friends, family, livelihood, home—and their forced migration. For Enver and his fellow CUP members, the end of the war was a personal, humiliating defeat. After the war with Italy, they had lost territory in Africa; after this war, they lost all of the Ottoman Empire's European territory, except for Thrace, the European province of Turkey near Constantinople (see Map 4).[42] Writers like Gokalp began to promote in earnest the idea of Pan-Turkism, the cultural and political unification of all people of the Turk race.[43] And the Committee listened. Enver himself was seething. To his wife, he wrote, "Our anger is strengthening: revenge, revenge, revenge; there is no other word."[44]

~ ~ ~

"The Turkish empire has slumped," declared Rev. Andrus of Mardin. "And the people have slumped with her."[45] He was right. Business was stagnant. Banks restricted transactions. People searched in vain for work, and were on the verge of starvation. There was a deep-seated feeling that government officials were corrupt. Brigands operated freely, robbing and killing at will, fearing no one.[46] Then came the devastating news from a Sivas outstation: Their former Talas colleague, Rev. Charles Holbrook, had been shot while asleep in the garden of an Armenian friend. The bullet had penetrated his lung and liver, killing him instantly. The investigation by local authorities, and later by a US State Department representative, was convoluted and full of conjecture as to the motive and assailant.[47] Everyone in the country was confused, jittery and discouraged. They were looking around for some sort of relief.

The Sheikh-ul-Islam, Ajemaleddin Effendi, tried to be the voice of reason about the growing violence in eastern Anatolia against Christian Armenians, Assyrians and Greeks. "The Muslim sheriat decrees the safeguarding of the life, honor and property of non-Muslim subjects, as well as Muslim subjects," he said firmly. He reminded his constituents of the constitution's purpose to promote harmony among all peoples of the empire. "Unfortunately, on the instigation of some evil-minded persons, ignorant ones of the population are committing murders and pillaging property, crimes forbidden alike by the sheriat and by common sense . . . Most certainly no person can approve of such doings."[48] Clearly, drastic changes were desperately needed to ensure the security of the Ottoman Empire.

5

The Reformations

When the war ended, everyone agreed that the empire was in desperate need of reform, and that the source of help had to be foreign instructors. In addition to reorganization of the gendarmerie and the police, an editorial in the *Jeune Turc* newspaper included

> the revival and good organization of our schools, our agriculture, our means of communication, our commerce and our industry. For otherwise, even with the best police in the world, a people that does not have good schools to train its youth, or highways to move about and send off its products, or industries and agriculture to keep it busy and feed it, will be irrevocably doomed to misery and to all the anti-social consequences of misery.[1]

But not everyone agreed on the specifics. The Pan-Turkism movement wanted a country where the words Turk and Muslim were synonymous. Ethnic political associations, such as the Armenian Revolutionary Federation (Dashnaks), and the Young Arab Society,[2] wanted education and legal reforms for their communities. The majority of Ottomans— whether Turkish, Armenian, Greek, Kurdish, Arabian or Jewish—were either peasants, craftsmen or small business operators; they just wanted peace, and steady prosperity for themselves and their families.

The Committee of Union and Progress also wanted prosperity and stability, but had proven, since coming to power in 1908, it was incapable of governing to achieve it. In a not-so-veiled accusation against CUP, writer Ahmed Effendi Aghaieff said, "Let us cherish no illusions about ourselves; this haughty arrogance has already cost us too dear. Let us at least have learned this hard lesson. If, for the past five years, we had had the grace and the modesty to have recognized our faults, perhaps we should today have been cured of them and could already dispense with foreigners."[3]

Of course, foreign powers had their own reasons for aiding the faltering Empire. The Ottoman debt had grown considerably after two wars, and the financial situation was now "far worse than it was before."[4] There were newly-discovered oil fields and vast business opportunities. Everybody wanted a piece of the resource-rich pie. *Ikdam* neatly summed up the situation: "The Russians want eastern Anatolia, part of central Anatolia, and an outlet on the Mediterranean Sea at Alexandretta. The Germans dream of reaching out toward Mesopotamia with their Baghdad railroad, and putting their hand on Adana and Palestine. England covets Arabia; France wants Syria, and Italy seeks an opening on the coasts of Asia Minor."[5]

It could have added American interests to the list. Missionaries wanted to "evangelize the world within this generation," Standard Oil Company of New York was trying "to secure a monopoly of the oil fields" in western Turkey, and businesses, such as the Singer Sewing Machine Company, American Tobacco Company, and International Harvester, wanted to sell their modern machines to millions of Ottoman customers.[6]

In November Kaiser Wilhelm had insisted, and King George V of England and Russian Tsar Nicholas II had agreed, "on the necessity of preserving the Turkish Realm in its present [political] form."[7] There would be no international interference in the governing of what was left of the Ottoman Empire—as long as the Committee moved forward with reforms. But before reforms could start, those culprits the Carnegie commission had warned about tried to incite people into enmity.

~ ~ ~

Following the publication of the gory details of wartime atrocities, tensions were running high between Christian and Muslim Ottomans. The call for an "awakening" for a national economy had been rising exponentially with the need for a national, that is, Turkish, consciousness. The boycott movement that had been so successful in its anti-Austrian and anti-Greek stances, now turned its focus on Ottoman Christians in general, especially in western Turkey. Jewish merchants had been warned to "put signs over their doors indicating their nationality and trade, e.g. Abraham the Jew, tailor,"[8] to avoid being picketed. In November, 2,000 copies of a pamphlet entitled "Especially for Muslims" were freely distributed in Constantinople and nearby vilayets. The audience was lower class Muslims and Turks, so the language was kept simple. It reminded readers of the atrocities committed by Christians during the Balkan Wars (omitting mention of any committed by Muslims), of the loss of imperial territory, and of children reduced to begging on the streets. The message was very clear: To make the Ottoman Empire great again, buy only Turkish goods. The pamphlet drew so much attention that another 20,000 were distributed. Soon after, another, darker pamphlet was published. "To Muslims and Turks" made a visceral appeal to its readers by talking about the "rotten skins" and "carved eyes" of the Muslim victims, and "about the enemies who killed their brothers with bayonets, raped mothers and sisters, and afterwards drank wine." Though the pamphlets were printed anonymously, the author was Ahmet Nedim Servet Tor, a bureaucrat in the Ministry of War. His brother was Edib Servet Bey, one of the ten members of CUP's governing board before the revolution. Tor had taken it upon himself to write and publish these and two other pamphlets because he felt the newspaper articles and other publications were not explicit enough in their promotion of the national economy, "and therefore were not effective."[9]

Most members of the boycott movement were low-ranking bureaucrats, and local gangs, consisting mainly of Muslim immigrants. They were paid for this work by Turkish guilds and the unions of Turkish merchants.[10] By February 1914, these boycotters were communicating with each other and Muslim merchants throughout the empire via telegrams, and boycotts were promoted in mosques, bazaars and public squares,[11] often twisting the truth to hammer home the message. *Tanin*, the unofficial organ of CUP, published an advertisement from a Muslim shop that read, "The fatherland is happy that the honorable Muslim merchants have come to understand, thank God, that the future and the independence of Pan Islamism depends on the financial situation." *Terjeman-i-Hakikat* wrote: "Everybody knows that until now it was the non-Muslims only that profited by commerce, industry, and all the economic operations of the country. The heedless Muslims never even thought of the fact that the dealers were of another religion. It was enough for them that they were Ottomans. As a result, the non-Muslims became rich, while for the most part our people stayed miserable."[12]

Three medical students gave public lectures on hygiene in Smyrna. "We are broken hearted at finding you Muslims are still asleep," they said. "The Christians, profiting from our ignorance, have now for ages been taking our place and taking away our rights. These vipers whom we are nourishing have been sucking out all the lifeblood of the nation. They are the parasitical worms eating into our flesh whom we must destroy and do away with. It is time we freed ourselves from these individuals, by all means lawful and unlawful."[13] This was the language of the new "science" of eugenics: The idea that racial purity and consequent prosperity could be achieved through selective breeding—or otherwise—to eradicate society of its bad seeds.

As time went on, picketing was not enough. Boycotters began to threaten, beat and even whip patrons of non-Muslim shops.[14] Both the Greek and Armenian Patriarchs made formal protests to stop the boycotts. The government ordered "local bureaucrats not to permit such aggression."[15] Though the boycott bruised international relations, the government did not seriously try to stop it. In fact, Dr. Nazim, a prominent CUP member, "was regarded as the organizer of the boycott movement."[16]

~ ~ ~

In addition to being negatively affected by the boycotts, Armenians in eastern Turkey experienced another kind of persecution—and it was long-standing. The war between the Ottoman Empire and Russia in 1878 had ended with an Ottoman defeat. The European Powers negotiated the terms of the Treaty of Berlin, that included Article 61, particular to Armenians: "The Sublime Porte engages to realize *without delay* those ameliorations and reforms which local needs require in the provinces inhabited by the Armenians, and guarantees their security against the Circassians and the Kurds."[17] The protection and freedoms of Armenians within the empire was known as the "Armenian Question." Despite the Article's directive "to realize without delay," the empire had mainly ignored it and the European Powers had paid lip service to it for the last 36 years. The Dashnaks had supported the Young Turks, hoping that a constitutional government would deal with the Question, but the hope had been in vain.

Half of all Ottoman Armenians lived in the six eastern vilayets of Sivas, Erzroom, Harpoot,[*] Diarbekir, Bitlis, and Van, the area which was their traditional homeland. These vilayets were populated with ethnic minorities: 1 million Armenians, 1 million Turks, 650,000 Kurds, and 350,000 others (Greeks, Nestorians, Arabs, and others).[18] As Article 61 noted in 1876, Circassians and Kurds were the main aggressors against Armenians. Little had changed since then.[19] In 1911 and 1912 the Armenian Patriarch had appealed to the government to stop the repeated incidents of looting, rape and killing in the area, but no action had been taken.[20] Now in 1913, in addition to making a formal protest about the boycotts, the Patriarch renewed his call for security. In the Bitlis area alone, there were twenty-seven murders in a month.[21]

Local Kurds were also dissatisfied with the inaction of the government, and wanted to "establish an independent Kurdish kingdom with Bitlis as their capital. Or, they say, they would gladly become subjects of England or Russia."[22]

Both western and eastern Turkey were becoming more unsafe with each passing day, and the situation in other provinces was no safer.

~ ~ ~

---

[*] Also known as Mamouret-el-Aziz

In November Susan wrote to her father, a veteran of the American Civil War, "War must be terrible at any time in any country, but *this* war was unspeakable. It was not the Muslims alone who were fiendish. The worst things were those outside the regular battles. The saddest thing perhaps is that no one is satisfied with the outcome, and another war will doubtless follow before many years. This country is not in good condition even yet." An old Turk named Ali, who had driven the station's wagon for decades, had been murdered on the road. He had been trusted and honoured by all who knew him. "Christians and Muslims alike," said Susan. "It has been a great shock to us."[23]

The Orient reported on Ali's death and on the "alarming increase of outlawry and crime" in Kaisarieh in general. The "indiscriminate use of firearms at all times of day and night" resulted in an increase of gunshot wounds and "ten or twelve" murders in November and December, "some of them peculiarly revolting." The victims were Turks and Armenians. Sometimes robbery was the motive, sometimes not. No one had been arrested for Ali's murder, and the mutesarrif appeared "to be acting very weakly in the matter."[24]

Dr. Kalfayan, an assistant physician from Aintab, had recently joined the Talas station. "He is of great value in relieving the stress," said Adelaide, "especially in the matter of dressing the wounds of the patients."[25] The non-medical work of the mission continued, too, but the compound was getting crowded. The Boys' School could accommodate 100 boarders, and there were now 98. There were also 65 day pupils: "139 Armenians, 20 Greeks, one Circassian, two Turks, and one American, who came from 44 different towns and villages."[26] Enrollment for the Girls' School reached 85. "This means that ten or so are sleeping on the floor in the room used for the sessions of the Annual Meeting last summer," Adelaide said. "We have ordered new bedsteads, and hope to have them before the coldest weather. But the return of soldiers is shutting off freight on the railway, and we fear both the bedsteads and the piano for the Girls' School will be delayed."[27]

There were three happy events during the year, however. The mission schools joined the Gregorian schools of Talas to celebrate the 1,500[th] anniversary of the Armenian alphabet, and the 400th anniversary of the printing of the first Armenian book. A kindergarten training class began with "seven young ladies, from Sivas, Hadjin, Aintab, and Diarbekir."[28] And a new baby girl, named Genevieve after her mother, arrived at the Irwin home. "That was a cause for joy to start the day!" said Susan happily.[29]

Every year the station made a grand occasion of the graduation ceremonies. The staff erected a large canvas over the tennis court, and set up a stage for the graduates. SOURCE: Susan Wealthy Orvis Papers.

But happiness was in short supply. It was a cold, bitter winter with heavy snow falls. Landslides and snow blockades on the Anatolian and Baghdad Railways interfered with freight and passenger travel.[30] There had been three years of harvest failure, resulting in high food prices. An economic depression offered little work for returning soldiers.[31] Combined with the increasing crime rate, the future was not looking bright. A serious change was definitely needed.

~ ~ ~

After running more or less unopposed in the 1913-14 winter elections, CUP was now free to run the Ottoman Empire as it saw fit.[32] All ethnic groups within the country acknowledged the need for modernization and applauded the government when it took steps to reform the various systems. In January both Enver and Djemal were promoted to the military rank of General and given the courtesy title of Pasha. At 32 years of age, Enver was made Minister of War, and Djemal became Minister of Public

Works,[33] and shortly afterwards, Minister of the Marine.[34] One of Enver's first tasks was to reduce the army's budget by £T 4 or 5 million, which he did by retiring over-aged military personnel. Scores of German officers arrived to reorganize the Ottoman military, with General Liman von Sanders in command of the army, and Rear Admiral Wilhelm Souchon in command of the navy.[35]

Wanting to build its own ships, the government negotiated with a British consortium to modernize the arsenal and dockyards near Constantinople, and build a large floating dock at Ismid.[36] However, in need of dreadnaughts immediately, they decided to purchase a £2.3 million ship currently under construction in England. It would be completed in June and named the *Sultan Osman*. A second ship, the *Reshadiye,* was also commissioned. To pay for half the cost, the government acquired yet another loan of 30 million francs from the Perier Bank of Paris, "which bought Ottoman treasury bonds, contrary to the advice of the French government." Not coincidentally, a few months later the bank was granted a railway concession to connect Smyrna with the Dardanelles.[37]

To pay for the rest, the charitable Navy Society ran fundraising events, and the public responded enthusiastically. There were door-to-door campaigns. Women donated gold, silver and jewellery, and even sold their hair for the fund. Children participated in plays and fairs, passing around collection boxes.[38] Prince Izeddin donated £T 60, Talat donated £T 20, Djemal, £T 15, and the Prefect of Constantinople's Police, £T 3. Bureaucrats in the Ministry of the Interior were "said to have given up claim to one month's salary for this same patriotic object."[39]

The government brought in forty instructors from France to reorganize the gendarmerie,[40] made it compulsory for girls to attend primary school, and opened "a number of courses" to women at the university in Constantinople.[41] While the government saw all these reforms as necessary, especially for the awakening of a national economy and a strong empire, it still did nothing about instigating reforms for its minority subjects. That took outside pressure.

In February, after months of sensitive international negotiations, the Russian-sponsored plan to settle the Armenian Question was finally accepted by the Ottomans. The government and the European Powers were "understandably suspicious"[42] of Russia, considering Russia had invested heavily in pro-Russian propaganda in eastern Anatolia in the past year.[43] Even so, the Armenian Reform Agreement of 1914 went ahead. The six vilayets were to be divided into two administrative districts, each supervised by an Inspector-General selected from a small, neutral European country. They would ensure the instigation of reforms concerning laws and regulations; criminal and civil court hearings conducted "in the languages of the interested parties"; proportional taxation and representation; and the safeguarding of minority rights.[44] In April two Inspectors-General were hired: Mr. M. Hoff from Norway, and Mr. M. Westenek from the Netherlands. They would move to Turkey to begin work in July.[45]

~ ~ ~

In the meantime, the European Powers insisted on investigating the reported violence and Greek deportations in western Turkey. Consequently, the International Commission of Inquiry was formed and included Talat as Minister of the Interior, and representatives from Britain, France, Austria, Russia, Italy and Germany. They toured the region from June 20 to July 11, followed closely by the press.

They found that rumours of murders of Greeks, including a priest, near Brousa were false, but that a village had indeed been plundered. They discovered from local Greeks that, thanks to the efforts of the village's *imam* (priest of a mosque or religious leader), the Muslims of Chukurkeuy refused to participate in the attack on Seyrekeuy, but that soldiers and gangs controlled many of the roads. It was true that Turkish officers forced Greeks "to sign a declaration stating that they were leaving the country on their own will, and that they would not make any claims on their possessions." And it was also true that Muslim refugees were now living in Greek houses, and the governor of Soma, who had tried to protect Christians, had been fired. German officers had "found the presence of Greeks on the seacoast of Asia Minor dangerous, and advised their expulsion." Though the Ottoman government had not ordered their expulsion, it had approved of it.[46]

Talat's purpose in participating in the inquiry was to convince the European Powers that his government was "trying to calm the prevailing nationalist fever."[47] He spoke to crowds every place the commission visited, and the press reported on his sympathetic response to the problems. He issued an official communiqué to both the Greek and Turkish press in Smyrna, announcing that "printing articles calculated to stir up race prejudice" would cease, and any newspaper that published such articles in the future would be prosecuted.[48] He announced that the anti-Christian boycott "had a harmful impact on the economy of the country, and wanted its end," and that he had tried to convince Greeks intent on emigrating to stay.[49]

A typical missionary's room and furnishings. SOURCE: Susan
Wealthy Orvis Papers.

Behind the scenes, however, Talat was actively working against any
reforms or security for Christians. Before the tour, he telegraphed the
governor in Tekfurdag, "Disregard the contents of the letter of
recommendation given yesterday to a delegation consisting of four to five
people that the Patriarchate is going to dispatch for purposes of
counseling. . . . The aforementioned people are to be kept under secret
surveillance, and . . . you will see to it that the various matters of concern
to us will fail to be realized."[50]

This kind of deception was typical of the underhanded methods that
CUP's opposition had been railing against for years. Talat was known by
friends and associates as a liar. His closest friend said he "would lie in both
state and political matters," and his private secretary said that he "did not
view lies or cruelty as immoral."[51]

Therefore, he was untroubled to say privately of the Armenian Reform
Agreement, "We shall not respond to the proposals the Inspectors may put
forward. . . . The Armenians are trying to create a new Bulgaria. They
don't seem to have learned their lessons. All the undertakings opposed by
us are bound to fail. Let the Armenians wait. Opportunities will certainly

come our way, too. Turkey belongs only to the Turks." While openly preaching against the boycott, CUP established the Law on the Encouragement of Industry, stipulating that buying Ottoman products was preferable, even if they cost 10% more than the imported equivalent.[52] And over the past few months, CUP was busy setting up "a sophisticated network of party branches in the provinces, directed by party loyalists who were dedicated to a new Turkification plan."[53]

~ ~ ~

The focus of the Talas missionaries in 1914 was on reforming their teacher's training. They had created the Talas Teachers' Association, and had hosted a three-day "Teachers' Institute" for 60 native teachers from their outstations.[54] Clara was especially proud that one young woman had travelled fourteen days from Diarbekir just to study in Talas. "They have a fine training class there," said Clara, "but it is all in Armenian, and this girl expects to teach Muslim children. So she comes here, because ours is the only Training School in the Turkish language in Turkey!"[55]

They had also started an Educational Club to relieve local women of their "everyday drudgery, who had nothing outside to interest or elevate" themselves. The first meeting had a lecture on the life of Socrates, a presentation on "seeing and hearing," and several musical interludes. It was held on a rainy night, but deemed a great success, "the only drawback being that so many men wanted to come," said Genevieve. "Some had to come and bring their wives and daughters, but the problem now is, how to get rid of the unnecessary men! Preachers, priests and male teachers were very much in evidence. Indeed the audience numbered about 150, and they were all so appreciative that they doubtless would like to come again; but it is hoped for the sake of the girls and young women themselves that the men will only take note and form a separate club."[56]

Alden and Esther Hoover left for their year's furlough, and Susan went with them as far as Constantinople to attend the Western Turkey Mission's AGM with 20 others. Dr. Fred MacCallum chaired the event, Rev. Arthur Ryan gave the sermon, and Rev. Theodore Elmer officiated at the Lord's Supper. The Fourth of July was "piously observed as a holiday" on the grounds of the American Embassy at the kind invitation of US Ambassador Henry Morgenthau.[57] While the Americans were celebrating, serious clouds of strife hovered across the sea. Days before, Archduke Franz Ferdinand of Austria was assassinated in Sarajevo. Days later, the Ottoman Empire began mobilization. It looked very much like Susan's prediction to her father was coming true: Another war was about to happen.

6

Mad for War

The July Crisis of 1914 was a month of frantic diplomacy as the major powers of Europe tried to avoid war after the archduke's death. The Balkan wars had shaken the political balance in the Near East,[1] but when Djavid Bey, CUP Minister of Finance, made his budget speech before the Ottoman parliament on July 4, he presented an optimistic vision. "I am not of those who consider our cause a lost one. My statements are therefore founded not on sentiment, but on practical observations. We have indeed, in the immediate past, a period blemished by humiliation. But we must not forget that back of that, we have another past, more glorious and brilliant, a past full of heartening examples. And I believe if we can now earn the right to live, and if we grasp firmly the duties imposed on us by this right, we may make this glorious past live again, and with increased brilliance."[2]

The wars of the last few years had been expensive, and the recent purchase of the dreadnaughts, the *Reshadiye* and *Sultan Osman*, "all of which was, of course, necessary for the safety of the Empire," had pushed the public debt to almost £T 140 million. The two highest items in the 1914-15 budget were the £T 15 million servicing of the debt, and the cost of mobilization at £T 6 million. "All this in addition to the big budgets for gendarmerie and the navy," lamented *The Orient*. "Oh, that the figures might have been interchanged, and ten or twelve millions been allotted to education and agriculture, while the army and navy stayed content with a million or so!"[3]

As nationalism and colonialism clashed in the region, world stock prices dipped, and diplomats continued their seemingly fruitless quest to avoid war, everyone hoped for the best, but prepared for the worst. Within the Ottoman Empire, the Minister of War began mobilization: assembling armed forces, industries, transportation, etc. for service to a war-time government. Though the German officers had been training the army for several months, more troops were needed quickly. Enver Pasha ordered all male Ottomans aged 20-40 to become soldiers. He also requisitioned most of the country's horses for the cavalry and artillery, large quantities of goods to equip the military, and all railways, at least for the time being, to be used solely for troop transport.[4] He was so proud he had raised a large army in little time "with practically no money" that he boasted to Ambassador Henry Morgenthau it was a feat "no other nation had ever done before." Morgenthau was not impressed. "I told Enver that this ruthless method of mobilizing and requisitioning was destroying his country." Morgenthau predicted that misery and starvation would soon begin to afflict the land.[5] It only took a couple of weeks for that to happen.

~ ~ ~

On Friday July 24, Winston Churchill, First Lord of the Admiralty, listened with astonishment as the Austro-Hungarian Empire's note to Serbia was read aloud in the British parliament. "It was an ultimatum such as had never been penned in modern times," Churchill said. "It seemed absolutely impossible that any State in the world could accept it, or that any acceptance, however abject, would satisfy the aggressor."[6] In other words, war was inevitable.

On Tuesday, July 28 Austria-Hungary declared war on the Kingdom of Serbia. That same day, Churchill requisitioned the *Reshadiye* and the *Sultan Osman* for the Royal Navy. Turkey had made its last payment on the *Reshadiye* days before, and 500 Turkish sailors were waiting on a transport in the River Tyne in northeast England ready to sail her home. "The Turkish Captain demanded delivery of the vessel, and threatened to board her and hoist the Turkish flag," said Churchill, who forebade the action—by armed force if necessary. "I took this action solely for British naval purposes."[7]

It was a wise military decision. Within a week, the world had gone mad. Due to various treaties, countries were obliged to ally with each other in case of war. On one side was the Triple Entente, consisting of the British Empire (England, Scotland, Wales, Ireland, Canada, Australia, New Zealand, South Africa and India), the French Third Republic, and the Imperial Russian Empire, in addition to Serbia, Montenegro and Belgium. On the other side were the Central Powers: the Austria-Hungarian Empire and the German Empire. Several nations declared their neutrality, including the Ottoman Empire.

The Ottomans were quite naturally outraged when Britain had confiscated the ships. These two vessels "represented a spectacular outburst of patriotism"[8] for them. Men, women and children had enthusiastically donated to the cause, and suddenly it was to be taken away? The *Tasfiri Efkiar* found it "truly astonishing and strange" that the British Empire, with millions of Muslim subjects in India, would "adopt a policy so openly hostile to the Muslims," and called it "an act of piracy so iniquitous that we are really powerless to find words to express the indignation and anger."[9] Both the Grand Vizier, Said Halim Pasha, and the Minister of the Interior spoke to British diplomat Henry Beaumont on August 4 "with some vexation" about the incident. Talat said that it was an "unfriendly act" because Turkey was not at war, and "referred to the very heavy financial sacrifices by which this ship had been paid for, with money borrowed at" an interest rate of 20%. Naturally they wanted to be reimbursed. Beaumont telegraphed British Foreign Secretary Sir Edward Grey the next day to report on the Grand Vizier's "renewed assurances that Turkey intended to observe strict neutrality,"[10] something the Triple Entente devoutly wished.

The Turkish press reported that the British government declared it would repay the cost of the ships, but this was not true.[11] Grey had promised "due consideration" not "due compensation" for the loss.[12] The Turkish government understood the political difference, but as the Grand Vizier said, they "had to pretend to the Turkish public . . . that they were taking a stronger line than really was the case."[13] On August 8, Churchill wrote the following internal memo: "The Turks should have back whatever they have paid—no more. And there is no hurry about this. They may join the Germans, in which case we shall save our money. Negotiate and temporise."[14]

The public felt betrayed, but what neither they nor the British knew was that Enver, Talat, Halim, and Halil Bey, President of the Chamber of Deputies, had been secretly negotiating since late July to ally with Germany. Not even other members of their own Cabinet were aware of the meetings. Some of the Cabinet were pro-British, as was the majority of the public. Talat was not convinced that a German alliance was the best course, but he did not believe the empire could survive "as a neutral in a war of the Great Powers."[15] A 1911 overture to Britain for a permanent alliance had been rejected,[16] and since Britain and France had good relations with the empire's historic enemy, Russia, the choice was down to the Central Powers. As a potential partner, the Ottomans could offer Germany little in the way of military and economic aid, but strategically they controlled the Bosporus strait; they could block the Russian navy from leaving the Black Sea. On August 2 they signed the secret deal, with a condition that annoyed the Germans: They insisted on maintaining a public show of neutrality.[17] This is why they "pretended" outrage before the Turkish public over the seizure of the two ships. While they appreciated the political and military reasons for the confiscation, they also recognized that it played in their favour—it was guaranteed to sway public opinion away from the British when the time came, and support an alliance with Germany and Austria-Hungary. However, everyone "except

Enver wished to delay an overt act against Russia until the progress of the war revealed some sign of its probable outcome."[18]

~ ~ ~

The effects of mobilization in Turkey were punishing. Because all passenger and freight service was halted, Susan and her colleagues were stuck in Constantinople. She visited friends, and busied herself helping out at Bible House, but she worried about not being able to return to Talas in time for the start of the school year. She was asked by the Gedik Pasha School in Scutari to teach there—if they had enough students to pay her salary. "It remains to be seen whether the patrons of the school can produce any ready money," said the principal, Anna B. Jones. The school's money was in an Austrian bank in the city, and it might be frozen.[19]

James McNaughton reported from Bardezag, 72 miles southwest from the capital, that food prices soared, and people feared a famine. "A very large part of the flour used in this region comes from Russia and Roumania," he said. "If war progresses, we cannot hope for supplies from those countries."[20] George E. White, President of Anatolia College, said the requisitioning in Marsovan was progressing "in the most relentless manner, . . . but the hardest immediate feature is the entire lack of money. None is in circulation and no checks can be cashed." He was worried whether they could keep the school open, but was hopeful. "Some parents regard the college as the safest and best place for their sons, especially for those from twelve to fifteen or eighteen years of age."[21]

During the second week of August Dr. Clarence D. Ussher was returning home to Van from Eastern Turkey's AGM in Moush. "The military had seized nearly all the foodstuffs, kerosene, and sugar" he said, "leaving many families without food, and only the women and children to care for the fields. . . . We saw almost no horses along the road, as all had been seized. Near the cities all oxen and ox carts had been seized and the people had no means of transporting or threshing their grain. At one place we saw the women beating out with clubs enough grain for their day's bread." When he arrived in Van he discovered a similar situation. With no cash available, they could not buy food. "The other day Mrs. Ussher had three cents in our treasury, and we were expecting to eat little more than bread and water, when the son of a church member brought us a basket of apples, which made a delicious addition to our fare. [Rev. Ernest] Yarrow has since got some money and distributed a lira to each household." He added that the mobilization affected everyone—Turks, Kurds and Christians alike.[22] Edward C. Woodley in Marash, agreed. "Relations between Christians and Muslims are not strained. In fact, their common trouble seems to have drawn them together."[23]

By late August, recruits from inland were finally making their way to the coast. In Aintab, John E. Merrill, President of Central Turkey College, described the exhaustion of the regiments from Oorfa and Marash as they marched through the city. "Without uniforms, dirty and tired from the journey, without weapons, possessed of a few lumber wagons and a group of ox carts, they look like refugees rather than the rank and file of an army. They are sturdy material, no doubt, but one cannot help wondering how and when they will assume the appearance of a military force." The War Ministry had made no arrangements for provisions, so the locals spent much of the evening distributing food and water to the men. "The Marash regiment is said to have lost one man by death, and a large number by desertion on the march," Merrill said. "The Oorfa regiment is reported to have left seven or eight dead by the way."[24]

This lack of organization was noted with anger and frustration by several other missionaries. Charles T. Riggs in Constantinople spoke for them all when he described the "vagaries" of the mobilization efforts as absurd. "Men are called out, then told to go home; called to report every day for a while at army headquarters, till their business is ruined, and then told they may be called later for service. They are told to bring five days' provision with them when they go to the barracks, and then not fed at all for ten days. The men from twenty-one to forty-five are called out; later those between forty and forty-five are told they are not wanted; but the next day all tinsmiths up to forty-five, or all blacksmiths, or the carpenters, or some other trade are called to report. They have sometimes called for volunteer seamstresses, which is, I suppose, for the purpose of making up uniforms, for they have not sufficient uniforms by a good deal for the troops they have called out. The worst thing is that they have not barracks or tents or shelter of any kind for many of their troops."[25]

"Certainly the situation is fraught with heavy possibilities," Nesbitt Chambers said. Having lived through the destruction in Cilicia in 1909, he was deeply concerned about the near future. "It makes my heart sick to think of the destitution and suffering. One of my prayers has been that I might be spared the experiences of any more relief work. It seems to me I have had more than my share. It is the most trying and stressful kind of work."[26]

~ ~ ~

Late into the night of August 3, Germany declared war on France. Admiral Wilhelm Souchon, commander of the two-ship German

"S. M. Panzerkreuzer Göben".

German battleship *Goeben*. SOURCE: Private collection.

squadron in the Mediterranean Sea, was notified. In the wee hours of August 4 he received orders to take the *Goeben*, his battle cruiser, and the *Breslau*, a light cruiser, to Constantinople. He knew there were 80,000 French troops in Algiers, making ready to sail for France, and decided to attack before heading east as ordered. The ships replaced their German flags with Russian flags, and approached the African ports of Philippeville and Bône. This kind of deception contravened the Hague Convention, of which Germany was a signatory, but was permissible in the *Kriegsbrauch* (German Conduct of War manual). The Germans fired on the ports, then took off in a north-easterly direction. There were 37 ships in the French Mediterranean fleet, and 27 in the British fleet. Surely they could capture the *Goeben* and *Breslau* quickly? When the British spotted them between Sardinia and Algiers, the chase was on. Assuming the Germans were trying to escape to the Atlantic, they set up a naval blockade. No one gave a thought that the squadron's ultimate destination might be the Black Sea. For four days the ships played a cat-and-mouse game as the Germans made an erratic but strategically clever dash for Constantinople. On August 7 the *Gloucester*, a British light cruiser, encountered the *Goeben* and *Breslau* southwest of Greece. There was an exchange of gunfire, as witnessed by a passing Italian liner, but unable to defeat the faster, more powerful *Goeben*, the *Gloucester* had to back off. On August 10, the Germans reached the Dardanelles. The strait had recently been mined, and Souchon had to wait not only for an escort through it, but permission from the Ottomans to enter. A warship to pass through the waters of a neutral country during wartime would be a violation of international law.[27]

To get around this sticky problem, German Ambassador von Wangenheim arranged for the ships to have been "purchased" by the Ottoman Empire for its navy. They were being delivered to Constantinople, he said, renamed the *Sultan Selim* and the *Medilli*, to replace the ships confiscated in such a dastardly fashion by the British. Souchon and his crew sailed triumphantly through the Dardanelles, across the Sea of Marmora, and into the Ottoman port. "They took delight in putting on Turkish fezzes thereby presenting to the world conclusive evidence that these loyal sailors of the Kaiser were now parts of the Sultan's navy."[28]

The deed was done. Weeks later Sir Louis Mallet, British Ambassador in Constantinople, telegraphed the British Foreign Secretary with a dire prediction: "It is not likely that the two German men-of-war will come out of the Dardanelles, but there are grounds for thinking that the German plan is to urge Turkey to attack Russia."[29]

~ ~ ~

By the time the Anatolian Railway resumed regular passenger service,[30] Susan and the American Board had decided that she would go home on furlough a year early. There was not enough time for her to gather her belongings in Talas and travel to Smyrna to catch the steamer to Italy. She was confident her possessions would be waiting for her upon her return; meanwhile, she could borrow clothes from her sisters, and even shop for new ones. Fortunately she had her passport with her, but she applied for and was granted an exit certificate from police headquarters, now required for all foreigners or Ottoman subjects wishing to leave the empire.[33]

Susan left Naples on board the SS *Critic* on Tuesday, November 3rd, travelling at her own risk. "On account of the war, the ship takes no responsibility about the journey," she noted in her diary. She shared a stateroom with a woman who had spent the summer with friends at Capri, and a dining table with several travellers, including a "frivolous girl" and "an exceptionally fine looking and distinguished" young man. There were some well-known Americans on board. She did not name them, but noted, "They must be of the non-panicky kind who did not fly from Europe on the first boats after the war began."

On Thursday the ship passed Sardinia, which was "rather barren and rugged. . . . They tell me the people of the island are rather a bad lot." The main topic of conversation on board was the possibility of being run down by a German cruiser, though all the passengers agreed that being captured by the enemy had a higher probability than a collision. In any case, they had been warned that the ship would go into a black-out mode after leaving Gibraltar.

On Friday, they arrived safely at "the great rock at the entrance to the Mediterranean, for the Allied navies of France and England are able to control this sea. No ship can pass through the strait of Gibraltar without being challenged and, if necessary, searched as to cargo and crew." Only two crew members were allowed to go ashore, but several men came aboard with items for sale: shawls, scarfs, lace and flowers. Susan sent a postcard to Stella. "I decided it must be written in Arabic Turkish because of the censorship, which will doubtless cut out everything in English now. What shall we do? I almost regret that I have decided on going to America," she wrote. "There might be something I could do and I am so anxious about the friends I have left."

After several hours, they set off again. "The sunset was wonderful as we steamed out into the West. It was as though we were going into the glory of it. Homeward bound! We are off for America!" Not long afterward, a searchlight honed in on the ship through the dark. It drifted back and forth over the deck. The passengers watched and waited nervously as the *Critic* chugged on. Finally they could see a boat coming towards them. Susan heard someone on the boat shout, "Where are you from?" The wind was strong, so she could not hear her captain's reply. Apparently no one on the other boat could hear a reply either. They called over the question four more times. Then they fired over the *Critic's* bow. The captain brought the ship to a standstill.

The searchlight boat came alongside, and someone asked again, "Where are you from?"

"We have just left Gibraltar," the captain replied.

"Where are you bound?"

"Boston."

"What is your cargo?"

"Fruit and spaghetti."

"All right, thank you."

That was it. The boat drifted off. The *Critic* hissed steam from its escape valve, and headed west. At dinner everyone talked nervously about the exciting, somewhat frightening, experience. That night in her understated way, Susan wrote: "We are very conscious that we are sailing the seas under very serious circumstances." When they reached the Azores on Monday, they took on 150 steerage passengers—"new recruits for American citizens." Then it was discovered that a Greek passenger had smallpox. Everyone on board either required a vaccination or was to be kept in quarantine for two weeks once they reached Boston. "I don't care much," Susan noted. "I was vaccinated in June."[32]

~ ~ ~

By early October, the CUP government had taken full advantage of the distraction of war. While the other countries were fighting one another, the officially neutral Ottomans were busy emancipating themselves from foreign control. Under martial law, and much to the consternation of foreigners, they had abolished foreign post offices and the much-despised capitulations. They ordered all foreign businesses to keep their books in Turkish, and pressured them to hire Turks as partners and employees. They had even replaced the street signs in Constantinople that were in French—the international language of the time—with Turkish signs,[33] much to the confusion of the city's residents.

"A number of ugly things seem to indicate that we are drifting toward war," William Peet, ABCFM Constantinople Treasurer told readers of the *Missionary Herald*. The government had seized goods from local stores to equip the thousands of soldiers who were pouring into the tent city growing on both sides of the Bosporus. He learned from friends who knew CUP members that the leaders were "mad for war."[34] However, in late October, Talat still thought that a war would end badly for the Ottomans,[35] and the Grand Vizier insisted that military action would not be taken without the "full assent of the Government."[36] The person who was mad for war was the Minister of War. Germany had been secretly transporting gold bars to Turkey, as a loan and enticement to enter the war. By October 23 an additional £T 3 million was in the Ottoman coffers.[37] Four days later, Enver confided to the Austrian Ambassador "that he was determined to have war, whatever his colleagues might desire. The Turkish fleet would be sent into the Black Sea, and he could easily arrange with Admiral Souchon to provoke hostilities."[38] The British could see this happening. "Enver, who is a willing tool of the Germans," said British Ambassador Mallet, "is now supreme."[39]

On October 29 it came true. The *Sultan Selim* (formerly the *Goeben*) led a squadron into the Black Sea, sunk a Russian gunboat at Odessa, and bombarded Feodosia.[40] The next day the British, French and Russian ambassadors turned over their passports to the Ottoman government, closed their embassies, and left. The American Ambassador accepted responsibility to care for British and French citizens in Turkey, and Italy agreed to care for Russian interests.[41]

Within two weeks the Ottoman Empire was officially on the side of the Central Powers. On pressure from the German Department of Oriental Propaganda, the Ottomans declared a jihad against their Christian enemies. It was a strange act, considering the CUP officials were mostly secular, only 5% of the world's Muslims lived in the Ottoman Empire, and its allies—Germany and Austria-Hungary—were predominantly Christian.[42] Still, whatever it took to save the empire was deemed worthy of pursuit.

On board the *Critic* Susan learned the news from the ship-to-shore wireless service. "Turkey has got into it at last!" she wrote in her diary. "Poor, deluded country. Why did she do it? We are very anxious about the foreigners in Turkey for fear of the trouble they may be in at this time, for there has been much anti-foreign agitation and the fanaticism of the Turks may lead to tragic results."[43]

7

Eve of Destruction

Minister of War Enver Pasha had such a passion for all things military that his friends called him Napoleonlik (little Napoleon), after his idol. He had graduated from the elite Imperial Academy of Military Science, and was always looking for ways to improve both himself and the Empire's defence system. He had served with an infantry battalion near Bulgaria and had learned all about guerrilla warfare tactics there. He was a man of decisive action—some called it recklessness—so when his uncle Halil introduced him to the Committee of Union and Progress, he saw his chance to make change.

After the 1908 revolution, he was appointed as a military attaché to Berlin and acquired another idol: Frederick the Great. He also acquired a fluency in German, a Kaiser-styled moustache, gold braid, and numerous medals, all of which stoked his vanity. Unlike many of his CUP colleagues, Enver was devoutly religious, and did not drink or smoke. He had married into the Imperial family, and though he had a certain hauteur in his small stature and his attitude, he had an unusually liberal view of women's rights. But he was also remorseless, ambitious, brave in battle—even audacious—and cold-bloodily determined to save the empire. "I shall go down in history as the man who demonstrated the vulnerability of England," he told Henry Morgenthau. "I am a man of destiny."[1]

To help him on this journey was a newly-developed force known as the Special Organization (SO). It was similar to the old spy system of previous sultans, but employed the modern "Western concept of a political and military intelligence agency that would both collect information and act upon it. In addition, this organization assumed the military role of recruiting and directing irregular, guerrilla units in military and quasi-military operations."[2] The SO was a loose collection of various units: some serving the Ministries of War and the Interior, some aimed at suppressing Arab separatist groups or terrorizing Greek or Armenian businesses, and some geared at fanning Muslim resistance outside of the empire.[3] The SO was also a secret organization, which operated outside the official army and police departments. Though high CUP officials, such as the Central Committee's Dr. Nazim Bey and Dr. Bahaeddin Shakir, were deeply involved, the Grand Vizier and others were kept in the dark about its existence.[4]

In the fall of 1914, recruitment for the SO intensified. There were several sources. Poor, urban, unemployed young men were often receptive to join *chettes* (bands of outlaws), especially on the promise of "carte blanche to pillage."[5] "We need people for purposes of brigandage in the Caucasus," read one telegram from the Ministry of the Interior. "Try to assemble as many Lazes and Circassians as possible, namely those who are most suitable for brigandage."[6] Similar calls went out for Kurdish and Circassian cavalry, led by tribal chiefs.[7] "Pay no heed to the age of the men," wrote a CUP party secretary to a chieftain, "merely make sure the individuals . . . are steadfast and sufficiently resolute that they would gladly die for their country and nation."[8] Recent Muslim refugees from the Balkans were actively recruited, for some of those men were considered "vindictive and ready for battle."[9]

Orders also went out to release certain convicts from prison to join the SO. In fact, Talat personally participated in creating a list of names.[10] These paramilitary units were trained and outfitted in Constantinople and along the Black Sea.[11] "I saw hundreds of men in Constantinople dressed in a peculiar uniform, being drilled, as I supposed, for military service," said Fred MacCallum. "On inquiry, I was informed that they were criminals condemned to penal servitude for life, but had been released from the prisons and given a certain amount of military training and then sent to take charge of the Armenians."[12]

Gendarmes were often used by the SO when policing was needed. They were not usually the most able or dedicated individuals. In response to a sympathetic question about how gendarmes could afford to live on a lower-than-living-wage, one replied, "Eh, we lie, and steal, and trust in God."[13] It was entirely fair to call the Special Organization a disreputable force of more than 30,000[14] opportunists and bullies, who demonstrated "the depths to which the Unionists were prepared to go to defend their despotic system."[15]

In late 1914 Talat removed another pesky bit of foreign control: he cancelled the Armenian Reform Agreement, and sent the European inspectors packing before they had even begun their work.[16]

Then Enver decided to ignore a lesson from history and do what Napoleon had done a hundred years before—attack Russia in winter.

~ ~ ~

Men who were not eligible for military service could not work due to the stoppage of industries. "This means poverty and suffering," Herbert Irwin said of conditions in Talas. "The requisition of the railroads and of all good traction animals has stopped the movement of freight.

Consequently many staples, especially sugar and kerosene, are almost impossible to find in the interior." In nearby Sivas, Ernest Partridge noted that the harvest was left in the fields and shepherds had been taken into the army, "leaving the flocks uncared for and alone. The government is making no pretense of paying for anything." Food, products or anything else that could be used by the army was confiscated. And the government was building barracks and schools using the free labour of men ineligible for service.[17] On request, William Peet sent an itemized list of mission hospitals to the War Department, and the missionaries, YMCA, YWCA, and Red Cross workers all readied themselves for an influx of wounded soldiers.[18]

Canadian missionaries were among the 36 other British subjects working for the ABCFM.[19] As belligerents, they were expected to leave the country. Herbert was a decorated veteran of the Boer War, therefore was able to make a calculated risk for Genevieve, their children and himself to stay.[20] Since Talas was deep in the interior, and the governor was not unfriendly, they felt relatively safe. Not so for James McNaughton, a minister and teacher in Afion Kara Hissar. He was seized by the local authorities, and was given twenty-four hours to report to Nicomedia for detention. According to the American Ambassador, who had assumed responsibility for Canadian citizens, Rev. McNaughton "was receiving harsh treatment." He pleaded with Talat for McNaughton's release.

"The man is an English agent," said Talat, "and we have the evidence for it." When asked to produce it, Talat said, "We'll do nothing for any Englishman or any Canadian until they release Ayoub and Zinnoun," (his friends).

"But you promised to treat English in the employ of Americans as Americans," said Morgenthau.

"That may be," said Talat, "but a promise is not made to be kept forever. I withdraw that promise now. There is a time limit on a promise."

After a lengthy discussion, Morgenthau managed to cajole the Minister into releasing McNaughton. A similar situation occurred later with Nesbitt Chambers in Adana. As Morgenthau noted, Talat had a mercurial nature: "fierce and unyielding one day, and uproariously good-natured and accommodating the next."[21]

Censorship was strictly enforced, but there were creative ways around it. One unnamed teacher at the Talas Girls' School sent a coded message back home describing the trouble they had had with government agents over taxation of its new building. She suggested her friend "might profitably read certain passages in the Bible:" 1 Kings 20:6, 1 Kings 20:11, 2 Chronicles 21:17a, Ezra 7:24, and Nehemiah 5:11-12.[22]

~ ~ ~

Soon after the declaration of war in November, the Russian Imperial army fought the Ottomans in the Transcaucasus near Kars. Enver decided to personally lead a counter offensive at the end of December at Sarikamish. It was a disastrous campaign. The deep snow caused him to leave his artillery behind. His 90,000 troops were forced to sleep in freezing temperatures. There was a shortage of food, an outbreak of typhus, and uncoordinated communications.[23] He lost the battle—and 78,000 soldiers, mostly due to "cold and exhaustion crossing a mountain ridge in the dead of winter."[24] Enver was deeply humiliated by the defeat, and blamed Armenians for the loss.[25] An Armenian militia from the Russian Caucasus certainly had fought with the Imperial army, but the CUP leadership believed *all* Armenians on both sides of the border were plotting against the empire. As early as 1913 there had been speculation that "the entire Armenian population there is supposedly fitted out with modern weapons and are prepared to launch an attack against the Turks at any time at a sign from Russia."[26] There was a grain of truth to them being armed. For a decade Dashnaks had "trained Armenians around Lake Van to use arms against preying Kurds, had generated propaganda, assisted threatened peasants, and administered reprisals against Turks and Kurds."[27] But most civilians simply wanted peace in their lives and in the region.

The area between Lakes Van and Urmia, and north to Julfa, was known as Persian Azerbaijan, and was strategically important because of the road-rail links for troops between Mesopotamia and the Caucasus,[28] and access to the rich oil fields of Baku on the Caspian Sea. All the belligerents wanted to control it. Since August the land had turned into a "killing field." The perpetrators were "a confusing array of forces made up of regular army, irregular cavalry, volunteers, and brigands ran amok." Persians, Russians, Ottomans, Kurds, Armenians and Assyrians were all guilty of pillaging, burning villages, destroying farms, and massacring their enemies, perceived or real.[29] The victims were—as usual—civilians.

Jevdet Bey, Enver's brother-in-law, was the leading Ottoman raider in the area. He had been appointed by Talat as temporary vali of Van in September.[30] Dr. Clarence Ussher of the American Board's Van mission disdainfully noted that Jevdet almost immediately "took bands of volunteers across the border to stir up the Persians against Russia and, by destroying and plundering many Christian villages, to arouse their lust for blood so strong that they might be incited to join in a holy war."[31] Jevdet was well known for his "anti-Armenian zeal,"[32] and though he may have roused local Muslims to his cause, the jihad was a failure. CUP and their German advisors had vastly overestimated Muslim antipathy to Christian imperialism.[33] As Dr. Fred Shepard of Aintab put it, "The Muslim population is friendly, and the attempt to stir up religious fanaticism has fallen flat; it is ridiculed by the intelligent ones and ignored by the rest."[34]

Around the same time the Ottomans suffered another major defeat, thanks to Djemal Pasha. As commander of the Fourth Army, he had failed to take the Suez Canal. He returned to Damascus as the military governor of Syria, and spent the rest of the war there, garnering the nickname *al-Saffah*, the Blood Shedder.[35]

The British and French navy attacked the Dardanelles in February and March without success.[36] There was no doubt they would try again, and very soon. If they could open the straits, they could supply Russian troops on the Eastern Front with much-needed food and equipment and perhaps turn the tide of the war. The Committee had no control over foreign enemies, but they could certainly do something about what they saw as the empire's greatest internal threat—Armenians. Talat appointed Jevdet as permanent vali of Van, and Dr. Reshid as the vice governor of Diarbekir. Reshid's first act as the new vali was to re-hire Chief of Police Memduh, who had been responsible for setting a terrible fire in the city's market, which had destroyed many Armenian businesses, and several shops owned by Turks. His second act was to "set up gangs consisting of infamous bandits and tribal chiefs in the area."[37] In other words, contribute to the Special Organization membership.

Then, with the stroke of a pen, Enver disarmed Armenian soldiers and transferred them to labour battalions, which were already comprised mainly of Greeks and Armenians. No longer combatants, they were to do the army's grunt work as "road labourers and pack animals."[38] On February 24 a homemade bomb exploded near Talas. It killed the Armenian bomb maker, and unleashed shockwaves throughout the empire.

~ ~ ~

Kevork Poshayan, an Armenian who had recently returned from the United States, was manufacturing bombs in his home in Everek, about 25 miles south of Talas. He had just finished making three, when he accidentally triggered a fourth. The local CUP branch had suspected such activities were taking place in the area, but now they not only had proof, they had the perfect excuse to conduct house-to-house searches throughout Kaisarieh. Initially government officials told the Talas missionaries they wanted to keep the matter quiet to ensure no trouble was "stirred up between Armenians and Turks."[39] The CUP government in Constantinople, however, was dissatisfied with the efforts and results of the kaimakam, and suddenly replaced him with Salih Zeki Bey. The Talas missionaries hoped for the best, but were soon horrifically disappointed. Zeki, who also served as the interim commander of the 15th Division of the army in Kaisarieh, was "virulently anti-Armenian."[40] What followed was months of cruelty and violence.

The entire male population in the village of Chomaklou above military age was arrested.[41] In Tomarza 400 Armenians were arrested, tortured, and sent to the prison in Cesarea.[42] Stella Loughridge estimated that 600 to 1,000 men from Talas and Cesarea were imprisoned. She knew from her many visits to the prison that they were "subjected to torture in order to force them to confess that they had arms concealed."[43] The prison was located in the large, ancient, imposing castle of Cesarea. Within its walls was a village which had "become a sort of inner dwelling-place of Muslim fanatics." Deep underground lay the dungeons—"places of despair . . . without light or opening to the air, but with ancient rusty ring-bolts in the walls and lengths of heavy much-rusted chain attached."[44] The torture was a particularly nasty and painful form. "The men, whether guilty of having had guns or not, were fastened with the head down and feet up," said Clara Richmond, "and beaten on the soles of the feet until the strongest would faint."[45] Frieda Wolf-Hunecke, a German missionary who worked at a British mission in Everek, said, "During Roman times, 40 blows was the highest, but here 200, 300, 500, even 800 blows were supposedly administered. The foot begins to swell enormously, then bursts open on top due to the repeated blows."[46]

"For weeks some of those whom I saw were unable to put on their shoes or walk without a cane because of their swollen feet," said Stella. "I visited the prison often, and saw six men confined for many days in a space not more than six feet square, with nothing to eat except what their friends were able to send in."[47] There was no sanitation, and when a man died, there was no hurry to remove the body. Clara and a colleague visited the home of Jebidelikian Effendi, a wealthy merchant and the father of a former student. He had been badly beaten, and his voice was so weak they could hardly hear him. "His house was practically in ruins," Clara said. "Floors, closets, cellar, all torn up in the search for weapons which he did not have."[48]

The Talas hospital's druggist did have weapons. Haig Effendi Haroutounian was beaten and kept in custody for three months until he revealed the location of the three guns he brought home from his service during the Balkan War. He had hidden them in a nearby garden. "We were surprised to find that he had a large quantity of ammunition," said Theda Phelps. "And that a good many others had also."[49]

Ambassador Morgenthau called this disarmament "senseless" because all Ottomans were allowed to carry guns since the re-instatement of the Constitution in 1908. During the violence in Cilicia in 1909, the government had even "appealed to the armed assistance of the Armenians, especially in the provinces, to fight the enemies of the Constitution. Moreover, the Armenians, as well as all the partisans of the new regime, found it absolutely necessary to carry arms on them, just for self-defence."[50] Johannes Ehmann, a parish priest in Harpoot, found that "the acquisition of permitted or forbidden weapons arose from a great short-sightedness—yes, an almost unforgivable stupidity—because it awoke the distrust of the Muslims and the government, who imputed other intentions to the Armenians with regard to the acquisition of these weapons,"[51] such as secretly plotting revolution.[52]

The cache of weapons accumulated in Kaisarieh allowed the Ministry of the Interior to develop propaganda that there had been an organized Armenian rebellion in the area. In all, a few hundred arms were found, including 24 empty shells under the roof of the local Armenian church. Dozens of Armenians were executed, including the leaders of two secret societies, one of whom gave up, under torture, the list of members. Talat claimed the unearthing of 400 bombs,[53] and published a photograph of the collection. Frieda Wolf-Hunecke said the government claimed to have found 5,000 Mausers and revolvers in Everek, but in fact, attempted "to enlarge everything 70 times."[54] Theda agreed. "We know there were Armenian revolutionary societies," she said wryly. "We know, also, that the government was quite capable of producing a composite picture."[55]

~ ~ ~

In March whispers of something nefarious began to spread among those with government connections. Nurses Thora von Wedel-Jarlsberg and Eva Elvers heard from an Armenian doctor in Erzroom that the government was "preparing for a massacre on a grand scale. He begged us to find out from General Passelt whether the rumour were true. We heard afterwards that the General (a gallant officer) had his own fears of it, and asked, for that reason, to be relieved of his post."[56]

Stella had a long conversation with the vali of Kaisarieh. "He stated to me emphatically that not an Armenian was to be left in the sanjak. About the same time, Ali Sabri Bey, the *tahrirat mudir* (tax administrator) of Cesarea, intimated to me very clearly that something terrible was to happen to our school girls and boys."[57] A Turkish official in Adana warned his Armenian friend, "A new storm is about to break upon the Armenians, and it will exceed anything that has happened before. You know I like you, so I hope that you will save yourself.... Go to Mersine, get on a steamship, and escape to Europe."[58]

Jelal, the vali of Aleppo, told local German Consul Walter Rössler that the CUP government was now seeing "all Armenians as suspicious or even hostile. He thinks of this development as a misfortune for his fatherland," said Rössler. "He begged me to persuade His Excellency the Imperial Ambassador to counteract this trend."[59] Jelal had direct knowledge of the government's attitude. The British had been clandestinely recruiting support among the residents of Cilicia to hinder Ottoman resistance if the British landed at Alexandretta. The new kaimakam in Marash arrested 40-50 Armenians in Zeitoon, accusing them of being part of a pro-Russian armed revolt.[60] Jelal investigated the incident, determined that it was in no way a revolt, and released those who were not charged. He was reprimanded for his efforts by the government by having Zeitoon removed from his authority. Within weeks, the villagers were deported to Konia.[61]

Deportation of Armenians was suggested more than a year before by von Sanders' predecessor, Baron von der Goltz. He believed the real agenda of the Armenian Reform Agreement was to dismember the Ottoman Empire. "In order to save Turkey from a new calamity," he said, "it is necessary to—once and for all—remove the half a million Armenians living in the provinces of Van, Bitlis, and Erzroom, contiguous to the Russo-Turkish borders, . . . to the vicinity of Aleppo and Mesopotamia."[62]

In Konia, Dr. Dodd gave a letter to Adelaide Dwight, who was passing through on her way to the capital, asking her to hand deliver it to William Peet, ABCFM's Turkey Treasurer. "Have you any means by which you can send me as much as fifty liras for relief of the Zeitoonis?" he requested. "The Government has now left them to starve."[63] Much like the fate of the deserted dogs of Constantinople.

~ ~ ~

From mid-April to early May 1915 the CUP government was pushed to the limits of its competence and tolerance.

"We were surprised April 11 by the arrival of a strong and well-equipped Turkish force," said Mary Shedd of the Presbyterian Board's

Front view of St. Cross Monastery of Varak in Van photographed c1910-1915.
SOURCE: Vartan A. Hampikian ©1923, US Library of Congress.

Urmia station. Halil Bey, Enver's uncle, commanded 20,000 troops, including 12,000 irregular Kurdish cavalry, to fight the Russians near Dilman in Persia.[64]

On April 16, Enver's brother-in-law, Jevdet, murdered the Armenian delegates who called on him to reaffirm their loyalty.[65] Convinced the Armenians of Van and area were going to launch a revolt, more than 10,000 Ottoman troops began to bombard the city on April 20. The local Armenians resisted in a kind of guerilla warfare. Special Organization units continued to harass, kill and plunder in the nearby villages. About 15,000 villagers poured into Van during the three-week siege, which was fine with the Ottomans. They "hoped the influx of refugees would deplete the Armenians' supplies and starve them out."[66]

At the same time, 60 miles south in the Hakkari highlands, about 80,000 Assyrians were massacred. The same number escaped to Persia.[67]

On April 19, knowing a British attack was imminent, the town of Gallipoli was ordered evacuated. The Greek residents were given two hours' notice to leave. "No one was allowed, by order of the police, to take anything away with him. . . . Soon after their departure their houses were plundered."[68]

On April 21 Armenian notables began to be arrested and imprisoned in a great number of cities in the interior. The arrests continued for four weeks straight.[69]

On April 23, the Patriarch held an emergency meeting with prominent Armenians in Constantinople to discuss what they could do about the dire activities in the interior.[70] It was futile. The next day, the government rounded up 235 Armenian political, religious, intellectual and cultural leaders in Constantinople, and imprisoned them.[71] The Ministry of the Interior also sent orders to the vilayets that all branches of the Dashnak and Hinchak parties were to be closed, their files seized, and their leaders, members of these parties, and any "important and detrimental Armenians . . . to be arrested and court-martialed."[72]

On April 25, British forces—mainly the Australia and New Zealand Army Corps or Anzacs—landed on the beaches of the Gallipoli peninsula, but Ottoman troops prevented them from reaching the high ridge.[73] Meanwhile the CUP leaders made a contingency plan to evacuate to Konia.[74]

On April 27, the Armenian Catholicos at Etchmiadzin petitioned the United States, Russia and Italy to intervene with the Sublime Porte to end the persecutions of unarmed civilians. In response, Talat blithely told Ambassador Morgenthau that the authorities in the vilayets had been instructed "to protect all innocent people from molestation."[75]

On May 2 the Russians, with considerable help from an Armenian and Assyrian volunteer brigade under the command of Antranik Ozanian, soundly defeated the Ottomans at Dilman. Thousands of troops had been diverted to Van during the siege, but Halil blamed the loss on the Armenians.[76]

Suddenly the possibility of the CUP leaders going down in history as the men who lost the Empire was very, very real. The only way to save it was to destroy their enemies. Enver as Minister of War concentrated on their external enemies. Talat as Minister of the Interior focussed on the Armenians. "He declares openly that their persecution is revenge for the defeat at Sarikamish, the Turkish expulsion from Azerbaijan, and the occupation of Van, all of which he lays at the Armenian door," said American diplomat Einstein. "The Committee of Union and Progress fear the Armenian organization. Added to this is the conviction that they cannot assimilate, and must, therefore, crush them."[77]

Part II: A Time To Mourn

8

Welcome to Hell

Susan Wealthy Orvis was blissfully unaware of the events exploding around her colleagues in Talas. She had arrived home in Dubuque in time for Thanksgiving with her mother and siblings. Her father had died a few months before she left Turkey, and her mother's health was now poor. But the family was happy for the long-awaited reunion. On January 5, 1915 Susan enrolled in graduate school at the University of Chicago.[1] She was going to make good use of her furlough year by learning how to train teachers, just as she and Stella Loughridge had planned.

As usual, a missionary on furlough was expected to drum up enthusiasm and dollars for the cause by speaking to groups and the press. Since Susan was under the auspices of the Woman's Board of Missions of the Interior (WBMI), and the Interior was the vast American mid-West, distances between speaking engagements could be quite long. In March, for example, she was asked to speak in Mattoon, Illinois to two groups on a Wednesday, the last day of the month—in the morning and in the evening—and then again on April 1 to another group. The town was almost 200 miles south of Chicago. "It will keep me away two days and I'll be tired out, but perhaps I can do some good," she wrote to her mother, discounting the travel time entirely. She ended the letter with "How are you today? I was sorry you felt so weak and tired. I wish I could see you this evening. My room here is very comfortable. With much love, Susie."[2] Mary Ellen Phelps Orvis was the only person to whom Susan did not always sign off with her full name. They had a close, loving relationship. Naturally she was quite distraught two months later when Mrs. Orvis died.

Susan arranged to defer her thesis until the summer, so she could spend time with her siblings in Dubuque. But there was an additional reason for her anxiety. North American newspapers began to report on the worsening conditions in Turkey. Even *The Rock Island Argus*, a small town paper 70 miles south of Dubuque, described the massacres occurring in the Lake Van district, stressing that "help is urgently needed."[3] For the first time, she felt real fear for those she left behind.

~ ~ ~

Susan had good reason to worry. By the time the Russian army arrived in Van on May 21, the destruction of Van was complete. They took on the task of cremating 55,000 bodies they found in the district.[4] Days later

Britain, France and Russia made a joint declaration with a new term [in italics]: "In view of these new *crimes* of Turkey *against humanity* and civilisation, the Allied governments announce publicly . . . that they will hold personally responsible . . . all members of the Ottoman government and those of their agents who are implicated in such massacres."[5] The CUP government officials publicly ignored it.[6] They were earnestly ordering the arrest and deportation of Armenians from all of the eastern provinces, and unleashing the Special Organization to implement a final solution to the Armenian Question.

The German consul in Adana reported to his embassy in Constantinople on May 18. "Hundreds of families are being exiled, the prisons are overfilled, and again early this morning several people were executed. With its barbaric methods, the government is obviously damaging the interests of the nation. In particular, the Deutsche Orientbank has suffered considerable damage and has asked me to put a stop to the deportation of Armenians."[7] German Ambassador Hans von Wangenheim replied to the Consul in Erzroom on May 19, "You are authorized to approach your local Supreme Command about the deportation of the Armenians and, if reversal of the measures is inopportune for military reasons, to advocate humane treatment of the deported, defenceless people."[8]

Often, Armenians were given the option of converting to Islam. Many did to avoid deportation. The ceremony included a Mufti (Muslim legal expert) reading from the Quran, then asking the converts, "Are you accepting the true faith, and are you giving up the controversy of One and Trinity?" When the answer was affirmative, they would be congratulated,[9] and their names would be listed on a certificate to change the government registration from their previous Christian denomination (Gregorian, Catholic, or Protestant) to "Muslim." The certificate also stated that they had "appealed to be honored with the glory of Islam, declaring that they are impelled to do this from conscience and their free will."[10] But by mid-June the government decided that, though these converts could stay together, they still "had to be distributed within the province or district."[11]

The deportation of Armenians left the government with the problem of what to do with their property. In most cases the deportees were only given a few days—or in some cases, a few hours—to be ready to leave. They could only take with them whatever cash they had on hand and possessions they could carry; they were not allowed to sell or rent their property. On May 30 the CUP Cabinet decreed that the value of the property the deportees had "abandoned" would be sent to them in their new location, and that Muslim immigrants would be resettled into their abandoned homes. The details of how this would work were outlined in an ordinance on June 10. The administration would be carried out by local Abandoned Properties Commissions. The deportees' lands, buildings, and businesses would be recorded, and the equivalent value forwarded at a later date to the owners, after any debts had been paid. All remaining perishable or moveable goods, crops, and livestock were to be sold at an auction. As quickly as possible, immigrants, mostly from the Balkans, would settle into the Armenians' abandoned houses, according to their needs, financial status, and ability to farm the land. Once the immigrants were settled, tribal families and nomads would be allowed to live in what was left. Buildings and businesses not suitable for immigrant resettlement would also be sold at auction. The Commission was accountable to the Ministry of the Interior, and all revenue from these sales or rents would be held in trust by the government.[12] That was the theory.

The government had been too busy ordering the deportation of Armenians to worry about legalities. In late May they retroactively drafted a provisional law giving sweeping powers "while the country is at war" to military commanders, and "commanders of independent groups" (which neatly covered the Special Organization) to "check all opposition . . . of any form whatever," including to "send away, either individually or in mass, the inhabitants of villages and towns, and install them in other places."[13] The law did not refer to Armenians specifically. The commanders did not need evidence to act, but only "suspicion of espionage or treason, and on military necessity." And rather than present it to Parliament, the Law on Deportations was ratified by the Grand Vizier and Cabinet alone.[14]

On June 4 the new kaimakam in Develi (in Kaisarieh), Zeki Bey, requested permission from the Ministry of the Interior to deport 160 Armenian families from the village of Injesu. His reason: They were connected to the Hinchak party.[15] In early May Johannes Ehmann, the parish priest in Harpoot, whom the German ambassador considered "a level-headed and well-informed observer," reported to the Embassy on the CUP government's "particularly harsh measures against the members of the Dashnak and Hinchak organizations." He believed that membership in those parties should not be a criminal offence, "unless it can be proved that the individual organisation or the individual person has leanings and activities which threaten the security of the state, or are rebellious."[16] But since suspicion was now the only criterion for taking action, permission was granted to Zeki, with a suggestion to send them to a place where there were no Armenians, such as Askerai, 140 miles to the west. This was done within two days, leaving about 300 Armenians and 222 Turks in the village. Ten days later, the mutesarrif "demanded the settlement of 160 immigrant households to replace the deported Armenian families" to prevent the destruction of buildings and to harvest the crops. The next day the Ministry telegraphed its agreement. But in the middle of the Injesu deportations, the government could foresee another problem: Eventually the deported Armenians would become the majority in their new destinations. Therefore, the deportations in Kaisarieh were temporarily halted until they could figure out a better solution.[17]

~ ~ ~

The order for all residents of Talas and Cesarea to turn over any and all arms they possessed came on June 7.[18] "They say that if arms are not given up, the offender will be shot on sight. Without trial," Genevieve Irwin said. "Everybody is commanded to do it. The Christians seem to be complying. The Turks, knowing that nothing will be done to them if they don't give them up are not, upon the whole." Herbert Irwin and Jane Wingate collected and turned in the mission's weapons: one gun, one rifle, two pistols, and ammunition.[19]

A week later on Monday morning June 14, the horror began. The missionaries were making final preparations for the week's Commencement ceremonies and children's programs. They had decided not to put up the large tent in the tennis court as usual because of the sorrow all around them.[20] That afternoon, just before they were to greet the arriving guests for the children's presentations, the sorrow deepened. News came that eleven Armenians had been hanged in Cesarea. Among them were Garabed Jamjian, a highly respected Talas merchant, and Minas Minasian, a member of the Hinchak party. Genevieve noted that the previous mutesarrif had been sent to Smyrna in May, but that everyone spoke well of the new one. "They say that through his influence the number of hangings was reduced from 60 to 11, and he would have done more, if he could."[21]

Nevertheless, "we were stunned," said Theda Phelps. "Some of us stole away up to the hospital garden to have a little time to think before we met the people."[22] They struggled through the program, not being able to bear the children's disappointment of a cancellation, but changed their plans for the rest of the week. They dropped all festivities, and only held the Commencement the next morning for the upper classes and their parents. "No music except hymns," said Genevieve. "The audience mostly in black."[23] "Much like a funeral service," Stella said.[24] After the diplomas were handed out, Henry Wingate preached a sermon. He ended by saying, "I am not ashamed of the Gospel of Christ, for it is the power of God unto salvation to every one that believeth." He expressed his hope that the graduating girls and boys would live a life based on this faith. His words seemed to comfort those in attendance.[25]

On Friday Stella, Clara Richmond and Fanny Burrage visited the homes of five of the men who had been hanged. They found Jamjian's wife and mother shocked by his death, but also terrified by a rumour that they were to be deported. The same fears were evident in every home they encountered. But so was the praise and love for Jamjian, who had been a kind and generous man. A Turkish official wept profusely in front of them for his friend. "He has done everything for me. I would have died for him."[26]

~ ~ ~

The Fourth of July was a subdued event at the Talas mission, not in the least because of the unexpected arrival of two nurses. Their reports of activities in the east were harrowing. Thora von Wedel-Jarlsberg, a Norwegian, and her German colleague, Eva Elvers, had been working in Erzroom with a German charity since October 1914.[27] In the winter, a typhus epidemic started to take hold in the region. Typhus had a 25-30% mortality rate, was highly contagious, had a sudden onset, and was difficult to fight.[28] Among its victims were sick and wounded soldiers, the underfed population, and the doctors and nurses who attended them. The government had confiscated the American Board's boys' and girls' schools in Erzroom, turning them into hospitals. The mission's doctor, Edward Percy Case, called for help from the Sivas mission when Rev. Robert Stapleton, his wife, Dr. Ida Stapleton, and two of their children, Elinor and Sibyl, succumbed to the disease.[29] Dr. C. Ernest Clark, Mary Graffam, Marie Zenger, and former Talas nurse, Lillian Cole Sewny, responded immediately. The journey from Sivas, which usually took 10 days, took twenty-one because of deep snow and bad roads. On arrival, "they found Erzroom one big hospital, every available building filled with sick and wounded." No sooner had they arrived when Lillian heard that her husband, Dr. Levon Sewny, who had been conscripted to the front lines, "was desperately ill of typhus at a village nine hours away." Mary went with her, near the war zone, hearing the "sound of the cannon most of the way." They arrived two days before the doctor died. "The horror and sadness of his death cannot be described," said Mary. "It took us two days to get the rudest kind of a box, which they finally managed by breaking up a door, and then we brought the body on a horse to Erzroom." Lillian had no time to mourn. On the day of their return, Dr. Case was infected. Ten days later it was his wife who succumbed, then the two nurses, Thora and Eva, and then the head Turkish doctor and the hospital's druggist. There were reports of typhoid and typhus raging in Harpoot and Mezereh, too. The hospitals were overflowing, with patients dying at a rate of fifteen per day. "Conditions were indescribable," said one missionary. But since typhus is typically a "cold weather disease," everyone hoped that by spring things would improve with the warmer weather and "more sanitary living conditions."[30] The tide did indeed turn. Many of the Sivas party were able to return home, though without Marie Zenger, who died on March 23.[31]

Thora and Eva recovered. However, there had been many staff changes in the hospital in the intervening time, and there was no work for them in Erzroom. The German Consul found them positions at the Red Cross hospital in Erzingan. In early June they were informed that the Armenian population in the city, roughly 25,000, were to be deported to Mesopotamia. The people were given a few days to sell their possessions, "naturally realised at ludicrous prices," the nurses told the Talas group. "The Red Cross staff were forbidden to have any relations with the exiles, and prohibited any excursions on foot or horseback beyond a certain radius."

By wagon and on foot, wave after wave of Armenians were led south to Harpoot, and supposedly on to their ultimate destination in the Syrian desert. A few weeks later the nurses heard directly from soldiers of the 86th Cavalry Brigade, and a few teachers who had managed to escape, about the slaughter of the deportees. Men, women and children were shot, stabbed with bayonets, smashed in the head, thrown into ravines, and thrown off cliffs into the Euphrates River. "The butchery had taken four hours," they said.

The perpetrators had been Kurdish brigands, Turkish irregulars, and local gendarmes—in other words, the Special Organization. The cavalry soldiers had also been ordered to participate in the killings once they arrived on the scene. "It was horrible," one young soldier told the nurses. "I could not fire. I only pretended." A forty-six year old Turkish cobbler, who had been forced into military service despite every year having paid the tax that should have exempted him, returned the next day with overwhelming grief. "I know the truth," he said. "They are all dead."

The executions had been pre-planned. "The soldiers told us that there were ox carts all ready to carry the corpses to the river and remove every trace of the massacre," said Thora and Eva. The next morning, they decided to follow another procession of deportees as far as they could. They walked for an hour to the edge of Erzingan. "At this point the scene turned into a regular slave market." There were few men among these exiles. Women begged bystanders to rescue them, or at least their children. Some children were rescued by Turks; some were taken without their parent's consent. "For our part, we took a family of six children," said the nurses. Their Turkish cook took a little girl, expecting to keep her in the home of one of the hospital's doctors until the nurses could fetch her. The cook was later beaten and the child thrown into the street by the doctor's Turkish adjutant.

The two nurses accompanied the children back to Erzingan, intending to take them to someplace safe outside of the city. They went to the hospital to collect their baggage, and were told by the Turkish orderlies, "You have done a good deed in taking these children." But after spending the night in a hotel—all eight of them sharing one room—they were snubbed by former Turkish patients in the hotel's café, and were told by the hospital's hodja who dropped by, "If God has no pity on them, why must you have pity?"

The women managed to obtain a meeting with the mutesarrif of Erzingan to ask for permission for the children to travel with them. While there, they also protested the vile treatment they had witnessed of the deported Armenians. The mutesarrif was furious. "Women have no business to meddle with politics," he shouted, "but ought to respect the Government!" Not only did he refuse permission for the children to travel, he told the women they had just been dismissed from the hospital, and ordered them to leave the city and go to Sivas. They were taken to the Armenian district instead of their hotel. "The whole of this extensive quarter of the town seemed dead. People came and went at will to loot the contents of the houses; in some of the houses families of Muslim refugees were already installed."

On June 21 the women set out in a carriage for the seven-day journey to Sivas, under armed guard. "During the first days of our journey we saw five corpses," the nurses said. "One was a woman's, and still had clothes on; the others were naked, one of them headless." One night they were awakened by the sounds of gunfire. The next morning they were told that ten Armenians had been shot. Later they passed over ground that was covered with clotted blood. It had been the last position of a 250-man labour battalion. A few days before arriving at Sivas their driver pointed to a ridge. They saw about 400 Armenian men lined up. "We know what happened after that," they said. They spent a couple of days in Sivas, and arrived at Cesarea, three days later, on the 4th of July.[32]

After visiting with the Talas missionaries, Thora and Eva prepared to continue their journey to Constantinople. It was not to be. A gendarme was posted at their hotel door. They were not even allowed to leave their room. When word of their predicament reached Talas, Herbert and Henry went down the mountain to speak to the authorities. They were able to arrange the release of the nurses into their care. "They all came back from the city," Genevieve wrote in her diary, "and we ate lunch prepared for them tonight, together on the lawn. . . . Postcards from Sivas indicate very serious conditions there."[33]

"We heard that there was trouble in Sivas," said Stella. "We thought it was massacre, and quickly gathered in the girls and teachers who were not in their houses, fearing that some disturbance might break out in the town, as there was great tension."[34]

"First from one side, and then the other, news would come of the villages [around Talas] being sent out," said Theda.[35]

"Then the report came of a little town just a half hour from us was to be sent away, because the people were accused of harboring deserters from the Army," said Stella. "I went with one of our women to the edge of this little town, as she wished to see a relative of hers who lived there." The woman received permission from the gendarmes in the town to talk for a few minutes. Meanwhile Stella watched the Armenians prepare for their journey. They sold whatever possessions they could to get enough money to hire a cart and donkey. Turks from surrounding villages were buying the household goods at the lowest possible prices, though Stella saw some stealing, too. "The next day we saw them start away, over the white, dusty roads under a scorching July sun, guarded on all sides by gendarmes, going they knew not where. A few days later we heard where. After a day's journey the men were separated from the women and children, taken down into a ravine and brutally murdered. The women and children were carried off by the Turks and Circassians to their harems. As the days went by we saw and felt these horrors creeping upon us there in Talas. Every day news would come of this village or that sent away."[36]

"Our nearest village, Derevenk, was sent, and we felt it was only a question of time until both Cesarea and Talas would suffer a similar fate," said Theda.[37] The man responsible for the deportation of Derevenk was Zeki, the kaimakam[38] whom Frieda Wolf-Hunecke called a "cruel and violent-tempered" man.[39] It took less than a week for Theda's prediction to come true.

9

In the Valley of the Shadow of Death

At 11:30 p.m., Sunday, July 11 Clara Richmond was unable to sleep.[1] Sorrowful tales of disrupted lives in the outlying villages in Kaisarieh had affected everyone. As she lay in bed, she suddenly heard loud voices outside the compound, and saw reflected on her walls flashes from lanterns. It was the gendarmes. They went to the house of Boghos Haroutounian, steward and buyer for the Talas mission, and brother of the Hospital's druggist, Haig Haroutounian. They hauled him off to the local jail. "I can never forget the screams of his old mother and his boy as they came to our American men for help," Clara said. "I then saw from my balcony Saibalian Effendi and his son taken from a house below us." The shouting and screaming continued as the gendarmes went from house to house, dragging off thirty-seven prominent men of Talas, including Horen Muggerditchian, head Armenian teacher in the Boys' School, and an associate pastor, Vartavar Garabedian.[2] At midnight Stella, Herbert and Henry went to the police station, but were not allowed to see them nor arrange their release. The next morning, the men were taken to the prison in Cesarea. In all there were about 90 leading Armenian merchants in the prison.[3]

"I saw the Governor at once, and begged that these men be given a fair trial—if charged with any crime—and asked to see that they were not killed," Stella said. "He assured me that he would look into the matter personally and that nothing would happen to them."[4] Turkish merchants tried to help, too. "They sent two telegrams to Constantinople imploring them to stop, and not send Armenians away," said Genevieve, "but it was useless." She noted that Sabri Bey implied "the worst is still to happen."[5]

That day the government in Constantinople sent a coded telegram to the authorities in Kaisarieh and other regions. It was an order for Armenian children who were now orphaned to be distributed "to notables and men of repute in villages and *kazas* (counties) where Armenians and foreigners are not found." It also ordered that a monthly payment from the special appropriations' fund for immigrants be given, for sustenance, for those "children who will be left over after the distribution." There was a warning included: Destroy the telegram after it had been shown to the necessary personnel[6]—no doubt, in case the Triple Entente made good on their threat to charge the Ottoman government with crimes against humanity.

The next day the men who had not been hanged were sent halfway to Sivas to the village of Gemerek. They were not charged with any crime. A few Armenians from that village, disguised as Turks, escaped to Talas with news that all the men and boys in Gemerek had been rounded up. They told the missionaries that 135 young girls had been separated from their families, and secluded on government grounds.[7] After two or three days the males, including Boghos and Horen, were marched out of town. Their clothes were returned, without the men. Mariam Hanum, a former maid in Stella's house, and some of her neighbours were witnesses. Takouhi Donabedian, a former student of the Talas Girls' School, was living in the house of Gemerek's mudir, an old Turk who wanted her to convert to Islam and marry him. She had steadfastly been refusing to do either. It was in his house that she overheard someone describe how the men had been taken to a valley behind Ihmal Oghlu Han, stripped, and shot.[8]

In the midst of all this, swarms of locusts descended on the region, from Syria and Cilicia, across the interior to as far west as Konia.[9] "The air filled with locusts," said Genevieve. "They settled in vineyards and fields in the plain." The government ordered people to collect them, promising payment, "which never came." Henry bought several large bags of the insects to feed the mission's pigs and chickens.[10]

The authorities had prevented the Misses Wedel-Jarlsberg and Elvers from travelling with some Austrian missionaries who came through Cesarea, so the women telegraphed the German Embassy in Constantinople to put pressure on the government to allow them to leave.[11] Perhaps the fact that Miss Wedel-Jarlsberg was of Norwegian nobility[12] helped them finally obtain permission to leave the district. Meanwhile the missionaries agreed that Adelaide Dwight, who had always struggled with her health, should start her furlough now, and go with them. As Theda said, they were counting on her "to get word to America and to let people know what was going on in Turkey." Jane and Henry Wingate decided, for safety's sake, their daughter, Dorothy, would leave with the three women.[13]

On July 16 the four of them travelled south to Oulou Kushla to catch the train to the capital. Along the three-day journey, they saw field after field wiped clean of fruits and vegetables. No doubt the nurses were reminded of the biblical verse, "If you refuse to let My people go, behold, tomorrow I will bring locusts into thy territory," when they wrote of these sights: "The Turks are already beginning to have some experience of the Divine punishment."[14] The women seemed to have forgotten that the

Cesarea castle entrance. Entrance to the imposing
Seljuk castle in Cesarea where the prisoners were
taken. SOURCE: John D. Whiting and G. Eric
Matson, Trip to Cappadocia, 1935, vol. I, US Library
of Congress.

destruction caused by the locusts affected everyone equally. Food would be
scarce for all in the fall and winter.

While they were travelling to Constantinople, Rev. Ernest Partridge
and his family arrived in Talas from Sivas. They spoke of how almost the
entire Armenian population of Sivas had been deported, and how their
colleague, Mary Graffam, had accompanied her school girls to the desert
to protect them from kidnapping or molestation. Even though "no order
had been given for deportation from Cesarea and Talas,"[15] local men
continued to be rounded up. "They were being taken from their homes at
night, kept in prisons from one to three days, and sent out," said Theda.
"Beginning with the wealthier and more prominent men, groups of from
20 to 30 men were gathered up every few nights until nearly all of them
were taken."[16]

"First the rich merchants were taken, then the teachers, lawyers and
others of the more educated classes, until it came to be understood that in

the eyes of the Turkish government, it was a crime to be rich or educated," said Stella. "One man, of fine character, a teacher in the Cesarea school for many years, known by everybody, Turk as well as Christian, to be a man of unstained integrity, said when remonstrated with for being seen on the streets so much, or for going out after dark, 'What have I to fear? I know that there is absolutely nothing for which I can be accused!' Not many days after this, he was gathered up with a number of others, probably as innocent as himself, and hurried off to Aleppo. But he never reached there, for he died on the road from fatigue and exposure."[17]

Genevieve wrote in her diary, they all found "tales of these days heart-rending."[18]

~ ~ ~

Ambassador Morgenthau. SOURCE: Henry Morgenthau, *Ambassador Morgenthau's Story*, Doubleday and Page Company, 1918.

In Constantinople, American Ambassador Henry Morgenthau was beside himself as he listened to the accounts of deportations from missionaries. "For hours they would sit in my office and, with tears streaming down their faces, they would tell me of the horrors through which they had passed. Many of these, both men and women, were almost broken in health from the scenes which they had witnessed. In many cases, they brought me letters from American consuls, confirming the most dreadful of their narrations and adding many unprintable details." They implored the Ambassador to try to persuade the government to stop the madness. Otherwise, they believed "the whole Armenian nation would disappear. It was not only American and Canadian missionaries who made this personal appeal. Several of their German associates begged me to intercede," he said.[19]

Even though he had no legal right to interfere, he certainly tried. On several occasions he discussed with Talat the Ottoman government's deportation policy and appealed to him on justice and humanitarian grounds for ending it. Talat responded with a variety of excuses: Armenians had enriched themselves at the expense of Turks, they were determined to establish a separate state, and they openly encouraged the empire's enemies. The destruction of the whole race was inevitable, he said.[20] On July 16 Morgenthau sent a telegram to the American Secretary of State in Washington, marked Urgent:

> Deportation of and excesses against peaceful Armenians is increasing and from harrowing reports of eye witnesses, it appears that a campaign of race extermination is in progress under a pretext of reprisal against rebellion. Protests as well as threats are unavailing and probably incite the Ottoman government to more drastic measures as they are determined to disclaim responsibility for their absolute disregard of capitulations, and I believe nothing short of actual force, which obviously United States are not in a position to exert, would adequately meet the situation. Suggest you inform belligerent nations and mission boards of this.[21]

~ ~ ~

There was enormous pressure on Armenians who were still in the Talas area to become Muslims to avoid deportation. In fact, Ali Ghalib Bey, a former member of Parliament for Cesarea and an old friend of Stella, told her privately that the only way to save their lives was to advise them to do it.[22] The hodjas were happy to have as many new converts as possible, and chose to ignore the reason for their conversion. The gendarmes who, as part of the Special Organization rounding people up for deportation, were happy when Armenians converted because it meant they did not have to work hard for their meagre pay. But conversion was not always a simple or easy decision for Armenians to make. Theda overheard some students behind the hospital discussing the ramifications. Even these young boys understood it was a matter of life and death.[23] The American Board was pleasantly surprised that the anticipated wholesale conversion of Armenians "to save their lives or their possessions" had not taken place. "A noble army have preferred death to denial of their Lord," the Board exclaimed.[24]

"I have been simply amazed at the heroism of some of these people," Genevieve said. "In cases where men would have turned Muslim, women with little children have said, 'No, I will go with my children, but will not give up my faith.'" She was particularly impressed by the refusal of the Talas druggist, Haig Haroutounian, to convert, and by Mme. Gulbenkian who was deported rather than give up Christianity. "We see so much pure gold these days, and from some whom we least expect it. And some from whom we expected more have disappointed us." She was "burning with indignation over the efforts they are making to turn Mrs. Arslan. Her father's family turned in Marsovan. Her husband, Dr. Arslan [a medical officer in the Ottoman army] has turned also, though she wouldn't believe it before. Poor thing! She looks like a ghost, and doesn't know what to do."[25]

However, it was the hypocrisy of Sabri Bey that really angered her and her colleagues. His wife was German, and was not required to become a Muslim because, Sabri said, "Germany was leading the world now." And besides, "Islam is simply as a waterproof [coat]—to be put on when it is raining, and discarded when the sun shines again."[26] He demonstrated this cavalier attitude toward religion again when he changed the record of his friend, Mibar Muncherian, a former pastor, from Protestant to Muslim in the government's registration. "To us it seems such a cowardly business," said Genevieve. "We are filled with humiliation. They say Mibar slipped out before the congregation rose at yesterday's service. May his heart be filled with such remorse that even yet he and others may turn back. He firmly holds that he has not turned, but to the world he is in that position."[27]

The conversions may have saved some Armenians, and may have strengthened CUP's commitment to Turkification, but as Faik Bey, a mudir in Talas, told Herbert, "Though the hodjas are pleased to have their new converts, the government isn't deceived. These new Muslims will be sent out later, too."[28] In many cases, he was right. The Ministry of the Interior generally viewed the conversions "insincere and unreliable, and as only being a response to the deportation order."[29] When the district governor asked what he should do about the villagers of Derevenk who had applied for conversion, he was told to continue the deportation even if they had become Muslims. However, in other areas Armenians were allowed to convert and be relocated in small numbers within the Muslim majority, where they would be "governable."[30]

An exceptional example of neighbours helping neighbours was in Tavlusun, less than three miles northeast of Talas. It was a small village of Turks, Greeks and Armenians who earned their living farming, breeding animals, and trading with the surrounding towns and villages. Of the 120 Armenians in 30 households, many were artisan plasterers. When the gendarmes came to deport them, the entire village banded together as one.

The Turks and Greeks declared that if the Armenians went, they would go, too. No one left the village—except the gendarmes.[31]

One of the Talas Hospital's native nurses had been in a nearby village when people were being deported. "She had her own children with her, and two little grandchildren," said Theda. "She was protected by a Turk whom she had previously helped by dressing and caring for a scalp wound he had had. Not forgetting her kindness to him, he helped her to hide while the others were being sent out, and then brought her secretly to her daughter's home in Talas."[32] Clara wrote about one of her former students in another village who had been protected by a wealthy Circassian, who had arranged for her to go to Cesarea to find her relatives.[33]

When Tateos Minassian, a trader from the village of Keskin in Kaisarieh, was working in Angora, he was rounded up with other Armenians and became part of a deportation convoy. As they passed through Keskin, he was able to get a message to his Turkish friend and fellow trader, Omer Effendi. Omer managed to extract Minassian from the convoy and hide him in his house. He also found a hiding place in the village for Minassian's wife and children. He told Minassian that once, when he travelled to Yozgat, he passed through a valley full of the corpses of naked women and children. He shouted his outrage at the people in the village nearby. "He could not accept the massacres. He could not reconcile them with the religion he believed in."[34]

Omer hid Minassian for three years, at great risk to himself because it quickly became apparent to CUP authorities that many Turks were opposed to the government's policies, and were protecting Armenians. Djemal Pasha was particularly concerned about this, and condemned the practice. On July 23 the following order was issued: "If any Muslim protect a Christian, first his house shall be burned, then the Christian killed before his eyes, and then his family, and then himself."[35]

The order put a chill on any caring Turk. He would have felt completely helpless to watch a scene described by Mirajan, a young graduate of the Talas Boys' School. He had been home in Chakmak when the gendarmes came to clear out his village. Because he was dressed in "a fine new European suit of clothes," the soldiers mistakenly thought he was the son of a Turkish official, and left him alone. They locked up Armenian boys and men in the church, and then, in groups of five, took them out and shot them. Mirajan saw his father shot. He saw Victoria Tavlian, another Talas student, running out of a burning house where she had been hiding. She was a beautiful girl, and was captured by one of the officials, who put her on a horse. Though she threw herself off several times, crying for Jesus to save her, she was eventually "driven away into slavery." While some soldiers were quarreling over which one would take Mirajan's new coat, he escaped. He wandered through the mountains with some companions for two months, sometimes creeping into a village at night to find food, sometimes "hiding under the heaps of dead bodies." One day he was "caught, beaten and left for dead." An Armenian woman who had turned Muslim found him and nursed him to health. He began working as a scribe for a Turkish officer who could not read or write. His job was to visit "the ruined villages, taking a record of the number of Armenians taken or killed." The sorrow overwhelmed him. He soon fled once more, this time making his way back to the temporary safety of the Talas mission.[36]

10

Pandemonium

"The thing we had dreaded for so long had come," said Stella Loughridge. It was August 8, her mother's birthday. "I was sitting in my room waiting for the breakfast bell, when Nellie Hanum Dakenian, our house mother, came slowly up the stairs and quietly announced, 'The order has been posted for Talas!'"[1] All Armenians had to be ready to leave in four days. The notice in Cesarea ordered them deported in ten days.[2] But neither schedule was followed as posted. Instead, the deportations dragged on for weeks in "a long, cruel 'cat and mouse' method," said Theda. Since most of the men had been deported in July, the deportees were mainly women, children, old men, and boys.

"Some families sold everything they had, prepared their bread, and then, as their names were not posted . . . to go on a certain day, they would eat up their bread and be compelled to prepare a fresh supply," Theda explained. "This happened several times over until they exhausted their supply or materials. And in not a few cases the order came for them to leave suddenly and they had no opportunity to prepare a fresh supply. Then we would send Greek women around the town to buy a little here and a little there, so they should not have to start without food."[3] Clara described the nightmare as living in an "agony of suspense, neither sleeping nor eating much, not knowing what might come at any minute of the day or night."[4]

The missionaries were told their students had to leave, too. As Mary Graffam had done in Sivas, they quickly made plans to accompany them.[5] Theda said, "We began at once to have Greek women sew for Armenian women, having cloth shoes with rope soles made, underwear and outside garments, and bags for them to wear as a sort of knapsack. We used any sort of material we could find, some of the productions being rare works of art. We bought what shoes we could from the market but they were only light slippers and only four or five dozen pairs at that." They also had large quantities of *peksamets* (a type of bread) made up. Because of its added fat, when it was baked hard, it kept a long time without spoiling.[6]

Then, before they could even hire wagons, new orders were posted. One, personally signed by Talat, stated that "all Protestants and Catholics were to be 'forgiven' and allowed to stay in their homes."[7] He had been under considerable pressure by the Vatican and by German religious leaders to end the persecution. He chose, however, to ignore appeals from

Etchmiadzin, the Holy seat of the Eastern Apostolic Church, to give Gregorians a reprieve. This edict applied to only Catholic and Protestant Armenians. The original telegram to the sanjaks contained orders not to deport them "if they are still there."[8] In many cases, of course, they had already gone.

The government was faced with another set of unanticipated problems. There were several families in Kaisarieh on the deportation list whose men were serving in the military as doctors and pharmacists. The district governor asked the Ministry of the Interior for exemption for their families. The military had already given exemption certificates to Armenian soldiers for their families, and now "some soldiers in the labor battalions applied to their commanders for conversion for themselves and their families to Islam." The district governor wanted to know what to do with these families. Zeki was vehemently opposed to any exemptions or postponement. He complained to the Ministry of War. The local civil authorities complained to the Ministry of the Interior of interference by the military authorities. It got quite heated. In fact, Colonel Sahabeddin complained to his superior in Angora that Zeki had falsely accused the Armenians of armed assaults. On August 15 there was a flurry of telegrams from the Ministry of the Interior. It requested of the military's General Staff that they order their local commanders "not to interfere in the matters of civil administration." It sent an official order to Kaisarieh to allow exemption for the families of Armenian soldiers and officers. It also sent another, private telegram ordering that "the conversion requests would not be accepted."[9]

In the end, it was all moot. "This mercy had come too late for most places," said Stella bitterly. "The majority of Armenian soldiers of Turkey had already seen their families deported and their houses desolated, while they were compelled to work on, half starved, with shovel and spade, slaves of the government that was destroying their homes." Many Catholic and Protestant Armenians were suspicious of the exemptions anyway. "They did not wish to remain, fearing some greater cruelty. But when they wished to go with their friends into exile they were not allowed."[10]

On August 22[11] the first party of 72 families was deported from Talas. "Never can I forget the terror on the girls' faces, as they struggled with their loaded donkeys through the crowd to say good-bye," said Clara. The gendarmes shouted at them and hit the donkeys to hurry them along. "From the old men, weak and hopeless, to the little children clinging in terror to their mothers' skirts, they had to go. Our neighbors told us that parties that went from lower Talas—where we could not see—went in terrible distress, with the blows upon their heads and backs instead of on the donkeys!"[12]

Not being allowed to sell property, the deportees could only sell household goods or moveable possessions to have some money for their journey. "Some of them . . . were able to sell a good deal," Theda said, "and to give away or hide many of their things."[13] But as Stella noted, the local Turks got their share of "good bargains from the distracted people."[14] Theda added, "The Greeks, as well as the Turks, took advantage of the Armenians, going to their homes begging, stealing or buying their things from them."[15]

Many people frantically appealed to the missionaries for help. They begged them to keep safe their rugs and other valuables. "It was impossible for us to do so," said Theda. "The Government was watching us very closely and asked us for a written statement of everything we had belonging to the Armenians."[16]

"Mothers and fathers came pleading for us to save their daughters from the fate of so many, many girls," said Stella. "One beautiful girl who had graduated just the year before, had been threatened by a government official and told that if she went out with her people on the road to Aleppo she would be captured. We did not dare to take her into the school, for if we did this under the eyes of the government, we felt sure we would lose everything—the girls and women whom we already had under our protection. So we had to refuse and to tell her to go bravely, trusting God, and be ready to accept as from Him whatever came."[17] The local government did allow the missionaries to accept children whose parents were Protestant, Catholic or military personnel. As the schools' principals, Stella and Henry tried to rescue as many as possible. "The days of choosing and deciding which ones could be taken were hard, hard days," said Theda.[18]

On August 28 the second group began the journey of three or four weeks to Aleppo. The mutesarrif told Herbert and Henry that eventually all Armenians, except those in the mission's compound would be relocated—"five Armenian families, and not more than one Protestant family to a village."[19]

"For days and days we saw the long processions starting over the hot roads," said Stella. "The women dressed in rough village clothes, and often covered by the charshaf (sheet) of the Muslim woman in hope of a little protection from that." Within weeks at least 20,000 Armenians in Talas and Cesarea had been deported.[20]

~ ~ ~

The 80-bed Talas hospital[21] had been limping along without Alden Hoover since May 1914. He and a native physician, Theda Phelps, and seven native nurses had cared for more than 800 patients, and handled more than 1,000 surgeries in the year before he left. The hospital was forced to close when the deportations started, though Theda continued helping the sick and injured as best she could.[22] In April 1915 Alden received an urgent appeal from the Board and the American Red Cross to return early from his furlough to help fight a typhus epidemic. However, rather than go back to Talas, they asked him to work in Constantinople, where he was most needed. He was happy to oblige. Alden had been at the Tash Kishla Hospital for three and a half months when he received another urgent telegram, this time from Talas. Genevieve Irwin was gravely ill with appendicitis. There was no doctor for hundreds of miles capable of performing the surgery to save her life. Would he come as soon as possible?[23]

Though he was willing to go, the entire interior was tightly controlled; any travel required special permission from the highest authorities, and was not easy to obtain.[24] Through the American Board's connections, Alden got permission from none other than Enver Pasha himself,[25] and raced to Talas. He arrived in the midst of the second round of deportations in August, just in time to perform the surgery. "The operation was eminently successful, and the patient is making fine progress," reported *The Orient*.[26] Genevieve was confined to bed for ten days of recovery. Herbert kept her apprised of the chaos in the mission and the town. Her heart ached, especially for women with little children. She wrote in her diary, "Going on the road with probable days of hunger and thirst, and perhaps dishonour and death before them—mothers in agony for fear of their daughters. I feel speechless over it all. And though sometimes the thought that God will doubtless use these thousand-fold tragedies in working out some blessing in the development of man and the Armenian people, yet often times, when I would like to help and give some word of cheer, I can only weep, thinking of some of these beautiful children, and what it would be if they were mine!"[27]

On September 9 Alden sent a postcard from Constantinople to let his former colleagues know he had arrived safely. He also let them know, in code, what was happening in the rest of Anatolia: "300,000 lambs and sheep are fertilizing the states to the East of you." Genevieve sadly supposed it was "only too true. It is said that of 800 families which left Yozgat at one time, all the men and boys over fifteen were slaughtered, and women and children scattered in the villages."[28]

The killings, kidnappings, deportations, and disrupted lives—it was all true. Of the forced marriages and sexual enslavement, Stella said, "At first it was too terrible to believe, and we were inclined to doubt, or consider it an exaggeration. But too soon we were forced to believe, for some of the stolen girls were brought to villages near us. Though we knew of their pitiable condition, we were powerless to help them."[29] They were also confused by how authorities in different regions interpreted the orders for deportation. They had not been allowed to accompany their students on the trek to the desert. Their friend in Sivas, Mary Graffam, had managed to get as far as Malatia with her girls, before her wagon was confiscated, and she was forbidden to go any farther with them. Mary had returned to Sivas in a terribly weakened state, but she had survived.[30]

Their friends Charlotte Willard, principal of the Marsovan Girls' School, and Frances Gage, a YWCA Secretary,[*] had a different experience. When Turkish soldiers stormed the mission compound and took 63 Armenian women and girls (teachers, students, nurses, and servants), they asked to accompany them. Their request was denied, too. They appealed—persistently—to a higher authority. It took three days before they obtained written permission and the necessary safe-conduct travel documents. "Taking all the money that could be raised on short notice, and accompanied by an interpreter and by one of the faithful Circassian guards employed by the mission," they frantically raced off with wagons and swift horses towards Sivas to catch up to the group. Within forty-eight hours, they had overtaken some of the party. Before they arrived, twenty-one young women—mostly servants and the poorer girls—had been separated at the village of Sharkushla, and sent south with another convoy of deportees. Charlotte and Frances were allowed to buy food for the remaining women, and pay the drivers "not to turn over any of their passengers to admiring citizens on the way." They negotiated for days with the Turkish guards, using persuasion, argument, "and the judicious application of large sums of money" to induce them to release their prisoners. It finally worked. The missionaries were allowed to return to Marsovan with the forty-two remaining girls and women."[31]

One day an Armenian woman arrived at the Talas Girls' School, and filled in some of the details. "She had escaped with a Muslim family from Sharkushla, where she and thousands of other women from the Black Sea Coast cities had been brought on their way to Mesopotamia," said Stella. "She said she had become a Muslim to save herself and her daughter, for

---

[*] "Secretary" was the title given to a YWCA or YMCA worker in the field.

the women and girls were being taken by the Turks and Kurds." She told them she had met many girls from the Marsovan mission there. "Many had already been stolen. If they went further on the journey they would surely be lost."[32] Indeed, most were never heard of again.

As international outrage and attempts at interference increased, so too did the escalation of deportations and massacres. On September 7, the day that became known as the "Great Drive" in Adana, 15,000 to 18,000 Armenians were deported along the southwestern road. When later asked about the attitude of Turkish citizens as they watched the houses being systematically cleared of women, children, the elderly and the infirm, Nesbitt Chambers recalled an older Turkish gentleman standing beside one of the mission's medical staff on a street corner, speaking "half to himself, half to the stranger. 'Allah cannot accept this,' said the Turk. 'This is not of Allah. Perhaps the men are traitors, who knows. But not these children and women and old ones. No, we shall see what comes to us for this. It is not Allah's will.'"[33]

~ ~ ~

In September 1915 a series of government telegrams indicated "there were no more Armenians to deport."[34] This may have been true in other regions, but it was playing with semantics in Kaisarieh. Despite the orders that came down from Talat, and despite the deportation of 20,000 Armenians, there remained more than 6,000 in Talas and Cesarea. And more than half of them were not Protestants, Catholics or the families of soldiers. In most cases, after the declaration of death to any Turk who helped an Armenian, it depended on how influential their friends were. Many artisans, such as blacksmiths and carpenters—anyone who was, as Genevieve said, "needful to the government"—were often given permission to stay.[35] Garabed Kasakian, for example, the *sandık emini* (treasurer) of Cesarea, was a valued member of the municipal administration. Among his friends was the mayor, Rifat Bey. Rifat appealed to the mutesarrif and obtained permission for Kasakian and his family to remain. Naturally, Kasakian's extended family included siblings, nieces and nephews.[36] Haig Haroutounian, the druggist of the Talas mission hospital, was well liked and well-respected by many Turkish officials and religious leaders, and was also allowed to stay.[37]

~ ~ ~

The school year began in Talas within a few days of the usual September opening, though the situation was anything but normal. Within a few weeks, in early October, the town crier proclaimed a new order: "All Protestants, Catholics and soldiers' families out of here by eight o'clock tomorrow morning!"[38] They were told they were not exiles. They could keep the keys to their homes, but must leave behind their household goods, which would be guarded. Of course, it was a lie. As soon as they left, their possessions were stolen.[49]

"So these poor women and children, for there were very few men left," said Stella, "were scattered about in the villages of the Turks, two or three in a village, and usually the very most barbarous villages were selected." The villages were from one to ten hours away from Talas, and considered the lowest of the low by the missionaries. "Villages beyond description for filth, ignorance, and degeneration," said Clara.[40] Most of the Protestant women and children whom Theda had been protecting in the hospital since the late summer were more fortunate; Herbert arranged for them to be exiled to Greek villages.[41]

There was a mad scramble to enroll as many children as possible in the mission's schools. "We were glad to save them from the villages, where many of them would have been frightened and forced into marriage with these half civilized Turks," Stella said. "We stowed them away in every conceivable place till our houses were full and running over. We took in all of our graduate girls that we could as teachers. Most of the girls were daughters of rich or very conservative and bigoted families, who would never have come to us in ordinary times. But now they were so thankful to come."[42]

The enrollment was the largest ever, with 125 girls, including nine day students, 160 boys, eight regular teaching staff, and the six young graduates who had formerly been teaching in outstations.[43] The girls' school and dormitories were crowded to overflowing, but Stella was pleased that, day by day, the snobby girls were becoming "delighted with the school and the spirit they found there."[44]

Though the missionaries tried to carry on as usual, on November 11 there was another government-issued order: All Armenians who did not convert to Islam would be deported. The Turkish friends of Cesarea's treasurer, Garabed Kasakian, advised him to convert. "Garabed Effendi, you don't lose anything," they said. "Let these bad days pass, and when the war is over, you return to your religion again. Don't go into exile." He and his family knew the terrible fate of many of the deported Armenians, and agreed.[45] Stella, however, was disgusted by this kind of advice. "This is only a political step," she said, mocking the words of Sabri Bey. "Only a raincoat put on in time of storm." She was especially annoyed "by leaders who should have helped them to stand true" to their beliefs.[46]

Talas' druggist Haig Haroutounian had a more difficult time. For months his Turkish friends had pleaded with him to become Muslim, but he had remained committed to his faith. Even when the decree was announced, he said he preferred deportation to conversion. But that night, Sabri Bey paid him a visit, telling him that he must either convert within the hour or face death. "The Turk walked up and down the room with his watch in his hand, pouring out a torrent of words," said Clara. "But Haig never wavered. Finally, as Sabri Bey said, 'One minute more!' Haig's mother, his murdered brother's wife and six children, and his fiancée's mother, all fell upon him crying to him to save them from the fate that would surely be theirs. He said to us afterwards, with the most wretched and hopeless face I ever saw, 'I gave my soul for them.'"[47]

As principal, Stella observed many mothers talking with their daughters about converting. "Some of the girls allowed themselves, without a thought, to be written by their parents in the government records as Muslim. Others protested and withstood their mothers' tears and prayers. Many were written so without being consulted at all."[48]

A young refined, gentle woman from the Cesarea Protestant church had been sent to one of the rough Turkish villages with her sons and her mother-in-law. One night ten Turks broke into her house. "After she had suffered at the hands of six, and her mother-in-law at the hands of four, she became Muslim in order to escape from the village and return to Cesarea," said Clara.[49] Faced with rape, deportation or death, it is no wonder many converted to Islam. "Many a poor broken-hearted woman has told us since that she would never have yielded, but with little children, no money for the journey, and no companions, she could not start out alone to starve with her children," Stella said. "Who can judge them?"[50]

Still, when the gendarmes marched into the mission to collect more than eight employees of the Boys' School, Genevieve was "thankful to see some who were willing to die rather than deny Christianity." One young teacher, Yervant, said to the group which was gathered to wish them farewell, "Pray for me, that I may be strong to the last."[51]

They were to go to the desert by way of Sivas, the route where so many Armenian men had been ambushed and murdered by Special Organization forces. For some unknown reason, "possibly to save them," the deportees were sent "not to Sivas but to Eregli, whereby the danger on the roads was less." Thus the party arrived intact.[52] "They went expecting death," said Genevieve "but so far God has kept them in safety."[53]

Then another threat descended on the Talas mission: "All who had turned Muslim must take their children from the school or they would be exiled." Some girls were removed, but most remained, even when high officials repeated the threats, and added a new one—any remaining girls would be carried off by the gendarmes and villagers. "We felt that these threats were only an underhanded way of trying to break up the school," Stella said. "We always counseled the girls, even those who had become Muslims, to stay. So nearly all of the girls remained. And some who had been frightened away returned after a few weeks. And work went on as usual."[54] By the end of the year, there were about 300 Armenian children still in the Talas mission and its outstation in nearby Zinjidery.[55] That would soon change.

~ ~ ~

It was not only a dangerous time for Armenians and Assyrians, and their Greek and Muslim friends and neighbours who tried to protect them. There were also Ottoman officials who opposed the government's extermination policies, and suffered for doing so—some with their lives. Jelal, the governor of Aleppo, had been reprimanded, and was probably saved from a worse fate because he was a great grandson of Sultan Abdul Hamid.[56] Others, such as Huseyin Nesimi, kaimakam of Lice, delayed deportations, and arranged fake marriages for Armenian women, in an effort to protect them. He was called to account by Reshid, vali of Diarbekir, and on the way to see him was murdered by a brigand, "because he did not comply with the policy" of CUP. The 25-year-old deputy kaimakam of Beshiri, Sabit Es Suveydi, was killed by a gang after he refused to participate in the Diarbekir deportations.[57] The governor of Basra, and three other officials in Müntefak, Midyat, and Bafra were also murdered for their opposition to CUP policies, and about twenty local officials were fired.[58]

Life was dangerous for missionaries, too. Dr. Ussher's wife, Elizabeth, died of typhus just before the rest of the ABCFM mission escaped from Van. Of the 15 Americans and 10 Armenian station members who travelled to Russia, almost all were lame or ill. Both Clarence Ussher and Ernest Yarrow were so weak they had to be carried out in carts. Nearing Russia, Martha Raynolds slipped from a cart and broke her leg. Within days it worsened; within weeks she died.[59] In the autumn, Helen Thom of Mardin, and Rev. George Knapp and Charlotte Ely of Bitlis died of disease.[60] In early summer Rev. Francis H. Leslie left his pregnant wife in relative safety in Aintab, and went to Oorfa. As the only American missionary there, he supervised the station's large industrial plant, a relief effort that employed several thousand people. He also acted as a consular agent, providing aid and monthly allowance payments for 300 British, French, Italian and Russian belligerents who had been interned there. As a young man he had trained at art academies in Chicago and Cincinnati before being called to the ministry. Nothing in his background had prepared him to deal with the stress of his current tasks and the violence that surrounded him. On October 30, he became "so mentally unbalanced with the threat of immediate death on the gallows that he committed suicide" by drinking carbolic acid. He died without ever seeing his daughter, Elizabeth Louise.[61]

11

The Need for Relief

Susan spent most of the summer of 1915 at the University of Chicago working on her thesis, "Religious Education in the American Schools in the Ottoman Empire." There were a few "interruptions," such as when she attended missionary conferences at Lake Geneva, Wisconsin, and Lake Okaboji, Iowa, and was called upon to speak at Woman's Board meetings "here and there."[1] She found the schedule "a heavy strain," and was tired much of the time. Still, in September she completed her studies and was granted an AM (*Artium Magister* or Master of Arts). One professor congratulated her for producing "one of the best theses ever presented to them for a degree." After her own year's furlough Susan told the WBMI she was anxious to return to her station to give Stella "the year of rest which she needs. We have a large work and it is growing better. Even this year Talas has been able to keep up the Girls' School in good shape."[2]

Like other Americans, she knew of the deportations and massacres along the border with Russia, but was unaware of the extent of the turmoil in the interior in general, and in Talas in particular. Censorship was so heavy the missionaries did not write anything contrary to the Ottoman government in their letters home. When someone inadvertently did, the letter arrived with large rectangular holes where the censors had cut out the offending text. *The Orient*, which Susan subscribed to, was not allowed to publish any negative details, though did report on the mission schools that continued to operate.[3] Telegrams from American consuls in the interior to the Ambassador in Constantinople were often intercepted, sometimes creating a lag in the time Morgenthau was aware of the exact situation in the regions. Talat was very open with Morgenthau about his reading embassies' correspondence "before consenting to their being forwarded to their destinations."[4] Even so, Consul Jesse B. Jackson in Aleppo was able to arrange for his coded telegrams and dispatches to be hand delivered to Morgenthau.[5] Consul F. Willoughby-Smith in Tiflis (in the Transcaucasus) also regularly sent messages to Morgenthau from ABCFM missionaries in Georgian and Armenian Russia, and from Presbyterian Board missionaries in Persia.[6]

In any case, Susan was prevented from returning to Talas because of "unsettled conditions"—the WBMI's genteel way of referring to the hazardous travel on the Atlantic due to submarine warfare, and the American prohibition to transatlantic crossings.[7] Consequently, Susan agreed to assist the Woman's Board by speaking to "as many Thank-offering and Association meetings as possible" in Illinois, Michigan, Iowa, Nebraska and Oklahoma. She would do it until she could return to her mission and her colleagues.[8]

~ ~ ~

On September 3 Henry Morgenthau sent a telegram to US Secretary of State Robert Lansing, saying, "Destruction of Armenian race in Turkey is progressing rapidly, massacre reported at Angora and Brousa. Will you suggest to Cleveland Dodge, Charles Crane, John R. Mott, Stephen Wise and others to form committee to raise funds and provide means to save some of the Armenians and assist the poorer ones to emigrate."[9] Morgenthau had tried to negotiate with Enver for some deportees to be allowed to leave the empire, but that did not come to pass. What did occur weeks later was a meeting in Dodge's New York office of several prominent men to discuss the urgent need for relief funds. Within hours they had established an ad hoc committee, set a fundraising goal of $100,000, pledged half of it themselves, and appointed ABCFM Secretary James Barton as chairman, educator Samuel T. Dutton as secretary, and the heir to the Crane plumbing company, Charles R. Crane, as treasurer.[10]

Barton was concerned about "the troubling lack of information on the situation" in Turkey. He believed it was imperative to their fundraising efforts for the public to know the facts. In early October he and Crane prepared the *Report of the Committee on Armenian Atrocities,* compiled from State Department's confidential consular reports. It contained "horrific descriptions of torture, rape, and trails of rotting corpses." The evidence was enough to convince the Rockefeller Foundation to immediately donate $30,000 to the cause.[11]

Two other committees had already been operating in the United States for a few months to support refugees in the Near East. In November 1915, it made sense to merge the existing Syria-Palestine Relief Committee and the Persian War Relief Fund with the Dodge-Barton committee to create the American Committee for Armenian and Syrian Relief (ACASR).[12] With the help of the US State Department, ACASR wired relief money from New York to Europe and on to William Peet, ABCFM Treasurer in Constantinople, for the missionaries to distribute.[13]

Enver Pasha was not pleased. "How can we furnish bread to the Armenians when we can't get enough for our own people?" he asked Morgenthau, ignoring that it was his mobilization, confiscation, and deportation policies that removed the workers in the fields, mills and factories, resulting in decreased food production and increased prices. "We don't want the Americans to feed the Armenians. That is one of the worst things that could happen to them. They must never know that they have a friend in the United States. That would absolutely ruin them! It is far better that they starve," he said. "And in saying this I am really thinking of the welfare of the Armenians themselves. If they can only be convinced that they have no friends in other countries, then they will settle down, recognize that Turkey is their only refuge, and become quiet citizens. Your country is doing them no kindness by constantly showing your sympathy. You are merely drawing upon them greater hardships." After much negotiation, Enver did allow "certain missionaries" to use the American relief money to help the destitute.[14]

Unlike the United States, the British Empire was at war. Its subjects had been sending food, clothing and money to the Red Cross for more than a year, and supplying relief money to support the 100,000 Belgian refugees who had escaped to England's shores after the German invasion. Nevertheless, after the Marquess of Crewe rose in the House of Lords on October 6 to address the plight of a quarter million "Armenian, Chaldean, and other refugees" who fled "appalling horrors," the British were moved to help. His Majesty's Consul at Batum had provided "a most horrible description of their condition, ravaged by disease, many of them starving. They have been dying at the rate of at least 100 a day." The Marquess praised the efforts in Persia and Russia trying to cope with the situation, but noted that "very much larger supplies of medical comforts and of foodstuffs are needed if the condition of the refugees is to be materially relieved."[15]

Little more than two weeks later Lord Mayor of London Charles Johnson, Viscount Bryce, the Archbishop of Canterbury, peers of the realm, and other influential men and women formed the Lord Mayor's Fund to aid the refugees. They immediately "telegraphed to H.M. Consul General in Moscow several thousand pounds," and began a campaign to raise more.[16] Within months the Lord Mayors of Manchester and Liverpool, the Lord Provosts of Edinburgh and Glasgow, the Armenian Relief Fund in Victoria, Australia, and the Armenian Relief Fund Association of Canada were also contributing to the humanitarian effort.[17]

~ ~ ~

Throughout the fall and early winter, conditions in Kaisarieh continued to worsen. A new, eleven-articled provisional law outlined in detail how the real estate and personal property of deportees would be handled. Their assets or money would be held in trust by "the treasury of the ministry of pious foundations . . . and the ministry of finance," though it was highly doubtful the government truly intended that the money would reach the owners. A "liquidation commission," was to be established in each region, which would dispense with the properties, either through auction, sale or distribution to immigrants. There was a complicated procedure for creditors, both foreign and domestic, to apply for payment on outstanding debts.[18]

Foreign creditors posed an awkward problem for the government, especially when their embassies got involved. In Cesarea the manager of the Singer Sewing Machine store had turned over the keys to the police as he was being deported. When the American Embassy asked the government to protect the store, the Ministry of the Interior made sure it was safe, "in order to prevent payment of a restitution to the company." Both German and Austria-Hungary formally expressed concern after storehouses and factories owned by merchants who did business with their citizens were sealed by city authorities. The Yosefyan store, for example, which involved Deutsche Bank, still had inventory valued at £T 15,000-20,000.[19]

Though the Ministry of Interior warned against profiteering, it became usual for Armenian properties and possessions to be bought at ridiculously low prices. There were so many complaints to the mutesarrif of corruption, that he complained to Constantinople about the management of the Kaisarieh Abandoned Properties Commission. He requested replacement of the chairman and several members. Months later Zeki complained about the replacements, and said "their mismanagement led to the corruption of lower level officials who were employed at the commission." The new chairman, Halim Bey, had swelled the commission to 25 members. One of the members, Tevfik Bey, was later removed for being corrupt.[20]

It seemed absurd that, with all the deportations and deaths sanctioned by the Minister of the Interior, he would be averse to profiteering and corruption. But he was. Ambassador Morgenthau had visited his house a few times and noted, "Although Talat was then the most powerful man in the Turkish Empire, his home was still the modest home of a man of the people."[21] His focus was entirely on what was good for the state. The Ottoman Treasury held the proceeds from the auction of abandoned properties; it was not for personal gain. Talat fired Reshid, then-governor of Angora, after he appropriated goods and jewelry for himself, and "tried to buy a waterside mansion with the confiscated funds."[22]

The women of the Talas mission knew exactly how unscrupulous some of the local officials were. When Sabri Bey and his mother took them on a tour of their home to see their new rugs, he explained to them that government officials were only being paid half of their salary in money, and had to buy goods with promissory notes based on the other, future half. "He must have had between 40 and 50 new rugs," Genevieve said. "Silk and wool. He had a young Protestant man ironing them, and his walls were being covered with them—being nailed up when we were there." There was a new piano, an elegant candelabra, a clock, and countless other furnishings.[23] Stella recognized some items from her visit in July to the village accused of harboring army deserters. The house was "simply crammed with beautiful and valuable things from the rich houses of this little town."[24]

An indignant missionary, whose identity the *Missionary Herald* kept hidden for fear of reprisal, described How to Make War on Nothing a Year. "All you have to do is to take what you need from your own subjects, giving them paper promises—where necessary—to be redeemed after the war. One firm I know was thus forced to furnish three thousand pounds' worth of shoes for the army. Another gave up a hundred thousand dollars' worth of suitings." But the promissory notes they received were for only half the items' value. "When it came to requisitioning hundreds of pairs of ladies' silk stockings, and yards upon yards of ribbon, the reluctant proprietors wondered why such articles were needed for the Ottoman army."[25]

A hodja had told Haig, the Talas druggist, that the government was going to raid the compound. "We have been very careful," said Genevieve. "But we have been very carefully watched." To the authorities the large number of boarders in the Girls' School alone, the possibility of seizing their bedding, clothes, and other possessions "must have seemed a good deal." Fortunately, the raid never happened.[26]

The internal squabbles among the Kaisarieh administration and military continued. Colonel Sahabeddin opposed the deportation of the families of soldiers and converts, an action Zeki firmly supported.[27] Sahabeddin was more fortunate than Faik Bey, the mudir who had confided to Herbert about the government not being deceived by the conversions. Faik also opposed the deportations, but was murdered for it, reportedly by Sabri Bey.[28]

Deportations and massacres continued into mid-December. As diplomatic pressure and humanitarian aid from foreigners increased throughout the fall, so did the speed and violence of the deportations. "Only the Armenians of Constantinople were spared, to demonstrate 'good will' to the Turkish allies."[29]

Some Armenians escaped into the mountains to hide, and a few were hidden by their Turkish friends. Most, however, did not survive. One young family—the husband in his twenties, the wife with cropped hair and dressed as a boy, and their son, all filthy—made their way to the Talas mission from Klenje after a month of wandering. The men and boys in their village had been shot, as had been many women who could not flee. "They had armed themselves with what weapons could be found, with stones, et cetera, and withstood the gendarmes for a couple of days," said Genevieve. "Then the government brought 200 soldiers and a cannon from Cesarea, and when this family escaped, they said that only one house was left standing in Klenje. All the villagers, men, women and children in the Bozock have been massacred."[30]

The missionaries had their clashes with town residents, too. Herbert and Henry were in Cesarea one day when they learned the mutesarrif's commandant and a few attendants had gone into the mission's kindergarten building and ordered the caretaker to clear it out, except for "such articles of furniture as they desired." The caretaker, Nishan Aga, told them he first must talk to the missionaries. The commandant replied that he might consult them, and if not, he would take it all anyway. Herbert and Henry protested directly to the mutesarrif, telling him that the building was the home of Clara and Fanny, and as such, was private property. The governor replied that if they did not hand it over, he would simply take it. The missionaries' threat of referring the matter to Ambassador Morgenthau had no effect. The governor said it would not make a bit of difference—he would take it anyway. When she heard the story, Genevieve was furious: "May his reign be short! Dark days, heavy atmosphere, thunder and lightning, ominous!"[31]

Her temper did not abate when she recorded in her diary that the hodjas who had confiscated a neighbour's house wanted the house next to the mission's school. "But we have it. They intended to turn the Armenian Church into a mosque, we understand, but they cannot get the cross down. It is said that they tried to get one down in the city, and it fell on one of them and killed him, and they are now superstitious!" She then added a most un-Christian-like note: "Hope it is true!"[32]

Days later Nishan Aga was approached by three gendarmes who tried to convert him to Islam. When he refused, he was deported. "We have every reason to believe that he was killed," said Genevieve. "The Catholic bishop said to one of our ladies tonight, 'I expect to be called for tonight, and killed.' He was our guest a few evenings ago with Sabri Bey."[33]

The local government opened an orphanage for the children of Ottoman soldiers, where they could also learn agriculture or a trade. The national government announced that physicians who were citizens of belligerent nations would henceforth be forbidden to practice medicine in

Norwegian missionary, nurse and midwife Bodil Biørn captured the deplorable state of dress in Moush (west of Lake Van), 1916. SOURCE: Bodil Biørn, Kvinnelige Misjonsarbeidere (Association of Female Missionaries), Norwegian State Archive.

Turkey.[34] Even though Alden Hoover was American, and the United States was not at war, he decided that he would not be able to do much work in the country, and returned home.[35]

So far the horrors had rained down on the Armenians and Assyrians. But as Genevieve astutely noted, "The Greeks are in terror for fear Greece will go into the war, and that will be their end."[36] Dark days. Heavy atmosphere. Thunder and lightning. Ominous.

~ ~ ~

In January 1916 as the Russians advanced from the east towards Erzroom, the Turkish commander ordered all Greeks to leave the nearby town of Hasankala. "It just seemed as though he sat up nights to think of something more wicked to do," said Dr. Ida Stapleton of the Erzroom mission. "It was zero weather; there was not very much snow, and few vehicles could be obtained even for large sums." Ida visited all forty Greek families before they were forced to go "to their death, from cold if from nothing else. All the rich Turkish families and, in fact, all who could possibly leave, did so. Many of the rich, influential Turks felt it was a great shame that the Armenians had been so treated, and repeatedly went to the government, but they were savagely told that if they secreted or helped one of that race they would be hanged in front of their own doors." When the Greeks begged to stay, the commander replied, "We must suffer, so must you."[37]

~ ~ ~

The Allied and Ottoman armies had been fighting at Gallipoli in the west for eight months when the Allies decided to withdraw on January 7-8. Realizing victory was not possible, the troops, which by now included Anzacs, French Corps expéditionnaire d'Orient, the Royal Newfoundland Regiment, Royal Irish Fusiliers, and British Indian Brigades and Gurkha Rifles, retreated from the Dardanelles at night under cover of dense fog. German General Liman von Sanders called the cost of the campaign "very high," corresponding to the duration and severity of the fighting. He was right. More than 130,000 died (about 86,000 Ottomans and 44,000 Allies), and an outstanding 262,000 were wounded (165,000 Ottomans, 97,000 Allies).[38] Of course, not all the Ottoman Fifth Army consisted of Turks. Most of the officers were German, and there were Armenian, Assyrian, Kurdish, Greek, and Arabian combatants and labourers, too.[39] One of the reasons for the high number of casualties in the Ottoman army was poor sanitation. "The sanitary situation was such that it seriously threatened the battle efficiency of the army. After the toil of the Dardanelles Campaign, many thousands had to be sent to the hospitals. The death rate from debility was terrifying," said von Sanders.[40]

Even so, there was much rejoicing in Constantinople when news broke of the Allied retreat. The Ottoman victory was celebrated with parades, flags and bunting, and numerous medals. Newspapers grandly announced, "We have at last driven the enemy back into the sea!" They also acknowledged that "unfortunately, we took very few prisoners."[41] But the Ottomans had little time for joy. Days later the Russians launched an unexpected offensive in the east against the Ottoman Third Army. A month after that, Erzroom fell. It was a bitter blow to Enver. "The loss of Erzroom was kept so secret by the Turkish headquarters," said von Sanders, "that it did not appear among the army news, and remained unknown for months—even to the Sultan and his entourage."[42] From the beginning there had been conflict between von Sanders, who was the chief of military missions, and the Minister of War. It came to a head in February when Enver circulated a letter to all Turkish armies, "wherein he decreed that from then on he alone would give orders about the employment of German officers in the Turkish army, without reference to the chief of the military mission." Von Sanders asked the Chancellor to recall him. His request was denied.[43] The resulting tension among German officers, however, seriously began to affect their relations with the Turkish soldiers under their command.[44]

12

More Evictions

Though travel throughout the interior of Turkey, and to and from Constantinople, was very difficult, if not impossible in some places, communications were still relatively open.[1] Letters from North America took months to arrive, and often looked like Swiss cheese, thanks to the censors. Telegrams and visits in the country, between mission stations, with Bible House in the capital, and with various American consuls, kept everyone informed of current events. On February 3 the Talas mission received a telegram about the suicide that morning of Crown Prince Youssouf Izeddin. He had been found lying in a pool of blood with his arteries slit. "We have our own opinion regarding the cause of death," Genevieve said wryly.[2] They were not alone. The heir apparent to the sultanate had been under house arrest in his villa due to his sympathies for the Allies and his extreme antagonism towards the Committee of Union and Progress. A French colleague of Henry Morgenthau declared, "'On l'a suicidé!' (They have suicided him!)."[3]

The Talas group were also aware of the comings and goings of their own colleagues. Fred MacCallum, who had been working in Constantinople, and George Gracey, formerly of Oorfa, had gone to Tiflis, Russia in the fall of 1915 on behalf of ACASR. They were tasked with helping the British and Armenians organize a massive relief effort in the Caucasus. They were soon joined by Dr. George C. Raynolds, Rev. Ernest A. Yarrow, his wife Martha, and the four Yarrow children, all formerly of the Van mission, and Bitlis mission's Rev. Harrison A. Maynard, his wife Mary, and their two children.[4] George's wife, Martha, had died from a broken leg while he was in the United States raising funds to build a college in Van. He had raced to her side as soon as he heard the news of her illness, but had arrived too late to speak with her. He returned home,[5] but after a few months was asked to be part of the relief effort there. He missed the Van community so much, he could not refuse. This group began working with Dr. S. G. Wilson, of Persia's Presbyterian Board, Alfred E. Backhouse and E. St. John Catchpool of the Lord Mayor's Fund, and Thomas Dam Heald from the British Society of Friends. They were going to set up a relief centre in Erevan for the estimated 234,000 Armenian and Assyrian refugees who fled from eastern Turkey and western Persia.[6]

Trebizond on April 21, 1915. SOURCE: Underwood & Underwood, Trabzon, Turkey, April 21, 1915, US Library of Congress.

~ ~ ~

By March, 1916, the Russians controlled Van, Erzroom and Bitlis, and were fighting in Trebizond, Harpoot, Diarbekir and Sivas. The *Missionary Herald* reported that this was good news for missionaries, who would likely be treated favourably by the Russian army: "If we may believe the reports that come from various quarters, Turkey is now in desperate plight. With the Russians victorious over her armies in Armenia, with defeat attending the Egyptian campaign, with impending union of Russian and British forces in Mesopotamia, with her German ally rendering small aid or support, and with internal dissensions weakening her counsels and policies, the Ottoman Empire seems to be tottering to a fall."[7] Though the Russians never did capture Diarbekir, probably due to the command of General Mustafa Kemal,[8] a hero of Gallipoli, von Sanders pointed out a major flaw of the Ministry of War: "The ultimate cause of the failure of this campaign, as of all offensive operations begun in Turkey throughout the world war, lay in the long and imperfectly organized lines of communications."[9] Trebizond was the next city to demonstrate von Sanders' theory.

For most of April the inhabitants of Trebizond heard the sounds of war to the east of the city. The governor left the city on April 16 to the care of the Greek bishop. The police soon followed, leaving no one on guard. "It was a time for thieves to reap a harvest," said Olive Crawford of the Trebizond mission. Two days later, the Bishop's representative and the American Consul, Oscar Heizer, waved a white flag in the quarter of the city that was under bombardment. "When they reached the summit of the hill where the flag could be seen by those on the attacking ships, the firing stopped! Can you imagine the relief it was? That was the end of it," said Olive. "The Russians could hardly believe that Trebizond had come into their hands without resistance."[10]

In the previous summer, almost 6,000 Armenians had been deported from the city. Many were marched south to the desert, but Special Organization forces also used a particularly nasty method to get rid of hundreds at a time: They loaded barges with men, women and children, headed out into the Black Sea, and returned without passengers.[11] Now Olive's husband, Rev. Lyndon Crawford, said, "We saw another pathetic sight. This time it was the Turks fleeing! Between forty and fifty thousand were leaving our city and leaving their homes and their shops and their goods behind them." It took a while for the Russians to catch up with the last group of fleeing residents and suggest they return to their homes "in peace, without fear." The Red Cross took charge of the hospitals, and the Russians set up a "wireless telegraphic apparatus" to resurrect communications. But the most remarkable sight for the missionaries was the return of Armenians. "They began to come in from the further villages, and from the woods and the caves and dens of the mountains," said Lyndon. "Over five hundred in all, to whom God had sent modern 'Obadiahs,' in the shape of some kind-hearted Turks, and some Greek men, but mostly Greek women, who, during the storms of the winter, had secretly come to the city to get help and then to bake and carry bread to the hiding places in the woods, week by week for all these ten months."[12]

~ ~ ~

The Russian victory in eastern Turkey only put a temporary halt to the deportation of Armenians in the east.[13] At the same time they began in earnest in the northwest. Swedish military attaché Captain Einar af Wirsén said, "One can observe that the persecution of the Armenians has now begun in Thrace and even in Constantinople itself, when the Armenians living in the eastern parts of the city have begun being transported away to Asia."[14] The Turkish authorities who had fled Trebizond when the Russians arrived had only moved westward along the coast. Now they began to deport Armenians—and Greeks of the Pontus region, north of Kaisarieh. "Our quiet was again disturbed by the coming of great crowds of exiles from towns and cities near the Black Sea coast, places which had not suffered in the first deportation, being protected by friendly officials," said Stella. "Thousands of men, women and children, worn, sick and despairing, passed our school building on the way to the *khan* (inn) where they were crowded into dirty little rooms and locked in. They were weak with hunger." At first, attempts to help them were rebuffed by the guards.

"But finally the local head man allowed us to carry them food, but not money. Our school girls and boys gladly gave up their hot supper and sent it to the exiles. One of the most earnest workers among the school boys . . . was a young Turkish boy, son of an official. There were many of the Turkish people who disapproved and deplored this cruel treatment of their Armenian neighbors." Like them, the missionaries hated feeling so helpless to change conditions or provide much help. "Sometimes relatives and friends of our school girls and boys would be found among these exiles, but nothing could be done to save them. They were in the hands of a cruel government."[15]

As the days wore on, it became an increasingly difficult sight for the missionaries to witness. Genevieve noted in her diary, "March 14: . . . This evening 264 surgouns* from Kastamouni arrived. Over 100 passed through Saturday, 400 more to arrive tomorrow. . . . March 28 . . . Over 500 today from Sinope, Sivas, Gemerek and other places . . . Until today, when Americans got a special permit, and took water to surgouns, gendarmes were charging 5 paras a glass!" She had a strong, visceral reaction to it all: "How we can understand the Old Testament these days, and how my being responds to the Imprecatory portion of it! 'Father, forgive them' is miles above me when I think of the Turks these days. My own desire is for them—or rather those of them who have actually participated in these horrors, and those who sympathize with it—to suffer as they have made others suffer!"[16]

They did not trust the lack of activity in April. It was too quiet. "We had grown almost superstitious and fearful of the times of calm, which so often had been followed by some more terrible calamity," Stella said.[17]

～ ～ ～

For months foreign embassies were made aware by their consuls of the deplorable conditions of the deported Armenians upon their arrival in the Syrian desert. German Ambassador Wolff-Metternich and American Ambassador Morgenthau, among others, had offered to provide money, soup kitchens, sanitary centres, and shelter to help them. In each instance the offer had been rejected by the Ministry of the Interior. In fact, the government went so far as to investigate and make arrests when anyone tried to help the deportees.[18] Even Jelal Bey, the governor of Aleppo, who had tried to prevent the deportations, had his suggestion of erecting shelters rejected, and was removed to Konia.[19] As conditions deteriorated, foreigners became more insistent to be allowed to provide relief. The

---

* from sürgün (lit. "expulsion")

government, in turn, insisted that it have control of all relief funds.[20] Of course, this position was absolutely unacceptable to the American Board. American consuls were directed "to leave all the relief work to the missionaries." The feeling was that a visit from a missionary would not raise suspicions of diplomatic interference.[21] Consequently, money was transferred to ACASR's Constantinople account for Treasurer Peet to distribute to the various missions quietly through their local banks.[22] Requests for funds increased exponentially as the weeks and months wore on. Without a doubt local authorities were aware of the relief work, but they did not interfere in any substantial way.

In the spring of 1916 Morgenthau went to the United States. His trip had three purposes: to campaign for his friend, Woodrow Wilson, who was running for re-election; to update ACASR's National Committee on the situation in Turkey; and to help inform the public, and rouse their sympathy and financial support for the relief effort. Before his ship arrived in New York, however, Morgenthau received a cable from Secretary of State Robert Lansing who asked him not to speak publically because newspapers might "misrepresent" his remarks. This order did not sit well with him. In March he resigned as Ambassador. In April, "his first act as a private citizen was a speaking tour for ACASR."[23] Morgenthau's replacement as Ambassador to the Ottoman Empire was Dr. Abram I. Elkus, a lawyer from New York. Elkus arrived in Constantinople in the fall, and quickly received "expressions of satisfaction" from the American Board missionaries.[24]

~ ~ ~

The only major victory the Ottomans enjoyed was in April at Kut, south of Baghdad, against the British Indian expeditionary force.[25] Otherwise, the war was not going well for them. The British were building strength in Mesopotamia in preparation for an assault on Baghdad, and were courting the Ottoman governor of Mecca, Sharif Huseyn, with the offer of supporting Arab independence.[26] There were rumours that the Ottomans were making overtures to Russia for a separate peace, because "Turkey seemed on the eve of disintegration" and a "fast approaching collapse."[27] A secret deal was also under negotiation since January between Sir Mark Sykes, aid to the British Secretary of State for War, and French diplomat François Georges Picot. The Sykes-Picot Agreement outlined how the eastern portion of the Ottoman Empire would be divided once it (inevitably) lost the war: Britain would get the vilayets of Baghdad and Basra, and the Mediterranean ports of Acre and Jaffa; France would get Lebanon, Syria and the oil-rich vilayet of Mosul; and Arabia would expand its present territory to include Medina and Mecca.[28] The political situation between the United States and Germany continued to deteriorate as Germany ramped up its "illegal" submarine warfare in the Atlantic, and the Americans threatened to cut diplomatic ties.[29]

But in the spring of 1916, the biggest threat to any Ottoman victory was the dismal health of its soldiers. The poor sanitary conditions of the military, as described by von Sanders, and the fact that they were often malnourished, left them open to a raft of diseases, including typhus, cholera, malaria, pellagra, scurvy and smallpox.[30] The military needed more hospitals, and they knew just how to get them: appropriate American mission buildings.

In Kaisarieh, they demanded the 394 children in the Talas and Zinjidery schools be transferred to government orphanages, so the buildings could become military hospitals. Not wanting to go against the previous orders by the Ministry of the Interior to maintain good relations with the American missionaries, the district governor asked permission from Constantinople on April 29 to transfer the children. The next day, the Ministry sent the following instructions to Kaisarieh and other regions about the remaining Armenian women and children:

Families without a man (gone because of deportation or military service) would be distributed to towns and villages where there were no foreigners or Armenians.

Young women and widowed women would be married off.

Children up to twelve years of age would be distributed to government orphanages.

If there were no space available in the orphanages, the children would be given to wealthy Muslims to be assimilated.

If there were not enough wealthy Muslims to accept the children, they would be distributed to villagers who would be paid 30 gurush per month from the immigrants' fund for their living expenses.[31]

~ ~ ~

"On May Day we decided to have a picnic to cheer the girls and relieve the long strain of work and anxiety," said Stella. "We had a delightful day—never to be forgotten—because it was our last happy play day together." A week later the mission compound was surrounded by gendarmes in civilian clothing. A few women wanted to remove their girls from the school because one mother was told by a hodja that it was going to be confiscated. Stella told them she had heard nothing from the government, and felt sure it was only a rumour. The next day, however, the gendarmes arrived.

Henry went to the local governor, and confirmed that the rumour was true. "Very well," said Henry. "We will give up the buildings, but let us take other buildings and go on with our schools."

The answer was an emphatic "No!" A government commission was going to confiscate the buildings. All Armenians, except those who could be classified as personal servants, would be handed over to the government. They had one hour.

Everyone had long dreaded the possibility that this day would come. "It *has* come!" Henry told his colleagues.

With great sadness Stella explained the situation to her teachers and the mission's two cooks, asking them to be brave and strong, and help keep the little girls quiet. "They were wonderfully calm," she said. "One or two smiled at me. One of the youngest broke down and cried, but all were quiet and self-controlled. We called the girls to the school room and told them of the order. Some of the younger ones began to weep, but the older girls and teachers went quickly to them and, putting their arms about them, tried to quiet them." They read the 91st Psalm together. After the house mother led a prayer for God's guidance and strength, the girls went to pack their clothes.

The commission arrived with several military officers. They told the girls they were to be taken to another school, and would be able to continue with their lessons. "The expressions on the girls' faces during this harangue were not especially encouraging to the orator," said Stella. "After their names and fathers' names and villages had been written down, they were arranged along the sides of the tennis court where they waited patiently until the gendarmes led them away to the wagons, which were waiting to take them to Cesarea. As they passed us, saying goodbye, tears were in their eyes and their voices were choked, but they still continued brave and quiet, and held their heads proudly." The students were taken from the Girls' School in the morning, and from the Boys' School in the afternoon. The women and children who had lived in the hospital, protected by Theda for so many months, were taken the next morning.[32] In all, 92 girls and 170 boys left the Talas and Zinjidery schools. The buildings and objects inside were turned over to the Sanitary Department of the Military.[33]

~ ~ ~

The appropriation of missionaries' buildings solved the military's need for hospitals, but it also signalled a change in the government's attitude toward missionaries. Once, if not revered, certainly respected, they were now seen as "foreign intervenors," even "microbes."[34] German

Ambassador Wolff-Metternich applauded this change, despite it affecting German missions, too. "The Turkish government has rightly recognized that schools and orphanages run by foreigners have had considerable influence on the arousing and development of Armenian national sentiments," he wrote to his Chancellor. "It is, therefore, only consistent from the government's point of view if it puts them under rigorous control or closes them down altogether."[35]

Two days after the Talas schools and hospital were appropriated, the same order was announced in Marsovan. The difference in this case was that the Marsovan compound also included Anatolia College and the King School for the Deaf, and the missionaries were told they must all go to Constantinople. Dr. George White, Charlotte Willard, Frances Gage, and their colleagues tried to negotiate, but after six days, "all the missionaries of the station were forced to leave in wagons engaged by the officials and under the escort of mounted, armed guards." They had cleverly sewn thousands of dollars of gold from the mission's treasury into their clothing, lest they be set upon by robbers during their eight days' journey to the capital. Interestingly, when the Turkish officials first arrived, they had insisted on opening the safe, and were surprised to discover so much gold. They had carefully, gently, passed around each piece, one by one, and then returned them to their rightful owner. They had just wanted the thrill of touching it.[36]

Meanwhile at the Sivas mission, a military commander announced that he would be taking over the buildings, and the missionaries "could go and take their orphans elsewhere." He suggested Constantinople. The missionaries appealed to the vali, who knew little. He told them he would investigate and get back to them within a few hours. Instead, he left town. Two days later the commander of the Tenth Army Corps told them Sivas was a war zone, and all the missionaries, except Mary Graffam and Mary Fowle, had to leave the city. Misses Graffam and Fowle were well liked, and were allowed to stay in a small building in the compound. The orphans would be transferred to the Turkish orphanage, and the rest of the buildings would be turned into military hospitals. "The day before they left, an official, accompanied by a detective and a policeman, appeared to insist on examining the letters of some of the missionaries." The missionaries were then transported in government wagons to Cesarea, in a truck to Oulou Kushla, and from there by train to Constantinople.[37]

The two Marys certainly had their work cut out for them. In addition to Armenian refugees, there were now Turks and Greeks, fleeing from the war in Erzingan and Baiburt, and in desperate need of relief. The women appealed for financial aid: "For the sake of our influence in the future and to show a really Christian spirit, . . . if there are any funds, please telegraph; and if not, please try to get some. It is an opportunity that we shall never see again."[38]

~ ~ ~

Though the Talas missionaries were not ousted from their compound, they were forced to adjust their accommodations. The mudir had informed Herbert that the government wanted to "rent" their Cesarea kindergarten building for £T 1 per year to be used as a hospital. "A military necessity," said the commandant. Polite protests fell on deaf ears. Fanny and Clara stored their furniture and most personal effects in the basement,[39] and moved into Henry and Jane's home in Talas. The teachers who had been living in the Girls' Boarding School, stored their possessions in the attic. Elsey moved into the Wingates' already cramped house, while Theda, Stella and three servants shared quarters in the gardens of the Talas Hospital. The Irwins were allowed to remain in their home.[40] Everyone was constantly under the watchful eye of a military guard. As other missionaries passed through Talas on their way to Constantinople, they felt more and more like prisoners in their own home.[41] "We all have most of our valuables and road things packed, ready for departure, if need be," said Genevieve.

Their activities were severely restricted as well. Two days after the students and Armenian teachers left the compound, Stella and Theda went to Cesarea to visit them. The girls had been installed in the Protestant and adjacent Catholic churches, which had been joined to make one orphanage. The boys had been sent away, and the women—the teachers and cooks—were locked in a guard house on the edge of the city. Stella and Theda were allowed to see the youngest girls, but were repeatedly denied time with the older ones. "We caught glimpses of the girls through the windows, and were able to exchange a few words with them until they were driven away by the woman in charge," Stella said.

With some difficulty, they were able to send in secret notes. When they received a troubling letter from Arshalois, one of the teachers, they went to the guard house to talk with her and the others through a window. The women explained that the governor himself had told them if they did not become Muslim, they would be sent to Der Zor in the desert. "We are ready to go," they said. "We shall never turn." When the governor asked how they wanted to go, they replied, "Just as you please." They were required to hire their own wagons, so the missionaries sent them money. Early one morning they were deported.

"Many of them had little children, some small babies," said Stella. "A few of them yielded, hoping to save their children by denying their faith, but many of them stood firm, giving up their precious little children to the mercy of a cruel government, and made ready to go far away."

Three weeks later, they telegraphed from Aleppo, "We all reached here safely." Some found work in a German orphanage, while others went on to Meskene. Clara wrote to the mission's faithful supporters back home: "These brave women and girls left everything—sisters, friends, children—everything, and without beds or food, started away amid unknown dangers." Genevieve called them "strong, brave, splendid heroines."

In a letter to her friends in Talas, Arshalois wrote, "I had often wondered whether I loved Jesus Christ enough to give up everything for Him. Now I know."[42]

13

A Door Closes

"The school boys were sent away!" said Stella. "The older ones to Angora for military training. The next younger to Adana to school, and the youngest to Evkere, to the orphanage where they are supposed to be taught trades and agriculture."[1] The boys in the orphanage were treated well, but one day, July 23, 1916 to be exact, Herbert and Henry were invited to a "circumcision party" on the mission grounds. A canvas sheet was erected outside in the garden of the Girls' School, and about 45 beds were set up underneath it. Once the operation took place, each boy was carried from the hospital to recuperate in a bed. It was also *Hurriyet* (Liberty) Day. There was a grand celebration all day. "Men, women and children filled the compound," said Genevieve. "Officials and their wives seemed to be having a special celebration in the evening." Herbert and Henry sent their regrets, and Genevieve took her children away on an excursion for the afternoon. "It was all so cheap," she said.[2]

Several boys ran away from the Evkere orphanage. Because the cost of food was so high, the directors were not inclined to pursue them very vigorously. The boys who were sent to Adana were pressured to become Muslims. "Sixteen of them refused, and fearing for their lives, ran away in different directions," said Henry. "One died of fever."[3] The goal, of course, was Turkification. Each boy was to learn how to read the Quran, sing patriotic songs with his classmates, and over time, forget he was Armenian.[4]

Back in Cesarea, the school girls were also pressured to become Muslims. "Every day their letters came to us," said Stella, "but we were powerless to help them much in a material way." Some converted because they were frightened, and some did so at the insistence of their mothers. Others held out, despite many threats. On any given day, the girls were scolded, separated from one another, given short rations, made to do hard labour, or told they would be deported, distributed among Turkish villages, turned out into the streets as "public women," or simply taken a short distance and then killed. Still they refused to convert.

One day the director of the orphanage brought in several "moohajirs" (rude, coarse men, "the worst sort of refugee Turks," in Stella's opinion). They were dressed up in fine clothes, complete with red neckties and canes, thanks to the inventory of confiscated Armenian shops. A number of the best looking, older girls were brought into the room. "The men were told to choose the girls they admired," said Stella. "At first the girls did not understand, but when they did, they began to scream—all together. Soon the official himself was so frightened that he hustled the men out as fast as he could." The girls were so angry they made a formal protest to the governor. He relented. They would not be forced into marriage. However, if they married a Turk, they would obtain their freedom. About thirty of them still refused, saying they were ready for exile or death. Instead they were put to work sewing four garments a day for the hospitals.

The younger girls were not given options. They were told they were too immature to know their own minds, and since their mothers had either become Muslims or had been deported, they would be given Muslim names and would accept that they were now Muslims. A few days later, when given permission to visit their homes for a day, several girls went to visit the Talas mission. Stella said, "We were glad to see them, but we told them that if they were determined not to be called Muslims, they must not accept the privileges of those who called themselves Muslims. This was a new idea and they looked very serious. A little later, we heard that six of those girls had gone to the superintendent and said, 'We are not Muslims, and we will never be, even if we must die for it. We want our Armenian names again.' Strangely enough, the man listened." After he assured himself they were serious, he changed their registration back to Gregorian. This made the girls very happy.[5]

Several women who had stayed with Theda in the hospital converted to Islam in the hope of keeping their children. It often did not make a difference. Some had their children taken anyway. Stella knew one woman who had one child taken by the mutesarrif, and another by a prominent Turkish doctor. Some women were forced to marry Turks, and some were exiled into villages without food or shelter. The governor knew that the missionaries continued their relationship with these women, often supporting them financially. It was also obvious to him that many of them did not follow a Muslim dietary regimen, did not work on Sundays, and continued to use their Christian names in their homes.[6] Stella knew that almost all who converted hid or destroyed their Bibles and made a pretense of learning the Muslim prayers.[7] "I think their condition from every point of view is worse than that of those who did not turn," she said. "The Turks themselves have no respect for them, which is quite natural."[8]

After five months of imprisonment, the girls who became Muslims were sent home. Fourteen of the sixteen girls who continued to refuse conversion were sent to the Red Crescent Hospital at Zinjidery as nurses, and the other two, who were senior girls, stayed in Cesarea to help care for small, orphaned street children. Remarkably, they were treated with respect from then on, and were not pressured to convert. In fact, the hospital administrator sent an organ to the house where the girls lived "and told them to sing all the hymns they wished." When an official complained about "those Armenian girls," he was admonished by the head doctor.[9]

To the missionaries, these sixteen girls had passed the ultimate test. "They are happy and free, for they know the truth, and the truth has made them free. The poor girls who failed in the trial of their faith are in their homes again, but they are not free. It is among them that the sad, unhappy faces are seen, as they feel that, before men, they have denied their Master and their nation, and have become the slaves of a lie. We cannot and would not judge them; their trial was hard—harder than we have ever known—but we must pity and love them with all our hearts and pray that this terrible experience may help them, and us all, to trust fully that Friend who never fails us."[10]

Still, they worried what the future might hold. Prices continued to rise. "Clothing, shoes, tea, coffee, sugar, etc., are out of sight. Flour is high and very hard to get," Henry reported to headquarters in November. "Meat is still cheap, but fat is very expensive." He was extremely conscious of the cost of living because the mission was now sheltering 21 people in all, and hinted that there were several Armenians hidden nearby. "We shall have to use some of the money sent for our people here, as they are penniless and in great need of clothing. Henceforth we shall also have to charge up the cost of feeding them." A part of the Girls' School had been demolished and a slice of land expropriated to widen the road.[11] The house where the Hoovers had lived was torn apart and the lumber was used to build 2,000 hospital beds.[12] Henry had tried repeatedly to obtain receipts for all the buildings that had been taken by the government. The governor kept promising he would comply. "But he never does," said Henry.[13]

Then came the disturbing news from Sivas that Mary Fowle was seriously ill. Since both Stella and Theda had had typhus, they left immediately—Stella to help with the relief work and Theda with the nursing. They were not in time to save her. Mary died on November 22, and was buried in the mission's cemetery next to Charles Holbrook, and little Robert Partridge, son of Ernest and Winona. Mary Graffam asked Stella and Theda to return to Talas. "Every movement we make attracts attention, and I think my being alone will serve to make it possible to do even more," she told them. She believed it. A few weeks before her death,

Mary Fowle wrote to her brother in Constantinople, praising her colleague, but worried for her, too: "I wish you could sit in her office for a day—any day—and hear the stories that come. Everything is thoroughly investigated. It is marvelous, the cool headedness and sense Miss Graffam displays. But the strain of refusing such great needs is telling on her."[14]

Everyone felt the strain. And as Henry said, "We have simply been sitting tight, never knowing what new wrinkle might develop."[15]

～ ～ ～

Back home, Susan had heard that an international refugee camp was being set up in Port Said, Egypt to accept the overflow of refugees from Aleppo and Beirut. In hopes she would be of use there, she began to study Arabic at the University of Chicago.[16] She also continued her speaking engagements. Her audiences were well aware of the ongoing deportations and massacres in Turkey, and wanted to hear details. She was often asked how she could stand to live in a country inhabited by such "unspeakable people," those vile Turks who had committed the atrocities. Her response was to try to separate average civilians from those in power. "What if you had to live under such conditions?" she asked. "What would you do? Would you want to be called an 'unspeakable person' because you had a bad government? I think not. You would hope for something better. The people there want something better." For her, the future could only be brighter. "We do not know what the end of the war will be, but we do believe that it is to mean better days for the Turkish Empire—that we shall have righteous government and opportunity to live a right life."[17]

The Swedish Ambassador to Constantinople, Per Gustaf Anckarsvärd, was not so optimistic. "It is only due to the war that an ultra terrorist regime, such as the present, can be upheld. The true nature of this regime has come to the surface in such a significant manner through the Armenian persecutions. That the same violent methods are still implemented is evident through the recent intelligence reports regarding measures for subjugating agitation among Arabs." He noted in a dispatch there were rumours that hundreds of thousands of Arabs in Aleppo were about to be deported. His assessment of the administration of the Committee of Union and Progress was that it was incompetent in solving the complex problems of a heterogeneous population, and was incapable of creating a better future. "The military successes, thanks to German aid, should not create the illusion that Turkey will be re-born thanks to the war. The stub is so corroded that a real regeneration is inconceivable.[18]

～ ～ ～

By the end of 1915 ACASR had sent nearly $250,000 for relief work and aimed at sending $500,000 more in 1916.[19] Much of that was thanks to the sophisticated fundraising methods of the Laymen's Missionary Movement, which had agreed to campaign for ACASR. In the 10 years since its inception, nearly a million men had attended the Laymen's conferences. As a consequence North American donations for missions had quadrupled,[20] despite their not directly collecting funds nor sponsoring missionaries. The secret to their success was in the training and organization of volunteers. District and local secretaries "gathered personal and financial information about fellow church members," trained canvassing teams on the facts outlined in ACASR's frequently updated bulletins, and instructed them on how to first solicit "those least able to contribute, in order to have their sacrificial example to set before wealthier prospects." ACASR organized committees in 16 states, which in turn created letter-writing campaigns, coin box collections, publicity materials, and solicitations of businesses to sponsor advertisements. President Wilson designated October 21-22 as Relief Days, "for Americans to express their sympathy for Armenian and Syrian refugees with contributions to ACASR."[21] A comprehensive publicity and fundraising manual that was distributed to all committees included a list of 35 ways to "Make the Most of Relief Days."[22]

Missionaries who were working on the relief effort in Russia, the Caucasus and Egypt were transferred, on the record, from ABCFM to ACASR. Any new relief worker was registered as an ACASR employee, such as Ethel Putney, a recent graduate of Columbia University, who was among the first to go to the Port Said refugee camp. She was soon joined by Mary Kinney, formerly of Adabazar, and Lilian Cole Sewny, formerly of Talas and Sivas.[23]

~ ~ ~

In January 1917 Greeks en masse "were accused of disloyalty to the Ottoman government" and had to be resettled.[24] American Ambassador Elkus tried to reverse the CUP government's decision to deport Greeks by emphasizing the negative impression "a repetition of the Armenian persecutions, but this time against the Greeks, would give in the entire civilized world."[25] As usual, Talat ignored what he saw as simply more international interference. And he could easily do it because he had become even more powerful. In February the Sultan appointed Talat the new Grand Vizier, and gave him the title of Pasha. Talat formed a cabinet with himself as Minister of the Interior and Minister of Finance, Nessimy as Minister for Foreign Affairs, and Halil as Minister of Justice and

President of the State Council. Enver continued as Minister of War, and Djemal as Minister of Marine.[26] And they continued the course they had set two years before.

The British were marching on Baghdad, and the United States had severed diplomatic relations with Germany. It seemed likely the Americans would soon enter the war. Those ABCFM missionaries who were still in Turkey were urged by William Peet to leave. When he sent a telegram to Talas that read, "Now suitable time," Stella, Fanny, Clara and Elsey agreed to go. The Wingates and Irwins decided to stay.[27]

On February 28 the four women, who had had their bags packed for a year, set off. They only got as far as Eregli, where they were forced to wait for permission to take the train to Constantinople. They waited eight days. No sooner they were allowed to travel than their train broke down at Eskishehir. The 24 hours it took for the engine to be fixed gave the gendarmes time to search the women's luggage. Their papers, including passports and residence permits, and their prized collection of photographs were confiscated. It took them 17 long days to reach the capital.[28]

In the meantime, Mr. Peet sent another telegram. "Now is a suitable time for vacations of Mrs. Wingate, Mrs. Irwin and families, and Miss Phelps," it read. They responded that they did not want to leave unless it was absolutely necessary. "The war was tightening about us," said Genevieve. "We hoped to see it through." But when his reply repeated the strong suggestion to leave, they knew there was "nothing else to do but go." On March 30, the women and children left Talas.[29] Herbert and Henry wanted "to stay at their post as long as possible."[30]

In Constantinople the others were able to reclaim their passports from the censorship office, after "long and persistent effort." On April 6, as they were preparing to leave the country, they heard that the United States had declared war on Germany. Americans were no longer welcome in Turkey. Ambassador Elkus closed the Embassy, and left the Ottoman Empire.

The American Board staff at Bible House had arranged to extricate its missionaries in small groups by train to neutral Switzerland. Clara travelled with a party of nine adults and three children. They spent the first night in a cramped compartment suitable for seven. At the Bulgarian border, they were searched once again. In Serbia they were arrested by Germans. Under armed guards, they were confined to a hotel for almost four days. They were then transferred into the care of two Austrian Secret Service agents, who accompanied them to Belgrade. After a night in Belgrade, they were sent on under guard to Budapest and Vienna. They spent two days in Vienna without a guard, and then travelled for two days more to Landeck, Austria. They were interned there for twenty days, though not treated unkindly, before finally reaching Berne, Switzerland. After a year living under the watchful eye of armed men, Clara exclaimed, "We are free, free here! You cannot imagine how it feels!"[31]

Eventually Herbert and Henry were required to close the Talas station and head for Constantinople. Henry and Jane, along with Stella, Fanny, Elsey and Theda followed Clara to Switzerland.[32] Herbert, Genevieve and their children, however, were not allowed to leave. As Canadian citizens, they were viewed by Austrian and German officials in Constantinople as belligerents. Technically, they were prisoners of war.[33]

A few ABCFM missionaries, such as Mary Graffam in Sivas, Olive Vaughan in Hadjin, and Charlotte Willard in Marsovan had insisted on remaining at their stations. Otherwise, relief work in the interior was left to the Red Crescent, and to the Swedish, Danish and German missionaries who were still there. The government had finally relented to allow aid into Aleppo, but was it a case of too little, too late?

~ ~ ~

On March 26, 1917 there was a rally in Sweden to protest against the massacres of Ottoman Armenians. Hjalmar Branting, Chairman of the Social Democratic Party, stated that "a fully organized *folkmord* has been carried out, and the events down there are unparalleled with all that which has happened during the war." It may have been the first use of the word "folkmord," which translates as "murder of a people" or "genocide."[34]

~ ~ ~

Conditions in the interior had deteriorated so badly the *Missionary Herald* told its readers the need for humanitarian aid was "past words to describe."[35] More than 750,000, mostly Armenians and Assyrians, had "perished by massacre, disease, and hardship." Millions more were in "dire distress,"[36] both within the Ottoman Empire, and in the refugee camps in the Transcaucasus and Egypt. Just before she left Talas, Stella stated bluntly, "There is no work. Bread is almost out of reach, even of the rich. And meat, which had been cheap, is now not to be found."[37] Months before, Genevieve had described the appalling sanitation system. After the hospital's toilets were (supposedly) cleaned, they were flushed out into the same streams that flowed through the streets to supply the town's wells. The odor was dreadful, the conditions dangerous. "Talas is full of typhus, typhoid, dysentery, about 20 dying every day in the hospitals here," she said.[38]

In addition to the untold thousands of civilians without adequate food, shelter and clothing, who faced death from starvation and disease on a daily basis, the Ottoman army also lived a precarious existence. In the winter many soldiers had no coats or boots, and were forced to wrap their feet in rags or go barefoot. They were often issued only a third of a ration, which left them badly undernourished and vulnerable to vitamin-deficiency, such as scurvy and pellagra. Their housing was filthy, unsanitary, and filled with vermin. There was little or no fodder for their draft animals, which often died. Their saddle horses only received a kilogram or so of barley, making them as weak as their riders. The soldiers were well armed, thanks to German supplies, but transport facilities were incomplete and inadequate. Their conditions were described as "lamentable" and "dangerous" by the German doctors who tended them. "No wonder that under such conditions whole detachments were found in caves dead from hunger and cold after blizzards or other heavy weather," said General von Sanders. In the warmer weather, malaria, typhus and cholera were added to their long list of ailments. The military hospitals were regularly filled to overflowing with sick soldiers. One doctor estimated that "as many as 900" were dying each month. Unsurprisingly, desertion was so common that by 1917 the Ottoman army was only at half its previous strength.[39]

This was the dismal situation when, in June, King Constantine, brother-in-law to the Kaiser, was forced from the throne by Greek Prime Minister Eleftherios Venizelos, and Greece joined the Allies.[40] It was now truly a world war.

14

A Window Opens

Susan Wealthy Orvis called her Field Secretary work in Illinois the 'Friendly Road.' "In contrast to the 'Unfriendly Road' of Turkey," said the WBMI's *Mission Studies* in May 1917. "Waiting in a small railroad station in Illinois somewhere is no hardship at all as compared to travel in Turkey, and she knows when her destination is reached the people will be kind and friendly, and she will be welcomed and refreshed."[1] All that was about to change. The ACASR team in the Transcaucasus had been working diligently for more than a year, and the influx of new refugees meant more work than they could handle. Workers were needed to start a new relief centre in Alexandropol, Russia. Susan immediately volunteered to go. Travel across the Atlantic was still prohibited because of German submarines, but the Pacific route was open, and was much safer. "Nearly twice as long as the other would have been," she told her family. "In fact, nearly two-thirds of the distance around the earth."[2]

After completing her scheduled speaking engagements, Susan only had a couple of weeks to prepare for an extended stay in Russia. She began with a whirlwind tour to say goodbye to her relatives. On July 1 she spent a few days with her beloved Uncle Gurney in Stanley, Wisconsin. She celebrated the Fourth of July with her sister Edith in Platte, South Dakota. Edith's husband, Dr. Edward Anderson, was preparing to join the army's medical staff. She also visited with her younger brother, Fred, who was enlisting in the navy. She then went south to Lincoln, Nebraska to see another sister, Mary Ellen Haines, and visit Stella's sister, Julia Loughridge.

Back in Dubuque, Susan was under no illusion she was not heading into danger. She got her affairs in order. She made the requisite medical appointments (doctor, dentist and optometrist), and was vaccinated (again) for typhoid. She applied for a passport, which took "time and trouble, for in war time they are very particular." She put her mother's brooch and a few other precious keepsakes in a safety deposit box at the Federal Bank, and gave the key to her brother, John. He was going to look after her finances, which included the $200 she had in a Turkish bank—if it were still there.

She could only take hand luggage with her due to "upset conditions" on the Russian railway. It was difficult to decide which kind of bags could withstand the long journey, but she finally settled on "one large suitcase, a telescope (expandable) suitcase, an ordinary suitcase, a black Gladstone bag and a lunch basket." She left the rest of her belongings with her sisters, Harriet Cook in Dubuque and Berd Wilson in Earlville, and set off by train to San Francisco.

Those "upset conditions" on the railway were caused by frequent bombings of the tracks and stations on the Trans-Siberian line. There had been a revolution in Russia in March, and the country was anything but calm.[3] The wily WBMI's Iowa Branch told its members, "As Miss Orvis goes into this work of more or less danger, let us bear her up with our prayers and our sympathy."[4] Members were then reminded that "traveling expenses are great in these days, and the journey by way of Siberia is long. All this comes as an extra drain on the treasury of our Board and must be met by extra gifts. Who is glad to have a share in this particular bit of relief work?" Below the address to send the money, there was a special appeal directly from "our own Miss Orvis: 'Please write often to Tiflis. It will be a lonely place. Write me in care of the American Consul, Tiflis, Russia.'"[5]

~ ~ ~

While Susan was travelling to San Francisco, the political and social situation in Russia was rapidly deteriorating. Rev. Fred Goodsell, former president of the Central Turkey College in Aintab, had left his home in Berkeley, California in February to work in Russia among Turkish prisoners and Russian soldiers on behalf of the International YMCA.[6] By June, from personal experience in Odessa, he had developed a certain level of distain for the Russian army. It had poor discipline, low morale and daily desertions. "Lasting and honorable peace with Germany can come only after decisive military victory," he said. He believed that the Y's "intensive educational program" could make them see reason. "The Russian soldier has been too busy to fight. Busy with mass meetings and committee meetings; busy with joy rides and liberty parades and holiday celebrations; busy with his hopes and fears for economic adjustment, whereby he may be able to get his little parcel of land as the great estates are divided up, or shorter hours and better conditions of labor." Fred agreed with many who thought the Provisional Revolutionary Government had made a mistake "in tolerating, for a day, the self-assumed authority of the socialistic Council of Soldiers' and Workmen's Deputies." The council had advised the soldiers that democracy extended to the army. They were now under no obligation to salute their officers, and should vote for whether or not they should be ordered to the Eastern Front.[7] The First Machine-gun Regiment voted to overthrow the government if it

Some of the group on the Trans-Siberian Express, (*from top row*): Susan Wealthy Orvis, Harry White, Irma White; (*next row*) Carl Compton, Ruth Compton, Ernest Partridge; (*next row*) Walter James, Harrison Maynard, Mary Maynard; (*bottom row*) George Raynolds, Martha Yarrow, Ernest Yarrow. SOURCE: US Passport Applications.

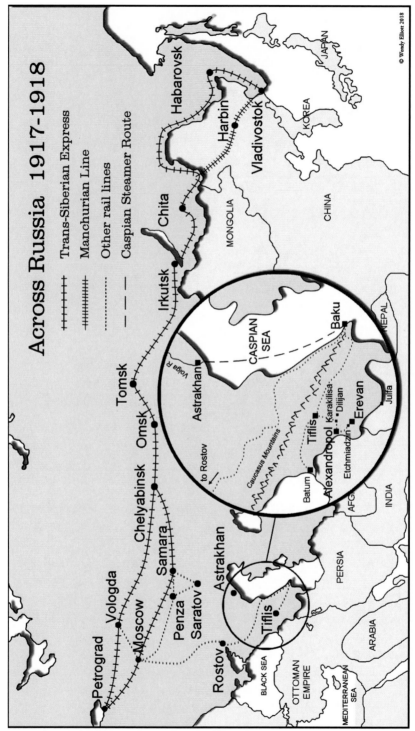

Map 5

proceeded with its "threat" to send them to the Front. Many other garrisons passed similar resolutions.[8]

Nevertheless, the government leaders took Russia's commitment to the Allied cause seriously.[9] Alexander Kerensky, the Minister of War, ordered an offensive against the Central Powers, with the help of the Kingdom of Romania. On July 1, Russian troops attacked the Austro-Hungarian and German forces. On July 16 they suffered a crushing defeat. That same day spontaneous demonstrations erupted in Petrograd. Lenin had urged them to wait until they—and the Bolsheviks—were in a stronger position to maintain power, should they be able to seize it. But the soldiers and armed industrial workers were too angry for restraint. The next several "July Days" were marked by violence and destruction of property, but did not result in the toppling of the Provisional Government.[10] However, "the Russian revolution is not yet achieved," Fred warned. "It is only fairly begun."[11]

~ ~ ~

On July 14, 1917 Susan arrived in San Francisco, and met up with her fellow travellers, most of whom she knew from Turkey. Rev. Ernest Partridge from Sivas was heading their ACASR unit. Rev. Theodore Elmer and Rev. Walter James were both from Marsovan. All three men were leaving their families behind in the United States. Carl Compton was also from Marsovan, having taught at Anatolia College. Carl was a newlywed. His bride, Ruth McGavren Compton, who had just been appointed a WBM missionary, was accompanying him. The other young man was Henry H. White, a graduate of Massachusetts Agricultural College, who had worked in Van and had escaped the massacres there in 1915.[12] Harry, as he was known, was accompanied by his wife, Irma.[13] This group of eight stayed in the city for three days, sightseeing, visiting old friends, shopping for the trip, and arranging for a visa from the Russian Consulate.[14]

"We decided to take our money for the journey across Russia in gold, as the rate of the rouble was likely to change," said Susan. They went to the mint and exchanged their money into five-dollar gold pieces. "I served up $300 worth of them in a case I had made to wear like an apron." On July 17, they boarded the small steamer, *Nippon Maru*, and headed for Honolulu and Yokohama. In her journal of the trip, Susan described several outfits she took with her: "a blue silk poplin dress with chiffon sleeves," an auto coat which she "wore over a blue mercerized sweater," and "a soft blue felt hat to match my other clothes." She also noted, "As the people on board were not given to fashion, we got along fairly well."[15]

~ ~ ~

While crossing the ocean, they began to "learn a little Russian," and occasionally received a wireless dispatch which kept them up-to-date on world events. One thing they did not know was when they could catch the train from Vladivostok to Moscow. They planned to stay in Japan for six days, to have their "laundry done and to see a little of the country," and then cross the Sea of Japan to the eastern Russian port.[16] Given the political circumstances, it was not surprising that their plans suddenly changed. When they arrived in Yokohama on August 7, they discovered that, at least for the next two weeks, the Trans-Siberian Express was not taking passengers—especially Americans. The reason was that Kerensky, Chairman of the new Russian Provisional Government, wanted to keep out Bolshevik agitators who were returning from New York.[17] Susan and her colleagues were staying temporarily at the ABCFM mission station, but were ill-equipped for the extremely warm weather in Japan. They had been advised that they could buy summer clothing when they got to Russia, so what they had packed was mostly suitable for fall and winter. Now they had to shop for lighter wear.

A few days later Fred MacCallum dropped by with some unsettling news. He had just arrived from Tiflis and was on his way to the United States. He advised them not to go to the Caucasus until they received instructions from the American Consul and members of the Relief Committee there. The political, military and relief situation were all uncertain. "He was especially dubious about the advisability of any women going there, and trying to live there under present conditions." They took his advice. They sent telegrams to Tiflis through the American Embassy in Tokyo. Then they waited. And waited. And waited. After six weeks without a word of reply, they had had enough of sightseeing. It was now mid-September, and they decided to be useful. Ernest, Theodore and Walter went to Vladivostok to investigate the situation first hand. The others volunteered to help out at the Japan missions. Carl and Ruth went to Kyoto, and Harry and Irma went to Kobe. Dr. and Mrs. Newell of the Matsuyama mission wanted Susan to teach English at the Girls' School there.[18]

Susan had visited Kyoto and would have liked to stay, but did not think her services were really needed. She had also been to Kobe College and the Evangelistic Bible Women's Training School in Kobe. "If only I had known Japanese I would have gladly taken work in the Training School," she lamented, "for that is what I felt prepared to do by my experience in Turkey and the special study in Chicago. But as all the work had to be done in Japanese, it hardly seemed worth while for me to begin. The language study would take too long." Therefore, she accepted the job in Matsuyama. It took eighteen hours by boat to reach the island of Shikoku, another half-hour by train from the port to the city itself, and finally a short rickshaw ride to the Newells' house. Susan was asked to wait before going to the school because the principal wanted time to "get the school girls tidied up" before greeting her.[19]

"I was tired and warm, and it was quite an ordeal to bow to so many," Susan said. "But I was pleased to be welcomed in this way." However, the thought of a formal greeting reminded her of the welcome she had received in Talas in 1902 when the Armenian and Greek girls came out to meet her. "The thought of those girls in Turkey and their present pitiable condition was more than I could bear." She went into the house, "quite exhausted." In the hall, the Newells immediately started opening a pile of letters from friends in the United States. She knew it was unrealistic to expect any letters herself because no one knew she had taken this detour, but facts were irrelevant at the moment. "I felt lonely and homesick and quite unhappy," she said. "I began to cry, and went off by myself."[20] It took a while before she was able to regain her equilibrium.

~ ~ ~

On November 6, Susan received a letter and a telegram. The letter was from the Peking mission, urging her to teach English at the Union Women's College. The telegram was from Ernest Partridge in Vladivostok, telling her she was "wanted in Tiflis." He had received a cable from the American Consul, Felix Willoughby-Smith, who had forwarded a wire from Erevan, signed "Yarrow, Maynard, Gracey," which read: "Work greatly increased. Your presence imperative. Let whole party come at once."[21] Susan immediately replied to Ernest that she was on her way, and reserved room on the next steamer. She hurriedly said her goodbyes in Matsuyama, travelled to Kyoto, where she raced around buying supplies requested by Ernest. Apparently it was hard to find tea, sugar and camera film in Russia, though she was unable to acquire the latter in Japan either.[22] At four o'clock in the morning of November 11, she headed off in a rickshaw to catch the train to Tsuruga.[23] Fortunately, she encountered a YMCA secretary on the platform. Ralph Brownell Dennis was also on his way to Russia.[24] He turned out to be "a poor travelling companion," but a great porter, helping her with her luggage on the train, and later on the steamer.

The trip across the Sea of Japan was cheap (30 roubles), but stormy. Susan lay "below, below" for two days, unable to keep much food down.

Wood being transferred at a railway station to heat the cars of the Trans-Siberian Express. SOURCE: US Library of Congress.

She was very glad to see Ernest waiting for her on the dock in Vladivostok because "the coolies around the boat were hard-looking specimens," and she did not know how to speak Russian. Still a bit unsteady on her feet, she managed to greet the Whites at the hotel, and have some breakfast with Walter James.[25]

The group kept busy over the next two days with last-minute shopping and re-packing. Before they left the port city they had an early Thanksgiving dinner with several YMCA secretaries in one of the hotels. They feasted because they had been warned that, from then on, there would only be cabbage soup to eat—"and not much of that."[26]

On Wednesday November 15 the group boarded the Trans-Siberian Express (see Map 5). They had "reservations on the International Sleeping Car all the way to Petrograd," which only eight months before had been known as Saint Petersburg. They had intended to transfer to a post-train that accepted passengers after Chelyabinsk, and go on to Samara and Tiflis. It would have been a shorter, more direct route. However, they had been advised to take the northern route as far as Vologda, then proceed southwest to Moscow, despite the riots and fighting happening there, because the American Consul could help them with transportation to Tiflis. Moscow was also the destination of the eleven YMCA secretaries, and there was safety in numbers.[27] Besides, the extra time on the International car would be more comfortable, which meant "a great deal in these troublous times."[28]

The Trans-Siberian railway between Vladivostok and Petrograd was only twelve years old. The 6,800-mile route had recently been shortened by a connection through Manchuria. Plans had called for a section of the track to go around Lake Baikal, but due to the "apparently bottomless marshes and mountainous regions requiring steep gradients," train cars still had to cross the lake by ferry.[29] The Manchurian section normally required stops for customs clearance both entering and leaving the country, but on this trip there was an extra delay while the train—and passengers—changed cars at Harbin. Susan noted that this task "was hard to do in the dark with so much hand luggage to transfer." They were fearful the Chinese porters would run off with the bags, because "there seems to be no law or order to depend upon." But the delay turned out to be fortuitous because, not long after travelling through the Russian city of Chita, they passed by Lake Baikal in daylight. The steep, rounded-topped mountains along the shore, covered in the distance with dark, vibrant greenery, sliding into the cool, brilliant blue lake was "one of the scenic points of the whole trip."[30]

The sleeping cars, located at the end of the train, were "as large as good staterooms on a first class ocean steamer." Each car had two compartments. Susan and Irma shared a room, with a toilet room separating them from the Compton's compartment. The ACASR and YMCA men were in other cars. On Sunday they all gathered together in Susan's car, dismantling the doors and part of the walls of the toilet area to create one large room for a vesper service. At least four of the YMCA secretaries were ordained ministers, so there was no shortage of oration. One of the men had brought a phonograph. They enjoyed lots of music and lots of singing. John Elder and William Young Duncan were especially good singers.[31]

To pass the time during the week-long journey, the groups often got together for concerts, to talk, and to play games. Susan had brought a set of dominoes with her, and discovered that some of the men were very fond of playing "42." The highlight of each day was going to the dining car, which was at the front of the train. "All the cars have double doors which must be opened and shut," Susan said. "We wear gloves to do it to keep our hands clean. Usually one man goes ahead and another behind to do this stunt, as it is hard work. The aisles are often quite crowded so we have to push our way through."[32] The platforms between the cars were also crowded, not with civilians, but with soldiers. They repeatedly told the travellers they would throw them off the train, though they "never carried out their threats."[33]

Russian peasants selling food at a railway station. SOURCE: James Maxwell Pringle, photographer, 1917-1918, US Library of Congress.

During the first part of the trip, the cars were lit with electric lights. Later, however, the electricity was cut and they only had candles—"and few of them." Because they were at the rear of the train near the stored water, Susan, Irma and the Comptons had a constant supply of hot water. The others were not so lucky. When the train stopped at a station, "everyone would jump off and run to the hot water tank to fill their tea kettles." No one dared to drink water that had not been boiled. People were also able to buy food at the stations, though fruit was scarce and expensive, "and vegetables almost unknown, except cabbage." It was dangerous to disembark "at many stations, where the crowds were ready to stampede the train and take possession."[34]

They were again reminded of the seriousness of their situation when they switched trains at Vologda for the relatively short trip to Moscow. Along the way they "had heard disturbing rumors, and had doubts as to the possibility of entering that city."[35] The notices posted by the government in the cars read: "Please do not shoot in the cars, or kill the engineers or guards. All the world will hear of it. Don't throw passengers out of the window while the train is in motion."[36] "We refrained from such violent demonstrations," Susan said.[37]

~ ~ ~

The train notices had been posted by the new Bolshevik government. Around the time Susan was leaving Japan, there was another revolution in Petrograd.[38] It had begun just before the meeting of the Second Congress of Soviets. The Soviet's Military Revolutionary Committee took over the telegraph offices and railway stations, set up roadblocks on the city's bridges, occupied key governmental institutions, and surrounded the Winter Palace, the seat of government. "They encountered almost no violent resistance. The streets remained calm, and citizens continued to go about their everyday business."[39] When the Congress met, there was support for the transfer of power from Kerensky's Provisional Government to the Soviets, but there was a serious wrinkle. The Bolsheviks did not hold a majority within the Soviet collective, and the Bolsheviks, led by Lenin and Trotsky, wanted power. A ten-day struggle ensued between the Bolsheviks and the other Soviets. There were skirmishes in Petrograd, but all-out fighting in the streets of Moscow. Military cadets and student volunteers in Moscow were loyal to the Provisional Government. They fought bloody battles against the local forces of the Military Revolutionary Committee, much of it in the vicinity of the Kremlin, St. Basil's Cathedral, and the nearby palaces and institutions. Armed fights occurred on the railway between Petrograd and Moscow, but Soviets in other provincial centres were too weak to take power in their regions.[40] Without military help, the tide in Moscow eventually turned against the Provisional Government's supporters. Lenin and Trotsky finally issued an ultimatum in favour of the Bolshevik platform, and the opposition gave up. Though the Bolsheviks were the victors, several of their own party resigned and published a protest in *Izvestia*, warning that a Bolshevik-only government would lead to a period of "political terror."[41] Another window had opened—but this time for a terrible civil war.

~ ~ ~

The weary travellers arrived in Moscow at sunset. They were greeted by a YMCA representative, and taken to the Y's headquarters. It was once a palatial residence, now rented to the Association by an oil magnate from Baku who had fled the revolution. The building was large enough to accommodate them all, which was fortunate because all the hotels were closed. The revolutionary fight had ended only three days before their arrival, and had badly damaged many buildings.[42] Evidence of the carnage was everywhere as they made their way through the city. "The crowds on the streets seemed to be sobered by the sight," Theodore Elmer said. "House walls scarred with bullet marks or smashed by shell explosions; buildings charred and gutted from fire; snow soaked with blood in the streets." The Y's building had not been immune from the battle. One of the secretaries had been trapped in his room for seven days. A shell had exploded next to him, but miraculously he had not been killed. "He has

Bullet-pocked building in Moscow, 1917. SOURCE: James Maxwell Pringle, photographer, 1917-1918, US Library of Congress.

now started on his journey homeward, a nervous wreck," said Theodore. "I saw the room where he was, and I am not surprised."[43]

Not one for unduly worrying her family, friends and WBMI supporters, Susan wrote to them about her "safe and comfortable journey through Siberia with no troublesome delays." They were staying at "a wonderful palace,"[44] and all Americans who were in Moscow on November 29 were invited to dine at the Y to celebrate Thanksgiving Day together.[45]

The reception did occur. The American Consul attended, but not many others ventured out because "everyone expected another battle to begin."[46] No doubt their thoughts were similar to those of President Woodrow Wilson, who asked of his fellow citizens while they rendered thanks for their bounties, "Let us pray to Almighty God that, in all humbleness of spirit, we may look always to Him for guidance; that we may be kept constant in the spirit and purpose of service; that by His grace our minds may be directed and our hands strengthened; and that in His good time, liberty and security and peace and the comradeship of a common justice may be vouchsafed for all the nations of the earth."[47] Susan had travelled 15,000 miles from Dubuque, and still had more than 2,000 to go to reach Alexandropol. She did not know what awaited her there, but Wilson's entreaty was devoutly to be wished.

15

Aiding in Alexandropol

After the Bolsheviks seized power, the Transcaucasian Commissariat was established to govern the Transcaucasus region. Some of the members wanted to create separate republics of Georgia, Armenia and Azerbaijan, though the area was still considered part of Russia. American Consul Willoughby-Smith requested financial support for the proposed republics from the US State Department. Robert Lansing, Secretary of State, refused. Neither Lansing nor President Wilson were in favour of dividing existing nation-states, nor did they think that doing so would prevent a civil war.[1] One of the first things the Commissariat did, however, was to negotiate a temporary peace with the Ottoman Empire. In early December 1917, the armistice of Erzingan suspended hostilities in the Caucasian and Persian Fronts. As a consequence, an estimated 100,000 Russian troops began to withdraw from Trebizond, Erzroom, Bitlis and Van.

"Every mother's son of them wanted to go home, and each individual wanted to be the first to get there," said Ernest Yarrow, head of the relief effort in Erevan. "They all had to come through the Caucasus, and very shortly the one single-track railroad was hopelessly congested. . . What would have taken weeks to accomplish under normal conditions, now took months under the 'every man for himself' rule." The breakdown of discipline and control made it difficult for Ernest and his colleagues to conduct their work. It was especially hard for the Home Orphan Department to visit families outside the city. "Home orphan" was the term ACASR had given to children who lived with their mother, but whose father had been killed during the deportations. These families were almost always destitute, but in their attempt to visit them, some relief workers had been thrown off the train, and others robbed.

No repairs were being made to the train engines and cars. They were kept running until they could run no more, and then simply abandoned. "In Alexandropol alone there were over a hundred engines which had been used up and were rusting to ruin, with no one to overhaul them," said Ernest. "Quite frequently a body of soldiers would reach the railroad and stop a train going in one direction, force the travelers to descend, throw out by the roadside the loads from the freight cars, and then, under threats of death, force the driver to reverse his engine and go back in the direction he came from."

Ernest Yarrow (*right*) allotting relief to Armenian orphans near Erevan, 1915.
SOURCE: Bain News Service, US Library of Congress.

On one trip, Ernest and Major George Gracey were invited by some Cossack soldiers to ride in the engine. When they entered, they found the entire crew drunk, with a Cossack—more drunk than the crew—supervising them in driving the train. "He was very active in his control," said Ernest, "pulling a valve here and putting on a brake there, the engineer not daring to say a word. Then he began to give us an illustration of how the Cossacks fought, first with the short dagger, and then with his sword, and finally with both of these weapons in combination.

"He would rip and dig out in all directions with his dagger, and then, placing that weapon between his teeth, he would take out his long, heavy sword, and parry and thrust and sweep wild and frantic circles in the air, whacking the roof, the engine, or anything else that got into its path. The poor engineer simply collapsed in a corner with fright, and the rest of us flattened ourselves out against whatever support we could find." Fortunately, Ernest and George lived to tell the tale, but during the months that followed, as more soldiers passed through the region, the situation worsened.[2]

~ ~ ~

In early December, Susan and the seven other ACASR workers travelled south from Moscow on an overcrowded train: 1,000 miles to

Rostov, then 1,300 miles to Baku, and another 580 miles to Tiflis.[3] They were met by Thomas Heald of the Friends' War Victims' Committee. He had been working in the region since 1916 on behalf of the Lord Mayor's Fund, where he helped refugees from Poland and Courland (western Latvia) who had "wandered to Moscow."[4] In February 1917 he joined two other Friends, Alfred E. Backhouse and E. St. John Catchpool, in Erevan to start an industry to make cotton clothes suitable for some 200,000 refugees in the Transcaucasus. Not long afterwards, realizing the need was great in Alexandropol, Thomas was asked to establish an ACASR refugee centre there.[5] It was a huge job for one man to supervise, so he was especially pleased to greet the reinforcements, and arrange for their accommodation for a three-day sojourn in Tiflis.

Susan's group stayed in two rooms at the International Hotel, one for the three women, the other for the five men. They had to move rooms almost every day during their stay, but felt lucky to have a safe place to sleep. The city was teeming with people, and there were few rooms available.[6]

Prices were high, too. Susan had always been careful with her money, probably because she had so little of it. The WBMI continued to pay her salary and the bare minimum for expenses to Tiflis, as did the ABCFM for the men in her group. At Tiflis, their expenses were taken over by ACASR, which provided enough for a basic outfit (bedding, dishes, cutlery, etc.). But "there could be *no* margin, no chance to save a cent," Susan noted. They had exchanged their gold for roubles "at a good rate of 13.95 roubles to the dollar," but were astounded at the cost of goods: sheeting was 10 roubles per *arshin* (an old Russian measurement, approximately 27 in.), and springs for a single bed were 200 roubles. Nevertheless, they bought the necessary equipment—washbasins, linen, beds and dishes—which was put in storage until they had an address for shipping it. It was agreed that Susan, Ernest Partridge, and Ruth and Carl Compton would go to Alexandropol with Thomas, and the other four would go to Erevan the next day to work with the Yarrows and Maynards.[7]

Before leaving Tiflis, Thomas arranged for them to take a scenic drive into the mountains. "It was like going from summer to winter in a half hour," Susan said. "It was an exhilarating ride, for the chauffeur was a wild driver. The car slid around on the snowy hills and dashed down the steep curves!" The next day, she experienced a different sort of thrill. They left the hotel in the dark in separate automobiles headed for the train station for the trip to Alexandropol. Susan was seated in the front beside the Russian driver. Their Armenian interpreter was in the back beside a pile of luggage. Not far from the station, the engine backfired and the auto stopped. "There we were for a half hour in a dark street, standing on the sidewalk shivering with cold and anxiety," said Susan. "I wondered what would happen if anyone demanded who I was, for I had no passport just then. It was the only time I had been without it. They had taken it to the consul to be signed and had not returned it." Her anxiety was compounded by the fact that "the interpreter knew no Russian."

The driver finally fixed the problem and got them to the station, where the rest of the group was waiting, anxious about Susan's whereabouts. They waited some more until an official came by with their papers, and with orders to take them "a long way in the dark down to the yards" and put them in a rail compartment. "After some time we were pulled up to the depot, and a struggle then began to hold our place," Susan said. "Crowds of soldiers packed into the train and we had to hold the door. The baggage was put in through the windows, which we had managed to get unscrewed and opened. Finally several soldiers were allowed to come in and they made the night dreary for us. One sick man sat in the corner and Mr. Heald sat between him and me. Mr. Partridge and Mr. Elmer occupied an upper berth and the Comptons another. Four soldiers sat opposite us. A girl came in during the night and talked all the time." In Susan's opinion, she was "a bad specimen." After twenty-one uncomfortable hours and 140 miles, in the middle of the night of December 13, amidst a blinding snowstorm, they finally reached their destination. At last their work could begin.[8]

~ ~ ~

Several local workers from the Relief Centre came to the station in Alexandropol and took the new arrivals by phaetons to the impressively-named Hotel New York. "This was the best accommodation to be found," Susan said. "It was the worst place I ever tried to sleep in." It was the only hotel not occupied by the military, but it had been abandoned. "It had shelter to offer—nothing else," she said. "No beds, no food, no service, no heat, not even a candle for light." Dinner in the restaurant was best forgotten. The noisy Russian soldiers and a tin-pan piano gave her a terrible headache. They ate at a different place the next morning. "It was even worse. After *long* waiting we got a little bad coffee and black bread. It was poor fare for tired, hungry, lonely mortals far from home," she said.[9] Her attitude changed significantly when Thomas took them on an inspection tour through the snow of "the many industries that provide work and employment for thousands of refugees." He and his team had done an impressive job.

Armenian women making quilts in Alexandropol. SOURCE: Bain News Service, March 7, 1918, US Library of Congress.

They had created a clothing industry with ACASR funds. It employed 2,000 refugees to clothe thousands more. They purchased wool and cotton from local farmers, and washed, carded and spun it into thread. The thread was woven into cloth on 30-35 simple looms. The fabric was then sent to tailor shops, or to women working at home, to be made into suits, dresses, shirts, trousers, coats, stockings and underclothes. Old men made moccasins of untanned leather. Approximately 15,000 orphans were provided with a complete outfit. The salary paid to each worker supported an estimated four other people.

The modest Relief Centre had also started a milk depot, where milk was processed and distributed free to babies and a few sick people. It needed work, and Thomas was hoping Susan would take on this task. "After seeing all this magnificent work," she said, "we felt as though it was worthwhile to have come to Alexandropol."[10]

~ ~ ~

Still, they were personally ill-equipped for life in Russia. At 5,000 feet above sea level, Alexandropol was especially cold. They had been told they could buy what they needed, including winter clothes, on their arrival.[11] That was before "the Bolshevik regime had caused everything to be hidden and nothing could be bought at any price," Susan said. "Money had no value." She had brought her old winter coat and muff, and a "black plush cape" which was "lined with a layer of paper material which kept out the cold better than anything else." Those items, plus an old steamer rug, two cloaks, and a blanket she had bought in Japan, saved her from freezing.

Food and housing for the new relief workers was neither easily obtained nor easily maintained. The town was overrun with refugees and Russian soldiers, all of whom needed a place to sleep. The Armenians who lived in the town had given their back sheds and spare spaces to refugees, or rented rooms to those who could afford to pay. Even so, entire families often lived together in one room. There were a few houses for rent, but most were small, single-storeyed, dark and cold. The ACASR group were fortunate to find three rooms in an Armenian family's residence, and took them immediately. It was not ideal, but it was a roof over their heads.

Ruth took on the job of housekeeper. "As she was a young bride, she wanted to do it alone with her 'hubby,' quite naturally," said Susan. "She had the glamour of romance to help her, but she was truly a brave little woman and kept up in spite of all difficulties. I think no woman ever set up housekeeping under more frightful circumstances. There was no furniture, no food, no fuel, no light, and nothing to be found for days." The first night was very cold because the stoves built into the walls did not heat the rooms well. They had borrowed some comforters from the Relief Centre, which they laid over their only furnishings—wooden bedsteads— which enabled them to lie down, even if there were no mattresses. They shared the kitchen with the landlord's family, but soon learned to put everything under lock and key. Even an armful of wood fuel brought in from outside had to be locked away or it would disappear.[12]

Thomas invited them to his home for meals until they were able to have their outfit shipped from Tiflis. They had been warned not to go outside after dark because "there was so much shooting and lawlessness on the streets." Of course, they had to eat, so they went out anyway, carrying a lantern and sticks to ward off the dogs, which "were too numerous to be pleasant." Susan expressed the sentiments of all when she noted that Thomas had "saved our lives by having us come to his place for meals for several days. His cook, Havasef, was able to feed us well, and we did justice to his cooking. It was a real picnic style, but there never was a time when food tasted better or when the host was more hospitable and eager to make us welcome."[13]

Over the next couple of weeks, they began to settle in. They bought a few dishes and pieces of furniture at second-hand shops. "The kitchen, which was shared by the other family, was outside the house. In order to

Alexandropol: SOURCE: Bain News Service, c 1918, US Library of Congress.

serve the meals we had to pass through their living room or pass the food through the Compton's bedroom window! The latter process was the quicker, but it was quite a performance." They had not done laundry since leaving Vladivostok, so they had quite a pile of it. They collected water from a nearby fountain and carried the heavy pails to the outdoor kitchen, where they had to use large quantities of soap before the clothes would come clean. "Soap cost 2½ roubles a pound," said Susan. "It was very poor soap at that. We had to dry our laundry inside at night because it would never get dry outside. It was so cold, and it was not safe to leave it out at night for fear of thieves.

"For our first bath in Alexandropol we borrowed Mr. Heald's rubber collapsible bath tub, such as the English nearly always carry with them when they travel in the East. We rolled it up and carried it home one evening and passed it around. My room was so near the freezing point, however, I did not enjoy my bath very hugely, even in this borrowed luxury of a bath tub, two feet in diameter and six or eight inches deep. I considered it a great feat when I finally got the water emptied out of it without putting it all on the floor." She had a little device she had bought in Constantinople, which she used as a daily wash basin, and since there was no closet in the room, she used nails and strings to hang her things. "I had to use my room for an office as well as a bedroom, so a screen was a great convenience. A pan of charcoal (a *mangal*) was my only stove. It was not very healthy, especially when I had to keep the room closed up tight at night. The one window opened out onto the sidewalk very near the ground. It was necessary to close the double windows and also the wooden shutters inside as soon as it was dark, as there were too many drunken soldiers about and no police or city government to help us."

They borrowed some kerosene for cooking because none was currently available in town. They were able to buy vegetables and occasionally some meat, but bread—"of the coarsest kind"—was rationed, and could only be purchased at a half-pound each day, and only with a ticket. Flour, too, was only available through a special licence. They did manage to buy a sack of flour "as a special favour," and hire two women to bake *lavash* (a flat bread) in the stable of the house where Thomas lived. "They turned the cows out for a day while they did our baking," said Susan. Thin sheets of dough were baked on the hot *tandoor* stove that was fitted into the floor. "We hoped they swept the floor well, but did not care to go to watch the process. We were only too glad to have piles of their sheets of bread brought over to us the next day." Much later they were able to obtain bread tickets, but "rarely secured any coarse bread, even for our servants." They did not seem to have particularly conscientious servants. One man was supposed to supply them with wood every day, "but often he failed and we nearly froze for lack of a fire," she said. "Haigaz, the cook, was a shiftless fellow who was too lazy to work. He knew English, but that was all he did know that was of any use to us."[14]

Still, Susan knew how fortunate they were. "The price was kept down on bread, but everything else was very expensive, and the poor had to go hungry when they could get no bread. They stood in line nearly all night in the cold street waiting to get a small piece for the use of the family." Her good fortune was reinforced during the next ten days when she surveyed the living conditions of the refugees.

~ ~ ~

Two young women in the Relief Centre escorted her around the town. They visited many "wretched stone huts, sheds and cellars," with stark, unplastered walls, dirt floors, and no windows. People were living in empty rooms, with only "a few pieces of dung dried for fuel, a few old rags for a bed, a few cups and spoons—this was all they had. Often there was no fire at all and no food. They were dressed in dirty ragged garments, which did not keep them warm." Susan thought she had seen poverty when she had done relief work in Muslim homes in Cesarea during the Balkan War. This was much worse.

They made as many home visits as they could. Susan was deeply concerned by the conditions of the "old people, who were even more pitiful than the children because they were so cold and miserable and sick

Refugees in Alexandropol, c1918. SOURCE: Bain News Service, c1915-1920, US Library of Congress.

and lonely and neglected." Four blind people lived in a desperately cold room with one old woman to care for them. They all huddled in bed to keep from freezing. "It was so depressing to see such utter misery, wretchedness, squalor and need, and not know any way to relieve it."[15]

Harrison Maynard had started the orphanage in Alexandropol in late 1916, and had inspected other orphanages in Karakilisa, Dilijan and Etchmiadzin. "We found the orphans well-fed and in clean, comfortable houses," he had reported. "The Russian government pays fifteen rubles per month for the care and provision and housing of each orphan. This is really quite a generous provision. The funds and orphanages are administered by various Armenian societies, of which there are at least seven." After the revolution in March, the funds stopped. The Armenian Church had generously made donations, but not nearly enough to meet the overwhelming need, especially when prices were so high.[16] On her first visit to the girls' orphanage one cold day, Susan noticed there was no fire in the entire building, except in the kitchen, where food was being cooked and laundry was being done. The situation had to change.[17]

She was not exactly sure what she was expected to do, where and how she could make the biggest impact and the best use of her skills. Local ACASR personnel were going to spend Christmas together in Erevan. It was not particularly wise to travel, but they "were willing to brave it once more for the sake of seeing all the friends, and talking over plans" for their work.[18]

~ ~ ~

In the days leading up to Christmas Russia began peace negotiations with the Central Powers. The Bolsheviks were bargaining from a weak position. The Russian army, already undisciplined, was getting worse by the day. The Ukrainians, who had formed a nationalist movement after the February Revolution, were seeking formal independence from Russia. Internally, the Ukrainian nationalists were fighting the Ukrainian Bolsheviks. Since Ukraine was rich in resources, especially food, iron and coal, both Germany and Russia had a vested interest in the outcome. The end of hostilities would be good for both sides, as it would free the Central Power to fight on the Western Front, and would be a promise fulfilled for the Bolsheviks. However, Russia was negotiating for a peace separate from the Allies, so it required time and a delicate touch.

Another party very interested in the negotiations was the Czechoslovak National Council (CNC). At the outbreak of the war, a unit of Czechs and Slovaks living in Russia was attached to the Russian Third Army to fight against the Central Powers. They wanted homelands independent from the Austro-Hungarian Empire. They had petitioned the Tsarist government to allow them to recruit their fellow compatriots from within Russian POW camps, but had been repeatedly denied. Once the Provisional Government was in power, and with the support of the American YMCA field secretaries who worked in the camps, the CNC was granted permission to recruit and expand the force. By November 1917, the Czech Legion, as it was informally known, totalled 35,000. This force did not want peace with the Central Powers without a concession for Czech and Slovak independence, which the Powers were not willing to give. Therefore, behind the scenes, the CNC began negotiations of its own with Russia to allow the evacuation of the Czech Legion eastward from Ukraine to Vladivostok, and on to France, since northwestern Russian ports were blockaded. This long journey to the Western Front was the only route they could take to continue their fight.[19] Christmas 1917 was not an easy time for anyone.

~ ~ ~

The Alexandropol group arrived via rail in Erevan in the pre-dawn hours. The normally dark sky was ablaze with a great fire in the distance. They watched it from the train platform for three hours in the chilly December air while they waited for someone to meet them and take them to the Relief headquarters. Even though Susan had worn a sweater, tights and gaiters, her winter coat, plush cape and a muff, she caught a cold. However, it was not going to stop her from celebrating Christmas with her friends, old and new. They learned later that the fire was in the Persian market. It had nearly burned to the ground.[20]

She and Ernest Partridge stayed with the Yarrows, and Carl and Irma Compton with the Maynards. Thomas, Theodore Elmer, and Walter James went to the house of the "bachelors," those single men or men who had left their families safely at home in North America or England. Susan was delighted to see Dr. William Kennedy, a Canadian who had passed through Talas years before, and who was setting up a medical clinic and a small maternity hospital, courtesy of the Lord Mayor's Fund.[21] They had just missed Major Gracey, now Captain Gracey, who had gone to Urumia to represent the British army at a conference.[22] Dr. Robert Stapleton, British Friends Alfred Backhouse and St. John Catchpool, and other ACASR people had been invited, but travel was not advised because of the brigands in the area. These days people took their lives in their hands if they even tried to go to the next station.

Surrounded by the warmth of her friends and the safety of the Relief station, like a true Congregationalist,[23] Susan "felt that a special Providence had watched over us all the way and prepared the way for us to get here at all. Surely there was a plan and a purpose in it all, else we never could have succeeded. Next there was a work for us to do which was of sufficient value to justify the effort and to repay the cost."[24]

Their hosts did everything they could to make their guests feel at home and part of the Christmas festivities. The family joke was that Mary Maynard should not be allowed out of the house because she brought home a new servant every time she went to the market. "But I had to help the poor woman," she tried to explain. "If I gave her a little work, I could give her food and shelter, too!"[25] Two things were especially memorable for Susan: the Yarrow and Maynard children, including baby John Maynard who had been born in August,[26] and a cherished letter from her family—which had taken two months to be delivered.[27]

Of course, an important component of this get-together was to make plans. There were a number of lively discussions as to how to carry on the relief work. Ernest Yarrow wanted to distribute clothes in the villages first, but Susan convinced him that the children she had seen in Alexandropol were just as worthy. There was much detailed talk of the various industries that were and could be established to give people employment, and who was going to be responsible for which project. The Yarrows, Maynards and grandfatherly George Raynolds would carry on with their work in Erevan and vicinity. Theodore Elmer would go to Etchmiadzin to continue the work George Gracey had started. In Alexandropol, it was agreed that Ernest Partridge would supervise the industrial work, Carl would see to the finances and accounts, Ruth would take on the centre's housekeeping, and Susan would oversee the creation of a hospital and supervise the medical program. The latter was no small task. The Centre had no doctor and no medical clinic. It did have one trained nurse, a man from Van, who visited the sick, and provided them with simple remedies. He was also in charge of the milk depot.[28] However, because malnourished adults became sick adults, there was an urgent requirement to provide the most desperate with decent food. They all agreed that, as much as possible, the relief activities were "based on the principle of giving work rather than money."[29]

With a rough plan in place, it was now just a matter of rolling up their sleeves and getting down to work. They were eager to get started.

16

Rolling Up Their Sleeves

Susan did a quick survey of conditions in Alexandropol and determined the top priority was to feed the hungry, because "often, food was more helpful than medicine." That required a kitchen. She found a pile of old bricks soldiers had left behind, and together with the Centre's nurse, Yeghia Azar, built one, brick by brick. She had nothing but praise for him. He had trained at the Mission college and hospital in Van, and was "most faithful," "a true Christian in his efforts to help others," and "one of the finest characters" she had ever known. Like those he administered to, he was a refugee. He had fled with his old mother and his wife, carrying his child on his back. "He never complained and was always ready to do anything we asked of him, and do it as well as he possibly could."[1]

Susan was fluent in Turkish, but the language was not common in the Caucasus, and she had only learned enough Russian to travel. She thought she should learn Armenian, and arranged to take lessons at night. "I was too tired to do anything strenuous, after rushing about all day, up and down, trying to get things to move along," she said. "Often the evenings were dull as we had nothing to read, till at last we got some *Encyclopædia Britannica* from Erzroom. Even that was not especially relaxing for light reading!"[2]

Once the kitchen was in service, she hired a team of helpers and organized three food programs: safe milk for babies, a soup kitchen to feed thousands, and for those who were housebound, meals-on-wheels. There were over a hundred cases where mothers were so malnourished they could not provide enough milk for their newborns. The plan was straightforward, but not easy to implement. First, they sent notices out to the surrounding villages to find farmers with cows—and cows that were fed well enough to produce milk. The supply was limited because few farmers could afford the high feed prices. Next, they paid men to carry milk cans on their backs into town, at one rouble per can. The daily trek was not an easy one on the cold, snowy roads. Some men were even attacked along the way. Susan soon discovered that not all the milk was pure. Several farmers tried to earn extra money by mixing old milk in with the new, which would make it curdle when heated. Some milk had been watered down. She quickly addressed these problems with a testing system.

Of course, it was important to sterilize the milk and the milk bottles, but they had a great deal of trouble finding fuel. The standard fuel was made from dung, but "it would not make a fire hot enough to make the kettle boil." They had to commission men to find wood—a very difficult task. After a few months they "were able to buy some crude petroleum," which they poured over the dung to produce a strong flame. "I had to watch everything to see that the bottles were properly washed and the milk heated right," Susan said. "It was so easy for the people to be careless when everything was so difficult." Ironically, the bane of the program was not the milk, but the bottles and corks. The "cheap pop bottles" they used were easily broken, and even though they implored the mothers to keep the corks, it seemed to be a losing battle. However, Susan was very proud that, after only four months, they were regularly supplying safe milk and a small quilt to three hundred babies.[3]

The soup kitchen shared the same fire and supply problems as the milk program. As she knew from her excursion on the Trans-Siberian Express, vegetables (except cabbage!) were in short supply. Bread was rationed, and flour was expensive. After the winter, "potatoes, grain and meat were on the market, but the prices were almost prohibitive." Therefore, the main fare of the kitchen was hot soup, and sometimes stew, with a hunk of bread. Still, it was enough to keep 2,000 refugees alive on a daily basis. For those who were not able to go to the kitchen, such as the very old, the infirm and the blind, she arranged for the kitchen to go to them by permanently "borrowing" the kitchen-on-wheels from the army. Every day this "war-machine" delivered soup and bread to the home-bound destitute.[4]

⁓ ⁓ ⁓

When Germany and Russia went back to the negotiating table in Brest there were divisions within the Bolshevik party as to their approach to a peaceful settlement. Trotsky wanted to take a hard line, but Lenin wanted the issue to be resolved quickly. It was looking more and more likely there would be a civil war, and Russia could not be waging it while fighting the Central Powers.[5] The old Imperial Russian army was rapidly disintegrating, so Trotsky began to form a new Russian army to combat the German threat. He drew recruits from the Red Guards. During the February revolution, armed workers sprang up to defend their factories. By the time of the Bolshevik revolution, they had been joined by peasants, ex-soldiers, and other industrial workers into a loose militia under local Soviet authorities. These Red Guards were mostly young, single, literate, skilled, and passionate about the revolution. Lenin had helped them form their "self-image as a workers' army, permanently on alert, to defend 'the revolution' against any threat."[6]

Trotsky also conscripted the bourgeoisie for labour battalions to dig trenches and clean out barracks. Soon it became common practice for local Soviets to round up aristocrats, lawyers, stockbrokers, artists, priests and former officials and factory directors, and force them to clear the streets of rubbish and snow, the sole purpose being "to degrade and physically destroy the genteel classes." Naturally, these and other events, such as skyrocketing inflation, shared housing, and long queues for bread, further divided the country into those who supported the Bolsheviks and those who did not.[7] As the Red Army grew, the "White" opposition grew, too.

Meanwhile, Germany was fed up with the stalling tactics and unrealistic ultimatums of Russia when it came to the peace talks. On February 18, 1918, German troops under the command of General Max von Hoffman, advanced into Ukraine and Russia. They met minimal resistance. Hoffman recorded in his diary that it was the most comical invasion he had ever known. "It is waged almost exclusively in trains and automobiles," he said. "We put a handful of infantry men with machine-guns onto a train and push them off to the next station; they take it, make prisoners of the Bolsheviks, pick up a few more troops, and go on. This proceeding has, at any rate, the charm of novelty."[8] It was beginning to look like they could easily take Petrograd, too.

At the same time, and in defiance of the armistice of Erzingan, the Ottomans decided to take advantage of the receding Russian army in eastern Turkey. They began to advance. On February 27, Rev. Herbert E. B. Case, a secretary with the American Board, wrote to Susan's family to reassure them about the current conditions in Russia. "The paper this morning rumors that Trebizond has been retaken by the Turks. It is possible that they will press their advance toward the Caucasus. In order to provide for every emergency the Board has cabled thro' the instrumentability of the State Department, advising our missionaries to use every precaution and to withdraw in case of necessity. As far as we know, everything continues well with them up to the present time."[9]

~ ~ ~

Reverend Case actually had no idea how Susan and her colleagues really were. And they were just as unaware of the state of the outside world. Since Christmas communication had been "entirely cut off." There was no working mail or telegraph service; no messages could get in or out of the area except through personal delivery. "There was no regular transportation," Susan said. "Military trains came and went occasionally, but there was no regular schedule. The trains were in the control of irresponsible soldiers . . . Every train was loaded to the utmost, even the platforms and the tops of the cars were packed with men. Windows were broken and all the furniture of the cars had been spoiled and mostly destroyed. The cars were filthy beyond description. No freight was carried and so no supplies could be obtained. The Tartars often tore up the track and burned the stations."[10]

Tartars were Azeri soldiers: Muslim, Ottoman allies, and enemies of the local Christian soldiers (Russian, Armenian and Assyrian). It was getting especially dangerous between Erevan and Julfa on the Persian border, and Tiflis and Baku in the north. "Under the guidance of Turks and Germans, Tartars began to arm and make petty attacks on all principal roads," said Ernest Yarrow. "Over and over again they assaulted trainloads of soldiers, and in many cases overcame and disarmed them."[11]

There was often firing on the streets of Erevan and Alexandropol, too. And it was not the Tartars who were dangerous to the civilians of these towns. "Thousands of Russian soldiers were passing through on their way home from the Persian and Turkish front, after the Russian army was disbanded," said Susan. "These men looted and stole to get what they wanted. They were unpaid and unfed, so one can hardly blame them."

To protect herself, Susan had embroidered a red cross on white flannel, and sewed it to the sleeve of her coat. "People knew that we were using large sums of money for our relief work, and that we kept it with us, as the banks were likely to be closed most of the time or, when open, to be out of funds. Everyone was supposed to go armed." She wished she knew how to use a gun. To her knowledge, her Quaker colleagues were without weapons, but she knew for certain the other men carried pistols. "On the streets one never saw a man who was unarmed, it seemed to me. I got so used to seeing soldiers with guns and bayonets, I felt quite at home in such surroundings."[12]

Like Alexandropol, the town of Etchmiadzin, the Holy seat of the Eastern Apostolic Church, was crowded with refugees and soldiers, but there was one significant difference: the soldiers and officers were part of the Armenian army, and they were preparing to fight again in eastern Anatolia. Their presence made it hard for Theodore Elmer to find accommodation, and single-handedly supervise the cotton spinning and weaving industries previously set up by George Gracey. He managed to do it, but not before he took care of a problem that reminded him of "Dante's description of hell." There was an old khan and a large stable on the grounds of the monastery. Most of the refugees were living in the khan in overcrowded, unsanitary conditions. Theodore hired some of them as labourers to clean up the place as best they could. "We removed one

Etchmiadzin: SOURCE: 19th century postcard. Private collection.

hundred and fifty dead horses from the stable," he said. "The Russians had allowed these horses to starve to death in there." He also hired a priest "to visit the sick, and perform the last rites over the dead, who were carried out every day, smitten with smallpox and typhus and dysentery." Only then did he feel he could tackle the other problems of lack of food, clothing and work.[13]

~ ~ ~

It was not only the relief workers who were cut off from the world. Banks in the region were also unable to communicate with national or international banks, or secure money. The 1000 rouble note, which the Russian government was "so fond of printing," was only good in some localities. Many cities and districts issued their own currency, and people began to hoard whatever money they still had.[14] By February the ACASR team had just enough money left to pay workers or supply food—but not both. They decided to pay with food.[15] Even so, "the local jealousies made this work difficult, as all semblance of central political authority was gone," said Ernest Yarrow. "We would get permission from the nominal head of a district to purchase and transport food in his district, but like as not, the 'Committee' of the first little village to which we went would refuse to acknowledge any outside authority." The negotiations with each district for payment in food became so time consuming that Ernest had to give up all his other activities, "with the exception of the Home Orphan Department," to ensure the payments were successfully made.[16]

When their funds ran seriously low, the Centre's treasurer, Walter James, decided to go to Tabriz in Persia to get money. William Kennedy and Mr. Welch offered to accompany him. It was a fortuitous decision because soon after their trip, the road between Erevan and Julfa closed, and the Tartars seized the rail line. The ACASR workers "came back in about ten days, looking like New York aldermen!" Ernest said. "They had 2,000,000 rubles in paper money hidden about their persons, and they had to ride back on top of the passenger car. It was a dangerous undertaking, but was well executed, and enabled us to continue our work."[17]

~ ~ ~

The German invasion gave the impetus to the Bolsheviks to move the capital from Petrograd to Moscow, and to end Russia's involvement in the war. On March 3, 1918 the Treaty of Brest-Litovsk was signed between Russia and the Central Powers. Russia agreed to give up the Baltic states, Poland, Finland, Estonia, Latvia and Lithuania, and recognize the independence of Ukraine.[18] Russia also agreed to cede the *oblasts* (provinces) of Kars and Batum, and the district of Ardahan, to the Ottoman Empire.[19]

Days before the signing, two important events occurred: the Czech Legion obtained permission from the Bolsheviks to travel across Russia to Vladivostok, and the Transcaucasian Democratic Federative Republic (comprising Georgia, Armenia and Azerbaijan) was created. Lenin had approved the Legion's evacuation plan, but he wanted them gone immediately, not in stages as the Czechs had suggested. One of the terms of the treaty with Germany was an exchange of prisoners of war, and the presence of the Legion could present a sticky problem for the Soviets. Now, 35,000 Czech and Slovak soldiers began moving from Ukraine into Russia in a loose convoy of 72 trains.[20] Now, the borders and stability of the Transcaucasian Republic were in question. The transfer of the government to Moscow had thrown Petrograd residents into a frenzy. "The railway stations were jammed with people trying to escape, while thousands left every day on foot. Law and order broke down altogether, as armed gangs looted abandoned shops and houses, and angry workers, faced with the evacuation of their factories, tried to recoup weeks of unpaid wages by pilfering from the factory stores."[21] In fact, the entire region was in chaos.

An ABCFM editorial summed up the concern and anxieties of the missionaries and relief workers in the region: "Trebizond, Erzingan, Erzroom, Van—these may all be taken back now without a struggle.

Czech Legion troops at a Trans-Siberian Railway station, August 1919. SOURCE: ARC, Siberian Commission, US Library of Congress.

Turkey may even march unresisted across what used to be the border into the district of Etchmiadzin and Erevan, with its large Armenian population, increased by the refugees who dragged themselves thus far and thought they had reached safety." It was a sure bet. Refugees from Erzroom began to pour in by the thousands to Alexandropol.[22] "Many came with frozen hands and feet," Susan said. "The greater urgency of the work then made us try harder to get the hospital ready to open. But food supplies were a great problem."[23]

"What fresh arrogance may not be apprehended from Turkey in her dealing with American missionaries in other parts of the country!" declared the *Missionary Herald*. "It cannot be denied that the situation is now darker and more ominous than heretofore, both for the subject races of Turkey and for mission interests in that land."[24] It might have expanded its comments to include the Caucasus, Russia and Siberia and the American position of non-interference. President Wilson had been apprised of the worsening situation, but refused to participate in an Allied expedition into the region.[25]

~ ~ ~

As Susan worked on establishing the food programs, she began the search for a doctor, a pharmacist and a building for the new hospital. Luck was with her, at least as far as the professionals went. There were two outstanding Armenian refugees in the area. Dr. Oksen Harutunian, a graduate of Van College and Syrian Protestant College's Medical School in Beirut, became the doctor-in-charge. He was able to recommend a good druggist, also from Van. By the time the kitchen was built, and with a certain amount of bureaucratic difficulty, Susan had located a large, old building that had been used as a barracks for soldiers. In her typical understated way, Susan called it "a bit of salvage." The windows were broken and there were no locks on the doors. There was no heat, but they "could not wait for warmer weather as the need was too urgent." The men she hired to extricate the ice, dirt and refuse needed shovels to remove it all. "All the workers employed were refugees, and most of them were too weak to do much heavy work," she said. "It required courage and patience, as well as constant supervision, to make things move at all. Scrubbing once or twice hardly made any impression, so great was the filth." In the bitter cold, she and they scrubbed and scoured the walls, floors and ceilings, then whitewashed them, then fumigated, then scrubbed them again. "It really did take a little heroism to get results," she said. In the end, the building housed a small hospital, a dispensary, offices for the industrial work, an Industrial School for 60 girls, and in the basement, a carpentry shop, a blacksmith shop, and store rooms.[26]

To equip the clinic, she had wooden bedsteads, stools and tables made in the carpentry shop. Her team spent many hours in second-hand stores trying to find furniture and equipment suitable for an examining clinic, a nursing station, a kitchen and laundry. She put in an order to the Relief Centre's weaving and sewing industries for mattresses, sheets, pillow cases, bandages, towels, and gowns for patients. Some women walked twenty miles on foot through the mountains to get wool and cotton to spin. "The whole countryside had a part in the preparation of that hospital," Susan said. The process took several weeks, but finally it was ready to open its doors.[27]

Meanwhile in Etchmiadzin, Theodore continued to expand the clothing industry. He employed 700 women to spin cotton yarn, and several hundred others to wind bobbins and prepared yarn for the looms. Forty people worked the looms to weave the cotton cloth, called *ghidao*, which was used for making underclothing for the orphans. He also started a similar industry in the town of Ashdarag, eighteen miles to the north.

"The monastery authorities, seeing the success of our cotton shop, asked me to take over their wool shop, which they were utterly unable to make go," said Theodore. "I paid their debts to 1,000 refugee women, who had spun wool for them for two months without pay, and took over the whole business. The Catholicos gave me two large rooms in the old refectory of the monastery, close to the cathedral, in which to carry on this work. My greatest difficulty was to find trustworthy men to oversee the work."

The people of Etchmiadzin had very little water, and had been trying for years to build an irrigation canal between the town and the river at Erevan. Theodore had hired an engineer to direct the work, and was ready to employ 1,000-2,000 labourers to begin excavation, when extreme circumstances forced him to stop.[28]

~ ~ ~

On the morning of March 18, 1918, Allen M. Craig, the YMCA Secretary in charge of the Caucasus, arrived to hand-deliver an order from Consul Willoughby-Smith: All foreign relief workers were to leave the area within 24 hours. The German army was approaching from the north and west, and the Ottoman army was rapidly advancing from the south. Neither was encountering much resistance. Within days the Caucasus would be entirely cut off. Two messengers from the consulate arrived the next day to accompany all the American citizens and British subjects. "We had to get on board a freight train for Tiflis with what few things of a personal nature we could gather up" said Susan. "We did not know how long we might be exiles and refugees."[29]

George Raynolds spoke for everyone when he said, "Our first impulse was to say, 'We can't leave this work and these people who need us more desperately than ever. We will stay with them and share their fate.' But we realized that if Germans or Turks were to come, or to secure control, we could not hope to afford protection to the people, as we have been able to do at different times in Turkey. Our presence might even make their condition worse."[30] Fortunately, they had had the foresight to set aside some contingency funds. "If we had not taken this precaution," said Ernest Yarrow, "I hardly know how we could have gotten along."[31]

They quickly made arrangements to turn over the administration of the relief centres and running of the industries to the local workers— "trained and faithful officials"—many of whom had been educated in mission schools. The hospitals had to close due to lack of personnel, but the orphanages had enough supplies to last for six months. It was hoped the Consul would be able to transfer ACASR money to the centres as soon as communications opened again.[32] Meanwhile, they turned over the rest of their funds to support the centres. But there was a dreadful sense of impending doom. Many of the locals told them, "It is not for your money that we want you to stay. It is that we may have some trusted friends with us when the end comes."[33]

"I said good-by to my beloved boys," said George, "and it was a scene long to be remembered. Tears and sobs showed the feelings of every heart. Mr. Yarrow and Mr. Welch were with me, and they succeeded in bringing wan smiles to most of the faces, and persuaded them to send me off with three rousing cheers. But it was with breaking hearts that on Tuesday morning we made our way to the depot."[34]

He wrote a hasty note for the consul to pass on to ACASR headquarters: "How much hope we can have that internecine war and general massacre can be averted, it is hard to tell. The general outlook is gloomy enough."[35]

Maynard Owen Williams, a photojournalist who joined the retreating party in Tiflis, was unabashedly cynical about the outcome: "The relief work supported by the American people has, during two years of efficient effort, kept alive thousands of men for the massacring, women for the torturing, and young girls for the ravishing, which the American Government has neither been potent to prevent nor willing to oppose."[36]

17

Eastward Ho!

It was no easy task to arrange the departure of 55 foreign nationals from Tiflis in only a day or two, but "Consul Willoughby-Smith was eager to get us through to Baku at once," said Theodore Elmer.[1] In addition to Theodore, the Americans included Susan Wealthy Orvis, George Raynolds, Ernest Partridge, Harrison and Mary Maynard and their three sons, Ernest and Martha Yarrow and their five children, Henry and Irma White, Carl and Ruth Compton, and Walter James, all from the Transcaucasus; Robert Stapleton and the YMCA secretaries from Erzroom who had fled northeast to Tiflis, barely ahead of the Ottoman army; Maynard Owen Williams, a writer and photographer who was in the region preparing an article for *National Geographic*; and a Mr. Samuel, an Assyrian-American merchant, and his wife and family. Among the British subjects were Thomas Heald, Alfred Backhouse, St. John Catchpool, Mr. Welch, William Kennedy, Mrs. Harrison, who was the wife of the manager of the Indo-European Telegraph Company in Tiflis and her two daughters, and a few English governesses to Russian families, including the Misses Renaud, Cuming, Creighton and Weld. There was also the Russian wife of a French military officer, and her little girl. Three relief workers who did not leave with the ACASR party were George Gracey, who was already in Persia, and two YMCA secretaries: John Elder, who had accompanied Susan and her group across Siberia, and his colleague James Arroll. Both of them insisted on staying in Erevan to do what they could to help.[2]

Though the relief workers were still worried about their decision to leave, they knew the value of doing so. "We found that Consul Willoughby-Smith's haste in getting us out was wise," said Ernest Partridge, "for within three or four days, travel over the road was completely disrupted."[3]

While the consul was busy securing two second-class train cars for the group, and arranging travel documents for them, they were busy buying food and organizing their luggage. As was usual for the ACASR workers, they created committees to divide the work and responsibilities. Maynard Williams, a graduate of Kalamazoo College, was new to this method of community decision-making. "The slaves and tyrants of our party were the Baggage Committee," he grumbled good-naturedly. Each person was allowed to take only what he or she could carry. For Maynard that was a roll of bedding, two suitcases, and "a year's accumulation of duplicate manuscripts, a typewriter, with paper and envelopes, a camera and films, a shaving stick, a handkerchief or so, and my medicine chest." He considered his manuscripts as being "rather light, but in the aggregate, the Baggage Committee considered them as weighty as a President's first message to Congress."[4]

Susan had given away most of her summer clothing to the refugees in Alexandropol before she left. She had lined her winter coat with her pongee silk cool weather coat, and wrapped her straw summer hat with the black plush ripped from her winter hat. She was able to pack them, her bedding and other clothing, including her next-best pair of shoes, into four suitcases. "These were numbered 1, 2, 3, 4," she said. "No. 4 was the first to be abandoned in case of great emergency. Then #3, and #2, and #1, in order. It was hard to decide which things to abandon first."[5]

Russia was in a state of anarchy, and there was no reliable news to be had anywhere. The Germans had supposedly taken Petrograd, Moscow and Rostov. The Turks were "said to be advancing on Tiflis from Sarikamish and Batum, threatening to go on till they met the Russian army, which would carry them to the North Pole."[6] Willoughby-Smith advised them to take one rumour very seriously. Due to virulent anti-British feeling in the area, he had them create signs that read "American Mission" and post them in each car to keep their British friends safe.[7]

It was storming the night they left Tiflis. Just before departure, the consul gave each traveller two sets of documents. One was issued by the American Consular Service and the other by the Russian Executive Committee of the Council of Workers and Military Deputies. Both certified the identity of the document holder, and requested military and civil administrations to assist and provide the bearer "lawful support."[8] He also gave them a hundred-pound bag of flour as a parting gift. A general consensus gave Susan the responsibility of guarding it.[9]

During the days and nights on the train to Baku, they saw several villages in flames. "Whether they were Armenian villages burned by the Tartars, Tartar villages burned by the Armenians, or Tartar villages burned by the Bolsheviks, I cannot say," Maynard Williams noted.[10] In any case, everyone agreed that the American consul had given them good advice, because Tartar guards inspected each car and arrested and hauled off the train five members of the British military from the Tiflis mission.[11] Almost all the train stations en route had been destroyed.[12] And it was very likely that, within days, all exits from the Caucasus would close.[13]

~ ~ ~

They spent their first night, March 29, 1918, in Baku camping out in a room that was used by the Armenian Protestant community as a church. Thereafter, they split up according to available accommodation. Susan, the Russian woman and her daughter stayed in a room above the church, where other rooms were occupied by some Armenians. Other Armenians had taken the Comptons, custodians of the group's stash of food, and George Raynolds and the Whites to one of their houses in the Tartar quarter. The Yarrows, Maynards, and the English women crowded into a few hotel rooms.[14] The single men stayed in the English Club, which was located near the shore of the Caspian Sea and the oilfields. These men had the best arrangements by far because the club had bedrooms with real beds, a shower, a 1,400-volume library, a billiard table, and tennis courts.[15]

They had been planning to hire a ship to take them north to Astrakhan at the mouth of the Volga River, and then take a boat up the river to connect with the Trans-Siberian Express to Vladivostok.[16] "We could get no further, as all traffic on the Caspian and on the railway to the north was stopped," said Theodore.[17] Thus the waiting began.

On Saturday March 30, Susan and the Comptons bought tickets to the opera. That evening, a few steps from the makeshift church, they heard gunfire and were driven back into the building by a mob running down the street. They had been told about the street fighting that occurred every few days between the Muslim Tartars and the Christian Russians and Armenians, most of whom were Bolsheviks. They had seen bullet holes in the walls of the church, and knew what to expect. So they huddled down behind a double-walled fireplace. "There we sat, waiting with our hats on, hoping it would soon be over, so we might not lose our tickets, which we had paid for," said Susan. "The attack continued for two hours. We did not go to the opera."[18]

The next morning the sun was shining. All was calm. Several members of their party attended a church service near the English Club, followed by an excellent meal in a nearby restaurant. After lunch, Maynard Williams took Susan to see "the flying machines at the air-drome." They were escorted around the airfield by a "bird-man," an English-speaking "White Russian" who hoped to visit the United States one day. It was late afternoon when they walked through the Municipal Gardens toward the city. The sun was glinting off the sea, and the air was fresh with the scent of violets and daisies blooming in the park. Suddenly a man near them fired a gun. A woman screamed. A street car raced across the park with its curtains flying. Panic stricken people ran for safety. Another fight had begun.

At the sound of machine guns Susan and Maynard "walked briskly" towards a corner, where they stopped to assess their options. "Our retreat was dignified, due to the fact that I let Miss Orvis set the pace," he said. "She evidently felt that American rush was uncalled for, under the circumstances."[19] Little did he know that Susan was not so much dignified as cerebral. Rather than praying to Jesus Christ with all of her might, she mused about William James's bear. According to James's theory on emotion, which she had studied in a psychology class, an encounter with a bear would trigger the emotion of fear, thus causing a person to run away.[20] "I thought I would be afraid if I tried to run or if I showed any fear," she wrote in her journal that night. "So I intentionally walked slowly, and we sauntered along. . . . I am glad to record that James is right. I was not afraid at all."[21]

Luckily they made it safely to the English Club, where they had tea and waited for Robert Stapleton to give the evening service at the church. While the Reverend spoke of his experiences in Van, cannons boomed in the distance. This was no street fight. This was the beginning of a war between Azerbaijan and Armenia. The cannons were on board two Russian battleships that had just sailed in from Persia.[22]

Several British and American residents of Baku opened their homes to the stranded ACASR workers. Susan and an English governess found themselves guests of a Texas oil man and his wife. The couple slept on the bed springs, while the two women slept on the mattress on the floor. "We heard the noise of battle all night," said Susan. "In the morning we could see the soldiers advancing over walls not far from us." One of the soldiers had dropped a cartridge belt near their front door, and Susan took a few cartridges as a souvenir of these harrowing days.[23]

"From the veranda of the English Club, we had seen and heard the machinery of war," said Maynard. The Bolsheviks and Armenians went up over the hill to attack the Tartar quarter.[24] "We could see the flash of the guns, the dust and falling walls where the shell struck, and then could hear the sound of the explosion and crash when the building was hit," said Ernest. "A good many fires were also started, and every night these lighted up the sky."[25] The Tartars had kidnapped the managers of the oilfield on the outskirts of the city, hoping to ransom them for a considerable profit. They also set fire to the oil wells. Maynard estimated the oil was "running to waste at the rate of five million gallons a day."[26]

The battle ended on the third day. "A great many people were killed," said Theodore. "The best part of the city was destroyed by artillery, and burned. The pavements of many of the streets were bespattered with blood and human brains. Corpses were lying everywhere."[27]

"Not one man in ten was a combatant," Maynard said. "Great wagons, driven by Austrian prisoners, were gathering up the ghastly remains of what had once been men. Young and inexperienced Red Cross nurses, pale and a little trembly, supervised the moving of the bodies."[28]

Susan accompanied a few of the men from the English Club across the city to the Compton's room to get some food. She was also hoping to be able to stay with them. They refused, fearing for her safety because the house was exposed to the elements. The night before, from their upper storey window, Carl and Ruth had witnessed the murder of four wealthy Azeris, who had been wrenched from the safety of their guard. They had also seen a crowd of Tartars rushing up to an Armenian house for refuge. "Both Tartars and Armenians hid their friends who were endangered," said Maynard.[29]

Henry, Irma and George had been staying in the heart of the Tartar quarter. In the midst of the fight, a military escort whisked them away. That night their lodging was burned to the ground, their belongings destroyed.[30] "Well, that settles my baggage difficulties," George quipped. But everyone knew the enormity of his loss. "Having left his heart in Armenia, where his life work had been done, this fine-spirited hero of missions now lost the last reminders of his beloved wife, who gave her life to the Armenians she loved so well," Maynard said. "The rest of us were going home. Dr. Raynolds was leaving his. Yet not a note of complaint passed his lips."[31] George eventually bought a large shawl, a chess set, and a large hatbox. For the rest of the journey, Susan noted, "in this hat-box he carried all his outfit, including the shawl."[32]

The local bazaar was burning. "The streets were cluttered with fresh and dried fruits, canned goods, dried fish and dead bodies," said Maynard. "There was no real looting but everyone helped himself to what he wanted to prevent it from being burned." Consequently, there was very little food in the city. Susan and the governess ate a meat-only dinner with the Yarrows, and a young Czech woman who had joined the party as an au pair for the Yarrow children.[33] "We had little else but boiled ham," Susan said. "It had to be eaten, so we tackled it and tried to save our other supplies for the ship." When three-year-old Ernest Junior said he did not like ham, Ernest Senior replied, "We are eating to exist, not because we like the food!" Eight-month-old John Maynard needed milk, but there was no canned milk available. A young Armenian boy who had known Harrison and Mary in Bitlis found some fresh milk and risked his life to bring it to the hotel for the baby. They were able to warm it with a Primus stove they brought with them.[34]

For a few days Susan shared a room with the Russian woman and her little girl. They would pass a Russian-English primer back and forth between themselves to communicate, and found it especially helpful when ordering a meal in a restaurant. Their main obsession was bread. They still had some of the tea and sugar Susan had purchased in Japan, and could add egg and cheese for breakfast or dinner, but they never had enough bread. Bread was rationed everywhere in Russia, and tickets were only issued to residents. "At the hotels we would get only two tiny slices of black bread with a meal, and one meal a day was all any hotel would try to serve. We saved the two precious pieces of bread and wrapped them up to keep them for the next meal, which we would eat in our rooms with or without the *samovar* to make tea." Susan was enamoured with the samovar, a decorative metal tea urn. She was also intrigued by the Russian method of serving the beverage. "They always serve tea in glasses. They refuse to drink it from tea cups. Then they never use milk in the tea, only sugar and lemon, if they can get it. The tea is always served very hot, for the water in the samovar is kept boiling by the hot charcoal. A tiny china teapot sits on the top and a few drops of the strong tea is enough for a whole glass of hot water to make tea for a crowd for one hour or two. When we saw people escaping from their homes in the burning city, we noticed that, if nothing else was saved, the samovar was carried along. It seemed like a household god and so it really is, the center of the house life of the family. I grew to be very fond of the samovar and its associations of comfort and cheer and friendly conversation."[35]

~ ~ ~

The group's Transportation Committee had a very difficult time arranging passage on any ship bound for Astrakhan. They had tried to negotiate passage with the Caucasus and Mercury Steamship Company as soon as they had arrived in Baku, but the company saw no need to hurry.[36] First, the clerks reasoned, the Volga River was still frozen. It would not be navigable until it was cleared of ice. Then there was the battle, which made embarking too dangerous. Even afterward, there was no rush because soldiers wanted to go north, and the local Bolshevik government believed soldiers had preference over the bourgeoisie. "The company was unwilling to send out the first boat for plutocrats like us, as it would involve it in endless rows with soldiers who wanted to go," said Ernest Partridge.[37]

The lengthy negotiating process gave the Food Committee enough time to scout for food to take with them on their sea voyage. Not only was food scarce and prices high, the Baku rouble was worth less than the old Kerensky rouble, which was worth about 10 American cents. Everything was very expensive. Still, the Comptons' room became more cramped day by day as the food supplies for their trip grew.[38]

Finally the company agreed to charter them a small steamer. "Our payment of 10,000 roubles had been divided among the several thousand sailors of the nationalized fleet of the Caspian," Maynard said. "This enabled the managers to open the season."[39]

"We were told to assemble in secret after dark at the English Club," said Susan. There were so many people trying to flee Baku the captain did not want anyone to know he was planning to sail. That night he also had an additional demand. "His crew had turned Bolshevik and were demanding a special bribe before they would consent to leave port."[40] It was not until the morning of April 9 that the ACASR group paid the extra fee and were able to board—as unobtrusively as possible. They quickly discovered that the wives and children of the crew had occupied all the first class staterooms, and hordes of people sat immobile on the narrow deck. Theodore was indignant. "We ourselves, who were paying for the ship, were obliged to go down to the bottom of the hold, with no accommodations whatsoever.[41] Actually, the men of the party slept in the hold. The women with little children slept in the dining room. "The rest of us slept on the deck outside or in the life boats above the deck," Susan said. "We had only our steamer rugs and very little to protect us from the chilly rains that began." The only food to be had was what they had brought themselves, and did not need cooking, such as cheese, raisins and some precious loaves of bread. Since the ship had a limited amount of fresh water, it had to be shared and rationed with the rest of the passengers and crew.[42]

The crew had not taken on cargo, so the ballast was off. The steamer rolled and pitched, and bumped into ice so forcefully most of the passengers became terribly seasick.[43] Little John Maynard was desperately in need of sustenance, and the milk they bought in Baku was sour. Susan had two cans of milk she had bought in Japan. "No one knew I had them. I had kept them for an emergency," she said. "Now the extreme need had come, and I was glad I could meet it." St. John Catchpool heated some water for the baby in the engine room. "With this we fixed the condensed milk for Master John and fed him from the bottle while his father and mother were lying flat with sea sickness." Susan managed to keep the contents of her stomach during most of the voyage, though it was often difficult. "One night I slept under the table on the floor in the lower cabin where the crew ate their cabbage soup. I think this was the hardest test I had, when I heard the men gurgling their soup. I came so near feeling seasick as ever I want to be."[44]

It took four uncomfortable days for them to reach Astrakhan. "The captain did not dare to stop at any port on the Caspian for fear his boat might be commandeered by Bolsheviks," Susan said. They had a close call when two men in a riverboat pointed a machine gun at them and ordered them to stop. "We stood there for an hour or more but were finally allowed to proceed. We never knew who or what they were."[45]

On the sunny morning of April 13, they arrived at the port city. They sat for a few hours on the dock with their luggage. They had nowhere else to go. Astrakhan had seen fighting similar to what Baku had experienced, therefore, no hotels were open for business. The Transportation Committee, headed by Ernest Yarrow, finally negotiated with the owners of a luxury steamer docked in the marina to let the group of fifty live aboard for the ten days or so it would take for the ice in the river to break up.[46]

A few of the men decided to carry on by land. "Delightful as was the prospect of living on velvet while the ice in the Volga melted, I felt it was my duty to see something more of Russia, and get on toward home and my work," said Maynard Williams. Joining him as far as Samara were Mr. Welch and St. John Catchpool.[47] Soon after, Earnest Partridge, Walter James, and YMCA secretaries Craig and Wells followed.[48]

Meanwhile the rest of the group coped as best they could. "It was a queer way to live," said Susan. "No beds, no food, no water, no light or fire. We were not allowed even to strike a match for fear of fire." For cooking and cleaning, they used a public kitchen, located a block from the boat. Each morning they would draw water from the river, and boil it in their own tin kettles for tea and coffee. The Food Committee would then go out into the city searching for food. "They would sometimes meet some peasants with a chicken or a bottle of milk or some few potatoes, beets or onions. This was all the market we could find. We divided the large group of about fifty into groups of five or six. Each of the smaller groups arranged to cook and eat together as a table." George, Carl, Ruth, Harry, Irma and Susan formed one group, and took turns cooking and washing dishes.

Susan was head of the House Committee. "No brooms, mops or brushes were to be found, but we finally did get a small broom and a

Travelling up the Volga River. SOURCE: Sergei Mikhailovich, photographer, 1910, US Library of Congress.

shovel, and a few pieces of coarse cloth to clean with. With such a large crowd of men, women and children, the place needed a good cleaning every day." She had been puzzled by the lackluster and infrequent help of the governesses in the party. One day one of them said to her, "Why do you work like a servant cleaning the boat? You will loose your social standing." For a moment, Susan was speechless. "Under the circumstances, it had never occurred to me to think about social position!" she wrote in her journal. "I said I thought my social position was not in danger."

On April 21, their last evening in Astrakhan, they were allowed to cook in the ship's kitchen. The river was now passable and a crew had fired up the engines, ready to travel north on the Volga to Samara. Susan served up a memorable dinner of chicken, vegetables, gravy, and even biscuits. She had also made a custard pie with the flour Consul Smith had given them in Tiflis. Considering she had rolled out the pastry using an empty milk bottle, and boiled the poultry and vegetables in tin pails, she was surprised at how good everything tasted, and how her table-mates praised the results. "We were all hungry and seldom had a good meal, so that may account for our appreciation of this one."[49]

It was a good send-off for their time in Astrakhan. In the morning they would head north to Samara to catch the train for Vladivostok. Unbeknownst to them, the entire Czech Legion was intent on the same thing.

18

The End of the Beginning

The trip that Ernest Partridge, Walter James and the two YMCA secretaries took to Samara was long, indirect and chaotic. They caught a train in Astrakhan bound northwest for Saratov. The Police Commissioner of Saratov helped them get tickets for a special car that was taking political delegates west to Moscow. Samara was east of Saratov, but they were to change trains at a junction, and head east. "We missed our connection, and slept again on our baggage," said Ernest. "Then we were put into a box car—a small box car, twenty-two feet by ten—in which sixty of us traveled for twenty-six hours covering ninety-eight miles!" They arrived in Penza in mid-April 1918, smack in the middle of thousands of Czechoslovakian soldiers.[1]

The Czech Legion had begun its evacuation from Ukraine weeks before, but in Penza, Russia, local authorities held up the trains, awaiting orders regarding possible disarmament of the troops. Then Trotsky, the Soviet's Commissar of War, got involved. He saw the 35,000 Czech soldiers as excellent recruits for the Red Army, and tried to negotiate with the Czechoslovak National Council and its French allies for the Legion's military cooperation. His request was denied. Then Stalin, Minister of National Affairs, got involved. He issued an order to the commissars in Penza that the troops must be completely disarmed. The Czechs were incensed, believing, not irrationally, they needed weapons for self-defence on the long journey to Vladivostok. Thus began a series of tenuous negotiations, which culminated in a signed agreement on March 25. The Legion would surrender four-fifths of their weapons, keeping only 168 rifles and one machine gun per train. It took so long to search the trains and disarm the soldiers that the first train did not leave until two days later. By the end of April, only 15 trains had moved on. "The National Council calculated that, at that rate, its last train would reach Vladivostok at the end of the first week of May."[2]

Ernest and his colleagues had arrived in the midst of this mess. After "various adventures," they were finally able to board an eastbound train for Samara, where they were met by the American consul, several YMCA secretaries—and more Czech troops. Three days before Susan and her group arrived in the city, Ernest and Walter said goodbye to Messrs. Craig and Wells, and hopped a train of fifty box cars, two second class passenger coaches, and 700 Czech soldiers[3]—just as Maynard Williams had done a few days previously. "I fell in love with them at first sight," said Maynard. "The Czech Bolshevik differs from his Russian brother in that he shaves, washes behind the ears, thinks before he acts, wipes off his chin, and pulls down his vest. Never have I seen snappier salutes and stricter discipline."[4] They were lucky to be in the company of such a tight corps, considering what lay ahead.

~ ~ ~

Meanwhile, Susan and her colleagues arrived in Samara under a full moon after a pleasant four-day, fair weather trip upriver. The city was much more stable than the southern cities had been, so everyone was able to find adequate food and lodging. Over the following few days, they all made arrangements for the next phase of their personal journeys. Carl and Ruth Compton decided to stay in Samara to work with St. John Catchpool and the YMCA. Several other YMCA secretaries, as well as members of the Lord Mayor's Fund and the Society of Friends remained there, too. Thomas Heald was one of the few who continued eastward with the ACASR party.

Their hotel had recently been taken over by the employees—Bolsheviks who maintained it and served good meals. "They refused all tips because they were now the owners," Susan noted. The Tiflis sack of flour was secured in her room while they shopped for food, some dishes, a Primus stove and other supplies. They also bought tickets on two second class coaches on the Trans-Siberian Express.[5]

The night before they were to leave, shortly after Susan had gone to bed, there was vigorous knocking on her door. Members of the Food Committee urgently requested the bag of flour. On the advice of some locals, they were going to take it to a baker who would turn it overnight into bread.[6] The next morning, the group left for the train station with several calico sacks filled with steaming loaves of bread.

~ ~ ~

Two weeks before, while waiting in the Saratov station for the passenger train from Moscow to Samara, Maynard Williams encountered two black American wrestlers. "One stuttered horribly, and this impediment to his speech made him one of the most accurate describers of Russian travel I ever met. When he said, 'd-d-d-dammed d-d-d-dirty' in describing the Russian cars, his profanity was justified by its accuracy."[7] Susan would have concurred. Her group occupied two very old second class cars on a very crowded train. Each car was divided into five compartments which opened onto the narrow corridor that ran along one

Soldiers on a crowded Russian train, 1918. SOURCE: James Maxwell Pringle, photographer, 1917-1918, US Library of Congress.

side of the car. "The cars were fumigated before we got on board," she said, "but one room was missed and *that* was alive with B flats [bed bugs[8]]. Women had been hired to clean the cars, but nothing had been touched, except the aisles. Under and around the berths, there were bushels of dirt, cigarette papers, stale bread, fish bones, cartridges, bayonets and such articles." Two items they had purchased in Samara, a broom and dustpan, were in constant use.[9]

For the first two weeks of their train journey, Susan's roommates in the four-berth compartment included her two former roommates from Baku—the Russian woman and her daughter. "She refused to have the window open, so I had to put up with the bad air at night," Susan said.[10] "We cleaned out the musty bread crusts and old fish bones and cigarette stumps, again and again, from around and beneath the berths, but always more would ooze out of the cracks." She finally used one of the calico sacks from the Samara bread to cover the filthy wall at the back of her berth. "That was luxury!"[11]

On this trip, no water was available on the train. The only food they had was what they had brought with them or what they could purchase at each station along the route. In their haste to leave Samara, they had left the warm loaves of bread in their sacks. "Before we knew it, it was mouldy!" Susan said. "And we had to eat it for weeks, dry and mouldy."[12]

Every day the train would make one stop. Robert Stapleton would get off and buy enough food for his colleagues. Local women had set up booths to sell bread, butter, cheese, chickens, fish, ham, fresh or boiled eggs, and sometimes cabbage soup. "We had two aluminum cans with covers that once belonged to a fireless cooker in Mr. Stapleton's house in Erzroom," Susan said. "Usually we could get some boiling water about once a day. They had great tanks of it, and all the passengers would hike up in a queue, and fill their tea kettles." Sometimes they would make coddled eggs in a pail of hot water. They were also able to mix coffee, water and canned condensed milk for a hot drink. "With some crusty bread, this would make our breakfast. The water that remained was used to wash the dishes and sometimes we could get enough to wash out the towels or do some other laundry." Once in a while they even washed the ever-dirty windows. "The dish towels were some pieces of Japanese cloth that had been given to me at the Bible school in Kobe, and had served as sash window curtains in our house in Alexandropol."[13]

And so the days passed. Susan spent a good deal of time in the corridor, looking out the window. "We had some beautiful scenery in the Ural Mountains, and saw the white marble monument which marks the boundary between Europe and Asia. There have been acres of wild flowers and beautiful birch and larch and fir trees along the way."[14] One day their train collided with a freight train. Due to the slow speed, no one was injured. "Our front engine had to be lift-piled on top of the rear car of the freight train ahead of us. With the other engine, our train was backed along the track to the next station back of us, and we went along on the other track and passed the wreck."[15]

They all had a lovely time during the twenty-four hours they had to spend in Irkutsk. They were able to buy some canned fruit and stale biscuits, but it was the restaurant that really made an impression. The beef steak was so good they had two meals of it. A previous battle had destroyed the newly-built bridge, so they took a boat across Lake Baikal.[16] But a little further on, at Chita, they ran into a problem.

~ ~ ~

Though Ernest and Walter had started out before their colleagues, they were waylaid several times along the way, and were now trailing them on a Red Cross train. As Ernest noted, the Russian Civil War was well underway throughout Siberia: "The Russians have gone absolutely to pieces. There are indecision and petty rivalries in every town. Just before we arrived at Tomsk, there was a Bolshevik uprising, which came very near succeeding. Just after we left Omsk, the government, on which all hope had been set, fell."[17] The movement of the Czech Legion across the continent was difficult and tense for everyone. Local Bolsheviks along the way had tried to recruit them for the Red Army, which angered both the Czech soldiers and their officers. Orders and counter-order from Trotsky made the authorities in each station confused and fearful. Even though the disarmament question had been settled, the Legion was expected to hand over more weapons each step of the way.[18] "These negotiations are really tiresome," said one Czech official. "The local Soviets do not trust us; they are afraid of us." Though the rail line was in good shape and functioned smoothly, it was not an easy trip.[19] At Chita, the Red Cross train encountered the same problem as had the Trans-Siberian Express: a blockade.

Normally, passengers at Chita would travel to Vladivostok through Manchuria, which shortened the trip by several days. It was now impossible to continue on this route because an anti-Bolshevik army, led by General Grigori Semenoff, blocked the line between Chita and Harbin, and cut off all communication. All east-bound trains were forced to go around Manchuria via the northern route along the Amur River to Haberovsk, and then south.[20] By the time Susan and her colleagues arrived in Haberovsk, it was mid-May. Wild flowers blanketed the valley. After three weeks on a train—two weeks more than it had taken them to travel to Moscow in the first place—they made good use of a day's layover to walk around the town. They visited a whaling museum, ate some decent restaurant meals, and talked with several Austrian and German prisoners of war who were confined to the city, but were free to earn their own living. They also made excellent use of a public bath. "The only bath we had along the way!" said Susan.[21]

It took another 24 hours to reach their destination. "We learned later that ours was the last train [that left Samara] to get through to Vladivostok," said Jane Yarrow.[22] They were met at the station by their former colleague Fred Goodsell, now YMCA Secretary for the city. Fred was described by a fellow secretary as "the 'angel' of not only American refugees, but of British, French and Belgians as well.[23] They were most fortunate to have his help in arranging lodging for the party because the city was overrun with thousands of Czech Legionnaires, Russian refugees, and international diplomats and military personnel. Fred managed to find a room for Susan and the Whites, though it was cramped. Harry slept on top of a long table, while Irma and Susan shared a single bed, with one woman's head facing the other's feet.[24] Despite the crowded quarters and jostling atmosphere, so different from their experience here in November,

A scene at the Vladivostok dock and the arrival of Czech Legionnaires. SOURCE: Riley Allen, photographer, 1919, US Library of Congress.

"we felt almost as though we had reached home, there were so many people speaking English," Susan said.[25] When Ernest and Walter joined them a few days later, they were finally able to report to ACASR not only of their safe arrival, but of the desperate need for more relief money.

~ ~ ~

The American relief committee had been fundraising steadily and earnestly for four solid years. Unfortunately they were very familiar with the concept of donor fatigue. At first they had appealed to Americans' sense of "Christian charity," and had raised millions of dollars. But by late-1917, public interest was waning. It was hard to support a cause year after year that was 6,000 miles and cultural lightyears away. ACASR had to come up with a different kind of appeal. The Committee needed a new approach. The solution lay with a young Armenian refugee, the sensational techniques of Madison Avenue, and the power of Hollywood.

The refugee was Arshaluys Mardiganian. As an exceptionally attractive 14-year old, she had been kidnapped from her home in 1915 near Harpoot during the deportation, and was subjected to sexual and physical abuse in a Turkish harem with other enslaved girls. She had witnessed the horrors of death, starvation and destruction all around her, but had managed to escape, been recaptured, and had escaped again. Finally, in 1917 Arshaluys wandered into the Erzroom mission and the safe arms of Fred MacCallum. He knew very well the trauma she had experienced as she tried to survive. Using ACASR money, he had been buying "thousands of Armenian girls out of slavery" from their Turkish captors for $1 each. "The Turks, knowing the Russians would liberate these captive Christian girls if they found them, were glad to sell them at this price rather than risk losing them without collecting anything."[26]

Learning that she had a brother somewhere in the United States, Fred had facilitated travel arrangements for Arshaluys to Oslo and on to New York. On her arrival at Ellis Island on November 5, 1917, she was met by an Armenian couple, "who took her in and placed advertisements in various newspapers" to help locate her brother. Reporters from the *New York Sun* and the *New York Tribune* picked up her story,[27] which is how "an extraordinarily talented hack journalist," Henry Leyford Gates, and his wife, novelist Eleanor Brown Gates, came to hear of her.[28]

Gates recognized a public relations gem when he saw one. Not long after her arrival, he bought her story for $50,[29] arranged for his wife to become her legal guardian, changed her name to Aurora, and convinced ACASR that her "autobiography" would make a wonderful fundraiser.[30] *Ravished Armenia* was published in December 1918. Its subtitle was "The Story of Aurora Mardiganian, the Christian Girl Who Lived Through the Great Massacres." H. L. Gates was listed as the "interpreter," even though he did not speak a word of Armenian. In the Acknowledgement section, he declared, "You may read Aurora's story with entire confidence—every word is true." Fortunately for the credibility of ACASR, this statement was softened in the book's Foreword. "Miss Mardiganian's names, dates and places, do not correspond exactly with similar references to these places made by Ambassador Morgenthau, Lord Bryce and others," wrote Nora Waln, ACASR's Publicity Secretary. She excused the inaccuracies by first blaming Aurora's young age and the trauma she had suffered, but then admitted that the "interpreter, in giving this story to the American public, has not attempted to write a history. He has simply aimed to give her message to the American people that they may understand something of the situation in the Near East during the past years, and help to establish there for the future, a sane and stable government."[31] Not only was the book a vehicle to raise funds, it was an appeal for public support of an American mandate for an Armenian homeland—an idea that President Wilson and ACASR both wanted. In January 1918, Wilson presented his administration's war aims with his "Fourteen Points" address to Congress.

Point 12 proposed to assure "a secured sovereignty" for residents of "the Turkish portions" of the Ottoman Empire. Though the right to self-determination for Armenians, Assyrians and other minorities was not specifically mentioned, that was its intention.[32]

The language of *Ravished Armenia* was an emotional appeal to Christian Americans. Armenians were "superior to the Turks intellectually and morally," "among the first converts to Christ," and "a noble race." When Aurora hugged the walls of a house, she gazed on "a beautiful sight": the stars and stripes waving in the rays of a searchlight. When she said, "The American flag is very beautiful to the eyes of all Armenians!", how could an American resist opening his wallet? The fact that Aurora had had to take "intervals of rest of several days,"[33] caused by the traumatic re-telling of her story to the interpreter, seemed to the producers a small price to pay for aiding her fellow refugees.

The book was only the first step. It was followed closely by a movie and a continent-wide promotional tour, coinciding with the launch of ACASR's $30 million fundraising campaign. Nora Waln was given credit for writing the "original" scenario for the "eight reel photo-play", though Frederic Chapin was credited as the screenwriter,[34] as was Gates. H. L. Gates and his wife whisked Aurora to Hollywood to play herself in the movie, for which she was paid $15 a week.[35] She had been exploited by her captors in Turkey, and now faced another kind of exploitation in the United States.[36] One can only imagine what she went through "as she retold her cataclysmic story a few years after it happened, watched as costumed strangers played her torturers in the film version, and then went on a press tour to promote the film until she suffered a nervous breakdown."[37] Both the book and movie presented "relatively sanitized versions" of what she had experienced,[38] but they were what the producers decided the public could accept.

The first showing of *Ravished Armenia*, known in Canada as *Auction of Souls*,[39] was in January 1919. It was promoted with a poster of "a brutish man brandishing a sword, gripping a struggling girl" under his arm. Dan Smith, the poster's artist, had modelled the drawing after the sculpture by Emmanuel Fremiet "of a gorilla carrying off a female." The depiction of "the Turk" as a primate, and the sexual undertones of a gorilla and a woman, were designed to draw in the salacious crowds.[40] Newspaper advertisements were created with the same intention, such as one in the *Toronto Daily Star* touting the movie as "the world's most sensational screen drama."[41] It worked. The crowds came and the money poured in.

~ ~ ~

(Left) The poster for *Ravished Armenia* designed by Dan Smith, *(far right)* a poster featuring Aurora Mardiganian, "the Christian girl who survived," and *(middle)* a newspaper advertisement for the alternative movie title *Auction of Souls*.
SOURCE: Armenian Genocide Museum Institute.

Despite signing the Treaty of Brest-Litovsk, the Ottomans continued their invasion of the Transcaucasus. The Armenian army successfully resisted them in battles near Erevan and Karakilisa in May, days after the Transcaucasian republic collapsed, and days before the founding of the Republic of Armenia.[42] Ottoman troops pushed on, and by mid-September, under the command of General Nuri, Enver's 27-year-old brother, and General Halil, Enver's uncle, they occupied Baku. Dr. Bahaeddin Shakir, head of the Special Organization, was with them. "After three days of unrelenting butchery" of tens of thousands of Armenians in the city, Nuri declared martial law.[43] It was all for nought. By the late summer, the outcome of the war was inevitable. The German army was being driven from France, and the British were advancing in Palestine. When a British-French expeditionary force defeated Bulgaria on September 29, the end was in sight.[44]

On October 3 Enver Pasha and Abdul Kerim, a former secretary to Sultan Abdul Hamid, met with Basil Zaharoff in Geneva. Zaharoff was a "colourful arms dealer" who referred to himself as Zedzed. He had been meeting secretly with Kerim for the last two years. In 1916 Kerim had claimed he represented Enver, who was willing "to open the Dardanelles to the British fleet in return for a substantial sum", possibly £T 4 million, and "safe passage to New York." Zaharoff reported this to the British, but Prime Minister David Lloyd George had had doubts "whether Enver was open to such bribery." As late as August 1918 Kerim had informed Zaharoff that Enver was interested in negotiating for an early peace. This time Lloyd George "seemed ready to contemplate a payment of $25

million to buy Turkey out of the war." The meeting in October with
Enver confirmed that Kerim had, in fact, been working on his behalf.
Enver suggested that, for "10 million francs for the Turks and 15 million
for the Hungarians," the Ottomans would leave the war. Zaharoff
"jumped at this suggestion" and offered to have 5 million francs placed at
Enver's disposal within the hour. Enver agreed, took the money, and left
for Constantinople. Whether or not there was a direct cause and effect,
three weeks later the Ottoman Empire and the Triple Entente began peace
talks.[45]

Knowing that "negotiations involving the wartime leadership (whose
members the Entente had branded as war criminals) would be difficult,"
the Cabinet of the Committee of Union and Progress resigned. The
Armistice of Mudros was signed by a new cabinet on October 31, 1918.[46]
On November 1, in the dead of the night, Talat, Enver, Djemal, Dr.
Bahaeddin Shakir, Dr. Nazim and three others boarded a German warship
and escaped to Odessa.[47] Ten days later, Germany sued for peace and the
world war was over.

～ ～ ～

Millions of people had died since 1914. Millions had been displaced,
and needed humanitarian aid, including an estimated 400,000 Armenian,
Greek, Assyrian and Turkish orphans.[48] The missionaries and relief
workers, so anxious for the war to end and for their part in the recovery to
begin, were scattered all over the world when the news broke. Susan
Wealthy Orvis, Harry and Irma White, George Raynolds and the Yarrows
were working at the American Board's Peking mission in China. Walter
James and the Maynard family were in Vladivostok with Fred Goodsell
and the YMCA. Thomas Heald, Allen Craig, Robert Stapleton, Ernest
Partridge and photojournalist Maynard Williams had gone to the United
States. Theodore Elmer was in Japan, waiting to join the first ACASR
contingent going on to Persia.[49] Nesbitt Chambers was in Switzerland,
acting as the treasurer for the relief workers, since William Peet's departure
for home.[50] Because they were British subjects Genevieve and Herbert
Irwin were detained in Constantinople, though Herbert was allowed to
teach at Robert College.[51] Stella Loughridge was a graduate student at the
University of Chicago,[52] and Clara Richmond was enrolled in a special
course at Oberlin College in Ohio. Fred MacCallum and Adelaide Dwight
were working in the New York office of ACASR.[53] They, and many
others, were just waiting for the word, "Go!"

Part III: A Time To Mend

19

Through A Glass Darkly

As soon as the war ended, missionaries inundated ABCFM's Boston office with letters and calls about returning to Turkey. "When it appeared that the earliest transports to be provided could not, in accord with the Navy's rules, take women as passengers, great was the consternation," the *Missionary Herald* reported. "There is just one cry from the men and women who are the American Board's Turkey missionaries in this country: 'Let us go back and have a part in this work of relief and reconstruction.'"[1] They would have to wait a little longer. Post-war demobilization and stabilization takes time.

Luther Fowle sent an urgent message from Constantinople on December 1, 1918 to James Barton, Chairman of the American Committee for Armenian and Syrian Relief. It read, "New relief conditions demand new men, bringing clothing, food, medicines, and transport facilities." It took 15 days for the War Trade Board in Washington, DC to grant Barton a "license" to receive the cable.[2] Despite planning for more than a year to conduct a tour of the Near East to assess the extent of the need, it took another 19 days before ACASR's Relief Expedition Commission embarked on the *Carmania* to Liverpool. The seven-man commission consisted of Barton; ABCFM Turkey Treasurer William Peet; ABCFM President and Harvard theology professor Edward C. Moore; Grinnell College President John Main; George W. Washburn, physician and son of the former president of Robert College; Deering Milken & Company Treasurer Harold A. Hatch; and Arthur Curtis James, grandson of the founder of Phelps, Dodge Co., of which ACASR Treasurer Cleveland Dodge was President. The group met with government officials and concerned citizens in London, Paris and Rome before arriving in Constantinople on March 12, 1919.[3]

Two naval ships left New York on January 19 and 24 respectively, carrying forty-five male relief workers and preliminary supplies, including vehicles, agricultural tools, and enough medical supplies for 10-15 hospitals. The US War Department was going to make arrangements as soon as possible for vessels that would transport women.[4]

Even though many missionaries wondered when they could return to Turkey, many had received telegrams from James Barton shortly after the armistice. Susan Wealthy Orvis, Ernest Yarrow, and Harry and Irma White, all working in the Peking mission, were asked to return as soon as possible.[5] Susan agreed immediately, but she had many arrangements to make first. "It meant that I gave up my study of the Chinese language, and turned over to another the classes I had been teaching in the North China Women's College," she said.[6] She gladly accepted help from both the American Ambassador and the French Legation to obtain a berth on the SS *Porthos*, which was "originally reserved for a French officer from Siberia!" In a letter written in Nanking, January 25, she thanked her sister Harriet for sending a trunk with some of her clothes, and apologized for taking so long to repay her for the shipment. "I couldn't seem to get ahead enough money to send," she said. "I'm hoping the Board may make me an allowance for the outfit." It was not an unreasonable wish, considering she had had to leave many of her things behind in Alexandropol. "But I've had no assurance of it thus far. They did not expect me to start quite so soon. I suppose that *may* be the reason." She expressed concern for her sister and family for a speedy recovery from influenza, which she herself had experienced. They were the lucky ones. The "Spanish flu" was turning into a dangerous pandemic, destined to kill 21 million people worldwide.[7] She expected to leave Shanghai on February 1, and signed off, as usual, "with lots of love, Susan W. Orvis."[8]

Clara Richmond had been in bed in Boston for several weeks, also suffering from the flu. But she was determined to join Stella Loughridge and Elsey Bristol as one of the first women on the relief ship to cross the Atlantic.[9]

~ ~ ~

After the armistice, what was left of the Committee of Union and Progress continued to run the Ottoman government. They mostly ignored Mehmet V, the new sultan who had taken over after his brother died in July.[10] Not all government members had known of the policies and crimes of their previous leaders until they were underway, and not everyone had approved or condoned them. Nevertheless, they were all left with the political taint, and the repercussions. The Liberal opposition now felt free to speak out and participate fully in Parliament.[11] The public also felt a freedom to speak, something they had not experienced since 1908. When they heard on November 2, 1918 that the officials responsible for the horror and destruction of the last four years had fled Turkey—without consequences—many were outraged. The same day, a Muslim Deputy made a motion in Parliament to begin legal proceedings against the former CUP Cabinet Ministers for their crimes.[12] As one parliamentarian said, "We inherited a country turned into a huge slaughterhouse."[13] A 20-member committee was created almost immediately to investigate the

View of the Bosporus and the Scutari area from Constantinople, 1920. SOURCE: Bosporus, Istanbul, Turkey, 1920, US Library of Congress.

charges. But by mid-December the public was so annoyed by its slow progress, Sultan Mehmet dissolved it, and transferred the job to the Courts Martial in Constantinople.[14] It took a couple of months for the Courts Martial to interview witnesses and gather the mountains of evidence for the first trial, which began on February 5 and concerned the deportations and massacres in Yozgat, specifically in Boghazlian, just north of Talas.[15]

Without waiting for formal demobilization, soldiers and public employees headed home. Train service between Constantinople and the interior "broke down completely owing to the desertion of train and station men, carriers, engineers, and laborers of all sorts."[16] The economy, health, agriculture and security of the country was in disarray. According to the terms of the armistice, Entente troops were granted the right to occupy the Dardanelles and Bosporus, which they did by November 9. They could also occupy any place in the Ottoman Empire considered to be a security problem.[17] This term was not only acceptable to the Ottomans, it was "sometimes even greeted with relief."[18]

By early January 1919 conditions in the capital had deteriorated such that Nesbitt Chambers cabled the US State Department to say there was a "great menace to health and grave nervous strain making return of families undesirable."[19] Indeed, it was so bad that British Vice Admiral Sir Somerset Gough-Calthorpe, "with a staff of British, French, Italian and American officers, took control of the police and sanitary forces of

Constantinople."[20] The police force was understandable. American minister, Rev. Loyal Lincoln Wirt, summed up the reason for the sanitation takeover: "If I could choose a task, I would like to be the sanitary engineer of Turkey—with power. What joy it would be to clean up these unhealthy cities! To spend money on water and sewer systems, or any public improvements, is the last thing in the mind of a Turkish public official. Earthen jars on a donkey is as far as he goes in providing a city's water supply. Yet sweet water is abundant almost everywhere and may be had for the piping." The systems may have been more advanced in Constantinople than elsewhere, but he insisted that "sanitation can be made popular throughout Turkey."[21]

Another issue raised in Parliament was the Special Organization. It was abolished in early November on the insistence of the Entente and the anti-CUP contingent.[22] But what was not generally known was that a few weeks before they left, Enver and Talat ordered the SO to "store guns and ammunition in secret depots in a number of places in Anatolia." They had also created the *Karakol* (the Guard), whose purpose was twofold: to protect CUP supporters from any revenge the Entente, Liberals and Christian communities might take, and to strengthen the "resistance in Anatolia and the Caucasus by sending able people, money, arms and supplies there from the capital." Soon after its abolishment, the SO was resurrected in Berlin under the name General Revolutionary Organization of the Islamic World. One of its aims was to "start guerrilla bands" in Turkey's interior. Since the area was full of brigands, this was not a difficult task.[23] Unfortunately, it was also the main reason for the delay in sending relief workers into the interior. It simply was not safe. The British army took the job of securing the interior. However, in Europe it "was rapidly disappearing" as soldiers went home, so there were few reinforcements to send to Turkey. Many of the units already there were Muslims from British India. It was necessary, as one commander pointed out, for Britain to have "a friendlier policy toward the Turks."[24]

～ ～ ～

About the task the Relief Expedition Commission was undertaking, the *Missionary Herald* wrote:

It fairly takes the breath away to consider what is being attempted . . . To enter a land so torn by war; depopulated, desolated; with towns and villages demolished, fields lying untilled, work animals destroyed; with the dreadful wreckage of battles and massacres, deportation and pillage visible on every hand, is enough to dismay the stoutest heart. . . . To seek to re-establish homes and industries, to repatriate hundreds of thousands of refugees, who have been driven far from their familiar places, to provide care for the destitute thousands of orphans, to establish hospitals and to set in operation medical service for all the diseased and debilitated sufferers from cruelty and want, to inspire hope, and rouse to renewed action those who have sunk into despair, and to do this over vast areas of country where means of transportation, always limited, have now broken down, and where bands of freebooters and brigands lurk along the highways of travel, is a task that might well seem impossible. Yet this is what is being attempted, with both courage and caution, by the backing of generous America, and the counsel and support of many of America's most representative men. If the expedition succeeds to the full measure of its program, it will be a modern miracle; if it accomplishes a half of what it is undertaking, it will mean the saving of a race and the restoring of a blighted land. In any event, it is a superb adventure in neighbourliness, the parable of the Good Samaritan wrought out on a gigantic scale.[25]

In late February and early March, the ACASR teams of commissioners and relief workers set out from Constantinople on their exploratory tours. President Main, Theodore Elmer, Clarence Ussher, and six other men went by ship to the Caucasus. Dr. Washburn, Mr. Hatch and several others went to Samsoun and Marsovan. Another team explored the Constantinople and Smyrna area. A twenty-car train left on March 6 on the Baghdad Railway with two teams. Professor Moore, his son John, Ernest Partridge, Herbert Irwin, Dr. Raymond C. Whitney, a young minister named Joseph Beach, and a few others, were going to investigate Konia, Kaisarieh, Talas and Sivas. The other team included James Barton, President Caleb Gates of Constantinople's Robert College, Harry Riggs, two young graduates named Means and Vrooman, and several relief workers. They were going to visit Adana, Tarsus, Aleppo, Oorfa, Mardin, Marash, Aintab, Diarbekir and Harpoot. All teams were taking with them as many supplies as they could handle. The British military controlled the railway and provided protection while the teams were on the train.[26]

Gardiner C. Means, fresh out of Harvard,[27] was on the Barton team. Because he knew how to drive an automobile, he was immediately given the job of chauffeur. He soon discovered there was more to being a chauffeur than driving. "About eleven one night, without any sort of warning, I got word to be ready to start at nine o'clock next morning for a ten days' trip up country, and to have a Ford on a flat[bed] car ready for an equal length of time. Also to have provision for that length of time for three people. Some hustling!" As the train pulled out of the station, Gardiner sat with two others in the Ford. They were guarded by six heavily-armed Sikhs on the flatbed, and other British troops with machine guns at the head and end of the train. The Berlin-Baghdad Railway had been extended during the war to actually reach Baghdad, but the roadbed was currently in bad shape. "Often we would get off the train to take a look at some particularly bad stretch," said Gardiner. Where the rails had sunk into the mud several inches, "they had to use pick and shovel to dig us out, as the mud had hardened. On the grades, one of the trainmen would walk along ahead of the engine and put stones on the track for the wheels to crush into sand. At one point we struck such a grade that the engine couldn't make it, so every one got out and pushed, and she went up all right then. Three hundred Turks and Arabs and Armenian refugees, in their varied costumes, pushing the train up over a hill was certainly a strange sight."[28] Another time on a steep grade, the train broke away from its two engines. "We started down the mountain," said James Barton, who was aboard the sliding train. "The engineer whistled for brakes, and two of our young men rushed to the tops of the freight cars and stopped the train."[29]

Lee Vrooman, a twenty-one year old graduate of the College of Agriculture at the University of Maine, who also travelled with the Barton team, wrote to his mother about the road conditions: "We entered the Taurus Mountains for fifty miles of the wildest riding I ever hope to do. The roadbed was fairly good, thank heaven, but it was narrow, just a couple of feet leeway for the Ford. On one side the mountains went up, on the other side they went down—no retaining wall—the road sloping down for drainage, and the whole thing a series of hairpin curves. At intervals, dirt had slid into the road, and every so often we would strike a place where the outer edge of the road had slid away. In several places we scraped the rock going up on one side, and the outer wheels rested just on the edge of nothingness on the other side. We twisted and turned and crawled around rocks, crept under overhanging cliffs, and climbed up and slid down. After some miles it began to rain and the road got slimy. Although we had chains, we skidded in spite of them. At last we got up into the clouds so we could not see far ahead. I claim to have a fairly steady set of nerves, but I never want to repeat that ride. To go around a corner with a one hundred and eighty degree turn in slippery mud, and when you can see only a few feet ahead of you, is no sport when one is several hundred feet above the first stopping place."[30]

The SS *Leviathan* in New York harbour sometime after a re-painting of its camouflage. SOURCE: Bain News Service, US Library of Congress.

~ ~ ~

About the time Susan was leaving Hong Kong for Saigon, Singapore, and Columbo in the Indian Ocean,[31] another ship—this time with women on board—was leaving New York for France. The SS *Leviathan* was the world's largest ship, refitted from a confiscated German battleship. It had transported American troops during the war, nine thousand at a time. Though it still had its camouflage painted pattern, it was now on a humanitarian mission. The *Leviathan* left Hoboken harbour on Sunday, February 16. On board were 241 people. Most were ACASR workers, a few were members of a Jewish society, and some were women headed for the YMCA in Paris.[32] During the week it took to get to Brest, at the northwest tip of France, the passengers were kept very busy. "The daily conferences and lectures, which had been held in New York before we started, were continued," said George White, formerly President of Anatolia College in Marsovan, and now ACASR's Director of Personnel. "Twenty classes were studying the languages of Turkey, under twenty able teachers." It was important for the newcomers to be oriented to the language and customs of Turkey as quickly as possible. The language instructors likely included himself, as well as passengers Stella, Clara and Elsey, who were now ACASR workers.[33]

Children in Constantinople photographed by the American Red Cross. SOURCE: American Red Cross, April 1919, US Library of Congress.

In Brest the party had to wait most of Sunday while their bags were transferred to the US Army Hospital Train, No. 64. "We got ashore about noon, and were entertained with unstinted hospitality at Red Cross headquarters," said George. "At ten o'clock that evening the roll was called by the group leaders. Every person was reported in his place. More than six hundred pieces of hand baggage were located with their owners; more than six hundred pieces of heavy baggage were stored in the freight cars." Five cars fitted with 36 bunks in tiers of three held 177 women, and two similar cars held the 56 men, all of whom were headed for Marseilles. They arrived in the port city on Wednesday, and were immediately transferred to the British Ambulance Transport, *Gloucester Castle*, that steamed its way across the Mediterranean to Salonica. There they spent two days, waiting to proceed.[34]

On Friday morning, March 7, they sailed past the Gallipoli Peninsula and entered the Dardanelles. The *Gloucester Castle* crept slowly through the still-dangerous waters, using its minesweepers every minute. The next morning, at 6 o'clock, after a three-week journey, the ship rounded Seraglio Point. "We found ourselves really in sight of Constantinople, after these two years away from it," Clara said. "We had been looking forward to having our new people see the city in the sunshine—in its beauty. But the skies were gray and the city anything but beautiful to them. To us old-timers, it was our Turkey again. And there was such joy in that." Clara then remembered all that had gone on in the intervening time, and was subdued as they pulled into the Constantinople harbour. "The thought of the friends that are gone, of the desolate homes and streets, of the misery, hunger and suffering, almost overcomes one. I want more than any place in the world to be there, but, oh, how much we will need strength and courage from above, and prayers!"[35]

~ ~ ~

While the *Leviathan* was still in the harbour, Dr. Peet went out to greet the passengers. "How good it was to see him once more!" said Clara. He described the present conditions in Turkey, which she found very discouraging. He also explained the arrangements that had been made to house everyone.[36] "Our friends in Constantinople exercised ingenuity in providing for the flood of guests whose arrival was known only a day in advance," said George.[37] Small groups of 15-20 relief workers had been expected and it was not until the *Leviathan* was in Salonica that they learned such a large party was on its way. Every hotel in the city was full, so they were to be billeted wherever there was an extra bed or two: Bible House, Robert College, the Girls' College, and Gedik Pasha School. One group of 70 was lodged in a German sleeping train. Clara, Stella and Elsey were going to go with 137 other women to Prinkipo, the largest and most beautiful of the Princes' Islands in the Sea of Marmara. It was a popular resort in summer, twelve miles from Constantinople by ferry, with decent accommodations. As the ship moved up to the dock, the trio spied Genevieve Irwin and Rachel North in the crowd. They had not heard anything of them for two years, and were thrilled to see them. Genevieve insisted her friends stay at her home on the grounds of Robert College. They had a grand reunion. They learned that Herbert was on his way to Talas, and that many of their old school girls were well and teaching or nursing right there in Constantinople. "Genevieve had some very encouraging things to tell us, and that did much towards cheering up our new recruits," said Clara. "She was a real blessing to all."[38]

For the next few days the women visited with twelve of the older girls who had been sent to the Red Crescent Hospital in Zinjidery as nurses in 1917. The others had gone to nurse in Konia, Adana and Aleppo after the armistice. In Constantinople, nine continued to work in hospitals, and three were teaching in orphanages. Their former teachers were delighted. "You cannot imagine how wonderful it was to see them after these years of separation, and of such experiences for them!" Clara said. "They are as round-faced and fat as if they had been most tenderly cared for." They all caught up on news of their former colleagues, too. Several teachers who had given up their children before being deported to Aleppo had been reunited with them. Fanny Burrage, now 67, was not returning to Turkey, nor was Adelaide Dwight who was working at ACASR's New York headquarters. Theda Phelps was nursing in Persia for the Red Cross, but would return as soon as possible. Henry Wingate was going to join them soon, but Jane had decided to stay at home with their children. The only person whose whereabouts was unknown was Susan Wealthy Orvis.[39]

Susan had been chugging her way through the Indian Ocean and north through the Red Sea towards the Suez Canal. To pass the time, she had exchanged French lessons with a young YWCA secretary who wanted to learn English. By the time she reached the Mediterranean, Susan expected to have a working knowledge of the language. "It is so easy compared to Chinese, Turkish and Arabic!" she wrote to her friends at home. She also added that she had arrived in Cairo just as the revolt started.[40] Days before, the British had refused to allow an Egyptian delegation to attend the Paris Peace Conference, despite a widely-circulated petition signed by Egyptians requesting the representation. Sa'd Zaghlul and two other ministers in the Legislative Assembly resigned in protest, and riots erupted in Cairo and other regions. After their arrest, the disturbances intensified. The new high commissioner, General Edmund Allenby, suppressed the riots,[41] but the animosity against the British overlords had intensified.

Susan spent two weeks in Cairo. She did a little shopping, visited the Great Pyramid of Giza, which she climbed in 15 minutes at sunset, rode a camel, and took a lot of "Kodak pictures." On March 24 she was finally able to take a heavily-guarded train to Port Said. From there, she found space on a steamer to Constantinople via Cyprus. "This has been an interesting trip," she wrote, "but I have no doubt there are other more interesting experiences ahead. I hope they will not be too interesting. . . . Yours with much love, Susan W. Orvis."[42] In another letter to her mission supporters, she reflected again on her immediate future. "The tremendous challenge of it all is inspiring. At the same time I feel overcome at the magnitude of the task before us. Only a complete confidence in the God of infinite power and grace enables one to undertake to go forward at such a time."[43]

Henceforth, the team going forward was known as the American Committee for Relief in the Near East or ACRNE,[44] because they recognized that the need for relief was well beyond Armenians and Syrians, and now included the destitute of every ethnicity.

20

Making Their Way Back

There were no accurate records of the number of people who died as a result of the reign of terror of 1915-18, but it was estimated that 1,500,000 Armenians,[1] 500,000 Greeks,[2] 250,000 Assyrians and Chaldeans,[3] and thousands of Turks, Kurds and Arabs perished from murder, starvation and disease. The vast majority of them were innocent, unarmed civilians. Now in early 1919, hundreds of thousands of survivors began returning to Turkey from the refugee camps in Aleppo, Beirut, Port Said and the Caucasus. Armenians who had lived in Anatolia and the interior provinces were shocked to discover their homes had been given to Muslim immigrants from the Balkans, and their possessions auctioned off. Their financial assets were recorded in the Ottoman treasury, but who had enough money to hire a lawyer to try to recover them? Protestant Armenians in the west were somewhat luckier. They had been the last to be deported, and there had not been time for officials to appropriate their "abandoned" property. "Most of them came back to empty houses. Some have been able to find their goods," said Sophie Holt, who herself had returned to her mission in Adabazar after the war. She noted that the local kaimakam (a Circassian) and a British lieutenant were doing all they could to restore missing property to the returning Americans and Armenians, but it was a huge task.[4]

In January the British and French pressured the Ottoman government to instruct all Turks in the country who had Armenian and Greek women and children in their households to turn them loose.[5] Officials and soldiers began to go door-to-door to ensure the orders were carried out. In many cases, it was an act of salvation. Minnie Mills, Dean of the American Collegiate Institute in Smyrna,[6] worried about the "great many stolen children and young maidens," and wondered "what to do with all these children and young women, who have been the victims of such evil deeds?"[7] James Barton was very angry when he wrote about the situation in Malatia. "Several thousand children and girls were suddenly thrown out of Muslim homes and orphanages, without food and with scant clothing. It was impossible for their own people to take care of them, and the Turks were asked to take them back, or some of them, until aid could be secured." He discussed the matter with British commissioners, who "secured an amendment to the order to the effect that at least four months' food supply must be given to every child or girl discharged, and officials are ordered to see that this is done."[8]

This wholesale rescue was not always the best policy for the individuals involved. One relief worker met a young woman whose wealthy parents had been killed by a Turk. The Turk had handed her over to his son. The young man forced her to convert to Islam and marry him. Now, when asked if she wanted to leave, she could not decide. She had a child to support. Her own people would not take her in. All her inherited wealth belonged to her husband. "Some scheme on a large scale should be immediately put in operation for the benefit of girls similarly situated," said the worker. "There must be hundreds, if not thousands, of cases such as the one cited."[9] In fact, there were. At every station, ACRNE workers soon set up what they called Rescue Homes for these women and children.

The same release order was also proclaimed by Emir Feisal for Arab and Kurdish households. Relief workers John Dunaway and Stanley Kerr went from house to house in the Aleppo region, accompanied by an American Red Cross nurse, Rose Shayb, who spoke Arabic. One day they heard of a Bedouin sheikh who had Armenians in his home. It was true, the man said. He had known the family for many years. "When I heard that the Turks were deporting the Armenians of Aintab, I went there and searched for them," said the sheikh. "The father and mother had already been killed, so I brought all five of the children—three boys and two girls—here to be members of my family." When the local kaimakam saw the girls, he wanted them for himself. The sheikh and his brother fought him off. The sheikh showed John and Stanley four bullet wounds in his abdomen and thigh, the result of the fight. He asked them, "Now are you going to take these children from me, after I have protected them during the past four years?" It was obvious to the relief workers that "the children loved this man as a father." Stanley reluctantly told him that it was an order from Feisal, and there was no other option. Everyone was heartbroken. The young women cried. The sheikh asked to accompany them to Aleppo to ensure they were going to be cared for. "The entire village came to say goodbye," said Stanley. "As we drove from the village the entire population ran beside the car shouting farewells, and weeping." He later felt that he had allowed his "sense of duty to override sentiment." Within months his team had visited "nearly every village within fifty miles of Aleppo," and had found 450 children. "Some Armenians estimated that we had recovered only a quarter of those who were actually in Arab homes in that area."[10]

~ ~ ~

Hired hands wrestling supplies into the American Red Cross warehouse in Constantinople, similar to what was taking place in the ACRNE warehouse in Derindje. SOURCE: Constantinople 1920, US Library of Congress.

Susan finally arrived in Constantinople at the end of March 1919, and reported directly to Bible House. It was hard to tell who was more surprised and delighted to see one another—Susan or her friends from Talas. They had just come from Robert College for a meeting only minutes before. They had a grand old time catching up with one another. The most recent news was that Herbert Irwin and the rest of the advance party were stuck in Konia. Allenby's division had not yet entered Kaisarieh, and the general was not allowing any relief teams to venture forward until the area was secure. Herbert said he would contact them when he arrived.[11] Rachel North, who had not seen Susan since leaving the Talas hospital eight years earlier, was staying at Bible House, and had room for a temporary roommate.[12]

It turned into a short stay for Susan because less than a week later, she and all the women and men of ACRNE who were not busy elsewhere moved to Derindje, fifty miles southeast of Scutari. During the war the Germans had constructed two large, five-storey buildings on the shore of the Gulf of Nicomedia. On one side of the buildings was the deep water harbour, with docks for the ocean-going vessels. On the other side were six train tracks with switching facilities, and a direct link to the Anatolian

Railway. It was the perfect location for ACRNE's central warehouse. While the site was ideal, the equipment and living conditions could have been better. The machinery for unloading ships and hoisting crates into the buildings had been broken during the war. "In consequence," said George L. Richards, ACRNE's Assistant Medical Director, "the cargo had to be carried on the backs of the native hamals from the ships to the various floors of the two warehouses and up many flights of stairs."[13]

Turkish porter (hamal) carrying boxes of kerosene. SOURCE: Turkey, 1920, US Library of Congress.

The warehouses were not really designed for living. "Yet we have what is necessary," said Susan. She described the women's dormitory as "one big bare attic room. We have bedsteads set up in two double rows all the way along each side. For each eight beds there is a shelf with two washbasins and a kerosene tin full of water. A wire above the shelf answers for a towel rack. Our baggage is under our beds and we have a few nails driven into the big pillars where we can hang our coats. There are a few benches and folding chairs and three electric lights." Their working days were long and busy: Breakfast in the mess hall at 7:00 a.m., work from 7:30 a.m. to 5:30 p.m., with an hour's break for lunch at noon. "I go to supper and then sit on a pile of timber or in one of the trucks, autos or ambulances for a little while till sunset," she said. "By that time I am glad to go to bed."[14]

The plan made in New York called for an orderly distribution of crates from the ships to the warehouses. Given the unloading problems, the plan had gone out the window and the workload had doubled. Dr. Richards said, "The entire cargo in both warehouses and the two large adjoining sheds was entirely rearranged, sorted, and put in workable order. Accordingly, the doctors, nurses and relief workers were organized into warehouse gangs and for the next three weeks the entire force at Derindje was occupied in rearranging and completely cataloguing the large amount of stores. To do this required large numbers of native hamals, and at a time 500 or more of these were employed in night and day shifts."[15]

Everyone was waiting for word from the British that it was safe for the crates—and the personnel—to be shipped to the various stations in the interior. Susan was ready to go, but she had trepidations. "I really do not have time to regret leaving Peking, though I do remember the lovely comfortable life there. If I did not feel that I am needed here, I should be very glad to live in Peking the rest of my life. Here one gets very tired, and there is a constant strain on the nerves and emotions that gets too much for us at times."[16] It was an emotion the few missionaries who had remained in Turkey for the last few years recognized well.

~ ~ ~

Fifty missionaries, mostly women, had refused to leave their stations when they had been ordered out of the Empire during the war. In each case there was at least one orphanage attached, and they would not leave the children behind. Now that communications had been restored between the interior and the capital, they were sending urgent requests for relief—not only for the basic necessities, but for replacements for themselves. They were tired. They were also very happy to learn their prayers would soon be answered.

Mary Graffam, who had been awarded the Order of the Red Crescent by the sultan in 1917 for her work at the Turkish Hospital in Erzroom, had been caring for 600 Armenian, Greek and Turkish orphans with help from her Armenian assistants. She had created jobs for local women to knit sweaters for soldiers, and had rented a farm, owned by the Kaiser, to supply grain and vegetables for the four orphanages in Sivas. "I am well and going on as best I can, with more or less ups and downs," she said.[17]

Serephina Dewey wrote from Mardin about herself, her 40-year old daughter Diantha, and their colleague Johanna Graf. "We three are here alone, as we have been for over three years. A little older, but not so worn as might be. We do not have time to mourn or to be lonesome, for we are driven with work and many cares. Both military and civil authorities have, on the whole, treated us very well, and we are thankful to have been kept through all until now. We can see the morning light coming, though very slowly."[18]

Olive Vaughan had been the only non-Ottoman in the isolated mountain village of Hadjin for the last few years. She had maintained diplomatic relations with the local Turkish officials, ran a small school, supported her teachers, fed the hungry, and cared for the sick. It was

Women waiting for work outside the wool room, Marsovan, May 1919. SOURCE: Tsolag K. Dildilian, US Library of Congress.

especially hard when the villagers came down with "Spanish fever," herself included. By April 1919 she was "nearly at the end of her strength."[19]

Dana Getchell had stayed in Marsovan the whole time with his colleague Charlotte Willard. She wrote to ask if the Woman's Board would send five American teachers for September because "the school needs them." But Dana knew that Charlotte needed them more. "Miss Willard must be relieved soon," he said. "I am troubled about her condition. It would be criminal to leave her, after all these years of brave, splendid service, to suffer in health or to lose her life because the Board fails to send the workers needed."[20]

Danish nurse Marie Jacobsen, a member of the *Kvindelige Missions Arbejdere* (KMA or Women Missionary Workers), had taken over the American relief work at Harpoot. By 1919 that meant caring for more than 3,600 orphans, "most of whom were hidden by Armenian widows among ruined houses and cemeteries scattered throughout the area." But every morning outside her house she "would find the bodies of 10 to 15 children who had died of hunger during the night."[21] The most difficult task for her was saying 'No' when she did not have enough clothes, food or medicine to distribute. She was understandably eager for ACRNE reinforcements. "Do you believe me, I have been longing so for you that when I now sit down and think about you so near, something fills my throat. Do come quick—it has been oh, so hard—two years full of fear, anxiety, and great responsibility! Can you realize what it means to be responsible for more than a thousand people, and all the work and workers? I have to be mother, teacher, doctor, and all. There is more than enough work for all who come. Your rooms have been ready since the beginning of March. I clean and dust them every two days, in case you should come unannounced!"[22] Her colleague, Nurse Sarra, described Marie's life: "Poor Miss Jacobsen runs from morn till eve, and sometimes loses sleep at night, in order to accomplish all her tasks. In the last two months she has lost twelve pounds and has grown pale, working incessantly, with but little rest. One minute she is here at the infirmary, the next at the sick bed of a child in an orphanage. Another minute she is comforting a wailing orphan in the street, the next minute she is at the cloth factory, bidding the weavers hasten, in order to clothe the thousands of shivering ones. Then to the wool-shop to rebuke the slow hands and order that yarn be more quickly prepared for sweaters and bloomers. Now, a call to the operating table to lance an abscess or give chloroform for a drastic treatment. Then she runs to prepare food and beds for the many American workers whom she joyfully expects."[23]

Fellow Dane and KMV missionary Karen Marie Petersen was the director of the Emaus orphanage in Mezreh, near Harpoot.[24] She, too, had a request for ACRNE: "Would it be possible for me to buy from your supplies stuff for dresses and underclothing for the children? They are almost in a worse condition than the children outside. I have been so ashamed to have them going around in rags! I have a few sick children I would like to give over to your care when you come. It has been a dreadful time—we could not get the most common of needed medicines in any of the pharmacies. I hope you will bring some toothbrushes, thread, garters, etc. Please come soon!"[25]

~ ~ ~

The United States had entered the war with the hope and expectation that it would be part of establishing a new world order. No one expressed this sense of destiny better than Rev. Loyal Lincoln Wirt. In addition to the new water and sewer system he would have designed for Turkey, he could barely contain his eagerness to create a whole new world within its territory—in the image of his own homeland. "Roads can be built; mines opened; city streets widened and kept clean; model houses can be erected; public finances honestly administered; Western agricultural methods introduced; industries encouraged; foreign markets opened; confidence restored; and the age-long system of graft, 'rake-off,' and baksheesh smitten hip and thigh. That would be a beginning. Let America give this land an honest government. Let our doughboys bring it security and equal opportunity. Then give our school teachers half a chance at every boy and girl, and the Eastern question will be settled—and settled right for all time."[26]

Right, of course, was understood to be American and Christian. As the WBM's *Light and Life for Woman* exclaimed, "Great hopes and expectations are heading up in this experiment for bringing in the new world order in Turkey. We are sure the prayers of the Christian church will follow them on their way."[27] But British archeologist Sir William Ramsay, who had level-headedly assessed the situation in Cilicia in 1909, injected a caveat into the plans for reconstruction and rehabilitation. "My conclusion is that Turkey must be taken in tutelage by the Western Powers, and that everything will depend upon the personal character and the knowledge of the men into whose hand the task of regenerating Turkey will be put. Foremost among those who are fit to be intrusted with this duty are certain American missionaries in the country—not, by any means, all of them, for I have known one who said to me with fervour that he had never been inside a Turkish mosque. Such as he may be eliminated at once. But many missionaries whom I have known are well fitted to be guides, as in their life, they are examples of economic management, and moral vigour, and of living on a high standard."[28]

It was a valid point. Though there were now very few missionaries-turned-relief workers in Turkey who vocally disdained Turks, it was common to hear generalizations. "The Turks are not pleased," Ethel Putney said, as if every Turk felt the same about the return of deported Armenians. "Their consciences are too unpleasantly active for them to enjoy seeing the people they have robbed. Now the English officer in charge of the occupation here is forcing them to give up stolen goods,"[29] as if every one of them had condoned the crimes of the last four years and had participated in them. Ethel was not alone. James Barton also made frequent generalizations.

Ramsay would have approved of the attitude of the Talas unit, as expressed by Susan Wealthy Orvis: "All people are really much alike at heart, wherever they may live. The differences are very clear at first, but resemblances appear better on further acquaintance. The school girls I've taught in Turkey and Japan and China and America are all just schoolgirls, not so very different one group from another when you look beyond the strange dress and features to the desires and hopes and difficulties they all have in common. There are good ones and naughty ones, and never any all good or all bad. They are just human. Like the rest of us."[30]

~ ~ ~

The American government fully supported ACRNE, but its interest in the reconstruction in Turkey was not totally altruistic. There were tens of millions of dollars of American assets to protect, in the form of $2 million in ABCFM property ($28 million today),[31] and even more millions in inventory and property of American companies, as well as potential markets for them. When the Bolsheviks withdrew from the war, they published details of the Sykes-Picot agreement[32]—much to the embarrassment of the major powers, and the anger of Ottomans—as to how the Ottoman Empire would be carved up: Britain would get Baghdad, Basra, Acre and Jaffa; France would get Lebanon, Syria and Mosul; and Arabia would get Medina and Mecca. But now that the war was over, other members of the Entente, including Italy and Greece, wanted some of the spoils. Unfortunately, both of them wanted the same part: the vilayet of Smyrna-Aidin.[33] For Greece and the large Greek population in southwestern Turkey, there was the long-held Megali Idea—the dream of regaining lands formerly belonging to the ancient Greek empire.[34] For Italy, it would be a strategic land hold in the Aegean. In March the Italians began to occupy with their navy and army "one point after another on the coast from Adalia northwestwards in the direction of Smyrna"[35]—without the consent of the Allies.[36] Italy was also pursuing territorial claims in the Balkans on the eastern shores of the Adriatic, which sparked a public disagreement with the other delegations at the Peace Conference in Paris.[37] The Italians withdrew from the conference on April 24, though they returned on May 5. This rash act did not help their cause, neither at the table nor with the various advisors. All nationalities in Turkey were growing alarmed by the encroaching Italian occupation. As British Foreign Office Turkey specialist Arnold Toynbee noted, "Lovers' quarrels between statesmen in Western capitals may produce more serious breaches of amity between their representatives in the Near and Middle East, who have been trained in jealousy for generations."[38]

Greek Prime Minister Eleftherios Venizelos had been campaigning heavily for the land across the Aegean Sea. He certainly had the ear of the British and French leaders because he had been instrumental in arranging for their forces to land in Salonica during the war, against the wishes of the pro-German monarch, King Constantine.[39] British Prime Minister Lloyd George favoured Greece in this contest as "a valuable counterweight to France and Italy in the eastern Mediterranean."[40]

Because Article 7 of the armistice allowed the Allies to occupy any strategic point if the security of the Allies was threatened,[41] and the on-the-ground Allied officials were feeling unsettled, it was not a difficult decision to permit Allied troops to occupy Smyrna. On May 7 at 23 Rue Nitot, Paris, David Lloyd George, Woodrow Wilson, Georges Clemenceau and Eleftherios Venizelos agreed that those troops should be Greek.[42] It was a fateful decision.

~ ~ ~

By late April 1919 the British military had still not secured the interior. However, knowing the need for relief was overwhelming, they relented, and authorized ACRNE to enter the region. On April 25 George White wrote to the relief workers who were assigned to Talas, Sivas and Harpoot, informing them that Herbert had reached Talas on April 16, and Ernest was now in Sivas. James Barton's team was on the way to Harpoot. The Turkish authorities were cooperating, helpful and friendly. In the opinion of the Relief Expedition Commission, it would be best for the relief units to proceed to those areas as soon as possible. "The doors are opening, but it is a clear question how far each individual feels ready to enter these fields, which are admittedly difficult and to some extent dangerous," said George. "Volunteers will be welcome, but it should be clearly understood that no one who hesitates to volunteer will meet any reproach or criticism."[43] None of the Talas unit hesitated. As Susan explained in a letter to her friends and family, "We plan to go in anyway, and trust to the protection of the Turkish authorities. . . . Naturally there is much unrest and lawlessness."[44]

It took a couple of weeks to organize the train transport and load the cars with supplies. The group left Constantinople for Talas on May 19, four days after the Greek army landed in Smyrna.

21
Suffer the Little Children

Susan, Stella, Clara and Elsey were on the first relief train leaving Derindje. There were twenty-one cars. On the flatbed cars were an ambulance, a German touring car, and seven REO trucks. In the freight cars were tons of supplies. The two cars reserved for the women were jammed with sleeping cots, an oil heater, packing boxes and personal luggage.[1] In addition to the four returning to Talas, there were two newcomers. Rachel King and Blanche Easton were 25-year-old nurses who had trained and worked together at The Presbyterian Hospital in New York City. They had come over on the *Leviathan*, and had worked in Smyrna for a couple of months before being re-assigned to Talas.[2] The car for men provided accommodation for seven: two drivers bound for Talas, three for Sivas, and two who were transport help.[3]

Susan had set up one car for cooking and eating. It contained a barrel for water, a two-burner oil-fueled cooking stove, a table and benches, and crates arranged to provide a working surface for food preparation. She devised a schedule for taking turns at cooking and washing up. Whenever the train stopped at a station, everyone lowered ladders, jumped off, ran to the cook car, and climbed another ladder for a meal. "It was exciting work to cook and wash dishes when the train was in motion," she said, "And still more exciting to try to eat. The enamelware dishes made such a racket we could hardly hear anyone speak, even if they shouted." The trip took four teeth-rattling days to reach Oulou Kushla.[4]

They were nervous as they unloaded their cargo into the ACRNE warehouse near the station. They had no guard for the warehouse, and no escort for the next day's journey north. Fortunately, the road had been vastly improved during the war. In good weather, it cut down the travel time to Talas from 2½ days to 6 hours. Unfortunately, that was only when conditions were good. They were not good now. The mud and washed-out bridges at the halfway point made it dangerous to travel in the dark. The team was forced to stay overnight in one of the notoriously dirty *khans* (inns).[5]

As the group approached Talas in the car and ambulance, followed by seven trucks filled with baggage, food and hospital supplies, Susan could not help but remember her first "triumphant" arrival in 1902. At least a hundred people had come out to greet her and Adelaide, carrying flowers and wearing smiles, the children laughing and clapping, so happy to see

New arrivals Joseph Beach and Raymond Whitney, and a familiar face: Henry H. Riggs. SOURCE: US Passport Applications.

them. Now, there was no such greeting. As the automobiles slowly made their way up the steep hill, she remembered the children she had seen in Alexandropol. Not children, really, but "wizen and ancient dwarfs, with wrinkled foreheads and those downward cheek creases which deepen when one smiles. Not that they were smiling, however; they had forgotten the way of that, long ago."[6]

Herbert greeted them warmly at the compound's gate. He introduced them to Raymond Whitney, the new doctor, and Rev. Joseph Wickliff Beach. During a bit of small talk, Susan was delighted to learn that Joseph was the nephew of Dr. Harlan P. Beach, her Uncle Gurney's roommate at Yale's Divinity School. She found him to be "a splendid fellow with a fine mind."[7]

But Herbert had disturbing news to deliver. His house was the only place fit to live. It had probably been occupied by an administrator or general, and had therefore been taken care of. However, the hospital had been used as a military hospital, and the girls' and boys' boarding schools had been turned into barracks. After the troops retreated from the Caucasus, the barracks had become state-run orphanages. The condition of the buildings was, Henry said, "indescribable. Dirt, filth, vermin, destruction everywhere."[8] He took them on a tour to see for themselves. He was not exaggerating.

The once-beautiful yards and gardens that had taken the missionaries years of work to create were now garbage-filled cesspools. The schoolrooms were strewn with trash. The furniture was cracked or broken, but mainly non-existent. The walls and ceilings were stained with smoke and water from burst pipes and leaky roofs. In many places the plaster had cracked and fallen in pieces to the floors, which were crusty with dirt and broken glass. "All the windows in one dormitory were carried off, frames, glass and all," Susan noted. Every building, except Herbert's, was crawling with bugs.[9] Naturally his house became their temporarily crowded headquarters and home.

"The people were crying for bread," Herbert said. He had surveyed conditions in the sanjak, and made a conservative estimate of those needing assistance: Of 40,000 Armenians, there were 30,000 needy, including 5,000 orphans; of 90,000 Greeks, there were 8,000 needy and 1,000 orphans; of 800,000 Turks, 50,000 needy and 4,000 orphans. In total, 88,000, mostly women and children, needed aid, and 10,000 of them were orphans—who needed everything.[10]

James Barton had appointed Herbert, Susan, and Henry Wingate to be the committee to guide the Talas relief work, with Henry as the unit's leader. Neither Jane Wingate nor Genevieve Irwin were going to return with their children, as it was deemed too dangerous for them to travel at the moment. Henry had been delayed in Constantinople for a week, but everyone agreed they urgently needed a preliminary plan, because there were "so many things needed all at once."[11]

As usual, they divided the work—this time mostly by committees of one. Susan would be in charge of housekeeping, Stella would organize the orphanages, and Clara and Elsey would set up soup kitchens. Herbert said, "To hand out the loaves without any return is poor charity, except where it is absolutely necessary."[12] They all agreed; they would certainly provide food for the desperate and starving, but their goal was to arrange employment for all who could work. Joseph's job was to establish industries that would not only employ people, but would provide essential clothing and shelter items. As soon as Susan's housekeeping job got the entire compound in good working order—with the exception of the hospital, which was the responsibility of Raymond, Rachel and Blanche— she would assist Joseph in building up industries. Herbert would oversee activities in the outstations, and would coordinate things until Henry's arrival. Henry would ultimately be responsible for the distribution of ACRNE supplies and money.

As Susan knew from her experience in Alexandropol, housekeeping entailed more than sweeping. Her immediate concern was to create a healthy environment for herself and her colleagues, so they could devote their energy to helping others. To do that, she hired a small army of men and women to help her. It took thirty men, working six days a week for two months to haul away the refuse from the gardens. It took fifty women,

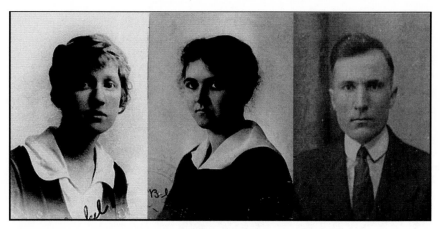

Nurses and friends Rachel King and Blanche Easton, and Edward Martin who came to Talas shortly afterwards. SOURCE: US Passport Applications.

working the same length of time, to scrub clean all the walls and floors, and remove the bugs. Herbert noted in his report to ACRNE, "It is no exaggeration to say that bedbugs and lice were swept down from the walls and gathered up by the quart. Finally, by a plentiful application of sand and soap and Dutch Cleanser, and barrels of hot water and plaster and whitewash, we managed to get our buildings back into something like their old appearance."[13]

While the cleaning was underway, Susan conducted a detailed inspection of the premises and found "school desks heaped up in the basement" and dusty, musty textbooks "piled up in the attics," some of them spoiled because of the leaky roofs. She had several bedsteads, and the dining tables and benches repaired. When she opened the door to her old storeroom, "it looked as though wind had struck it," she said. "The mice had made their nests among the confused mass of stuff, and everything was in a frightful mess!" Her clothes and shoes had vanished, but she did have a delightful surprise. "Out of the chaos I finally pulled a good number of my books and various articles that are of value to me. Among them my college diploma!" Later she uncovered her dear grandmother's diploma, too.[14]

Susan reclaimed from the military depot every item she could that had belonged to the school. There were dishes, bedspreads and pieces of furniture, but one important piece of equipment was missing: the large reservoir for heating water. She went directly to the mutesarrif to ask him to recover it. Perhaps anxious to quickly establish good relations with the relief workers, he "sent out an order to have it hunted up." Not surprisingly, he was successful. Susan then hired a tinsmith to mend it and a blacksmith to mend their stoves, which were "in one grand heap of old iron." Within days both were back in business.[15]

It was a good thing, too, because on May 31 twelve relief workers dropped in from Oulou Kushla on their way to Harpoot. "Their telegram did not get here in time, so we had a big surprise party!" said Susan. "It made us hustle to provide beds and meals for so many, for we were hardly ready to live there ourselves yet." They were lucky to have a good cook, a young Armenian woman who had worked for Herbert's family for several years. Even so, "it was no easy matter to get up meals for twenty-four Americans and ten native people with one small cook stove built for six."[16]

~ ~ ~

As a former principal, Stella knew how to manage hundreds of children. She now had to draw on her considerable emotional reserve to handle the 200 orphans in her charge in Talas,[17] and help support the other 787 in Cesarea. They were filthy little creatures, not much more than skin and bones, covered with lice and sores. They were dressed in dirty rags, most probably the same clothes they had on in 1915. Some of them were almost naked. She started them off with a bath, a haircut, and a clean set of underwear. This monumental task required a legion of women, gallons of hot water, hundreds of cakes of soap, and thousands of pieces of donated clothing from ACRNE.[18] Many a tear was shed, especially by the girls, as they gathered up their shorn hair, unable to believe that it would eventually grow back.[19]

The children desperately needed safe shelter and nutritious food. Breakfast and suppers consisted of vegetables and pilaf with a little meat sprinkled in. Lunch was a piece of bread, and fruit, whenever possible. It took weeks for all of the dormitories in eight buildings to be equipped with adequate beds, so some of the children slept on the floor, now clean and dry thanks to Susan's hired troops.[20]

Adelaide Dwight's role with ACRNE in New York was administrative. She was to help families reconnect with their surviving relatives, and facilitate placements for orphaned boys and girls. She started the task by taking a six-month tour through Turkey, Lebanon, Syria, and the Caucasus to assess the situation and explain the organization's method of record-keeping for this purpose.[21] Naturally she stopped by Talas for a brief but emotional visit with her old friends.[22]

Stella complied with ACRNE's method by dividing the children according to age and gender, and recording as much of their particulars as they knew, in their own words, onto index cards. For example:

My name is Mariam. I am almost eleven years old. My father's name was Manoog. My mother was Mariam also. My birthplace is Erzroom. When they killed my father in Erzroom, I began to cry all night and all day. I ran away with my mother and grandmother. The murderers saw us on the way. They took my mothers both, tied their hands with a rope and threw them into the water. They took me to Arabkir. A Turk lady named Zernoolas took me and I served her for a long time. When she died, a man called Ismayel-Hakie Bey took me to Boghazlian with him. He was about seventy years old. He wished to marry with me. I ran away during a dark night. I heard of the ladies of Talas, of the American Mission, and the orphanage. I was saved from the dangers.[23]

Some of the youngest only knew their own name, and of course the babies didn't even know that. Stella further divided them by their maladies. Those who had contagious diseases, such as scabies, favus and trachoma, were sent to a building nicknamed "Ellis Island" to be detained for medical treatment. Those who simply had lice were deloused, thanks to a machine donated by the local government. Most of their clothing was burned.[24]

~ ~ ~

When Theda Phelps had turned over the hospital to the military in 1917, it had been clean and well-equipped. By the time Raymond Whitney arrived in mid-April, it was almost as filthy as the other buildings in the compound. Raymond had handled a few emergency cases in the month before Rachel and Blanche arrived, but it was in no fit state to open a clinic. Now that they were here, Raymond inspected the medical equipment and Red Cross supplies that had arrived with them, and supervised the hiring of native medical help: four English-speaking nurses, five "uneducated" nurses, and two orderlies. He also helped set up the x-ray equipment, which was to be a major asset in locating "bullets and other foreign bodies, as well as in the diagnosis of fractures." Rachel and Blanche hired women to clean the building thoroughly—three times—and paint the walls twice with calcimine. Carpenters repaired the holes, fixed the leaks, installed new plumbing and electrical systems, set up fixtures and equipment in the operating room, and new beds in the wards. "Before the beds were up, the bedbugs appeared," said Rachel. For the next few days several women were given the task of "picking up the insects and putting them into pans of water while the medical staff squirted kerosene or bichloride into the cracks" of the furniture and walls. Then the nurses made up the beds with fresh bedding and the hospital was open for business. "Patients came quickly," she said. "Most of them were surgical and their conditions extreme. There were many bad chronic infections. One young man came in with a large bullet hole in his thigh. It was nearly a week old and for several days had been stuffed with scrambled eggs. Many cases came in ox carts from surrounding villages, riding thus, sick or wounded, for a day or two. They were certainly most grateful for the clean soft bed that awaited them."[25]

Rachel remembered their first Muslim patient, a little girl named Fatima, who had been found half starved on the street. "She was covered with rags, scabies, lice, favus and sores." Scabies and favus were the two most problematic and prolific skin diseases of the orphans. Scabies is caused by a mite that burrows under the skin and produces ulcers and a terrible itch. The treatment was even worse: The ulcer had to be opened, the scabs rubbed off, and a mixture of sulphur and lime applied over the wound. "Many of the little things screamed from pain, but never hesitated to come forward, and all begged to be the next."[26]

Favus, or kel-head, as the children called it, was an especially nasty disease of the scalp, caused by a fungus and acquired by neglect. The odor emitted from the dry, yellow encrustation was awful. In some cases the pus-pockets that formed killed the hair follicles, leaving bald patches on the head. The prescribed treatment was an x-ray, but it did nothing for the first two patients. The recommended ointments proved no better. The staff then decided to use the native method of treatment: applying tar to the shaved head until it formed a cap, and after a week or so, pulling the cap off with the hair follicles attached.[27]

"Miss Easton and I tried tar caps, pulling them off under anaesthesia," Rachel reported. "We found that the sores became badly infected under the caps and very little of the hair came out." The children were begging for relief, saying "Save us from the kel!" Having heard of two native experts on tar caps who had some success in the Cesarea orphanage, they decided to hire them. The experts certainly knew what they were doing, but according to Rachel, they "were two heartless women. Each week they came and pulled off the caps—with no anaesthesia—scrubbed the heads, and applied new tar caps. They disregarded the infections, which seemed to heal up somehow, and claimed their cures were due to some secret medicine which they put in the tar, together with the occasional application of a stewed apricot poultice. The real value of their treatment was the fact that they had the knack of pulling most of the hair out with the cap . . . The hair grew in naturally again, except where the disease had

217

Some of the youngest children only knew their own name. SOURCE: Bodil Biørn, Kvinnelige Misjonsarbeidere (Association of Female Missionaries), Norwegian State Archive.

entirely killed it. Sometimes as many as fifteen or twenty caps are necessary, and it is a harsh treatment which most people could not undertake. The children are grateful, however, and they forget the treatment quickly."[28]

~ ~ ~

"Food, clothing and bedding come first," said Susan. While she got the kitchen staff running smoothly, Joseph's priority was to have beds and clothing made for the orphans as soon as possible. He bought wool from local sheep farms, and had it trucked up to the streams above Talas every morning to be washed, beaten and dried by about 15 women. The clean wool was then sent to be spun by hand into strands of various thicknesses. He hired women to knit stockings, paying them 40 piasters (100th of a Turkish lira) per pair. The immediate goal was to make stockings for 1,000 orphans. He also established an Industrial Department in the old Boys' School, where weavers created cloth for clothing, and rugs for sale. Susan took charge of the tailor shops, where adults sewed suits for boys and dresses for girls. In those early months they had limited sources for dyes. Soot from cleaning the chimneys made a khaki-colored dye, and walnut hulls produced an olive green or brown color.[29]

Meanwhile, Joseph worked diligently to create adequate beds and bedding. He set up a factory in Cesarea to weave a coarse cotton cloth, and had the cloth sewn into bed ticks (cloth cases), which were filled with wool because straw was too expensive and not as warm. Most of the school's old iron bedsteads were gone, but some had been returned and repaired. Old boards and cupboard doors were placed over the iron slats, and the wool mattresses on top provided a bit of comfort. In July he and Stella took three weeks to tour their northern outstations. "We found 265 children in Boghazlian, who were being cared for by a former graduate of the Talas School," Stella reported. "They have neither beds nor clothes, and scabies is almost universal." In Yozgat, which had experienced more destruction than any other community in the area, they found 365 orphans, all but 10 of whom had scabies. The building supposed to house them was "so infested with vermin that all the children slept in a paved courtyard." Stella and Joseph scouted out another building, and hired more workers to bathe the children, apply the scabies treatment, burn their clothes and give them a new set. "There are from 2,000 to 3,000 children in dire need, requiring food, clothing and shelter," Joseph estimated. By August, he had arranged for shipments of blankets from America to arrive by the fall; he had also created employment for more than 600 people. It was a good start.[30]

Neither Clara, the former kindergarten teacher, nor Elsey, a former Boy's School teacher, had any experience preparing food for hundreds. That did not deter them. Within days they organized a soup kitchen in Talas. Within weeks, Henry had arrived, and they organized one in Cesarea. Each month Henry gave them £T 1,000. With that they hired cooks, and bought wood, *kerpidge* (dried manure fuel), potatoes, onions, beans, fat, *boulgour* (boiled, dried and ground wheat), cheese, and enough other items to feed almost five hundred per day (100 in Talas, 300-400 in Cesarea). "My family is big. I feel somehow as if they all belonged to me— all my little old women, decrepit, blind, sick, the children and all," said Clara, as cheerful as ever. "I am having quite a novel time."[31] Elsey, fifteen years her senior, was perhaps a bit more staid, but no less capable.

~ ~ ~

Everybody in the Talas unit was focussed on providing relief, but there was one important aspect of life that still needed attention: education. Schools in Turkey had been closed for most of the war years, so the younger ones could not read or write or do simple mathematics. "Many of

219

the children of twelve and fourteen years of age had never been to school a day in their lives," said Susan, who had been elected by the others to open the schools. The buildings had been cleaned, but they were unfurnished. "Our school desks were all tumbled together in the basement, but we succeeded in setting them up in their proper places once more." There were 150 of them, not nearly enough for all the pupils. The Armenian school in Talas had not been able to open, so Susan tried to take in all the Armenian children she could into the primary and day school. Many of them were home orphans. There were a large number of Greek students in different grades, and a few Turkish pupils, too. Most of the Greek students paid a tuition of £T 1 per month (a little more than $1), which helped defray the operating costs. In the middle of all this, Susan was helping the Armenians get a school started in their own building, reasoning that she could then send part of her surplus of pupils to them.

"Forty-five miles is a long way to walk, but sixty of our boys and girls walked the whole distance in order to come to Talas for the two orphanage schools we have opened. They had to spend two nights on the way without beds of any sort." She also arranged for 75 of the older, more promising girls from the four orphanages in Kaisarieh to come as boarding students. All this meant finding more beds and bedding, which she somehow managed to do. It also meant crowded classrooms. In the early fall, she reported to ACRNE: "At present, we are badly overcrowded, with eighty or ninety in a primary room intended for fifty. There are about one hundred twenty in the larger room, which provides for only one hundred. She felt fortunate to find two Greek and five Armenian teachers for the different grades and courses. "My teachers are all just splendid in trying to help every way they can and we are happy to see the children so eager to come to school. What a contrast it is to some people I have heard about in our favored America! Here it is a great privilege to go to school."

The only books that had not been destroyed in the intervening years were a few readers and arithmetic manuals, and the old high school textbooks. The high school books were useless for the vast majority of students, who were still at the primary level. Susan ordered books from Constantinople, but it would take months for them to arrive. Meanwhile, lessons were taught from the blackboard, and the readers were passed around. It was a start.

When she wrote to her supporters back home, Susan described how the students were currently walking around barefoot, and how badly they needed shoes. She made a special appeal to the women in the mid-West congregations: "All our orphan girls are dressed in dark grey Japanese crepe

Mary and George Richards, and another doctor who practised in Talas later, John O'Meara. SOURCE: US Passport Applications.

aprons with gray outing flannel dresses and muslin underwear. It is good to see them thus decently covered, but I find it very depressing to see them all alike in such sombre colors. I wonder how it affects them, since, in this country, they all do love bright colors so much. If only I could get some bright ribbons or beads or aprons that are pretty, it would surely cheer them up. It is one of my pet notions that it is not good for girls in their teens to be kept on a dead uniformity, in dress or anything else. It prevents the development of a free personality and discourages any individual initiative. I wonder whether anyone at home could help me out in this perplexity?"[32]

~ ~ ~

In September Mary Richards, a member of the WBM Board of Directors, and her husband, Dr. George Richards, ACRNE's medical director in Derindje, made an inspection tour of Talas, Sivas, Malatia and Harpoot before going home to Fall River, Massachusetts. This was a planned visit, and Talas was their first stop. Everyone met them at the gate, and walked them around the compound. "We were at once in New England in the summer, with a green lawn, a miniature fountain, trees, and a tame stork," said Dr. Richards. They were treated to simple but delicious meals, comfortable beds in the guest rooms in the Cesarea kindergarten building, and a bath. "Yes, a bath in a tin tub, with at least two pails of hot water allowed," he said. In the evenings they read out-of-date copies of *Literary Digest,* or gathered around Henry at the piano to sing hymns and songs. "For real hospitality, the Waldorf Astoria cannot touch it!"

They visited the soup kitchens, orphanages, schools and kindergarten, industries, and the hospital. "When I learned what a small proportion the cost bore to the output, I became enthusiastic," said the doctor, amazed at the progress in such a short time. "Here was a genuine oasis in a barren land, where literally the desert was being made to blossom as the rose." But Mrs. Richards was in no doubt how devastating it would have been for the returning missionaries to arrive at the ruins: "We marvel at their splendid courage in beginning so much of it all over again."[33]

22

Order and DisOrder

While those in Talas were busy reconstructing and rehabilitating their little corner of the world, the rest of Turkey was being "reorganized" too, though sometimes in unhealthy and unproductive ways. On May 15 the Greek army landed in Smyrna. It was not an invasion. It was, however, an occupation. The troops disembarked from boats in an orderly fashion, with Allied warships in the harbour behind them. They marched along the wide quay "towards the *konak* (government offices), with a mixed crowd of local civilians—Greeks, Armenians, Jews, and Turks—looking on. As they approached, the atmosphere grew electric. When the head of the column came within a few hundred yards of the building, somebody fired a shot." Some of the troops returned fire. While no individual was ever identified as the first shooter, it was "certain that the Greek troops fired promiscuously into the crowd, killing and wounding Christian as well as Muslim civilians." The Greek soldiers, unfamiliar with the Ottoman habit of wearing a fez no matter what one's ethnicity, attacked citizens wearing one. "Not only in Smyrna but in villages within a radius of half-a-dozen miles from the city, local Greeks—suddenly possessed of arms—raided their Turkish neighbours' houses, stripped them of their furniture, and lifted their cattle." The killings happened during the first two days, but the looting went on for two weeks.[1]

Word spread quickly of mass atrocities committed against Turkish civilians throughout the vilayet. Clifford Heathcote-Smith, who worked in Constantinople for the British High Commission and the newly formed MI6,[2] reported that accounts of the violence "came as a great shock to the Turks, and had an unifying effect on the various factions" in the empire, even though tales of the atrocities had been exaggerated.[3] The exaggeration was confirmed by American Consul George Horton in Smyrna, who found that two hundred people had been killed in Smyrna. He was impressed by the new Greek governor-general, who "suppressed the disturbances completely in a very short space of time and severely punished the evil-doers," some by a firing squad.[4]

Still, the rumours of massacres continued. Tempers flared. Emotions ran high. In July Turkish chettes in Aidin attacked the Greek quarter. "Women and children were hunted like rats from house to house, and civilians caught alive were slaughtered in batches—shot or knifed or hurled over a cliff. The houses and public buildings were plundered, the machinery in the factories wrecked, safes blown or burst open, and the whole quarter finally burnt to the ground." Raping, kidnapping and killing went on for several days before the Greek army gained control.[5]

The Allies sent in a commission, led by Admiral Mark Bristol, United States High Commissioner at Constantinople,[*] to investigate, stop the fighting, and determine who was responsible for the atrocities. The report was not released publicly,[6] but there was plenty of finger pointing, especially at the Turks. Toynbee admonished the judges:

> In judging Greek and Turkish atrocities, Westerners have no right to be self-righteous. They can only commit one greater error of judgment, and that is to suppose that the Turks are more unrighteous than the Greeks. Much mischief has been done in the Near and Middle East by this common Western opinion. The argument generally advanced is that Turks have committed a very much greater number of atrocities upon Greeks than Greeks upon Turks since the two peoples first came across each other. The fact is true but the deduction is fallacious, because a second factor has to be taken into consideration, and that is the opportunities enjoyed by the two parties for respective ill-treatment.[7]

He laid the blame at the original decision to allow the Greek army to land at all: "There is no doubt that the Big Three were morally as well as technically responsible for the consequences of this particular decision, for they cannot plead that they were badly informed."[8]

Heathcote-Smith had been right about the news being a catalyst for reunification. Four days after the Greek landing, Mustafa Kemal, the Ottoman army commander who had distinguished himself at Gallipoli, began to organize a national resistance.[9]

~ ~ ~

Even though there were Ottomans who were grateful for the order the British patrols were bringing to the interior, others were decidedly disturbed by their presence. Army officers, such as Mustafa Kemal, had fought hard for what was left of the Empire, and did not want to see foreigners dissect it. Article 5 of the armistice had called for the immediate demobilization of the army, except for troops that were needed for surveillance and maintenance of order—the number and location "to be determined later by the Allies, after consultation with the Turkish Government."[10] The army was considerably smaller after four years of

---

[*] The United States no longer had an ambassador in the Ottoman Empire.

war, disease and desertions, with about 60,000 left in various pockets of the country.[11] When Kemal was ordered by the government—no doubt on the insistence of the Allies—to deplete the army further,[12] he was not happy. He arrived in Samsoun, heard about the Greek army in Smyrna, and contacted the other commanders to discuss the situation. On June 21 there was a meeting of several high-ranking military officials in Amasia where they issued a circular, which "was sent to all civil and military authorities in Anatolia. It stated that the country was in danger, that the government in Constantinople was unable to protect it, and that only the will of the nation could save it." They would organize a national congress in Sivas in September, with provincial representation.[13]

Naturally the government in Constantinople was astonished and worried by this faction. No one wanted another war, and certainly not a civil war. Kemal was reduced to half-pay and recalled to the capital. When he refused to comply,[14] Interior Minister Ali Kemal issued a circular of his own: Mustafa Kemal was fired and no longer had any military authority.[15] The government also issued an order to arrest him. The commander who received it, Kazim Pasha, "refused to obey, and made it clear that he still regarded Mustafa Kemal as his superior."[16] Politically embarrassed, Ali Kemal resigned.[17] At a regional congress in Erzroom in July delegates elected Mustafa Kemal as president of a "representative committee." This action was duplicated at the national congress, which had 38 provincial delegates.[18] It was the beginning of a national resistance movement. The members were known as Nationalists. And they had a slogan: "Turkey for the Turks."[19]

In September Ferid Pasha's cabinet fell, and Ali Riza Pasha became Grand Vizier.[20] The new government began talks with the resistance leaders. They ultimately reached an agreement that the resistance committee would approve all candidates running in the Ottoman Empire's general election in December. Of course, the consequence was that all the new parliamentarians were supportive of the resistance. The Nationalists moved their headquarters to Angora, which was connected to Constantinople by rail, but more centrally located,[21] "and far from the sea and the guns of the British Navy."[22] Now there were two governments: a puppet at the Bosporus and a master in the interior.

~ ~ ~

In September, Dr. Mabel Elliott, an ACRNE worker in Marash, heard that the British were withdrawing from Cilicia. "This was a thunderclap. Two weeks earlier the British in Marash had been building stables and preparing quarters for the winter. The British occupation had seemed to

The Parliament Building in Angora. SOURCE: Turkey, US Library of Congress.

every one to be as permanent as the mountains. Now, without notice, they were leaving. Cilicia had been given to France by treaty with England, early in the Great War; now the French were to hold it. But how, in less than two weeks, could the transfer have safely been made? And why were the British withdrawing so suddenly, without notice, without time for the French to establish themselves and take command of the situation?"[23]

Ernest W. Riggs, President of Euphrates College in Harpoot, also had questions. "What is going on in Turkey? . . . First, the government has been overthrown. Almost the whole of Asia Minor is in the grip of a military autocracy, with one of Enver Pasha's former generals at its head." Second, the new government vowed to "maintain its sway over all of its dominions and all of its territory." Third, it was going to do so by fighting. A relief worker had seen troops drilling, and vigorously recruiting. Fourth, instead of sending in reinforcements and exerting pressure "to stop such activities," the British were withdrawing. Fifth, "the remnant of the Armenians are fleeing the country with all haste, for they say that all signs point towards further massacre. . . . Why is nothing done about it?"[24] He did not have an adequate answer.

~ ~ ~

Nevertheless, the work of ACRNE continued in earnest. As of May the American Committee had raised $22 million of its $30 million goal, much of which was cabled to William Peet. Lee Vrooman, now attached to the Harpoot unit, noted that Harry Riggs had travelled from Constantinople with $85,000 worth of gold. "It weighed over three hundred pounds.

Some cash, I'll tell the world!" he hooted.[25] Four ships borrowed from the US Navy carried food and supplies for distribution.[26] Another ship of relief workers arrived from New York. Among the passengers were Fred and Lulu Goodsell and their three children, bound for Constantinople, and Nina Rice, who was returning to Sivas.[27] In June ACRNE also started a newsletter, *The Acorne*, to keep their workers informed of the work going on throughout Turkey, and provide a place to share ideas for better aid. Its first issue reminded readers of the danger of their work: three workers recently died as a result of a train accident, influenza and typhus.[28] During the second half of 1919 it was evident to all that each region was dealing with the same issues: the need for food, supplies, clothing, clean-up, orphanages, shelter, and work.

Nina arrived at the Oulou Kushla train station to find the mission's "battered but faithful Ford" and a group of exiles returning to Sivas. "Among them was one of my former little school girls, tattooed by her Arab captors on brow and chin with an indelible brand of slavery, and soon to bear a child, whose coming will bring back all the horrors of the past years. May love come with it to heal the wounds!" A few young men of ACRNE's transportation service took them in a convoy of supply trucks to Talas, where Nina spent the day visiting her Talas friends. The next day the group moved on to Sivas. Mary Graffam and Lillian Cole Sewny were there to greet them. Ernest Partridge, however, was not. He had "broken down under the strain, and had to return home for a few months' rest," she said.[29]

In addition to the regular relief work, "I really run a hotel," said Lillian. "Often eighteen or twenty trucks will reach here late at night and the men will have to have supper. Last week it was three in the morning before the last ones arrived. Seven young Americans were with the convoy. They stayed two days with us and then twelve of the trucks went on to Harpoot and the rest back to Oulou Kushla for more supplies."[30]

One of those young men was Edward F. Martin of Peshtigo, Wisconsin. He had joined the American Expeditionary Forces in January 1918 and fought in France until the end of the war. After an honourable discharge he joined ACRNE.[31] In August he was assigned to the Oulou Kushla supply depot and began regular visits to Talas, Sivas and Harpoot.[32] It was not long before a certain nurse at the Talas hospital caught his eye.

～ ～ ～

When 20 ACRNE trucks of supplies arrived at Harpoot, Maria Jacobsen was at last able to relax. She had suffered from typhus fever and cerebrospinal meningitis, and had witnessed countless deaths during the previous four-and-a-half years.[33] Lee Vrooman was so impressed by her accomplishments, he wrote an effusive letter to his mother about her. "When she started she had absolutely nothing to work with, except American financial backing and her nerve. She could not get food enough this way, so, though she knew nothing of farming, she rented a farm and had her orphans raise much of their own foodstuffs. She could get no cloth, so she bought wool and had the girls knit garments. But of course they were not satisfactory for underclothes, so she rigged up a little cotton mill, bought cotton, and made cloth. She also made her own shoes, and of course had to grind her own flour." He went on and on, and finally concluded, "Believe me, she did a wonderful work, and she is just a youngster herself.[34] It was quite a compliment. Marie was 36 years old; Lee was 21. Within a couple of months she was home in Denmark for a well-deserved rest.

Mary Graffam in Sivas was encouraged to join Dr. Barton on his journey to Samsoun, and then by ship to Constantinople for a rest.[35] She agreed, but within a short time was back in Sivas to continue her work. As Major General Harbord said, she had a "forceful character" and was one of the "strong influences in this whole region."[36]

James Lyman of Marash was the first to reach Olive Vaughan in Hadjin. "What that woman has endured these years, and how she has kept on in spite of all the difficulties, would fill a book and read like a dime novel," he said. "It is a piece of heroism such as is not often heard of, even in the annals of missionary work."[37] Olive, however, did not see it that way. A few months later, when she was visiting her college friends at home in Minnesota, she said, "Everybody is so good to me! Only I wish they wouldn't sometimes think I had been heroic. I just did what any other American woman would have done in my place. I'm thankful the Lord trusted me to be of some help."[38]

～ ～ ～

Fifteen Rescue Homes had been established in Turkey for young women who had been residing in Muslim households.[39] In Harpoot, Dr. Ruth Parmelee examined 680 of these women in one year, and diagnosed more than 15% with a venereal disease.[40] In Talas, Theda Phelps, who had recently returned from her nursing job in Persia, was supervising a rescue home.[41] All but one of the women there had had a bad experience. Stella had rescued two on her first visit to Yozgat. "One of them is just out of the hospital a week or two. Her child was stillborn," Susan reported. "What depths of gloom there are in the life of this wretched place! It is wonderful to see the patience and faith which they show through it all, and the courage with which they face life again."[42]

Elizabeth Webb had a similar feeling when two girls from mountain villages came to Adana. "Thirteen and fourteen years of age, and each the wife of Turks for three years past. I can't tell you how forlorn they looked. Then came the day they first went down to the yard, and their happy voices came up in a real game of ball! How we rejoiced that they had again gotten back their lost birthright of childhood play!" Rather than create a Rescue Home, her team built a "Trade School" because "the right thing is to teach them trades that they may be independent and able to earn a living for themselves." It was difficult to find a house and furnishings. "I think even Booker Washington's famous school did not start with less furniture," said Elizabeth. But they were creative in setting it up: empty milk cans for drinking glasses, used gasoline boxes for clothing storage, and filed pieces of umbrella frames for knitting needles. "The life of each one of these twenty-nine girls has its own tragedy. One of them, in order to free herself from an evil house in which she was confined as a prisoner, broke open a door and jumped from a second-story window. Another, after attempting to run away from the man who claimed her as his wife, stood up in front of him while he pointed his gun at her ready to shoot, absolutely refusing to return to his house. Her life was saved by the intervention of some Arabs, who told her husband the Government was killing and hanging all the Armenians, and to let her go, since she would be killed later anyway." Elizabeth was heartened by the week-to-week progress she saw in the girls' appearance and character, but noted, "They have been grievously sinned against, and many will suffer through life for it."[43]

~ ~ ~

After six months travelling with the Relief Expedition Commission "from Constantinople to Cairo" and almost every place in between, James Barton said, "Turkey is looking up. As she is so much in a hole, there is no other way to look. The upward look, however, is not a look of courage, hope, or hardly of expectation. Many of the blackest-hearted leaders in the atrocities are still in power, while others live openly in the places where they are well known. It is true that now and then one has committed suicide; a few have been hung; more are waiting trial, but most are still defiant."[44] In late May the British had taken prisoner 64 officials who had been indicted for war crimes, and sent them to await trial on the islands of Malta and Mudros.[45] But Barton was correct that most of those responsible had neither fled nor were cowering. Dr. Jemal Shehabeddin

Bey wrote in *Alemdar*, "Those who have even slightly open minds can understand that at all levels of the country, the mortal disease of Unionism continues to rage."[46]

The Commission spoke to Ottomans of all ethnicities, and determined that there was no money for any kind of reconstruction. "Not a hopeful note has been struck by a single Turkish official. They all say 'the country is bankrupt'." Barton did not mince words. "The entire system is rotten to the core, without purpose and destitute of capacity [even though] the present Turkish officials are vastly superior to their predecessors." He gave the example of the new governor of Malatia, Halil Rami Bey. "He is a Kurd and is no friend of the Turk. His people have suffered much persecution at the hands of the Turk during the war. One of his first proclamations after his arrival was to the effect that all Armenians should come personally to him if they had a grievance that was not receiving adequate attention. Such men welcome the coming of American missionaries and relief workers, and all seem to entertain the hope that somewhere, and soon, America will become the saviour of this disordered country."[47]

The Commission's conclusion was that education must follow humanitarian aid for there to be any hope of reconstruction. Of course, that would be American education. "I am confident that we can rely upon the hearty cooperation of most of the leading Turkish officials in putting American educational institutions well upon their feet, and in enlarging them to include modern agriculture, mining, engineering, and other practical departments," said Barton. "The people of Turkey need help of every kind now. This is the strategic hour to move and to move powerfully. Adequate means, used by consecrated men and women under God, can make this mourning land a blessing to the world."[48]

He would have had no problem with Marion Harlow's approach to teaching her primary grade pupils in Smyrna. Every day she began the class by having them repeat a psalm they were learning, then sing a morning prayer. "And then, as I want John to grow up a real American, we follow with the salute to the flag, such as is done in all American schools. But as there are only three American children out of the nine, and little Scotch Jimmie Ferguson strenuously objected to saluting any flag but the British, I solved the problem by holding up an American, a British, an Armenian, and a Greek flag, and the children repeat the same words but each salute their own flag. Then we sing one verse of *America*, and for Jimmie's sake and to keep peace, follow that with *God Save the King*. After that the three Rs claim our attention." Her husband, Mr. S. Ralph Harlow, was organizing a YMCA club in the city and was asked by the Greek Boy Scouts association to guide the work of their leaders. "The Greeks realized that their movement was too military. They begged him to take it over and put into it the American ideals for development of character," Mrs. Harlow said.[49]

No sooner had Barton and the Commission finished their tour of the Bulgaria-Greece-Thrace region and were about to depart for the Caucasus, than Ernest Yarrow sent a cable on August 5 from Tiflis to ACRNE New York with the disquieting news: The British were pulling out. The impending result, Ernest implied, would be political chaos, possible massacres of Armenians, and danger to the relief workers, particularly the women. He added that the locals strongly felt that the United States was responsible for the situation. Though the other Entente members had signed the Treaty of Versailles, the Americans had not, and were seen as delaying the peace process.[50]

~ ~ ~

The first court-martial of the main perpetrators of the "crimes against humanity" continued through February and March. The accused were Kemal Bey, 35, who had been the kaimakam of Boghazlian and interim mutesarrif of Yozgat, and Mehmed Tevfik, 44, the commander of the Yozgat gendarmerie. The Boghazlian deportations were notorious because the majority of deportees had been murdered. Though Kemal Bey declared, "We deported the Armenians for military reasons," he denied ordering any killings. Among the many witnesses were 18-year-old Eugénie Varvarian, who testified about the massacre of most of her fellow deportees, and civil inspector Nedim Bey, a colleague, who swore that Kemal "was the author of these crimes." On April 8, they were found guilty. Kemal Bey was sentenced to death; Tevfik Bey was given 15 years of hard labour. Even so, these two criminals had their supporters. The presiding judge resigned in protest of the verdict. Two days later, Kemal was executed in Bayazid Square in Constantinople before a crowd of 10,000. Among those attending were the commander of Constantinople's gendarmerie with an honour guard, the chief of police, the military governor, Constantinople's mayor, several leaders of chette squadrons, and many other high-ranking officials. They were there to witness the execution of a "martyr." Indeed the next day at his funeral, a bouquet laid on his tomb read, "For the innocent Muslim martyr." Just before his execution, realizing he could no longer deny his guilt, Kemal still denied responsibility: "I carried out the orders I was given."[51]

The trial and outcome were a microcosm of the current political situation. The new Ottoman government wanted to distance itself from the CUP leaders who orchestrated the deportations and massacres, demonstrate "good faith by punishing the guilty," and prevent the empire from being dismembered. The Nationalists, who accused the government of "collaborating with foreigners" were defiant in their show of force, unity, and "refusal to assume responsibilities."[52]

The trials continued. Evidence showed many high-ranking officials of the CUP government either participated in the creation of the Special Organization or did nothing to prevent it, gave orders to dress bandits in regular army uniforms, and released criminals from prisons for use by the SO. It was found that the Special Organization's mission was to exterminate the Armenians.[53] In July, Talat, Enver, Djemal and Dr. Nazim were condemned to death in absentia[54] "for joining in the war and for the Armenian, Greek, and Syrian atrocities and deportations."[55] Most people believed it was unlikely they would ever pay for their crimes.

23

On Their Own

November 1919 brought the first snowfall to Talas. The relief workers were grateful for the late arrival of winter. They were now directly caring for 200 orphans (100 boys and 100 girls), and had to provide them, and many of the home orphans among their 400 students, all the basics. This was after sending 300 orphans to Smyrna and 200 to Adana during the summer. These transfers were due to fear and political unrest in the outlying villages, the anticipated difficulty in finding fuel for the winter, and "to make room for incoming children." It was a wise decision. ACRNE warned that relief workers "must stand ready to care for those children who will soon be turned adrift in large numbers by their Turkish masters, as the fall work on farms is finished and winter comes on." In Yozgat and Boghazlian, the number of orphans doubled in September alone.[1]

Susan wrote to her sister, Harriet, "It has been a task to get enough things made to keep them from shivering these cold days. It surely will be a blessing if the winter is mild, for the poor people here are absolutely destitute of bedding and clothing. They cannot get food, to say nothing of fuel and other necessities."[2] This was no exaggeration. Houses were being torn down for firewood. Of the 360 houses in one Armenian quarter in Cesarea, only four were left standing. "An old, deaf woman woke up one morning to find that nothing was left of her house except the room she was sleeping in."[3]

The Talas group was responsible for relief in a vast area, and the need was great. There were six orphanages in all, with Stella supervising the care of 1,681 children, and Theda caring for the 200 in Talas.[4] There were also thousands of people, mainly women, who needed help. In July-August the unit provided direct aid to 3,351 Armenians, 1,008 Greeks and 1,305 Turks. Including hospital and clinic visits, soup kitchens, industrial work, and other kinds of treatments, there had been 10,831 instances of aid in total.[5] But the workers were worried. "Our appropriations have been cut down 60%, and our money is all gone," said Susan. "The Relief Committee is a whole month behind in sending us money that has been promised us. You may imagine how hard it is to be here with no funds and so much distress all around us that we cannot relieve." Still, thanks to an entire summer's work, they had enough wool to keep employing women to card, spin, and knit or weave thousands of garments.[6]

The hospital was doing a brisk business, but for several months without a doctor. Raymond Whitney had moved on, and ACRNE had not be able to secure his replacement. Rachel and Blanche carried on as best they could, consulting medical books often. When government officials became aware of the situation, they ordered the hospital closed until there was a doctor on the premises. "We then hired a native Greek doctor in order to keep it open," said Rachel. "He had the true spirit of a doctor, and often showed good judgment but had many strange methods. He usually respected our opinions, but one day I came into the ward to find he had made many cuts over the back of a bad eye case, and ordered cupping. His idea was to take the inflammation from the eyes by bleeding the patient." Rachel had been treating the patient for two months without signs of progress. "As it happened, a few days after the cupping, the eyes began to improve and grew steadily better. The doctor looked very wise. What could I say! For necessary operations, we called in a Turkish surgeon."[7]

Herbert Irwin had gone to Constantinople to pick up Genevieve and their children, and return to Canada. They had been in Turkey continuously since 1911; it was now time for a long-overdue furlough. After checking in with ACRNE headquarters in New York, they were planning on travelling west to visit Susan's family in Iowa,[8] and then north to their own family in Winnipeg.[9] Meanwhile a new worker had joined the team. Katherine Fletcher was a graduate of Smith College, with a master's degree from Columbia University. She had taught school for several years, and had attended business school during the war.[10] They could not have asked for a more suitable colleague.

Henry Wingate had been waiting for his wife to return to Talas, but when it became clear that Jane was not well enough to travel, he, too, made plans to go home. Unlike Herbert and Genevieve who expected to return, Henry decided to remain in the United States permanently. He was 54 years old and had come to Turkey three years after graduating from Carleton College in 1887. After a brief stint as a tutor in Marsovan, he had joined the Talas mission in 1893, soon becoming the Boys' School Principal. Perhaps 26 years of service, a horrible two of them served during the Armenian deportations, was enough.[11] However, he would wait until the spring to leave, as there was much to do beforehand. The political situation was still in limbo, highway robbery was on the rise, and the misery was still overwhelming.

Susan had also considered leaving. "I think if I got another invitation to go to Constantinople, I should accept it," she confided to her sister. She thought the work there seemed "more hopeful" than in Talas, and there were others who could do what she was doing. "But I hardly expect to make any change. It has been a satisfaction to be here thus far, and to take part in so many lines of work that help the people. We have had a most congenial group of workers in our unit, and it has been a happy year in spite of the hard things. I try to forget the work in the evenings and get rested for the next day." Knitting, mending, and her new interest in chess helped to distract her. She shared one other item with her sister: "driving our Ford over the frightful roads between here and Yozgat. I really know a lot about a Ford since then. I feel as though I could nearly make one myself."[12]

~ ~ ~

On January 28, 1920, the Nationalist-approved majority of parliamentarians voted, in secret, to adopt the National Pact. It was a statement of political principles "for the creation of an independent Turkish Muslim nation-state." On February 17 they made their decision public. It worried the Ottoman Christian minorities, but it was untenable for the Allies. They were still at the conference table in Paris talking about "the terms of the peace settlement they meant to impose, [while] the Ottoman Chamber of Deputies, without being asked, had defined the minimum terms they were prepared to accept." British Prime Minister Lloyd George and French Premier Millerand were warned by their generals that vastly more troops would be needed to impose the conditions of the proposed peace treaty on the Nationalists. Lloyd George was unmoved. He preferred to meet force with force.[13]

While they were contemplating their political choices, Dr. Mabel Elliott was trudging in a long column with thousands of other refugees through mountain snows to escape the siege of Marash. "What were the statesmen of England and France doing at that hour?" she asked. "Comfortable men—men who had eaten, men who had roofs under which to sleep, men whose wives and children were safe and warm—they sat playing the great game of international politics on the chessboard of the world, while the world bled lives and sweated anguish at every move."[14]

~ ~ ~

Around New Year's Day 1920, the British withdrew from Cilicia, and the French arrived, as per the agreement following the war. The locals wondered how the French would be able "to establish themselves and take command of the situation" in only two weeks.[15] James Lyman, who was touring villages near Marash, said, "We found both Christians and Muslims alike greatly disturbed over the coming of the French. In

Gerksun we saw the governor, and he told us that there were more than
sixty Kurdish and Circassian orphans in his domain, and wanted to know
if we would open a place for them, similar to what we were planning for
Albustan, a larger town." They attended a local Nationalist meeting, and
visited Kurdish and Circassian tribal leaders, to gain their support for
ACRNE-run orphanages.[16] Everyone was in favour of the idea, but within
days, the point was moot. When a battle starts, it does not matter to
civilians of any ethnicity where the bullets come from.

The shooting started between the French and the Nationalists in
Marash on January 21. Over ACRNE's protests, the French had installed a
machine gun on the top floor of the hospital. Dr. Mabel Elliott heard the
gunfire, and raced there "to find bullets whistling through it." One just
missed her head.[17] The 175 staff, patients and visitors were under attack.
At the Boys' Orphanage across the city, nurse Frances Buckley opened the
doors to people fleeing the fighting. Within hours, "every corner of the
house was filled with refugees."[18]

Both women kept a diary during the three-week siege. "Our telephone
wires were cut . . . the French have no wireless, so Marash is completely
cut off from the rest of the world," Mable wrote. There was "a constant
fusillade. Bullets never cease their whining, and the cannon shots rattle our
windows. . . . Every hour produces a new big fire. One by one, the French
are picking out the Turkish houses and burning them. . . . I have ordered a
tree cut down. We have hardly any wood left. Cooking only two meals a
day, for patients and all." An airplane dropped fliers in French and
English, which said that the fight was not a local movement, but a national
one, "and that the Turks of Marash could not stop it . . . In other words, it
is Mustapha Kemal's movement. . . . News came from one of the big
churches; there are nearly two thousand Armenians there, safe so far. And I
feel they will be. Dr. Artine is with them. . . . a thousand Armenians are in
the American college compound now. They are being fed one meal a day
from our supplies. . . . There is fierce fighting on all sides of us this
morning, and we are having the worst snowstorm of the winter. . . . News
came to me yesterday that Miss Buckley was killed on the first day. . . . I
do not believe it; I could not bear to believe it."[19]

Fortunately the news was wrong. But Frances's situation was just as
bad. "My apartment has many bullet holes. . . . There is no surgeon, so
Miss Tim will amputate an arm in the morning. . . . At three o'clock, two
bombs hit the house. . . . The civilians who are tearing down the houses
near us, to protect us from fire, are bringing in food. They have brought
enough to supply the people for a couple of weeks. . . . The eighth baby

was born today. . . . Bombs from Turks again today at three. Two struck the house and one came through the attic roof. The second floor is not safe, so about fifty people came to the kitchen. . . . Machine guns mowed the people down as they tried to leave the city. A tunnel has been made under the street. There are holes in the house across the street where they try to set us afire with a long pole and kerosene cloths."[20]

Mustafa Kemal. SOURCE: Frank and Frances Carpenter Collection, 1923, US Library of Congress.

At one point the hospital's pharmacist, who had once been in the Ottoman army, ventured into the courtyard across from a group of Nationalists. "You are not to fire on the hospital!" he yelled at them. "You know it is not permitted to fire on a hospital. The Director Doctor Madame is very angry about it, and will hold you responsible. The Director says you are to stop firing at once!" Mabel wrote in her diary, "Would you believe that the Turks stood there, and swore up and down by all the prophets that they never had fired on the hospital, and never would fire on it." All the while, the hospital stood "before his eyes, looking like a colander from their shots!"

On February 10 the French decided to retreat. Frances decided to stay, otherwise "it would mean certain death to hundreds of underfed and poorly clothed people. We must keep on trusting in our good Lord."[21] Mabel decided to leave and help as many patients as she could along the way. They left with the French in the dead of night. "It was difficult going, as soon as we left the buildings behind us, for the darkness blinded us and we did not follow the road, but went across rough fields, guided by hundreds of other marchers as lost as we were. We were not taking the long road to Aleppo, but were to strike out over the mountains in an attempt to reach Islahai." After three days, through deep snow, "our line was wholly demoralized; some stopping to rest, others trudging on. As they passed, I kept asking for Dr. Artine. No one had heard of him. This, I

British troops marching by the Nusretiye Mosque as they occupy Constantinople, March 1920. SOURCE: Turkey, 1920, US Library of Congress.

thought, is the way Armenian families are broken up. This is the way they tramp the roads of Turkey, asking for news of each other. I am a refugee. This is what it means. If I had been born in Marash instead of in America, all that I know, all that I am, would not keep me now from this; hunger and cold and heartache, refugee camps and lines of refugees, bread lines, dirt, disease."[22]

She later learned that the 2,500 Armenians in the church "held a meeting to consider how they should die. They could fight one day more, or they could try to make a dash for escape. If they fought, not one would live; if they made a quick dash some of them might get through." They decided on the latter. They threw open the doors, ran past the trenches of Nationalist troops, who began firing. Two hundred of those who left the church "got past the trenches alive. One hundred and fifty reached Islahai," including her colleague, Dr. Artine. He was never the same again.[23]

~ ~ ~

In mid-March, the British occupied Constantinople. They declared martial law, dissolved Parliament, replaced the police, and arrested and sent to Malta 150 Ottoman military officials and civilian leaders, including 14 elected deputies. Mustafa Kemal urged the rest of the parliamentarians to join him in Angora. By April 23, 92 of them did. With 232 representatives of resistance groups, they formed a national assembly, and elected as its president the 39-year-old Kemal. The Sultan and his government were essentially powerless, though they condemned Kemal and his colleagues as traitors.[24]

In addition to the fighting between the Nationalists and the Allies, there was another kind of danger: brigands. Bands of men roamed the country, robbing and killing at will. Some were semi-autonomous warlords, some were "great landholding families seeking to reassert their interests, but there were also marauding groups of nomads and refugees."[25] Every day travel became more unsafe, no matter one's nationality or ethnicity. On February 1 two YMCA secretaries, James Perry, a graduate of Colby College,[26] and Frank L. Johnson, of Ohio University,[27] were on their way from Aleppo to Marash to help start a YMCA centre. They were bringing mail from the outside world, and equipment to show newsreels and movies. Their bodies were found, "riddled with bullets, in the wreck of their car, with the dead chauffeur. The moving picture outfit had been torn to pieces and scattered for half a mile along the road. Their boxes had been broken open, their clothes taken."[28]

"The whole country swarms with brigands," said Edith Parsons of Brousa. A man from a nearby village told her "that, a few days before, brigands had descended upon the village, had driven everybody out, had completely looted the place, and had taken everything they possessed."[29] Many of the brigands were in it for their own gain, but "much of the brigandage has been carried on in the name of the Turkish nationalistic movement," said George White of Marsovan.[30] The three-month siege of Hadjin, and weeks of attacks in Adana and Oorfa were conducted almost entirely by local chettes.[31] Some fought with the Nationalists in Marash, but other brigands were allied with the British, French, Greeks or Russians. For the time being, it was best not to wander too far from home.

~ ~ ~

Amidst the chaos in the country was a chaotic exodus, mostly Christians in Cilicia who could scrape together enough money to leave. They were going as fast as possible to Beirut, and in many cases on to the United States. Beirut was rapidly becoming one large refugee camp, desperately in need of humanitarian aid.[32]

"Perhaps the most pressing practical need is for a regularly organized emigration system," said Henry Wingate. Family members did not have a reliable method of finding each other, whether in Turkey or in other countries. He knew of "scores of women and children" in Kaisarieh whose relatives in the United States were sending funds, and offering rooms in their homes. In response to his and similar suggestions, ACRNE created a new department called *Relief and Inquiry* to reunite families. "We propose to assemble these people at Talas as fast as possible, in order to have them ready to move on, as soon as opportunity affords." By that, Henry meant as soon as the transportation situation improved. "Because of the present unrest in the interior, travel is practically at a standstill"[33] He soon experienced the frustration for himself. After saying good-bye to his colleagues for the last time, Henry waited at the Oulou Kushla station for six weeks before he could catch a train for Constantinople and home.[34]

Joseph Beach succeeded Henry as Director. He had been asked by the governor to find work for a hundred Muslim women, refugees from Erzroom. He put them to work spinning thread for wool, and found they were extremely good at it. "Many children came with their mothers and sat idle all day, with no chance to learn anything or to find any occupation," he said. "A school has been opened for them, with two Muslim women as teachers. The officials are very eager to cooperate with us in this effort, and the mothers shower blessings on our heads."[35]

As Superintendent of Schools, in one month Susan opened that school, and two others in Cesarea. "It keeps me hustling to get books and other equipment enough for them all. The teachers are not very competent sometimes, but the children learn what they can." Stella was straining under the work of caring for even more orphans, so Susan accepted responsibility for the 125 orphaned girls in Talas. It took up a lot of her time. "They have to be taught everything, even though they are big girls, most of them. They have had no home training, and have been driven about like cattle for several years. But they are improving wonderfully, and look so nice and attractive and intelligent now. It has been worthwhile to do this year's work."[36]

And the work kept growing. "We have now in Talas and Zinjidery about 550 orphans, and more are coming daily," said Joseph. Within three days 70 orphans walked 50 miles from Boghazlian. More were expected the next day. "The distribution of clothing in the orphanages amounts to 2,829 pieces, and 60 blankets sent to the Turkish refugee orphans in Boghazlian." They had opened another weaving factory in Talas, with six looms made partly with homemade parts. They were able to make most of the winter clothing they needed, but Joseph was worried about not being able to buy the sheared wool that was to be ready in a few weeks. It was becoming much more difficult to get money from Constantinople, and

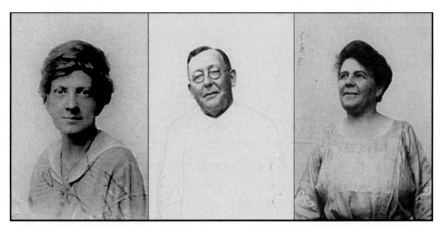

Katherine Fletcher (1919), and Charles R. and Ruby Pearl Gannaway (1923).
SOURCE: US Passport Applications.

they needed to pay for 1,500 boys' suits, 1,500 girls' dresses, 10,000 pairs of stockings, 3,000 sweaters, and 1,500 knitted boys' caps.[37]

In February, after much finagling, Talas finally got an American doctor in the form of John O'Meara from Samsoun.[38] Rachel and Blanche were going home for a break, but after waiting two weeks at the station in Oulou Kushla, and learning about the horrible political situation, they returned to Talas and extended their service. "The doctor of the Talas Unit is looking for Mustafa Kemal Pasha, that he may shake his hand!" said Joseph. But he also had a personal reason for enthusiastically welcoming the nurses' return. In *The Acorne*'s Personnel Notes column was this little gem: "The engagement has been announced of Miss Blanche S. Easton and Mr. Joseph W. Beach."[39]

~ ~ ~

The first act of the new National Assembly had been to send an emissary to Russia. The Nationalists wanted, if not friendship, at least a working relationship with Lenin's Bolsheviks.[40] After all, they were the best outside source of money and military supplies.[41] Since his escape, Enver had been given refuge in Berlin, and had been trying to organize support for his goal of Pan-Turkism.[42] He thought to unite with the Nationalists in their cause against the Allies. He thought wrong. Kemal wanted nothing to do with Enver. The British, however, did not know this. They also misunderstood his pursuit of the Bolsheviks, and did not understand that Kemal was not acting on behalf of the Sultan, which was why they had imprisoned the ruler.[43]

The details of the proposed treaty between the Allies and the Ottoman Empire had become known, and the Nationalists were against the still-official government accepting it. The French recaptured Aintab, but Marash and Oorfa were controlled by the Nationalists. On June 1, despite months of urging by ACRNE, ABCFM, WBM and dozens of others of concerned organizations, the "United States Senate refused to give the President authority to assume the mandate of Armenia."[44] It was looking less and less that eastern Turkey would become western Armenia.

On June 14-15 Nationalist troops attacked the British near Constantinople. The only troops in the area who were in a position to help the British was the Greek army in Smyrna. Venizelos was willing to send in a division, on condition "the Allies also authorized Greece to advance" beyond Smyrna. On June 20, 1920 Lloyd George and Millerand consented.[45] Thus began another war.

~ ~ ~

"We realize that in many places nearby there is serious trouble," said Susan, "but we go on hoping that here we may be spared."[46] They felt isolated and very much on their own. Their only news came from the occasional traveller or those who delivered ACRNE supplies. In June it came through a mountain pass from Hadjin. After three months of fighting between Turkish chettes and Armenian bands, the Armenians retreated and the compound was overrun by the chettes, who immediately began to loot the place. "We six Americans and our two Turkish girls took refuge in a dark storeroom," said Edith Cold. The chettes gave them one hour to leave. "We went on foot up the mountain, carrying saddles, saddle bags, bundles, and hurried every step of the way. For two nights we were guests in the commander's tent, and the following day two of their men conducted us to Talas." They were lucky to be alive, and deeply mourned those they were forced to leave behind.[47]

While they rested, the Talas unit continued to work. The industries kept local women working. Clara cared for 40 orphans in her kindergarten. Susan supervised the schools, now with a total enrollment of 2,000. Dr. Charles Gannaway, who knew Susan's sister in university in Iowa,[48] arrived with his wife to replace John O'Meara, who was moving to Sivas.[49] Two other workers were also leaving Talas. Rachel King and Edward Martin were going home to New York to get married, as soon as the roads opened and it was safe to travel. Everyone was very happy for them—especially because they planned to return. Work increased every day, and they needed all the help they could get.[50]

The American compound in Hadjin is in the foreground (in position but enhanced), with the village in the valley below. The only way out was on the road to Sis and south to Adana, or northwest over the mountains to Talas. SOURCE: The Missionary Church Archives and Historical Collections, Bethel College, Mishawaka, Indiana.

"It is impossible to rest here, but I'll have to make the best of it. I don't want an enforced rest," Susan wrote to her brother, John. "There are so many problems to face that we don't know which way to turn. Every day brings new difficulties. We only go on in trust, and try to do the best we can. I will not repeat the news, for fear you may not get this letter at all if I do. We live from day to day, not making any plans.

"It is hard to be patient when there is so much that is wrong in the world," she concluded. "I have my things packed up and arrangements made so I can start at a moment's notice, in case it seems wise or necessary. Do not be anxious about us here more than you can help. Please give my love to all the dear home circle in all the different places. Yours with love, Susan W. Orvis."[51]

24

No Pleasant Place To Be

On August 10, 1920 the second Ottoman delegation signed the Treaty of Sevres.[1] The first had refused to accept the harsh terms: the massive carving up of the Ottoman Empire. The newly-established League of Nations had created a mandate system, whereby certain countries could legally administer another territory on behalf of the League. The treaty gave Britain mandates in Palestine, Syria and Mesopotamia, and France in Syria and Lebanon. Italy got land in southwestern Turkey, and France in the southeast, as "spheres of influence." The Republic of Armenia was expanded to include eastern Anatolia, and Greece was given Eastern Thrace and the Smyrna area. The Bosporus became international waters.[2] The only land left for the residents of Turkey was Constantinople and some of the interior. An editorial in the *Missionary Herald* was blunt in its assessment:

> The agreement . . . is a surprising and saddening revelation at this time when we are hearing about new and 'open' diplomacy. For back of the thinly-veiled pretense of working for the welfare of the country and for the peace of the world are the old, unlovely figures of conquerors dividing the spoils. Each must get his portion. . . There is not much of cheer or forward-looking vision to this document. The problems of adjustment between the different races and religions of that disturbed land; the allaying of the jealousies and suspicions that are rife; the providing of those just and righteous foundations on which ordered government may rest—these things are little dealt with. It seems doubtful whether they have been much regarded. The interest of the conquerors is what obtrudes, and it promises a continuance of hostility and even violence in the path of its attainment. It is hard to see any promise of peace and prosperity in the grasping agreement.[3]

The League could not have provided a better motivation for the average Turk to support Mustafa Kemal if it had tried. Other editorials noted that 90% of Turks supported him in his scorn for the treaty and his preparation to fight it. They felt that their land was "being taken from them,"[4] and saw the Sultan's government "to be acting under coercion, and therefore not to be obeyed."[5] In Constantinople, "by some kind of agreement, all public transportation was suspended for five minutes at noon, work in stores . . . came to a standstill, and Turkish flags were half-masted."[6] Everyone, whether for or against the treaty was asking, "What prospect is there for an era of peace?"[7]

British and French military and intelligence officers asked the same question. Though "it was almost unthinkable for the military leaders to go to the civilians and admit that they could no longer guarantee victory,"[8] they did not have any confidence the terms of the treaty could be enforced effectively. They advised their governments accordingly.[9] Prime Minister Venizelos offered the Greek army as an enforcer, even though there was enormous political pressure in Greece to demobilize. Seeing no other option, the Allies accepted.[10]

Though Woodrow Wilson had championed the League of Nations, the United States was not a member, therefore had very little say in a peaceful outcome. The *Missionary Herald* reminded its readers that their country had "a big stake in this problem: over five hundred American workers, whose safety is a matter of concern; millions of dollars' worth of American property involved; and a prestige and influence which should count immeasurably, for the remaking of that part of the world is imperilled and possibly to be destroyed by the setting up of these new foreign overlordships. It is a serious hour for America's influence in the Near East."[11]

~ ~ ~

On October 23, 1920, *The Acorne* announced its new name was *Near East Relief*, because "the old initials A.C.R.N.E. officially disappeared when the American Committee for Relief in the Near East assumed its present name,"[12] which was Near East Relief (NER). In fact, the organization's name had officially changed in August 1919 when it incorporated through a charter granted by the US Congress.[13] For the humanitarian workers, it was irrelevant. They had been using the name casually for years anyway.

When Stella and Joseph went to Angora on business for the orphanages, they were exhausted by the travelling.[14] In fact, transportation on the Baghdad Railway was so bad that the NER decided to close the Oulou Kushla warehouse altogether. They began to ship supplies from Constantinople to Samsoun on the Black Sea, and from there transport them via motor, araba (wagon) and camel to the interior stations. They also made plans to charter their own boat because the commercial lines were "uncertain and inadequate."[15]

Susan had returned to Talas in September feeling well rested after a two-week vacation in Zinjidery. Daily horse rides around the village, accommodation in the old monastery where the bones of John the Baptist were supposedly buried, and visits in the cool shade with the boys in the orphanage had put her in a good mood.[16] But a new edict from the Turkish Superintendent of Education suddenly made her job more difficult. Foreign schools could only be established "if there are enough of their own nationality to make such schools necessary." Under a Special School Law, "education can be continued in the orphanages which are opened by the Near East Relief, if formal permission shall have been granted in the sake of a person of Turkish citizenship."[17] Susan scrambled to obtain said permission, and kept her schools open. At the same time, because the refugees were never-ending, she supervised the opening of more schools in the mountains. "Repairs and white-washing have been going on this past week," she wrote to her brother, John. "Our old buildings were badly damaged during the war and it requires a long time to get them restored. I'm trying to fix up a new kitchen now after a year of smoke and consequent distress. One of our walls is about to fall down and we shall have to pull it down and re-build it."[18]

Foreigners suddenly had to pay new taxes, too. "They have made us pay taxes on all our property—the schools and hospital and everything—though such property belonging to native people is free from tax, and we never had to pay on them before," she said. When the relief workers insisted on waiting for word from NER headquarters before they complied, the government seized the unit's automobile and held it until the taxes were paid. Even then, they did not allow the auto to be released. They told the workers it would be delivered later. "We said we would wait, if that was the order, but that we would stay in the car," Susan said. "We sat there as long as we could, till about ten o'clock. They finally dragged us down from the seat, one by one, and put us into a wagon, and sent us home with two mounted men to guard us. Just imagine your sister being laid hands on in such fashion! We Americans have never been treated with such disrespect and discourtesy here before!"[19]

By September they had more work, but fewer workers. It was so difficult and dangerous to travel that replacements were hard to come by. They were hoping the Irwins would return in the fall, but it seemed unlikely. Several workers were scheduled to leave in the next few months. In addition to overseeing the orphanages, Stella was going to take on the supervision of the Boys' Industrial School, which had grown to include a factory.[20] "Putting up supplies of food for winter is one big task here. That is keeping us busy at present," Susan said. "I am supposed to be general manager of the commissary to decide what is needed and how much for all the orphanages and institutions. This week I plan to open most of our schools and get things going if possible." Police were searching all visitors entering the compound. People in Talas without proper papers were arrested and often detained a day or two before being sent back to their villages. She told her brother, "It is no pleasant place to be in now."[21]

~ ~ ~

Two significant things happened in the last months of 1920 that had dire consequences for everyone in the region: Negotiations between the Nationalists and the Bolsheviks reached a standstill, and King Alexander of Greece was bitten by a monkey.

The Bolsheviks had been supplying the Nationalists with arms since late 1919, and with gold bullion since May.[22] But they were currently disagreeing about the land ceded to Armenia in the Treaty of Sevres. The Nationalists wanted it back, and the Bolsheviks did not want to jeopardize their relationship with the Dashnak government of Armenia. At the end of September, sensing the Bolsheviks did not care about the town of Sarikamish and the Allies would not interfere, the Nationalist army, led by Kazim Karabekir, faced weak Armenian resistance and easily captured it.[23] In late October, they captured Kars. By mid-November, when they were about to enter Alexandropol, the Armenian army admitted defeat. On December 2 they signed a treaty delineating the border between Turkey and Armenia. Van, Bitlis, Kars, and Mount Ararat now belonged to Turkey.[24] On the same day, with the Red Army hovering in Azerbaijan, Armenia and Russia signed a treaty. The democratic Republic of Armenia ceased to exist. It was now the Armenian Soviet Socialist Republic.[25]

On September 30 King Alexander was bitten by his pet monkey. Infection set in. Three weeks later he was dead. Constantine, his pro-German father, returned to the throne. At the same time, the Greek general elections ousted Venizelos and brought in Demetrios Gounaris, who was anti-British. France and Italy promptly withdrew their support of Greece, "and, by implication, from the Treaty of Sevres." In early 1921 the Nationalists and the Soviets resumed their negotiations. Britain, which had been talking with the Nationalists about a prisoner exchange, was anxious to detach the Turks from their growing ties with Soviet Russia. Thus, within a few short months, Britain, France and Italy moved closer to recognizing the Nationalists as the new government of Turkey.[26]

The *Missionary Herald* wondered how much freedom to act the missionaries and relief workers would have in the new regime. We must recognize that Americans will be somewhat discounted on account of our failure "to do our bit" over there, and also in view of the fact that other nationalities, more or less rivals of ours in business and diplomacy, will be in the ascendency. To what extent we shall have an open door in business and in mission activities, and in other ways, is as yet an exceedingly difficult question.[27]

~ ~ ~

In the late spring, Edward Martin had taken a group of boys, a farmer, tools, six oxen, and a Case tractor to the 1,600-year-old Armenian monastery in Evkere, and started a farm. By June they had cultivated 35 acres. By the late summer the terraces below the monastery were lush "with the green of two thousand fruit and nut trees." In the fall they harvested the hay, vegetables and grain crops, to provide the orphanages with food for the winter. It had provided employment for several dozen people, too.[28]

But more aid was needed. This time the refugees were Greek. There had been widespread looting of Greek homes north of Kaisarieh. Joseph had spoken to the Greek Bishop of Zinjidery. "It seems that many wealthy Greeks in Yozgat have been reduced to the condition of refugees," he said. "Those who were formerly in need of relief are even more miserable." Near East Relief funds helped their immediate needs, but "much more will be required to carry the Yozgat Greeks through the winter, since they are said to have not even their bedding left."[29]

In September, Stella, Joseph, Edward and a new relief worker, Miss Schaefer, obtained permission to travel southwest 86 miles to Nigdeh to inspect a prisoner-of-war camp. There were 598 French soldiers and officers from Algeria, and two British officers. Though the conditions were crowded, the prisoners were allowed to bathe and wash their clothes in the local stream, and they had a decent amount of food to eat. Those who had money could buy sundries from the camp's canteen. Their only complaint was a lack of warm clothing or any bedding. Joseph obtained permission to carry "censored mail and small packages" to and from the prisoners, and arranged for the NER to receive money from their families, which he would forward. "I'm glad to report that, in our judgement, the prisoners have been very well looked after by the military," he said. "They have been under the care of high-principled and humane men."[30]

Meanwhile, Charles Gannaway, with the help of his wife, had started an eye clinic in Talas. In the first six days he examined 867 patients and gave 2,655 treatments for trachoma, conjunctivitis, and too many corneal ulcers for his liking. "What might be considered, under ordinary circumstances, a somewhat trivial trouble," he said, "under the prevailing conditions of poor hygiene and low resistance, passes from bad to worse, until a small superficial ulcer in the beginning becomes a deep slough, the only result of which can be partial or even total blindness."[31] In addition to the eye clinic, the hospital and medical clinics in Talas and Cesarea, he and his staff regularly handled more than 1,000 cases per month.[32] The Talas hospital was assessed by the NER Medical Director "as one of the most important institutions in central Anatolia." Which is why it was such a tremendous loss when it burned to the ground in October.[33]

No one was sure how the fire started, but Charles, Rachel and Blanche supervised an emergency evacuation. All the patients were moved to safety. Sadly though, in trying to save some of the medical equipment, two of the native staff died of smoke inhalation. Only one-third of the portable equipment was saved. A makeshift hospital was created in one of the buildings in the Talas compound, and work went on as usual. But it was a big blow to everyone.[34] The following month, Charles was requisitioned by NER Beirut, and the hospital was once again without an American doctor. He did, however, teach the native doctor his special eye treatments before he left.[35]

Another worker left the interior, but not by his own choice. Harry Riggs was evicted from Harpoot on orders from the Nationalists. He was accused of being "partial to the Armenians," "unfriendly to the Turks," and "too friendly with the Kurds, who are disloyal to the Turkish government." He suspected the real reason was that a certain Turk was a close friend of the vali. The man had announced that he would kill Harry some day for "rescuing" his Armenian "wife" who was refusing to return to him. When Harry arrived in Constantinople, he paid a visit to the American High Commissioner. "I was rather taken aback to find that Admiral Bristol took the validity of these charges for granted, and read me quite a lecture on the necessity of adjusting our course of action to the present political situation." It seemed that Bristol would not let anything interfere with his goal of having good relations with the Turks to protect American business interests in the region.[36]

The Americans in Talas, ten in all, had plans to celebrate Thanksgiving on the last Thursday of November, as was the new custom. They had been feeling a bit lonely. No workers were expected to arrive during the winter,[37] and no visits with their compatriots at other stations were possible, because, by then, the Nationalist government had forbidden "all travel by foreigners."[38] The mail was not getting through either, so there

Harpoot missionary compound before 1915. SOURCE: Private collection.

was no news from home.[39] Just as they were about to sit down to dinner, about 50 gendarmes arrived at the door. "They searched every building from attic to cellar," said Susan. "We were kept busy till nearly midnight, and the roast turkey and pumpkin pies were left to get cold on the table." One officer opened a drawer and discovered a box of old springs-belts used to open and close windows that had no weights. "The man evidently thought they were cartridges. He was greatly excited and ran to call the chief official. A whole troop of men came rushing up to the attic to see the terrible thing we Americans had hidden there." Two mechanisms for closing doors quietly were thought to be bombs. "They also found a lot of old apparatus that had been used before the war in the Physics classes," she said. "Some broken electrical batteries and wire—a pile of junk, as anyone could see. Well, they packed it all up and took it to the government. They thought it was a radio outfit!"[40]

Susan recalled the anxiety of that night. "I remember eating a chunk of coarse bread after dark, while I stood in the Girls' School for a few minutes to quiet the fears of the teachers and pupils, who naturally remembered the terrible experiences of former years when some of them had been carried off." She had had a few anxious moments herself. As soon as she realized the gendarmes were going to search the entire compound, she slipped up to her room to retrieve the cartridges she had picked up in Baku as a souvenir. All evening she carried them around in her pocket, hoping she would not be subjected to a body search. "I decided that it was time to get

251

rid of them," she said. She later gave them to Edward Martin, who conveniently "lost" them in the vineyard.[41]

~ ~ ~

"With the exception of Constantinople and Smyrna, the whole country has been in upheaval," the American Board declared in 1921. It was true. Harry Riggs had been forced to leave Harpoot, and the Nationalists were trying to evict Drs. Ruth Parmelee and Mark Ward as well.[42] In Marsovan, they had searched the Pontus Club, a Greek literary society at Anatolia College. They suspected the members were connected to a Greek revolutionary group in Samsoun. Although they found no weapons,[43] they arrested four teachers and two students on political charges. After their court martial, the mutesarrif from Amasia said that, because it had been proven the college "sheltered political propaganda," he was closing the college, the girls' school, and the hospital. "All Americans must leave the city, and the country, except two, who would be permitted to remain and guard the property." In all, 29 workers were deported,[44] under the authority of Nationalist General Nureddin, a man who despised missionaries.[45] Susan's colleagues from Alexandropol, Ruth and Carl Compton, elected to stay.[46]

The Allies had been meeting with representatives of the Ottoman government and the Nationalists in London to talk about revising the Treaty of Sevres. Neither the Turks nor the Greeks would give an inch from their positions over land claims. The British would only agree to exchange prisoners with the Nationalists. Though the French had taken Aintab in February, both they and the Italians agreed to withdraw from Turkish territory within the year.[47]

Rumours of an immediate French withdrawal and an imminent attack on Aintab by the Nationalists caused panic throughout Cilicia. People feared another massacre. Those who had enough money to leave— Armenians and Turks alike—left.[48] Of course, knowing the withdrawal was scheduled for November, the Nationalists did not attack. But in the west, the war with Greece intensified.

Lloyd George had told the Greek leaders "that if 'they felt impelled to attack Kemal's forces, he would not stand in their way.' The Greek government took this as permission to resume the war, and launched a new offensive on March 23."[49] However, when asked to lead an offensive, General Ioannis Metaxas had refused. It was a war the Greek military commander did not believe in. "They mean to fight for their freedom and independence," he said of the Nationalists. "They realize that Asia Minor is their country and that we are invaders. For them, for their national feelings, the historical rights on which we base our claims have no influence. Whether they are right or wrong is another question. What matters is how they feel."[50] When the Greek army fought at the village of Inonu near Eskishehir, they lost to the Nationalists[51]—at least, temporarily.

~ ~ ~

On March 15, 1921 Talat Pasha was assassinated in Berlin.[52] The news that he had been shot in the street by an Armenian was shocking, but not surprising. He had been tried and convicted of crimes against humanity, but had escaped a legal execution. Before the end of the war, he had accepted full responsibility for the deportations and massacres, and had said, "I absolutely don't regret my deed."[53]

The former Ottoman leader had always anticipated a violent death. "I do not expect to die in my bed," he once told Henry Morgenthau.[54] Enver was in Moscow when he heard the news. He showed no emotion, saying only, "His time had come."[55]

~ ~ ~

For five months no one had heard a word from the Talas unit. Finally "Annie Allen made a six-day journey in mid-winter from Konia to bring the Talas workers their mail and to take their letters back to a place where they could be posted." Everyone was well, but "working to the limit of time and strength." They were desperately hoping for new recruits in the spring. "The greater burden rests on the few Americans in our unit," Susan reported to the Woman's Board. Rachel and Edward, and Blanche and Joseph would soon be going to the United States to get married. "That will leave us in a bad situation. They have all stayed long over time as it is, to fill the great need here. They have been just splendid about it." The loss of the hospital had been hard, but so too was the loss of the doctor. "There is not a doctor of any kind in Talas, and no one we can call, even in an emergency." Due to the increase in refugees, the number of orphans in their district had grown to 4,000, with 2,000 of them to be directly cared for by the relief workers. "Under these circumstances," said Susan, "you can realize what a burden of responsibility has rested on our nurses. When the two nurses leave, the first of April, Theda Phelps will be the only medical person left. She has supervision of a large orphanage and a woman's [rescue] home, but will have to take up the nursing when the others leave."[56]

The schools continued, and there was a new kindergarten in Talas, sponsored by the Woman's Board. Several churches in the region were still holding services, but it was not easy. "In Yozgat, our one ordained pastor left in this field preaches to 500 or 600, besides being the head of an orphanage with over five hundred children." And, with the exception of one Bible woman, "Clara Richmond is absolutely all that Cesarea has in the way of a missionary preacher, Sunday school worker or leader in Christian work of any kind. You may imagine what a difficult situation we are in."[57]

Missing from the report were Susan's complaints about the inability to buy stockings or a fountain pen. Relief worker John Warye, who had been with the Talas unit for a year and a half, recently returned to the States and sent a note to Susan's sister. He had found a pen in Samsoun for Susan, and had sent it back to Talas with the NER supply truck. "I will be very glad to do anything for you in return for the kindness and assistance she gave me in every way while on the field," he wrote. "There is no need to worry. The folks there are afraid that their friends at home are worrying."[58] It was a natural assumption.

25

A Greek Tragedy

Four rites of passage occurred in the summer and fall of 1921 for those associated with the Talas team. The first was the celebration of Mary Graffam's 50th birthday. Friends from far and wide went to Sivas to pay their respects. Joining the festivities were Dr. and Mrs. Talboy who were on their way to join the NER unit in Talas. One of the highlights of the party was a speech by a representative of the local Armenian community. He thanked Mary "for befriending them and helping them for twenty years, sharing their troubles, and in fact sharing her life with them. As a token of their love for her, they presented a little bag containing 50 Turkish gold pounds." Mary was deeply touched, knowing what a sacrifice it was for them "to collect the money at the present time, when even the wealthiest families are poor." She told them it was not necessary to have given her a token of their love; she knew it and felt the same for them.[1]

The second was Mary's untimely death. Not long after her birthday celebration, she discovered a lump in her breast. After six weeks of observation, she underwent surgery to remove it. She came through the operation fine, but died of fever and complications eight days later. Lillian Cole Sewny had been waiting in Samsoun for permission to travel back to Sivas, and ended up arriving two days after Mary was laid to rest. "I know she was heart-broken not to be here," said their colleague, Nina Rice. "It was a touching funeral, attended by crowds of poor people and orphans, and by government officials and a military escort. The people feel themselves sheep without a shepherd, and we have much to do to keep up their morale."[2]

The other two events were much happier. Blanche and Joseph sailed on the SS *Acropolis*, arriving at Ellis Island, New York on June 25. They married shortly thereafter, and Joseph took a temporary job in NER's New York Office.[3] Edward and Rachel spent the summer in Constantinople and did not arrive in the United States until October. They were married in November in the Presbyterian Church in Rachel's hometown of Little Britain, New York. The neighbourhood had decorated the pulpit with ferns and chrysanthemums. Blanche—now Mrs. Beach—was the matron of honour. The local newspaper reported all the glorious details: "The bride entered on the arm of her brother, Everett. She wore a gown of white satin and georgette, and carried a shower bouquet of white roses and lilies of the valley. Her veil was caught by a band of orange blossoms. Her only ornament was the gift of the groom, a handsome aquamarine set in a breast pin of green gold. The stone had come into the hands of an American merchant of Constantinople from a Russian refugee. The ceremony was performed by the bride's father, the Rev. J. Scott King, pastor of the church, assisted by the best man, Rev. Joseph W. Beach." After a brief honeymoon to visit Edward's family in Peshtigo, Wisconsin,[4] the Martins were going to Derindje, where Edward would become the Director of the Warehouses.[5] The Talas team would miss them, but could hardly wait to see Blanche and Joseph once again.

~ ~ ~

James Barton was angry. As the Chairman of Near East Relief, he had first-hand knowledge of the current political landscape. In an editorial for the *Missionary Herald* in May 1921, he accused international leaders, their cabinets, and their foreign and war offices of being morally bankrupt. "Expediency seems to dominate everything, while each country aims at securing for itself, of advantage of acquisition, the most possible," he wrote. "The official attitude of all the countries is undisguised selfishness." He recognized that European armies were "physically exhausted," European currency was discounted so much that foreign trade was "almost prohibited," and taxation was "paralyzing," but that trust between nations was gone, too, even regarding signed agreements. "Idealism has suffered shipwreck as the nations drift apart into secret intrigue." He lambasted France for "secretly negotiating with Mustapha Kemal" regarding Cilicia on the one hand, while discussing the Treaty of Sevres at the conference table on the other hand. "Italy had been selling arms and munitions to Kemal," he said, "which he was using against the French in Cilicia, the Greeks in Anatolia, and the Armenians in Armenia." Britain did not have the resources to restrain the Nationalists' "unbridled ambitions," nor protect the Armenians and Assyrians in Turkey, Western Persia, and Mesopotamia.[6]

Barton did not spare words for his own country or its new president. Warren G. Harding had been elected on a platform of opposition to the League of Nations and American membership in it.[7] Barton believed there was only one answer to halt the "disruption and disorder" in Turkey. "This is one of the most tragic situations confronting the world today, and, so far as one can see, there is no power in Europe or in Asia to change it for the better," he stated. "In talking with representatives of these countries and governments, it was pathetic to witness their conviction that, if America only would, she could save the day."[8] As Barton saw it, American "disinterestedness" and "sense of justice" would be recognized, accepted, and "in due time, followed," thus lifting "the standard of Christian idealism."

Unlike President Wilson, however, President Harding did not see Christianity as part of US foreign policy, and held a protectionist attitude regarding American interests, particularly American commercial interests.[9] He publically supported the work of Near East Relief,[10] but that is as far as it went.

~ ~ ~

From the end of March the western Turkish countryside was filled with fire and brimstone as the Greek and Nationalist armies fought each other, brigands went on killing and looting sprees, and civilians on both sides got involved in the animosity. Mabel Elliott, who had survived the siege of Marash, was now the Director of the NER medical work in Ismid, Derindje and Bardezag. She continued her diary. On April 9, she noted, "We heard the big guns booming all day yesterday, last night and to-day. . . . It was a sight to see the fires burning last night. We counted seven villages burning all about Bardezag, and for three days the refugees from these villages have been pouring in. At least two thousand new refugees are here."[11]

Nursing instructor Grisell McLaren had worked at the Van mission in 1915, and was therefore understandably bitter about the fighting that was all around her in Ismid. "The Nationalists are about their usual business of destruction and murder," she wrote on April 13. "The Greeks have promised safe conduct for all Christians should there be trouble here. The Turks are said to have threatened to set fire to the Christian quarter, but since about 100 of them have been arrested, there seems to be no further talk. Here we sit at the foot of a smoldering volcano, and no one knows when it will pour its fire upon us."[12]

Arnold Toynbee of the British Foreign Office had been in the peninsula between Yalova and Gemlik with his wife, and witnessed atrocities committed against Turks. "We not only obtained abundant material evidence in the shape of burnt and plundered houses, recent corpses, and terror-stricken survivors. We witnessed robbery by Greek civilians and arson by Greek soldiers in uniform in the act of perpetration. . . . My strongest impression during this horrible experience was of something inhuman both in the bloodthirstiness of the hunters and in the terror of the hunted."[13]

In May an inter-Allied commission conducted enquiries into "excesses committed against the Turkish population" in the Yalova and Gemlik regions, "a hilly peninsula containing about forty villages, thirty-five of which were exclusively Turkish." They acknowledged an "age-long hatred existing between the various races," exacerbated by the influx of about 5,600 refugees: 2,000 Armenians "who suffered greatly at the hands of the Turks during the war," and 3,600 Greeks "many of whom witnessed the atrocities committed by the Nationalists." Even so, they did not believe the increase of refugees was "the determining factor of their destruction on so general and rapid a scale." After an extensive investigation, the commission made two conclusions: There was "a systematic plan of destruction of Turkish villages and extinction of the Muslim population," and that this plan was carried out by brigands of Greeks and Armenians, which appeared "to operate under Greek instructions, and sometimes even with the assistance of detachments of regular troops." The report contained gruesome details of the burning, looting, killing and mutilations, so it is not surprising that the commission was "of opinion that the atrocities reported against Christians on the one hand, and Muslims on the other, are unworthy of a civilised government, and that in the region occupied by the Greek army, the Greek authorities, who are alone in authority there, are responsible, and, in the region under the Nationalist regime, the Turkish authorities" were responsible.[14]

On June 22 the Greek government "replied with a polite refusal" to an Allied offer of mediation.[15] Less than a week later, after many months of occupation, the Greek army left Ismid. "The Greeks had kept their threat and were burning the city behind them as they evacuated," said Sophie Holt, director of the Nicomedia Girls' Orphanage. "Practically all the orphanage force decided to stay on and share the fate of the orphans, whatever that might be." For two nights the children slept in their clothes, ready to go at a moment's notice. Everywhere Sophie looked, she saw pandemonium. Fortunately, not all of the Turkish section was burned. "Every Christian in the town had departed, many leaving all their household and personal goods on the shore, being unable to take anything with them at the last moment." The American navy sent an officer and three sailors to the orphanage to help protect it. When the Nationalist soldiers arrived, "they came in without massacring the very few who failed to escape." But as Sophie wrote her report of the incident, she added, "At the present moment there is a group of men in the road, looking up at the building and planning to rob us of the few cattle we have here. . . . Everything is in confusion, with everything to be done at once. We are trying to put things back into their normal order."[16]

The Greek army went from Ismid to Eskishehir and Afion Kara Hissar to reinforce troops already there. They fought the Nationalists for a month and finally won. The Nationalist army retreated as far as the Sakarya river, about 50 miles southwest of Angora. Mustafa Kemal took command and began to prepare for a defence of a lifetime. As General Metaxas had said, "They mean to fight for their freedom and independence. Asia Minor is their country and we are invaders." Kemal requisitioned 40% of food, cloth, horses and farm animals from local inhabitants, and gathered all the arms, munitions and recruits he could muster. His troops dug trenches high in the ridges and bare hills of the Anatolian steppes. By mid-August the Nationalists had the high ground advantage. Still, it took two weeks of intense fighting for them to win the battle. When the Greeks began a weary retreat westward in mid-September, they were not followed. Both sides were exhausted. For almost a year afterward, the Eskishehir-Afion Kara Hissar line remained static.[17]

But there were still pockets of fighting in the countryside, and an especially horrible anti-Greek campaign that had started in the northeast. Of all the brigands that had been part of the Special Organization, the one led by Topal Osman had been the worst. He was the leader of one of the squadrons that had drowned en masse thousands of Armenians in the Black Sea five years before.[18] He was known for his brutality—certainly against Armenians, but also against any Turks who opposed him. After the war, "he had been used to round up deserters, some of whom he enlisted in his band."[19] Now Topal Osman was working for the Nationalists, and began to raze the Greek villages in the Pontic region near Samsoun, deporting and massacring at will.[20]

An NER worker travelled across Anatolia at that time. "For 120 miles, we passed one unbroken stream of humanity: squads of recruits or prisoners, caravans of guns, ammunition or food supplies; but for the most part, refugees or deportees—poor, suffering, ragged women, old men and little children, and countless babes in arms; crawling and struggling across the blistering plains, and on and over endless mountain ranges and down again to miles and more miles of desert. It is all the same story of repetition of the worst conditions in 1915."[21]

Ethel Thompson from Boston joined the NER in August, and was shocked by similar scenes. "Dead bodies of those who had dropped during the hard tramp were lying by the roadside. Vultures had eaten parts of the flesh, so that in most cases merely skeletons remained," she said. "Upon arriving in Harpoot, we entered a city full of starving, sick, wretched human wrecks—Greek women, children, and men. These people were trying to make soup of grass, and considered themselves fortunate when they could secure a sheep's ear to aid it, the ear being the only part of the

Helen and James Talboy, and Annette Munro. SOURCE: US Passport Applications.

animal thrown away in Anatolia. The Turks had given them no food on the 500-mile trip from Samsoun."[22]

That trip, under the blistering sun, went through Cesarea, Talas and Sivas. One group had left Samsoun 14,000 strong. "When they reached us, there were just three hundred of them, mostly sick and diseased," said Helen Talboy, wife of the new Talas doctor. "Where they were going they scarcely knew. They were just stubbornly, courageously, keeping moving in the hope that somewhere, sometime, they would find a place where they could settle down in peace."[23] Though the NER workers gave them food and water, there was a limit to what these poor people could carry. "It would have been more humane to give them a bullet than bread, because death would come in any case sooner or later," Ethel said bitterly.[24] The devastation went on and on and on.

～ ～ ～

"Typhus came to Cesarea with the refugees who are constantly entering the city," said Dr. James Talboy. The increase in sickness made it necessary to rent space outside the compound, and open a 25-bed annex hospital. They also pitched tents for tuberculosis and favus patients, and a separate tent for suspected contagions. Altogether there were 100 beds. "Although the Near East Relief workers provide hot baths and clean underwear for the refugees upon entering, it has been impossible to keep away typhus."[25] The medical staff, which included a new American nurse, Annette Munro, and several native nurses, continued to operate the eye clinic that Charles Gannaway started. It ran three days a week and averaged 100 treatments each day. It had such a good reputation that people came, often on foot, from more than a hundred miles away, some making a six-day journey to get there. The doctor and nurses worked long hours, sometimes into the night. "However, it was often impossible to finish a clinic," said Annette. "Crowds had to be sent away with tickets to come again on the next clinic day. Camping outside the gate and waiting a day to obtain a ticket did not discourage these people in their hope of receiving treatments from the American doctor."[26]

Though Helen Talboy had gone to Talas as, she joked, "excess baggage", she was promptly put to work, too. "My official duty, besides accompanying my husband, was as general housekeeper for the orphanage at Talas," she said. "Being married, it was taken for granted that I could keep house. It just happened that was the one thing I had never done. I was a bit daunted. Much more daunted by that prospect in fact, than by the news that I would be marooned in the heart of Turkey with a war creeping up on all sides of me." The orphanages in Talas and Cesarea now cared for 2,400 "pitiful youngsters." "Well, I learned how to keep house. At least I think I did. I never was entirely certain that the number of other duties also urged upon me was a sign of my efficiency at housekeeping or a suggestion in other lines of endeavor. At any rate, I did them all, whatever was asked, and it's surprising how much you can learn if you have the inspiration."[27]

Helen also helped with the industrial work, and was impressed with the ultimate goal of making people self-supporting. "Unfortunately we could give work to only the merest few," she said. "We could never give work to one woman for more than two days a week. We could employ no woman who had a husband—despite the fact that it might be utterly impossible for him to get work—and we rarely took one who didn't have children to look after. For her two days' work we paid her twenty piasters, which at the present rate of exchange is just about 12 cents. And they were the lucky women!" She was very concerned by the "excessive export duty" of 60%, which "was putting a stop to what work we could give them. Such destitution as exists there is almost inconceivable." Within six months, the stress was too much for Helen. She became so ill, she was ordered to go home. "It was not until she had parted with thirty-six pounds, however, that she consented to leave."[28]

Annette Munro left Talas around the same time. She ended her final report by saying, "I felt as if I had been working in that compound for at least a year, instead of six months, as we had taken care of so many in that short length of time."[29]

Women in Talas busy with the industrious work of quiltmaking. SOURCE: Susan Wealthy Orvis Papers.

With James and Helen's departure in mid-September, once again Talas was without a doctor. Susan took the opportunity to send a letter with them to her brother. She filled him in on the unit's workload, and hers in particular. "It is a big business and requires all the time and energy I have to keep things going," she said. "Do not be anxious about us here, only don't forget me when there is such a long silence. I think of you and of all the family circle and look forward to seeing you someday." She signed off with "I am glad to be so well and happy in the work. Yours with love, Susan W. Orvis."[30]

NER Turkey was always trying to fill positions with new recruits or by moving people around to address the greatest need. In Joseph's absence, Barton Plimpton was appointed Director of the Talas unit. But the team was saddened to lose Theda. She had been a lifesaver—literally—for all of them. Apparently Sivas needed her more.[31]

~ ~ ~

In November, the long-feared evacuation of Cilicia by the French became official. They would withdraw from the region by January 5, 1922, handing over its administration to the Nationalists. "One thought,

New relief workers to Talas: Albert and Elsie Dewey and their baby; Barton Plimpton; and Henry Murphy. SOURCE: US Passport Applications.

and one only, seemed to take possession of the whole Christian population—to leave the country, sacrifice *every* thing, but get away," *The Orient* reported. "In Adana merchants quietly packed up their goods and shipped them out of the country. Household furniture was sold at any price . . . Streams of humanity poured down to Mersine. . . . Soon thousands of people were camping in the streets of Mersine. Many had started with only a few liras, and almost immediately began to feel the pinch of poverty. Heavy rains and black smallpox added to the distress. The Mission, Near East and YWCA came to their aid, as far as possible, with shelter, free clinic, soup kitchen and milk for babies."[32]

A delegation of Armenians, Syrians, Chaldeans, Greeks, Turkish, and Fellahins appealed to the French for "effective protection, or permission and facilities, to emigrate en masse." They represented approximately 100,000 Christians and Muslims in the Adana district who felt themselves in grave danger by the withdrawal. Given the events of the past six years, the Christians' fears were understandable. Armenians, in particular, felt threatened. A recent issue of *Yeni Adana*, published in Bozanti, the Nationalist "capital" of the Adana vilayet, contained an article, printed entirely in crimson red ink, that read, "We hear of preparations by the Armenians to emigrate. Have patience. When we come, we will have accounts to settle, after which you may think of emigration." Muslims who had been loyal to the French also had reason to fear for their safety; they were seen as traitors by Nationalist supporters.[33]

An anonymous American described the situation: "This killing of hope, this absence of confidence, this dread of revengeful action, this threatening attitude, this desperation of the thousands of non-Muslims, this stagnation of all business, is causing a paralysis that is of the very gravest import. It is not that we anticipate massacre on the arrival of the Nationalist forces. The danger that threatens is the absolute impossibility for these communities to live in any sort of confidence and tranquillity under the present circumstances without the presence of a paramount power that would hold the balance fairly even."[34]

The result of the withdrawal was a desperate and massive migration. By mid-January more than 20,000 Armenian refugees entered Beirut. Not all stayed as some continued to Damascus, Aleppo and other cities. "For a time the authorities arranged a camp for them in the swamps outside the city. As rains were then falling their hardest, the lot of the poor people was indescribable. The docks were piled fifteen feet high with bundles of luggage, soaking full of rain. People who had left baggage to seek shelter, often in distant parts of the city, returned to find the baggage stolen."[35]

Thousands of Greeks poured onto steamers headed for Smyrna. Dana Getchell, who had been expelled from Marsovan, was now heading the NER unit there. "The Greek Government is not giving wholesale permission for the refugees to land here," he reported. "Our committee began its work very cautiously, trying to get refugees off from the steamers." He had to obtain special permission for relief workers to board the ships and distribute food. "But O, the suffering and the heartache of it all! One steamer came into the harbor, and the two thousand on board were crying for bread and water! For fourteen days this crowd had not eaten a hot meal, and for two days they had not eaten even bread or had a drink of water." He estimated that 20,000 people had passed through the Smyrna harbour. Some were allowed to land at Mytelene or other islands, some at Cyprus and Piraeus, and some went on to Constantinople. "What is to be the end?" he lamented. "We need relief money as never before, and yet we learn that America is tired of hearing the cries of suffering Armenia!"[36]

26

Prelude to a Denouement

The Near East Relief was indeed struggling to raise funds for the ever-increasing need, and an unfortunate setback the previous year had not helped. Despite raising hundreds of thousands of dollars with the book and tour of the film, *Ravished Armenia*, the NER received some peripherally bad publicity when Aurora Mardiganian sued her guardian for money she was owed. After her breakdown over the trauma of re-living her terrible experiences for the film, her guardian, Eleanor Brown Gates, and Henry Gates had installed her in a convent school and hired imposters to pose as Aurora for the advertised personal appearances at the film's showings. Almost a year later, Aurora "escaped" from the convent and contacted Laura Low Harriman for help. She met Mrs. Oliver Harriman when the high society matron co-hosted the 1919 New York premiere of the film and ACASR benefit. Details of the arrangements with Gates came out in February 1921 in New York Surrogate's Court. Aurora had been paid $15 per week as the leading actress, but had also been paid $7,000 for the film, though she had not personally received the sum. Though Henry Gates had bought her story for $50, he had sold it to International Copyright Bureau for $700, with Aurora to be paid 10% royalties on the book sales. Gates and his wife testified that there was only $195 left in Aurora's account because she had lived so luxuriously in Hollywood, with "a chauffeur, nurse, housemaid, and messenger." In fact, he claimed, he had paid an additional $6,000 of her expenses from his personal account. The courts found in favour of Aurora and eventually awarded her $5,000.[1] But it was yet another exploitation she had been subjected to in her young life.

Ravished Armenia was not the only film produced for NER fundraising. *Alice in Hungerland*, modelled on Lewis Carroll's famous tale, told the story of an American girl whose father was a relief worker in the Near East. The adventures this Alice had included stowing away on a boat laden with NER supplies, finding her father in Constantinople, and accompanying him to "Hungerland." There she saw incongruous sites: little children who were "parentless, homeless, ragged, starving and ill," some "lying dead in the street for want of actual food," and others "living in caves with dogs because there was no roof in all that desolate land to shelter them." In sharp contrast, she also wandered through the gates of an NER orphanage to find "hundreds of healthy children at long tables, eating," and others in "classrooms and workshops, industrious and happy." But when she learned how much flour it took to make enough bread for the thousands of needy orphans, and how one bowl of food provided nourishment for only one day, she understood that more was needed. "For all America's generosity, there was not enough to go 'round."[2] The message was clear: Give more.

Child star Jackie Coogan lent his name and effort to the cause. SOURCE: Lewis Wickes Hine, photographer, 1924, US Library of Congress.

In March Edwin M. Bulkley, the new chairman of the NER's executive committee, announced the launching of a special appeal. Though he mentioned the Chaldeans in southern Persia, the main focus was on saving Armenians, not just from starvation alone, "but starvation coming after six years' destruction, wrought by a war that has never ended, that today is not ended. It is starvation following pestilence, hand in hand with death from exposure, from violence or from disease."[3] This innovative appeal from the Lenten Sacrifice Committee was in the form of a 60-coupon booklet. Each $1 coupon purchased "will feed one of the wards of America for a week; a page of coupons will feed a child for a month; the entire book valued at sixty dollars, will cover a full year."[4] President and Mrs. Harding, and Massachusetts Senator Henry Cabot Lodge bought a whole booklet each to demonstrate their support.[5] Mr. Bulkley reiterated NER's message: "We shall see an entire nation disappear from the face of the earth before our eyes if we withhold our hand now when the call comes to us *to save by giving*, or by inaction, to condemn to death."[6]

Hollywood was a very young industry, but celebrity endorsements were beginning to influence the public's habits. Ever since Jackie Coogan had played in "The Kid" opposite the world's most famous actor, Charlie Chaplin, he became the world's most famous child actor. NER deftly turned the "infant phenom" into a philanthropist by getting him to endorse "Bundle Day," a national used clothing drive. "There are altogether too many clothes in this house," said Jackie to his father in the publicity materials. He and dozens of other (adult) celebrities donated "carloads" of clothing, which was shipped by rail to NER warehouses in New York, the freight charges being donated by the railroads.[7]

Near East Relief tried many creative ways to raise public awareness and money for the humanitarian effort. Service clubs pledged their support;[8] the American Radio Relay League, which had 6,000 wireless operators throughout the United States and Canada in its membership, broadcast bulletins to publicize NER's campaigns;[9] and each of the 26 ministers who attended the Missouri Methodist Episcopal Conference pledged to support an Armenian orphan for a year on behalf of his church.[10] But after six and a half years of intense fundraising, the North American public was once again experiencing donor fatigue. Perhaps it was time to intensify efforts overseas.

In January 1922, Dr. Wirt—he of the sanitary engineering fame— embarked on a world tour on behalf of NER. He had sold his ancestral home for the cause,[11] and as a Congregational minister had become a gifted speaker. He was the perfect man to be NER's International Commissioner. The tour took him to Hawaii, Japan, China, New Zealand, Australia, the Philippines and Korea, among other places. Smaller groups in these countries had already been contributing, but Wirt's efforts raised hundreds of thousands of dollars.[12] In addition to money, by September Australians had also sent their first shipment of relief supplies, including canned milk, flour, and leather and woollen goods, on a 8,700-mile journey to the Near East. His stated mission was "to 'forge a chain of mercy' from one end of the world to the other." It seemed he succeeded.[13]

~ ~ ~

By Christmas 1921 the Talas unit finally had another doctor: V. W. M. (Valentine William Murray) Wright.[14] Due to government regulations, he was not supposed to practise medicine until the trunk with his diplomas arrived as proof he was a real doctor. Talas also had an American nurse with the return of Lillian Cole Sewny. She had switched places with Theda, who was now in Sivas, and everyone was happy to have her back. In the month of December alone, the Talas medical team performed what seemed like an enormous number of miracles: 953 surgeries, 750 procedures and 1,205 eye treatments. The clinic in Cesarea dealt with 1,393 cases, and additional 193 in home visits. Another smaller team in

Evkere performed 75 surgeries and 121 procedures, and treated 206 eye problems. "The patients treated at these clinics are the refugees and poor of all nationalities in the Kaisarieh district," said Lillian. "An epidemic of typhus fever broke out in the Evkere orphanage, and two experienced nurses were sent from the Talas hospital to take charge of the cases. They were able to stop the disease from spreading, and it is hoped that it will soon be stamped out."[15]

Dr. Wright still found time during the month to repair the hospital's sterilizer and X-ray machine, and build a delouser.[16] Scabies had been raging in the orphanages, and they had to run the delouser often to deal with the infestation. Because of the war and the attacks on the Pontic Greeks, there was enormous pressure on the Talas unit. "There is a great need for surgical and medical work," said Lillian. "It is hard not to have enough space. Our quarters at present are so limited that by squeezing I can only take in fifty patients." The Director told her he might be able to free one of the school buildings to use for the hospital, and "double up the orphans." That was unlikely if Stella had anything to say about it. She had spent the fall preparing for the winter care of more than 3,000 orphans "of all nationalities." There had been another large intake of refugees, and the added expenses of their needs and extensive repairs to buildings to accommodate the orphans had been huge. "This was no small task when three-fourths of them are outside of Talas, and many are over one hundred miles away," Stella said. She had done a fine juggling act. She had moved the children from poor conditions in Ak Dagh, distributing them among the orphanages in Talas and Cesarea, as space allowed. In the summer, at considerable expense, she had renovated the monastery in Evkere to winterize the buildings, and moved children from Cesarea there. "The place is ideal in many ways for an orphanage, and the children who have been shut up in the city houses are now showing the effects of the air and sunshine of the country," she said. "Our greatest enterprise this fall has been the taking over of the orphanage at Zinjidery. For some time the Unit has supplied a large part of the clothing and some food to this orphanage, but it became clear that the children needed better care than could be given by the local committee." She was confident the orphans would now receive that level of care.[17]

At the end of December word came from Sivas that Theda was gravely ill with typhus. She was not the only one. There was an outbreak in the Sivas-Harpoot region. When Annie Allen in Konia was told by authorities that the situation was dreadful, she replied, "That is why I must go."[18] Stella and Barton Plimpton felt the same. They were there for a month.

Theda eventually recovered,[19] but Annie did not. She had been forced to travel from Harpoot to Sivas "on horseback because of the deep snow," unknowingly already infected with typhus. In her weakened condition, she did not regain her health. She was 53 years old, and deeply mourned.[20]

While Stella was away, Susan took over the supervision of the orphanages.[21] This was in addition to her other duties as Director of Education, head of the Purchasing Department and, lately, Treasurer of the station. She supervised 60 teachers, organized teacher training sessions, and ensured appropriate instruction for 3,000 students. A few were beginning to work at the high school level, which she considered real progress. "One of the chief difficulties has been to get books for the schools," she said. "None are to be bought here, and those we ordered have not arrived for two years. So we have a hard time. I make charts and try to get along doing memory work and so on, with one book for four or five pupils."[22]

Purchasing was a big job, too. With one assistant, Susan had to order and pay for all the unit's supplies. "Flour, wood, meat, cloth, stone, lumber, and hundreds of smaller items appear on my accounts and thousands of liras pass through my hands. We bought 50 bolts of the Dwight A. Cabot muslins from America. The standard muslin is not found here in this market. It is cheap now, and we got it at 10.30 liras (about $6 a bolt of 40 yards). It takes many bolts to make underclothes for 3,000 or more orphans, and the sick and poor people." She bought 3,000 sheep for their meat supply, and beef cattle, which were put out to pasture in the mountains. She also ordered suits for 75 boys sewn in the unit's tailor shop, and 1,500 wooden clogs for the children, made from willow and poplar trees in the village.[223]

"This Relief Work certainly is wearing on one's nerves, and is harrowing to the feelings," she told her brother. Now that food was not so scarce, she had been using it to relieve stress. "No matter how hard I work, I continue to gain flesh till I am getting to the point when I really must diet or have a whole new set of clothes made!" Dashing off her letter to give it to the American attaché who had been visiting Talas, she asked John to pass it around to friends and family. "I'd like to run home and see you, each and every one," she wrote, "especially all the nieces and nephews I have. Love to each one, from your own Susan W. Orvis."[24]

~ ~ ~

In the spring of 1922, the Angora government's anti-Greek campaign was in full swing, moving in an easterly direction. "The Armenian villages were long ago destroyed. Now has come the turn of the Greek peasants," wrote *Christian Science Monitor* correspondent Herbert Adams Gibbons. "I find that Trebizond is being cleared of the remaining Christian population. Two years ago there were 25,000 Greeks here. To-day, between the ages of 80 and 14, the male population numbers 6 priests and 10 civilians." He accused the Nationalist government of "following a deliberate and ruthless policy of extermination of the Greeks."[25]

Dr. Mark H. Ward concurred. "At first the male inhabitants were sent to the interior near Sivas and Harpoot, where I was stationed, and set to work on the roads. There was no shelter and little food, and during last winter men succumbed in large numbers. The next step was to clear out the women and children from these same villages, and the men from the coast cities of Samsoun and Trebizond. Of 30,000 deportees who were driven from their homes in Sivas, only 20,000 arrived in Harpoot. All were destined for Bitlis, a heap of ruins left from the war, and in the centre of a barren, mountainous country unfitted to provide food for even one-tenth of the refugees."[26]

~ ~ ~

The one bright event of the year occurred in early March when a mailbag was delivered to Talas. Letters and packages spilled out from friends and families. Susan responded immediately. "Such a great treat I have had today! Letters have come, and now I have new hope and will proceed at once to write to my friends. For such a long time no word has come, and how lonely and forgotten I have been feeling! You perhaps have felt that I also had forgotten. I think that now the letters will come through alright if written on one sheet only, on one side of the paper, typed preferred, to make it easier for the censor. And I am sure they will send this to you. It is such joy to know that our friends do think of us." She asked her friends to send old magazines, such as *Harpers, Century* and *Literary Digest.* "I need reading matter more than I need food or clothes."[27]

Her response to her sister was about her personal life, increasing weight, and her wardrobe. Harriet's Sunday school class had sent Susan a pattern and enough blue silk for a blouse. "It is the longest time since I've seen a new fashion. Do send me a roll of fashion sheets, will you? It will be so nice to have some new white blouses and collars, handkerchiefs, etc."[28] She also wrote to John, telling her brother she had applied for a furlough and expected to see him in the summer. She downplayed her tiredness. "Do not be concerned about me. I am not sick, but only wish to have a rest and change." She wrote excitedly about her plans to visit "everyone of the home circle," which meant more to her than he could know. She was especially looking forward to being with his family, and meeting his one-year-old daughter: "Just think, I have never seen little Wealthy yet!"[29]

In April the happy thoughts of going home and the blossoming of spring with its eternal hope lightened her mood. She wrote again to John. "Looking from the window from where I am sitting I can see the loveliest view of blooming fruit trees and tall poplars with their tiny new leaves like a lace veil of green, through which I can see the white snow covered mountain, our glorious Mt. Argeus, with the fleecy clouds hanging above it. The sun has just shone an hour after a rainy day with heavy dark clouds. You can imagine how beautiful it is." She also told him that NER Constantinople gave permission for her furlough and would pay her expenses, but that she would have to wait until NER headquarters in New York approved. Still, she was wondering which route she would choose for her homeward journey. She put the letter aside, and did not send it until September, when she added a short note that her request had been denied. "Instead of July, it must be maybe November."[30] She had been given no reason for the delay.

Though Dr. Albert Dewey and his wife Elsie, who had been ousted from Marsovan, had "no prospect of getting into Talas to their work,"[31] and travel still required a government permit, a new relief worker, Henry R. Murphy, had arrived from Lawrence, Massachusetts,[32] Katherine was given permission to go on a three-month trip to Egypt and Palestine, and ultimately to Beirut for a special eye treatment, and newlyweds Blanche and Joseph Beach had finally returned.[33] Work was as busy as ever. Katherine supervised the two large orphanages in Talas, but while she was away, Susan took over her job, in addition to being "general helper of other untold activities."[34] She trained a new Matron of the Girls' School, expanded classes to include a large intake of new orphans, and supervised classes of 300 students each in the Boys' and Girls' schools from kindergarten to grade nine, the higher grades with "departments for Turks, Armenians, and Greeks, music, dressmaking, sewing, rug-making and various industries." There were also regular Church services in Talas, Cesarea, Zinjidery, and one outstation.[35]

Henry Murphy became Director of Orphanages, which freed Stella to deal with the government in Angora, and make regular visits to the Yozgat orphanage where 500 children lived. Henry was based in Talas but spent four days per week at the monastery in Evkere, which also housed 500 children. Years earlier, the monks had built gardens and a big swimming pool. "The gardens have been abandoned, but we have repaired the swimming pool—to the great joy of the children, and the relief workers as well," he said. "All through the hills on which the monastery stands, there are innumerable caves and many miles of subterranean passages, constructed long ago for safety's sake. Entering one of these passageways that connect with the monastery, one finds great boulders which can be rolled in place blocking the entrance. It is all very medieval. As to the orphanage work, I like it very much. I am on the best of terms with the orphanage boys, and whenever I return to Talas, after my four days at Evkere, they fairly fall over themselves to greet me. We are very proud of our large family of more than 3,000 children."[36]

In late July Susan became sick. She told her sister that she had been given the chance to stay in her room to "enjoy tonsillitis." As usual, she downplayed her illness, but did admit that it added to her general feeling of weariness. It left her with little ambition.[37] A month later she admitted that it had been a bad attack. She could hardly wait for her furlough, date still unknown. "It is so good to think of having a home with you," she said to Harriet, "where I can rest and visit and do what I like for a time."[38]

Her furlough would come soon, but not by her choice. As the *Missionary Herald* ominously stated, "There are indications that Kemal's government is not friendly to missionaries."[39]

~ ~ ~

In August 1922 newspapers reported on the previous leaders of the Ottoman Empire. Enver Pasha had escaped to Berlin, later moved to Moscow, and had his offer of aid to Kemal politely but firmly rebuffed. The *Ileri* compared him to a chameleon: "Enver is passing through every stage of metamorphosis—Pan-Islamist in Turkey, Bolshevist in Russia, and anti-Bolshevist in Bokhara. To him there is no difference between the principles of nationalism and internationalism, of religion and atheism, of conservatism and liberalism. We assert that he is suffering from the Napoleonic disease, though there is a large difference between heroism and bravado." It asked, "Who knows how many innocent victims Enver will make in the region of Touran?"[40]

The *Bosphore,* reporting on the recent assassination of Djemal, stated: "After asserting that Djemal Pasha cannot have fallen victim to Bolshevik bullets, since he was on such excellent terms with the Soviets, Hussein Djahid Bey loudly proclaims that the former Minister of Marine could have been killed only by the same hands that destroyed Talat, Behaeddin Shakir, etc. This is possible, and in our present ignorance as to the real authors of this crime, we will not uphold the contrary." Hussein Djahid also claimed that anyone who believed that killing Talat or Djemal was akin to killing "their spirit in the Turkish nation," was practising gross

The Talas team c1922 (*l to r*) Stella Nelson Loughridge, Susan Wealthy Orvis, Blanche Stewart Easton, Elsey Lois Bristol, Edward F. Martin, Henry K. Wingate, Joseph Wickliff Beach, Katherine Fletcher, Clara Childs Richmond, unknown, Rachel King, Theda Phelps, Henry Murphy. SOURCE: Amerikan Bord Heyeti (American Board), "Personnel Records for Susan Wealthy Orvis," American Research Institute in Turkey, Istanbul Center Library; online in Digital Library for International Research Archive, Item #15359.

self-deception. For every CUP leader who was killed, there would be "hundreds of Turks ready" to take his place. The editor stated this was never in doubt, and that he might never have reported it except for one significant fact: "After four years of war and three years of armistice, and especially after such frightening misfortunes as have fallen on Turkey, this assertion is made by one of the chief Union and Progress men."[41] Clearly, in certain circles, the spirit of the Committee was still alive.

Hussein Djahid had been guessing about a plot to kill the convicted CUP leaders, but it was indeed true. A group of ex-patriot Armenians living in New York had been outraged by the escape from justice of the masterminds of the 1915-1916 deportations and massacres of Armenians. In the absence of the Ottoman courts carrying out the death sentences, they decided to take matters into their own hands by launching a secret operation called *Nemesis*. They had coordinated several militant activists, including the Ottoman Armenian, Soghomon Tehlirian, most of whose family had been killed, to assassinate Talat Pasha in Berlin. He would then give himself up to force a trial to expose Talat's criminal deeds—something the courts-martial in Turkey had failed to do adequately.[42] And something that would never happen, now that the Nationalists had abolished them entirely.[43] So far, other assassins in Operation Nemesis had eliminated Said Halim Pasha in Rome, (December 5, 1921), Behaeddin Shakir and Djemal Azmi in Berlin (April 17, 1922), and now Djemal Pasha in Tiflis (July 21, 1922).[44]

Another secret operation was about to be launched. Mustafa Kemal was readying his forces for a surprise attack on the Greek army.

27

The Burning of Smyrna

For almost a year the Greek army had held the 400-mile front, cutting off western Turkey from the interior. In late August Mustafa Kemal secretly travelled to the Nationalist army base near Afion Kara Hissar to supervise an attack on the Greek troops. It was the most strategic spot to break through the line. The Greek army was slightly larger, with more guns and better transport. The Nationalists had more heavy guns and a much stronger cavalry, but they also had the element of surprise. By August 30, 1922 the Nationalists had encircled two Greek corps near Dumlumpinar, and had captured two generals, 500 officers, 5,000 men and hundreds of guns. Kemal treated the Greek generals with respect, and honoured his own officers. He promoted Brigadier-General Nureddin, the man who had closed down Anatolia College, to Major-General, but the commander had "refused to add a star to his uniform, saying that he had been badly treated by Kemal." Kemal "had indeed imposed his authority on Nureddin, and even issued orders directly to his troops," but had done so to maintain order. Nureddin had a reputation as "a thorough fanatic and a rabble-rousing demagogue."[1]

The majority of Greek soldiers had escaped capture. Kemal knew exactly where they were headed: west through the Meander valley to Smyrna. Months earlier, journalist Herbert Gibbons had written about the exhaustion of those soldiers: "Their strength was worn out in the foolish campaign towards Angora." He railed against the corrupt Greek military administration, the "wicked" Greek government, "unwise tactics, an unavoidable fatigue . . . and a disappointing propaganda, both foreign and Greek, as to the uselessness of all efforts, since there was to be an evacuation in any case."[2] These soldiers were demoralized, without leadership or discipline. Six months previously, British High Commissioner in Smyrna, Sir Harry Lamb, had warned that the retreating army had decided "to leave a desert behind them, no matter whose interests may suffer thereby. Everything which they have time and means to move will be carried off to Greece; the Turks will be plundered and burnt out of house and home."[3] They had no time to remove anything, but they could carry out a scorched-earth policy on their retreat. And in their rage, they did.

They burned hundreds of towns and villages in their wake. From Ushak to Manisa, they set fire to buildings, often with people still in them.

Part of busy quay in Smyrna, 1915. The arrow shows the location of the Custom's House. SOURCE: New York World-Telegram and the Sun Newspaper Photograph Collection, March 21, 1915, US Library of Congress.

Of Alashehir's 4,500 houses only 200 remained, and 3,000 people were killed; of Manisa's 14,000 houses only 1,400 remained.[4] The 31st Greek Infantry Regiment passed through the area a while after their undisciplined comrades. They saw "many corpses, which smelled horrible in the fire and smoke," said Eleftherios Stavridis, leader of the regiment. "Who was to care what corpses they were? We passed through hurried, stooping, like ghosts, amid the smoke."[5]

Like most residents of Smyrna in late August, Garabed Hatcherian, an Armenian doctor, paid little attention to news of the battle in Afion Kara

Hissar. However, he soon began to treat civilians who had been wounded in Dumlumpinar. Then more patients confirmed that the "Greek army set fire to Ushak before leaving, and committed a series of atrocities against the Turks."[6] Turks, Armenians and Greeks fled their homes in the Meander valley, fearing retribution from either the Greek army, the Nationalist army or both. Many took to the mountains to hide, but thousands fled to Smyrna in hopes of sanctuary.

~ ~ ~

For centuries Smyrna sat on the shores of the Aegean Sea, shimmering like the central jewel in a brilliant crown. Home to Homer, and rebuilt by Alexander the Great, Smyrna was a commercial centre for trade among the Greeks, Turks, French, Dutch, Italians and British. Snuggled at the end of a long gulf, with Mount Pagus rising behind it, an ancient fortress on top, the city had a harbour that was "one of the best in the world, comparable to that of Vancouver." Along the waterfront was a two-mile long quay, fronted by a beautiful architectural collection of cinemas, hotels, banks, office buildings, consulates and shops.[7] At the north end was the Levantine quarter, Levantines being those of European descent. The neighbourhood was nestled next to the Greek and Armenian quarters. At the south end of the city was the Jewish quarter, and next to it, uphill, was the Turkish quarter.[8] There were approximately 250,000 residents, about 40% Turks and 60% non-Muslims.[9]

Constantinople was an international city, but Smyrna was truly cosmopolitan. Gulfem Iren, who was seven years old at the time, remembered the residents' harmonious life. Her grandfather had a magnificent garden with plants from all over the world. "A day would come when all would bloom. And on that day, everyone would know, the Greek, the Armenian, the Jew, the Muslim, that in Mehmet Shevket Bey's house there is a flower show. Friends and strangers would tour the house, and when ready to leave, they would be offered the juice of whatever fruit was in season."[10]

But as much as the residents loved Smyrna—known as Izmir by the Ottoman government—it was called "*gavur* [infidel] Izmir" by non-resident Muslims. The reason was likely because of Smyrna/Izmir's non-Muslim majority, but "also because of the dominance in the city's economic and socio-cultural life of the Levantines."[11] In any case, gavur was a pejorative term.[12] And the vast majority of Nationalist soldiers who were on their way to gavur Izmir were non-resident Muslims.

~ ~ ~

Smyrna 1922 - Cosmopolitan city. SOURCE: Private collection.

Friday, September 1: Alexander MacLachlan, the Canadian president of International College in Paradise, a suburb of Smyrna, found it hard to believe the news: "Each day it became more evident that we were approaching a crisis that was likely to have far-reaching consequences."[13] Greek High Commissioner Aristeidis Stergiadis sent a circular telegram to his regional staff, ordering them to bring all their archives and papers to Smyrna, and to do so "in absolute secrecy."[14] Major Panagakos reported to headquarters from the field that the Greek army was dissolving: "Throughout the whole valley, a rabble is moving westwards with no thought in mind but to get to Smyrna."[15]

Saturday, September 2: Alexander's Turkish friends confirmed that there were about 5,000 chettes south of the city who might enter Smyrna before the expected arrival of the Nationalist army. By afternoon it was confirmed that they had been warned by the military to wait. Alexander was grateful to avoid "serious trouble with these irresponsible freebooters."[16] Garabed Hatcherian saw carloads and trainloads of wounded soldiers arriving, moment by moment. He thought it unlikely that any atrocities could happen in Smyrna, because there were so many Europeans, "who have been good friends of the Turks."[17] Olive Greene, an American teacher on vacation in Athens had difficulty finding a place to stay because the hotels were "full of Smyrna refugees—the rich who ran over to Athens in case of possible trouble."[18]

Sunday, September 3: Reports of the Greek army burning Nazilli and other villages, and committing atrocities against civilians filtered in. Smyrna residents were afraid of the Greek soldiers who were now "swarming the streets, openly selling their arms and uniforms for a pittance."[19]

Monday, September 4: "News was confirmed that the whole of the Greek army was ordered to evacuate Asia Minor at once," said Grace Williamson, supervisor of the British Nursing Home. "You can imagine what confusion and panic there is in this place. Refugees from all over the country coming into the town all day long, the trains coming in as fast as it is possible, day and night."[20] There was standing room only on the trains, and panic in the streets as 7,000-10,000 Greek and Armenian refugees poured into Smyrna daily.[21] The quay was filling with people, their meagre belongings, military equipment, horses, cows and sheep.[22] "The church yards, schools and all empty buildings are getting packed, and yet more and more are coming," said Grace. "What will be in a day or two?"[23]

Tuesday, September 5: American Consul George Horton had been telegraphing the US State Department, insisting that warships come to Smyrna to rescue his compatriots. "If there was ever a time when a situation demanded the presence of naval units, this, I thought, was that occasion. Though our colony was not great, our business interests and property holdings were very considerable indeed, to say nothing of our large schools with their staffs of teachers and professors."[24] There were a few French and Italian warships in the harbour, as well as several private yachts,[25] and four British ships, including the *Iron Duke*.[26] "Today an English boat is to take as many English as care to leave," Grace said. She thought many would go.[27] It was a good thing, too, because food was becoming scarce.[28]

Wednesday, September 6: In Ak Hisar, northeast of Smyrna, Greek military authorities advised all Christians to leave because "orders had been received to set it on fire before retreating." The local Greek, Armenian and Turkish community leaders got together and swore on their holy books that they would form a temporary government to protect *all* residents. The military and civil authorities left, and the telegraph wires were cut.[29] In Smyrna, Grace was annoyed by the attitude of some local British men. "I think they are responsible for the scare. And of course the Greeks, seeing the English are taking fright, are in a blue funk, and every one wants to go! How can they? There are over two hundred thousand, Major General de Candolle told me. And where are they to go? Greece can't take them all. What a ruination this has been!"[30] George Horton finally received notification that two small destroyers would be sent to Smyrna.[31] What he did not know was that the commanders of those ships had been given strict orders by Admiral Bristol: "Be neutral. Protect only Americans. Don't cooperate with the Allies. Don't lead the way."[32]

Thursday, September 7: All Greek officials left Smyrna. "Mr. Stergiadis had but a few steps to go from his house to the sea, where a ship was awaiting him," said George Horton, "but he was hooted by the population."[33] A large group of Greek soldiers walked through the city. "They tried to hearten the people by carrying the flag along the streets," said Grace. She was struck by a significant lack of response. "Such half-hearted shouts, and mostly from children."[34] "The city was now without a government of any kind," said Alexander.[35] He was surprised there were no reports of lawlessness.[36] But everyone was on edge.

Friday, September 8: The Nationalists were expected in a day or two. There were dozens of ships taking on Greek soldiers as fast as possible. "The soldier, in his hurry to get off, pushes and scrambles, and drops his rifle and everything he can, so the town is strewn with guns, and strings and strings of camels, and carts with solid wheels drawn by bullocks—full of things that looked like loot from the towns," said Grace. "You should have seen how the army hurried. It became a frantic run. Dropping everything!" The mad dash continued long into the night,[37] before the ships headed further south to Chesme. Garabed was warned by a friend in the French Consulate to stay home when the Nationalists arrived, and to make sure he had enough food to tide him over, but he really had nothing to fear. "This time, the Turkish army will enter the city in a most orderly way to demonstrate to the whole world that the Turks are a civilized nation," said his friend.[38] The British had arranged for a special night train to travel from Boudjah through Paradise to collect any British subjects who wanted to go. Alexander and the rest of the College staff—British, Canadians and Americans—all decided to stay. But they accepted the offer of 20 American sailors from the *Litchfield* to guard the campus compound.[39] The YMCA, Near East Relief, Red Cross and American Collegiate Institute all requested guards, too.[40] The precautions were wise.

In the afternoon, those Greek soldiers who had kept their discipline were only 25 kilometres outside the city when they received an order to abandon the idea of defending Smyrna. They were to veer south, and head for Cheshme to board ships bound for Greece.[41] The residents and refugees, now totalling half a million, were to face the Nationalist army on their own.

Saturday, September 9: Grace awoke to find her sitting room full of sleeping men who had arrived on the night train from Boudjah. She was not happy. "More and more people crowding into the clinic! I don't feed them; they have to provide their own food and bedding. But what a fuss it creates."[42] Alexander awoke to the sounds and sights of a Greek regiment camped outside the campus; they had taken a wrong turn in the dark and lost "five or six precious hours" in their retreat.[43] Meanwhile, at the north end of Smyrna there were different kinds of sounds. "Stepping to the door of my office, I found that a crowd of refugees, mostly women, were rushing in terror upon the Consulate, and trying to seek refuge within," said George Horton. "One glance from the terrace, which overlooked the quay, made evident the cause of their terror." About 400 soldiers of the Nationalist cavalry, with sabres sheathed and rifles slung across their backs, were riding along the quay in an orderly fashion to the Konak (government house) and barracks at the south end of the city.[44] The Turks had arrived.

~ ~ ~

There was an eerie quiet in the city that day. Someone in the crowd threw a bomb at the cavalry as it proceeded along the quay. An officer was slightly injured, but rode on, seemingly unconcerned.[45] There was no attempt at reprisal. Groups of mounted patrols moved through the streets, calling out, "Don't be afraid! Nothing will happen!"[46] And nothing did—likely because of the high regard the soldiers had for Mustafa Kemal. They knew he liked order and expected discipline.[47]

But it was the calm before the storm. Late in the afternoon, Kemal handed over command of Smyrna to General Nureddin. One of the general's first acts was to summon Greek Archbishop Chrysostomos to the Konak. In 1919 he had been dismissed from office due in part to the archbishop's influence, and Nureddin was now bent on revenge. After a brief meeting where he accused Chrysostomos of treason, he called down from the balcony to the crowd of Muslims outside, telling them to judge the archbishop and deal with him however they wished. "It was an invitation to mob rule."[48] They grabbed him, spat on him, tore his beard out by the roots, beat him, and stabbed him to death.[49] It was the beginning of the end of Smyrna.

That night there was shooting and looting in the Armenian quarter. During the next three days there were outbreaks of violence throughout the city. Hundreds of people were killed. Many were arrested, including Dr. Hatcherian.[50] Thousands tried to seek food and shelter with foreign agencies, until their buildings were bursting at the seams. Alexander MacLachlan and his military guard, Sergeant Louis Crocker, were attacked outside the campus gates by chettes, stripped naked, and beaten with the butts of rifles. Only their calm manner, pleading from a Turkish college student, and the chance passing of a Nationalist officer saved their lives.[51]

On Wednesday September 13, fires were deliberately set in the Armenian quarter and various points in and around the city. The chief of the Smyrna Fire Department, Paul Grescovish, usually dealt with one fire every ten days. Five in one day, and in such widely-separated places, was highly suspect. When the Nationalists arrived, the chief had applied for more fire fighters and equipment. On learning that the department employed 12 Greeks on its 49-man crew, Nureddin promptly denied the request, and arrested the Greek workers. Therefore, when the fires began, the department was ill-equipped to deal with them.[52]

There were accusations against the Armenian residents for starting the fires. Petroleum-soaked rags had been discovered "in several of the institutions recently deserted by Armenian refugees."[53] However, Minnie Mills, Dean of the Collegiate Institute, said, "There was not an Armenian in sight." She had seen men in "smart" Nationalist uniforms carrying tins of petrol into houses.[54] Using binoculars from the college tower in Paradise, instructor Anna Harlow Birge "could plainly see Turkish soldiers setting fire to houses. I could see Turks lurking in the fields, shooting at Christians. When I drove down to Smyrna from Paradise . . . there were dead bodies all along the road." Another American said, "I myself saw a chette carrying a load of firewood on his back up an alley, from which later came the fire that caught our building."[55]

Mark Prentiss, who had recently arrived on the USS *Lawrence*, reported on the carnage: "Turkish soldiers, armed with rifles and machine guns, were guarding every street in the Armenian quarter, and every man, woman and child who was in this section of the city as late as mid-afternoon on Wednesday, was either burned alive or shot down while attempting to escape."[56]

The fires grew. Due to the direction of the wind, the flames headed away from the Turkish and Jewish quarters towards the rest of the city.

September 1922: Viewed from the deck of a warship in Smyrna's harbour, the city burned. SOURCE: Armenian Genocide Museum Institute.

Late in the day, after repeated requests for more men, the military finally relented and gave the fire chief 100 soldiers to help him try to check the spread. They used bombs to destroy the burning buildings,[57] but it was too little, too late. Smyrna was beyond help.

So, too, were most of the hundreds of thousands of residents and refugees. The captains on the foreign ships ordered their nationals to evacuate the city. At first only the women and their own children from the International College were sent to Smyrna to board the American ships, but soon the men followed. In town, US Marines came for the staff of the American Collegiate. They had been sheltering 1,200 Greeks and Armenians, and were prepared to stay to fight the flames. But when a "band of robbers" set fire to the building next to them, they realized they were fighting "a losing game," and left. Minnie Mills refused to leave her girls, even when a Marine told her if she did not go with him, he would carry her out. After a short argument, it was agreed the girls could go with her. "As we moved toward the door, the screams that came from the crowd within was something beyond description," said one of the teachers. "All followed, as best they could, to the street, and then the robber bands began to shoot. We moved on, but as it happened the crowd pushed us in the wrong direction. . . . I can never describe that mad flight for our lives, the fire on one side and the robber bands on the other, but Miss Mills and I, with some of the girls, did reach the quay." They finally managed to board a ship, but only after Minnie had another argument, this time with the captain about taking on non-Americans.[58]

Similar scenes were taking place all along the quay. The British Nursing Home was evacuated by two officers escorting Grace and her staff, and fifty sailors carrying the home's patients to the *Iron Duke*.[59] Morley draped herself in the American flag and led "120 lone, frightened little girls" through the burning streets, jostling crowds, and whiz of bullets.[60] As people clamoured to get on board ships, there were frantic arguments between relief workers and the ships' crews to take on non-nationals. Many crew members argued with their captains, who were maintaining the strict orders they had been given. There was one remarkable exception. A Japanese freighter, laden with cargo, entered the harbour just as the fire began. Marion Harlow was very impressed with the captain: "He ordered every bit of that cargo thrown overboard into the sea in order that he might use all available space for taking away refugees."[61]

The inability to save everyone was devastating. Turkish journalist Falih Rifki Atay saw people rushing from their neighbourhoods to the quay, some of them jumping into the harbour to cling to small boats. "I was watching this unique tragedy with my heart aching," he said. "Izmir was burning and along with its Greekness, the peoples of the first civilizations, the ones who passed the Middle Ages with the Muslims, those who were living in their homelands and homes in comfort, those who held up Izmir's and all of Western Anatolia's agriculture, trade, and the entirety of its economy, those who used to live in palaces and konaks, now, at the twenty-second year of the twentieth century were dying for a piece of boat to take them away for good."[62]

Lieutenant Tip Merrill, Admiral Bristol's intelligence officer on the scene, noted that "to attempt to land a boat would have been disastrous. Several boats tried it and were immediately swamped by the mad rush of a howling mob."[63] At least one large group of refugees crowded onto a boat only to burn to death when Turkish soldiers torched it; the shocking sight of charred bodies was something Emily McCallum,[*] Fred MacCallum's sister and President of the American Collegiate Institute, would never forget.[64]

Four days later the situation was unchanged. "What I see as I stand on the deck of the *Iron Duke* is an unbroken wall of fire, two miles long in which twenty distinct volcanoes of raging flames are throwing up jagged, writhing tongues to a height of a hundred feet," wrote Ward Price for the

---

[*] Emily insisted on spelling her name differently from the rest of her family.

The title of this photograph is "Smyrna's Wall of Humanity - Portion of 300,000 people caught." Days after the fire, refugees on the quay were still waiting for help. SOURCE: Bain News Service, US Library of Congress.

Daily Mail. "The sea glows a deep copper-red, and worst of all, from the densely packed mob of many thousand refugees huddled on the narrow quay, between the advancing fiery death behind, and the deep water in front, comes continuously frantic screaming of sheer terror as can be heard miles away."[65]

On Tuesday, September 19, the British finally allowed refugees onto two ships, but that effort only rescued a few thousand. "It seemed as though the awful, agonizing, hopeless shrieks for help would forever haunt me," said YMCA worker Asa Jennings. Unable to stand the international complacency any longer, he decided to do something about it.[66] He successfully negotiated with Nureddin for an evacuation of the refugees within ten days.[67] He was eventually able to persuade the captain of the Italian *Constantinopoli* to take a group to Mytilene. He then used every trick in the book to move the international community to action—including blackmail, when he threatened the Greek government that unless they sent rescue ships to Smyrna, he would send an uncoded message to the world of their reluctance "to save tens of thousands of ethnic Greeks facing certain death."[68]

Other relief workers had been creating a lot of bad press for their own governments, which helped spur their participation. Within a week more than 240,000 Greeks, Armenians and Levantines were evacuated, though many died before, during and shortly after the process.[69] Garabed Hatcherian and his family were among those who survived.[70] It was fortunate Asa Jennings acted when he did, because a military revolution broke out in Greece days later, resulting in the resignation of the government and the abdication of the king,[71] and because Nureddin was preparing to cleanse Smyrna of infidels: Hundreds of Greeks and Armenians in Ak Hisar, Manisa and other places were raped, hanged or shot[72] and all Christians were to leave the area immediately or would be deported.[73]

One could argue the burning of Smyrna by the Turks was retribution for burning the towns and villages of the Meander valley by the Greek soldiers. Or that it was a continuation of the centuries-old animosity between Turks, Greeks and Armenians. But Atay may have had it right when he saw a sense of inferiority in the destruction. "It was as if anywhere that resembled Europe was destined to remain Christian and foreign, and to be denied to us," he said.[74] Neither Nureddin nor his soldiers nor the Turkish chettes were from Smyrna. Perhaps their burning the gavur city was a symbolic act of purification[75]—a signal that the Ottoman Empire was dead, and a new Turkey was rising from the ashes.

Part IV: A Time To Uproot

28

The Expulsion

The Ottoman was not the only crumbling empire. The British Empire was starting to show cracks. While Smyrna was burning, Mustafa Kemal continued his march toward British-occupied Constantinople. He ran into British troops at Chanak near Gallipoli. Fearful of once again facing the closing of the Straits, Britain informed each of its Dominions of the Cabinet decision to defend its position, and requested their military aid. New Zealand and Newfoundland agreed. South Africa did not respond. Both Canada and Australia refused; they did not want to participate in another war, especially without prior consultation. It was a major fissure in the constitution of the British Empire. The Chanak Affair, as it became known, signalled a growing independence among its Dominions. Ireland was already well into the process. Left with little support, the stand-off between the British and Nationalist troops continued while the Lloyd George government negotiated an armistice in the town of Mudanya. Details would be ironed out at a future conference, but the Allies agreed to withdraw and to give Kemal what he wanted: an independent Turkey that included Anatolia, Eastern Thrace, Constantinople and the Dardanelles.[1] Lloyd George resigned.[2]

Upon hearing the news of Kemal's victory, the *Tevhid-i-Efkiar* proudly proclaimed, "The contents of our National Pact, in which we have laid down our program, can be summed up in the phrase: We are determined to be masters in our own house."[3] A Nationalist committee made a pilgrimage to the tomb of Sultan Osman I in Brousa, "amidst a popular ovation."[4]

Others were not so joyous. "We cannot believe that Mustapha Kemal will persist in a policy that will undoubtedly tend to separate Turkey more and more from the progressive nations of the earth," said the American Board. "Until Turkey has proven to the world that she can govern wisely and well peoples of other faith and blood, she can never be satisfied with her attainment as a government; nor will she receive the recognition that she believes is her due." The trustees were worried about ABCFM's freedom to pursue evangelism and the continued ownership of its valuable properties. They insisted that the United States should be part of the upcoming negotiations because "the whole matter is far above the plane of partisan politics." In fact, "the soul of America is at stake."[5]

Though he did not specifically refer to the work of Near East Relief, James Barton declared that "hundreds of thousands of people of all races have come to associate the name of America with deeds of kindness and mercy." He strongly believed "that the rights of Americans in Turkey are defined by the Capitulations, which are assumed to be operative until something equally satisfactory takes their place." He also believed that "there are many powerful influences calculated to restrain the Nationalists from committing overt acts against Americans and their interests."[6]

Mustafa Kemal clearly had other ideas.

~ ~ ~

NER Talas had recently expanded by two couples, formerly of Marsovan: Dr. Albert and Elsie Dewey, and Carl and Ruth Compton. The Deweys were stationed in Talas for medical work, and the Comptons in Zinjidery, where Carl was Director of the orphanage.[7] The whole team continued their work, "in spite of deportations, hostility of the Turkish government, difficulties of obtaining permits to travel, and genuine danger."[8] The level of danger was highlighted in October by the murder near Aleppo of Rev. Lester J. Wright at the hands of bandits.[9] At every turn, relief workers faced life and death situations—their own as well as those they cared for. Sometimes they felt as though they were prisoners, constantly under surveillance. It was also difficult to be isolated from friends and family; not one personal letter was delivered to the Talas group in all of 1922.[10] They lived with their suitcases packed and some money always in their pockets, not knowing from one minute to the next what might happen. "Our great fear was that we might be deported, and the thousands of Christian orphan children under our care would then be sent out on the roads to die of starvation and cruel treatment," said Susan. The thought of no one else to help them was too terrible to contemplate. But they remained steadfast. "One thing we could always rely on was that life would never be monotonous. The unexpected was always happening so fast we could hardly get our breath."[11]

On November 7, a version of their greatest fear did happen. They were notified of the government's planned announcement for November 14 to give "permission" to all Christians to leave Turkey by December 13.[12] There would be widespread panic as those Armenians and Greeks still around prepared to pack, find passage on a ship, and hope for a nation willing to accept them. Staying meant being "hounded back into exile or perish of hunger, cold, and sheer bitterness of disappointment." Even the average Turk was surprised by the edict. As one man in Constantinople put it, "We are astonished that Europe takes so easily what we have done to the Christians. We have massacred them, and deported them, and Europe does nothing. Some years ago they would have gone to war on less provocation."[13]

The Talas group had a few days' head start to arrange the transportation of 3,000 children out of the country. In 1919 they had found 10,000 orphans in the district, but in the almost four years since, that number was halved as they reunited thousands with relatives, either in Turkey or through emigration, and sent others to orphanages in Beirut or elsewhere. The government had established orphanages for Turkish children, who were safe from this new deportation order. Of the original 6,000 Armenian and Greek orphans, 3,000 were left in Talas, Cesarea, Erveke, Zinjidery and Yozgat.[14] The NER team was determined to ensure government compliance with the "suggested" exodus, and avoid a repetition of the previous years' traumatic massacres. But they were also concerned about the coming winter. Snow would soon make travel very difficult. Any delay could lead to disaster.

The unit held a quick and decisive meeting. The children would leave Talas in convoys of wagons, travel for four days to Oulou Kushla, where they would board a train for Tarsus, and be transferred to Adana or Mersine. In Adana they would go east by train to Beirut; in Mersine, west by ship to Greece or one of the islands. They would be guarded every step of the way by Armenian and Greek staff, who would leave with them. Joseph would coordinate the evacuation from the compound, where he had access to the telegraph. He would organize the staff assignments and wagon transportation. Susan would leave immediately for Adana, making arrangements en route for accommodation for the children in khans as far as Oulou Kushla. She would proceed to Tarsus to connect with Rev. Paul Nilson, whom Joseph would ask "to take charge of the receiving and forwarding" of their orphans in Mersine. Susan would go on to Adana to see about further train transport. Albert Dewey was to go to Oulou Kushla to negotiate train transport to Mersine. Henry Murphy would go to Mersine to rent a large factory as a temporary transfer centre. The others on the team—Stella, Clara, Elsey, Lillian, Blanche, Elsie Dewey, and Carl and Ruth Compton—would prepare the children to leave. That in itself was a huge task: gathering the children from distant orphanages, informing them of the journey, and preparing their clothing and possible documentation.[15] Blanche and Elsie would do what they could, which might not be a lot since they were both new mothers.[16]

The plan was spontaneous and highly flexible. Not having received an immediate reply from Tarsus, Joseph told Susan, "If I receive a reply I shall wire immediately to Oulou Kushla to catch you there. If no word comes, please proceed to Tarsus and Mersine. Try to persuade Mr. Nilson to take over the work. You are authorized to offer him a salary from the NER of $150 per month for this service until it is finished. If Mr. Nilson is unable to accept the work, Mr. Murphy will stay in Mersine and Dr. Dewey will stay in Oulou Kushla. It is however highly desirable for either Dr. Dewey or Mr. Murphy to get back here at the first possible moment as I myself have too much to do satisfactorily. I should have Dr. Dewey here to act in my absence at the city or elsewhere. You may stay in Mersine till Mr. Murphy arrives, but please return to your work along the road and to be ready to evacuate the G.S.O. [Girls' School Orphanage] at the first possible moment. It is highly essential that you be on the road between here and Oulou Kushla as much as possible. I had rather have Dr. Dewey return here from Oulou Kushla as he is the one more likely than anyone else to remain here after the others of us leave—if and when we do leave. Good luck."[17]

Within hours Susan had a passport permitting her to travel. She set off with Dervish, their Turkish driver who had been in Herbert Irwin's boys' club in Cesarea years ago. They had packed supplies in their three-quarter ton REO truck to drop off at the Oulou Kushla train depot, and enough extras to see them on their 250-mile trek to Tarsus. They stopped at four places along the way to reserve accommodation for a few hundred children per trip, and arrange space for food preparation. It took them two days to reach Oulou Kushla, and another few days to reach the coast. Susan said, "It was a pleasure to visit our mission stations at Tarsus and Adana and to meet our workers there. They all helped me in every way they could."[18] On behalf of Paul Nilson, Paul Bobb of the Tarsus station accepted the assignment to greet and forward the children to Mersine.[19]

Within four days of Susan's departure from Talas, the first convoy of 570 children started out. Joseph arranged for drivers, wagons, and Armenian and Greek workers to accompany them. Six or seven of these native workers stayed at each of the stopping places, ready to receive the children and cook them a hot meal. Mealtimes were crowded but adequate. The children slept in the wagons or on the ground, huddled together to keep warm under blankets. The convoys were also accompanied by Turkish gendarmes, and at least one guard was posted at each khan, because there was an increase of bandits on the road.[20]

Susan and Paul Bobb loaded the REO with cooked beans and as much bread as they could pack in, and drove north to Oulou Kushla to meet them. While Albert Dewey and Paul loaded them onto the train, Susan

The road to Mersine from Talas had been improved during the Great War. SOURCE: The Missionary Church Archives and Historical Collections, Bethel College, Mishawaka, Indiana.

paid for their tickets. She was rather annoyed at having to pay "full fare for our children to ride in six inches of snow in open freight cars to Mersine," but she shared the ride with them.[21] Meanwhile Paul drove to Adana to fuel up the truck. He picked her up and returned to Oulou Kushla, where he took over for Albert, who rode back to Talas with Susan. It was an exhausting first week.[22]

The convoys continued to leave Talas at a rate of three per week, but with less than 200 children at a time. Everyone agreed that fewer children were more manageable to organize and feed. It was also easier and safer to guard, too. Susan spent most of the next few weeks riding back and forth along the convoy, in the cold, either on horseback or in the truck, to make sure everything was progressing smoothly. Once in a while she was able to stay for a day in Talas. It was hard to see her students getting ready to leave. "I shall miss them very much," she said.[23]

~ ~ ~

November 30, 1922 was the last Thursday of the month. It was American Thanksgiving Day, but the Talas unit was too busy to celebrate. Susan was on the road, as usual. She had set out at 5 o'clock in the morning with Dervish for Oulou Kushla. Their large automobile was full of enough food for the orphans to get to Mersine. They had one passenger, a Turkish official. They were giving him a ride to Nigdeh as a special favour. Wrapped in quilts to keep warm, they drove for an hour through the snowy foothills of Mount Argaeus. As they turned a bend, they suddenly saw a long, thin column of people staggering towards them. Moving closer, they could see most of them were women and children. There were a few old men in the line—a line as far as the eye could see. A lone Turkish soldier rode on a donkey in the middle of them.

"Such skeletons," Susan later reported to the NER. "Such great, hollow eyes. Such bare legs and arms of little children with skin stretched over the bones, with a few tatters of old stocking still hanging about the ankles. Such hands like claws. Such hair matted with straw and weeds. Such shivering, tottering specimens of human life. Eight hundred women and girls, dying of starvation, yet still moving forward, till one by one they should drop dead by the road. This was what I saw that day. Such a spectacle of horror and misery that it is fixed in my memory."[24]

It was starting to rain. The air was chilly. The only thing the people had to protect themselves were rags of burlap or old aprons to hold over their heads. As much as Susan wanted to stop to help them, she dared not. Her armed passenger would undoubtedly deny her permission. Besides, the orphans needed the provisions for their exodus. As they moved past the pathetic parade, Susan asked the official, "Who are they?"

"They are from the area about Smyrna," he said. She could tell from their clothing they were from another region.

"Why are they coming here now?" she asked.

"They are being deported to Cesarea as a punishment."

"Why? What have these women and little girls done that they should be punished in this way?"

"The Greek soldiers have done terrible things to our people, the Turks. The things they did are a sin against God, and no religion teaches that it is right to do such cruel things."

He began to innumerate some of the atrocities of the late summer, but Susan interrupted him. "Yes, whoever does such deeds sins against God. But is it not also a sin to make innocent women and children suffer as these are suffering here?"

He tried to persuade her that they were being kindly treated, but she could not get over the fact that these people had walked 500 miles from Smyrna. They had been walking for two months. "What a column of agony!" Susan said to herself. "There were 3,000 in the column when they started. Groups had at intervals been diverted to other roads, and many weaker ones had died by the roadside." She remembered village gossip of deportations after the Smyrna disaster. "Here it was in its awful reality. I had never imagined such a ghastly procession. Every face had a death-like pallor. Women carried babies in arms, and were stooped from weight of all their earthly possessions on their backs. The majority were barefooted. All were unutterably miserable, but they bore themselves with remarkable fortitude."

When they rounded a bend, they came across a boy, about twelve years of age, alone at the side of the road. "People never dare to be alone on the roads in Turkey," said Susan. "Even a strong man on horseback feels nervous if he travels alone." She ordered the car stopped. When she asked the boy what he was doing there, he said, "I-I- could not walk." She asked her driver and the official to help, and was surprised when the man lifted the boy into the car. The boy's thin, cotton garment was so torn he was nearly naked. His body was so wasted he looked like a skeleton. It was a pitiful sight. "It went to the heart of this Turk, who had been trying to excuse the deportation. He took this dirty, starved boy and wrapped him in his own quilt, and held him gently in his arms till we reached a khan." Susan handed the boy over to the Talas workers there, warning them not to give him too much food at first. "But they knew better than I about feeding a starved person," she said. "Poor Armenian teachers of ours, they had been through such experiences themselves!"

After dropping off the official at Nigdeh, and the supplies at Oulou Kushla, Susan and Dervish returned to the khan within two days. On the way they spotted a pile of old clothes discarded by the side of the road. When they stopped to collect it—for even old clothing could be put to use—they found two little yellow-haired girls huddled together beneath it on the snowy ground. Dervish thought they were dead, but one of them stirred. They made a bed on the floor of the auto and carefully laid the girls onto it. When they arrived at the khan, the workers tearfully told them the boy they had rescued had died. They had buried him next to many other children. Knowing these girls needed hospital care, Susan went to the commander of the gendarmes, and asked to be allowed to take the girls to Talas. Permission was granted,[25] and they drove on.

Hours later, they arrived at the Yavash Khan. In the yard eight young women and girls were lying down. An old woman was beside them—the only one of the group who could stand. They were stragglers from the long procession of Greeks bound for Cesarea. There were also several empty wagons in the courtyard, stopped for a rest on their return from Oulou Kushla. Susan arranged with the drivers to take these women, and any others they encountered along the way, directly to the Talas hospital. She also gave the old woman a lira, and went into the khan to pay the *khanji* (innkeeper) to feed them soup and milk.[26]

As she and Dervish drove on, they saw quite a few dead children and old men. Not far from the khan, a boy and a girl scrambled out from a culvert. Susan called back to a wagon driver to pick up these children. Further on, a small boy, sitting on the side of the road, asked them to take him with them. Susan tried to explain that a wagon would come along to pick him up, but he crawled to the car, saying over and over, "They won't take me, they won't take me!"

"Let us take him with us," Dervish said to Susan. "It will be late before the wagons reach here." He lifted the boy up into the car. Susan could never forget "how the little fellow's face shone with joy!" In all they collected six children.

When they pulled into Injesu, six hours west of Talas, they encountered 750 Greek deportees outside the khan. They had stopped walking for the night. Some had gathered dry weeds, and were attempting to start a fire for hot water and a bit of warmth. Most were huddled against a wall, too weary to move. Susan asked the commandant of the gendarmes to whom she should report the children in her car.

This is the document written in "old" Turkish, that Susan received from the commander of the gendarmes giving her permission to take the girls to Talas. See Endnote 25 for the translation. SOURCE: Susan Wealthy Orvis Papers.

"It is not necessary to report them," he said. "No count is kept of them." He granted her permission to feed the crowd, and took her into a corner of the large courtyard where she could set up cooking facilities. He had refused to let her use the khan's kitchen. "They are too dirty, and covered with vermin," he said. "The khan must be kept clean for the Turkish soldiers." But he did give her four gendarmes to help keep the people back until the food was prepared.

Susan then went to the local Greek school, which was the first night's stopping place for the Talas orphans. With help from the workers there, she brought back four large copper kettles, pails and dippers, wood and food. "We had to build a barricade around our corner to get a chance to work," she explained. "The thought of food made these starving people crazy. The mob crowded around, crawling under and around the wagon and automobile, and through the ropes we had put across in front of the kettles. It seemed as though they would fall into the kettles of boiling soup in their eagerness. Finally we began to distribute it, dipping it out in the utensils they brought—old tin cans and broken water jars. One had a sardine tin, another a plate, and several had nothing but an old piece of handkerchief or a piece of cloth! They pushed and jostled each other so badly that we often had to stop, and yet that did no good, they only fought the more fiercely for fear the supply was about to be exhausted. When the kettles were empty, they wiped out every drop and even licked up the soup that was spilled on the stones. They jumped over each other and tore at each other in their wild attempts to get the food. One old man fought his way through the mob several times and carried bowls of soup to those too weak to come. . . . I ordered bread baked at the ovens so that we had enough to give out to them in the morning, before they started on the day's march in the cold and rain."[27]

Susan later told her friends, it was "the greatest Thanksgiving dinner I ever shall see."[28]

29

The Exodus

One of the six children Susan and Dervish took to the Talas hospital died almost immediately. The other five had their heads shaved, were bathed and fed, and put to bed in clean linens. They survived. But Susan was worried when the wagons she had commissioned had not arrived with the other stragglers.

"They will not bring them," said Dervish. "They will be afraid of disease." He offered to drive back to pick them up. After talking it over with Joseph, who agreed, Dervish made two trips that night. He rescued nineteen women and children who had been left by the wayside. "Of the twenty-five taken into the hospital in Talas, only ten were saved," Susan said. "The other fifteen were too far gone. They had starved to death. All our efforts were in vain."

The rest of the "column of agony" eventually arrived in Cesarea. They were taken to the Greek Church. Their fellow Greeks in the city did what they could to help, and the government asked the NER team to provide food, which they did. "At first we thought we could take them into the school buildings just then being vacated by the orphans," said Susan. "But an order from [NER] Constantinople made us hesitate. We were afraid we would not have support from them." By support, she meant not only money but staff. All their native workers were either helping out in the khans, or were supervising the children, and leaving the country with them.[1] The Talas unit would soon be down to a few personnel, and those remaining would close the station.

~ ~ ~

In early November *The Orient* reported that "little short of half a million souls" had left Anatolia. There were rumours the Greek government would "require every householder in the interior towns to take in refugees numbering at least half of the number already in his house." The problem for host countries to feed and house these refugees was staggering.[2] And the exodus was speeding up as the deadline to leave Turkey loomed closer.

In mid-December the president of the Armenian National Union sent a telegram to NER headquarters from Aleppo asking for immediate aid: "Fifty thousand Armenian refugees already arrived, thousands on way. All robbed, naked, wounded, girls violated, misery indescribable. Help urgently needed." In the north, winter had brought extreme cold and deep snow. Thousands of children and the elderly were dying on the mucky roads, and on board the rescue ships on the tempestuous Black Sea. One relief worker said, "I saw a crowd of broken civilians more depressing than an army in hard-pressed retreat. Women about to become mothers tramped in snow up to their knees. Tired children dropped weary by the wayside, and girls of tender years bore men's burdens." The quays and waterfront streets in Constantinople were clogged with Christian refugees. Another relief worker sent a telegram from the capital: "Fresh shiploads arriving daily. . . Majority do not know where they are going. Sad picture, broken-spirited people who have lost everything."[3]

Fortunately for the Talas unit, there were orphanages near Beirut where they could send their children. In January Maria Jacobsen had returned from her rest in Denmark, and had landed in a "nearly indescribable" Beirut. "Everything was in chaos. Mobs of people with bundles on their backs were suddenly gathered in one place, where they had to raise tents or find a corner to sleep, or gather their families, find food or do cooking amid rain and mud as pools of water flowed everywhere." NER workers had pulled orphans from camps of refugees who had fled Cilicia, and given them to Maria's care. By July she had 208 orphans, and the number kept growing. NER also ran an orphanage in Djoubeil (Byblos) Lebanon.[4] And in nearby Antilyas, the Australasian Orphanage had recently been established with funds from Australia and New Zealand. Anzac veteran Captain John H. Knudsen, and his wife, Maria, were its directors, initially caring for 1,700 Armenian children.[5]

~ ~ ~

The pace of politics was no less frantic. In early October Britain, France, Italy and Greece invited Turkey to the conference table in Lausanne to negotiate the terms of a new peace treaty. Though there was a brief power struggle within the Nationalist camp, Mustafa Kemal had retained the presidency. When Grand Vizier Tevfik Pasha asked him to send a representative from the Nationalists to Constantinople to coordinate the actions of the two governments with the Allies, he curtly replied that "the Turkish Grand Assembly was the only legitimate authority in Turkey; any other bodies would do well to refrain from causing confusion in the country's policy." He sent Ismet Pasha, a loyal and trusted colleague, to lead the Turkish delegation to Switzerland.[6]

On November 1 the Assembly abolished the sultanate. On November 4 the Grand Vizier resigned, along with his government in Constantinople.[7] The Sheikh-ul-Islam also resigned.[8] That same day, Ali

Kemal, the former Minister of the Interior who had called for the arrest of Mustafa Kemal three-and-a-half years earlier, was kidnapped and shipped to Smyrna. There, Nureddin treated him as he had treated the Greek archbishop. "As news of Ali Kemal's lynching became known, the British High Commission was flooded with requests for asylum," including the deposed sultan, Vahdettin. He and his family were smuggled out of the palace on November 17 in British army ambulances, and out of the country on a British ship. As soon as word came that Vahdettin was in Malta, the National Assembly declared his cousin, Abdul Mejid, to be the new caliph—but not, of course, the sultan.[9] In the name of the Grand National Assembly, Refet Pasha took over authority in Constantinople.[10] Shortly after, the government was permanently moved to Angora. The Ottoman Empire was officially dead.

~ ~ ~

Susan had been on the road for weeks. She checked in regularly with the workers at the khans to take their orders for supplies, and deal with any problems they encountered. She maintained friendly relations with the gendarmes to make sure they protected the children. One day she had to rescue a girl with a broken arm. The wagon the youngster had been riding in had turned over because two drivers had been running a race on the rough, slippery road. Another time a convoy had been robbed mid-route. No one had been hurt, but everyone had been badly frightened. It was a necessary but exhausting job.

The work was made all the harder because Susan was hiding a secret. Not long after the treks began, she was stricken with a terrible pain in her abdomen. She carried on in silence because the work had to be done, and there was no one else to do it. Everyone else was as busy as she was. As the days and nights grew colder, it was difficult to keep warm, and the pain in her kidneys and bladder grew worse. Still she carried on.

By December 13 the Talas unit had accomplished their task. They had removed 3,000 Armenian and Greek children from the orphanages in Kaisarieh, and seen them all safely out of Turkey. The remaining native workers and three NER personnel had accompanied the last few convoys. Katherine supervised the transport of the Armenian orphans from Adana to Beirut, and Lillian, Henry, Carl and Ruth took the Greek children by sea to Athens. When the fifteenth and last convoy left Oulou Kushla for Tarsus, Susan returned to Talas. "The last trip I made was very hard, and cold, and I suffered a good deal before I could get home," she later told her sister.[11] She also had to make the "strongest representations to authorities for protection against soldiers who tried to carry off our oldest girls."[12]

Armenian children being evacuated by American Near East Relief workers by ship, 1922. SOURCE: Armenian Genocide Museum Institute.

Fortunately, they listened, and the girls continued safely on the train to Mersine. When she got back, Dr. Dewey diagnosed her with acute nephritis and cystitis, brought on by the severe conditions of being on the road. He ordered immediate bed rest. "However, I did not rest, but worked in my room on accounts, and then packed up—a big task, when I felt so used up."[13]

It was decided that Susan and Stella would leave in a few days. Stella would go to Athens, while Susan would head to Constantinople and home, finally to begin her long-awaited furlough. Joseph, Blanche, and their baby, Dorothea, would stay for a short time, with Albert, Elsie, and their daughter Frances Elizabeth. Clara and Elsey were going to stay over the winter, too. It would take all of them to close down the station and dispose of the supplies that were left.

~ ~ ~

In December *Renin,* a Turkish daily, reported on "extensive anti-Turkish propaganda" going on in the United States. The Anadolou Agency wanted to draw "the attention of all impartial Americans, who are in our country and can see at close range the facts in the case." According to the agency, the fact was "that it is the American missionaries and the Near East Relief workers—to whom the Turks have always been so kind in every part of Anatolia—who are at the bottom of this propaganda, and have gone so far to show such foolishness and lack of intelligence, or of

302

justice, as even to incite their country to make war against the Turks. The strange thing in it all is that all their charges are wholly baseless."[14]

The agency's assessment of propaganda and baseless charges was a matter of opinion, but it did get right the marked unhappiness of the missionaries and relief workers. The group in Talas had always conducted their business with as much tact, diplomacy and grace as they could muster. But as their last act as a unit, they felt compelled to write a manifesto to the American Board of Commissioners for Foreign Missions, entitled "Resolutions adopted at Station Meeting of Talas Station, by vote of the Station, December 15, 1922:"

Resolved that the future of Christian Missionary work in Turkey requires that the American Board remonstrate and protest in the strongest possible terms to the Angora Nationalist Government for their cruel, unrighteous, and unjustifiable treatment of their subject peoples, it having resulted in unnecessary wholesale suffering and death by massacres, deportation and starvation, for which the Angora Nationalist Government is morally responsible to God before the eyes of the world. Unless these acts are condemned officially by the American Board by means of open communication to the men responsible for them, the moral basis for future work in Turkey is undermined.

Resolved that the American Board would be most unwise and should refuse to re-open its work in Turkey without the reestablishment of the rights and privileges that were secured to us under the former Capitulations.

Resolved that to continue work under the present conditions requires so much deception, evasion and currying of favor from wicked men on false presentations of friendship, as to tend to destroy the moral influence of any work the American Board is attempting to do and eventually to undermine the Christian character of the workers themselves.

Signed by members of Talas Station:
Joseph W. Beach
Susan W. Orvis
Stella N. Loughridge
Blanche E. Beach
Clara C. Richmond
Albert W. Dewey
Elsie G. Dewey[15]

~ ~ ~

Susan and Stella departed two days later. Saying goodbye to their colleagues was hard, but they knew they would be in touch later. Saying farewell to the place they had called home for twenty years was harder. They took their belongings, and all their precious memories, and left Talas forever.

The weather was cold. They drove all day "through a frozen cloud which made every weed and blade of grass a thing of beauty." They stopped for the night at the khan in Kiz Hissar, which was the site of the ancient village of Tyana. "The owner exerted himself to get everything for us," Susan said. "He professed to be greatly impressed by the work we have done for the poor and the orphans. He said that nothing could be too good for such kind people as we. He especially noted that I had been on the road so much with the children. It was a satisfaction to find such appreciation."

The next day they went through the Cilician Gates, the historical pass through the Taurus Mountains. "It was beautiful all the way, and we left the winter and snow behind us. With the exception of the few mud holes, we had fine roads and the car coasted down the long slopes only stopping to let the camel trains have time to huddle themselves against the wall to give us room to pass. The road is so narrow in places that we have to wait for a wider bend in the hillside. On one side there was always the beautiful stream of water, and rising high above us on either side of the narrow gorge were the high mountains covered with evergreen trees. On the peaks we could see plenty of snow. About an hour after dark we reached Tarsus, and were made welcome by friends at the American school there."[16]

They were both so tired, but pushed on the next day to Mersine. The road was bad, the day was long, but the arrival was sweet. They were met by 600 of their Talas friends, who were still waiting for the train to Beirut and the steamer to Athens, which were both scheduled to leave in a day or two. Stella booked passage on the ship to Greece, and Susan bought a ticket on the SS *Umbria* to Constantinople.[17]

"We are very thankful that all got through alive and well and safely," said Susan.[18] It was December 20, 1922, her 49th birthday.

30

The Cost

While Susan sailed to the United States, and Stella to Greece, the rest of the Talas team began to close the station. It was a monumental task. The job required taking inventory of every single item in every building owned by the American Board, and of all the supplies of Near East Relief. Every piece was marked with a numbered tag, and every number was recorded on a list that would be sent to NER headquarters. "We had a tough time closing up," said Clara. "Miss Bristol and others worked night after night in the office until 1:00 a.m. and after."[1]

Personal possessions that they intended to take with them were packed in steamer trunks and sent ahead by wagon to Mersine. All other things were to be wrapped and stored in attics or basements, since it was not clear whether the station would be re-opened some time later. Clara left the furniture that belonged to her and Fanny Burrage in the upper bedroom of the Kindergarten building in Cesarea, "wardrobe, china closet, organ and all." All furniture belonging to the others, except the Irwins' piano, was stored in the upper levels of the Boys' School in Talas. The hospital's furniture and equipment were moved there, too, as was the entire library of the Girls' Boarding School. The numerous organs and pianos were moved to the Primary room. Joseph and three native workers carried everything else to the basement of the main building, even the kitchen range, tables and benches, and cooking equipment.[2]

Albert took care of the remittance and inquiry work, and organized his helpers to get rid of the remaining goods. "They are giving a three-month allowance to the home orphans, partly in money and partly in supplies," said Elsey. "That is one way of closing out the supplies." By mid-February she was feeling the pressure. "It is a most confusing situation. I am still at work closing the January accounts. Then I'll send the report. . . . We must pack all the vouchers and books and correspondence, and take them out. All I can say is that I hope this will be the last job of this sort for me to have a hand in. It is not inspiring."[3]

In the meantime, Lillian Cole Sewny and Henry Murphy sent several telegrams from Greece to Joseph and Blanche, urging them to "come quick." They were in "desperate need of new recruits" to handle the continuous in-pouring of refugees. Finally, on March 5, 1923, the Beaches, Clara Richmond and Elsey Bristol were ready to leave. The Deweys were staying behind to study the language, and there were many

Armenian and Greek workers who had decided to remain in their homes. One young woman named Yeranuhi wanted to emigrate, but her papers were not in order. "There were serious difficulties in her case under the newest conditions," said Clara. Joseph arranged for her exit as a nanny for his daughter, Dorothea. After a farewell every bit as difficult as Susan and Stella's had been, they were driven south to Mersine by the ever faithful Dervish.[4]

~ ~ ~

Between September 1915 and December 1922, Near East Relief sent more than 25,000 tons of food, clothing, medical supplies and other items of humanitarian aid to those in need. More than a thousand workers, many of them volunteers, delivered it: "300 office staff, 46 physicians and surgeons, 95 nurses, 48 secretaries, 39 engineers, 13 mechanics, 56 supply and transport workers, 17 industrial experts, 14 bacteriologists, 46 army officers as organizers, 20 agriculturalists, 285 orphanage and general relief workers, 19 teachers, and 32 administrators." The total value was approximately $73,000,000.[5] Of course, the need continued.

In Mersine, Clara, Joseph and Paul Bobb from Tarsus worked at the transport depot they called the Factory. There were 4,500 refugees still in the city, many from Smyrna, most looking like famine victims. More than 3,000 of the refugees were housed in the Factory. They were all waiting for a ship to take them away. It was a particularly dangerous place for a woman. Clara was grateful Joseph refused to leave her alone. "The filth of the place has been awful. We are working so hard to get them to clean it up," she wrote to Stella in Athens. "Do not be afraid for me. I am well, and very careful. I change my clothes, use naphthalene bands, have men with sticks to keep people off me. I am very careful, but go everywhere except into the smallpox room. We had 6 cases, but they are practically well, and it is not spreading. The dysentery is the worst. Their water is terrible there. We are trying to clean out a slimy well, and a soup vat in which we can boil water for them to drink. All my petty troubles have flown away."[6]

What disturbed her most was that the terrible conditions and suffering had cost many of the refugees their sense of decency and humanity. She was careful to point out that not everyone was "devoid of character," but she was shocked and saddened nevertheless. "Many of them have almost ceased to be human beings," she said. "I had several men just beating them back from me with sticks. More than 2,000 almost mobbed me for soup tickets." The doctor from one of the ships told her he had seen many awful sights in his life, but nothing as bad as this. "Oh, how they slander each other, and blackmail, go to the police with false charges, etc.!" Clara said. "Such depravity of human nature brought on by lack of training and real Christianity, years and years of exiling, and hunger. Greeks telling on Armenians, and vice versa." She said she would never forget that time as long as she lived. It was Easter 1923.[7]

Near East Relief continued to provide emergency aid for another seven years. In 1930, recognizing that the need for relief had lessened, but sustained, long term development was required in the region, the organization once again changed its name. It became known as Near East Foundation.[8]

~ ~ ~

The last fifteen years of the Ottoman Empire had been bloody and costly: two coups d'état, four regional wars, a world war, a war of independence, and a crippling national debt. Most of the Ottoman army had been recruited from the peasant population of Anatolia—the "soldier mines of the empire"—with little regard for their lives or the lives of the families they left behind. About 2.5 million Muslims had died.[9] Ottoman state policies of extermination against entire ethnic groups had been implemented. Since 1914 more than 3 million Armenians, Assyrians and Greeks had either been deported, murdered, died of starvation or disease, or fled. Only a few hundred thousand were left by early 1923, but they had chosen to stay.[10]

However, according to the terms of the Treaty of Lausanne, there would be an "Exchange of Populations" between Greece and Turkey. The Angora government had insisted on it as a way to further reduce the country of Christians, and to increase the number of Muslims. By the end of 1924, another 143,000 Greeks were forced to emigrate. There was a technical argument about how many additional Greeks were to leave Constantinople, because of a clause that stated "all Greeks who were already established before October 30, 1918 . . . shall be considered as Greek inhabitants of Constantinople," and could remain in the city. NER and other agencies had been working in Greece for more than a year, therefore, while the number of refugees was overwhelming—an estimated 1.5 million—and conditions were crowded, there were systems in place to help.[11]

It was not the same for the Muslims leaving Greece for Turkey. Most of the 353,000 deportees "went against their will. They were not ill-treated in Europe and had no wish to be uprooted and transplanted to a ruined country." The idea was that they would move into the empty houses of the Greek deportees, but the majority of Greeks in this "exchange" had left a year and a half previously, "during which time the government took no steps for maintenance of the empty houses." The buildings had deteriorated to the point of being uninhabitable. Neither had the government put support systems in place for the new arrivals. These people quickly became destitute, living in temporary shelters, susceptible to disease, without work, relying solely on a "dole of 50 piasters (25-50 cents) a day," not enough to live on. The economy was failing without adequately skilled industrial and agricultural workers. By expelling the Christians from Turkey, the government was closer to attaining its goal of a unified "Turkey for the Turks," although the Muslim immigrants of the past decade were not Turkish. As one observer noted, "This unity is costing her dear: the remedy bids fair to kill the patient. The rulers of Turkey will need great application, care, and skill to heal the wounds they themselves have opened."[12] Once again, with the sweep of a pen, men in power decided on the fate of civilians. And once again, they caused incalculable misery. "Immigrants in both Greece and Turkey felt like and were treated as outsiders for generations."[13]

~ ~ ~

When Susan arrived at the dock in New York on February 10, 1923, who should be waiting for her but Adelaide Dwight.[14] It was so fitting. Twenty years and five months before, they had set sail together on an adventure of a lifetime. It had turned into more than either one of them anticipated—or wanted. Now they were older, wiser, and a bit worse for wear.

A reporter interviewed Susan on the pier while she waited for her bags to clear customs. The article about her saving the orphans was published in *The New York Times*.[15] Adelaide booked her into the Hotel Albert, and gave her an armful of letters from friends and family, which had been undeliverable for more than a year. Susan read them voraciously, catching up on births and deaths and all that she had missed.[16] A few NER workers were going to Chicago and had agreed to take her three steamer trunks with them on their ticket. She wrote to her brother, asking if he would arrange to have them shipped from Chicago to his home in Dubuque. She expected to see him there on February 24.[17] First she was going to spend a few days in New York, visiting the NER office and shopping with Adelaide. Then she would see Joseph Beach's parents to inform them of their new grandchild, and take a quick side trip to Boston to check in with her colleagues at the American Board and the Woman's Board of Missions.[18] She was also going to try to squeeze in a visit with Theda Phelps in Philadelphia.[19]

Her plans changed drastically when, three days later, she landed in Bosworth Hospital in Brookline, Massachusetts. The nephritis Susan had suffered on the cold road between Oulou Kushla and Talas had finally cleared up, but the cystitis had worsened. "The rush and excitement of New York was too much for me, in spite of the fact that I was very careful," she wrote to her sister. "Seeing people and talking wears on me, and travelling in cold weather is bad for me, of course. I am in hopes that the Near East Relief may be willing to pay for this hospital bill since Dr. Dewey gave me a statement to the effect that this trouble was the direct result of exposure on the road when I was taking out the orphans." She had been in pain for months, and now she was forced to do something about it.[20] Three months later, she was still being treated, having been transferred to Memorial Hospital in Worcester. Her spirits were as optimistic as ever, and she kept busy with reading and correspondence, but regaining her health was a slow process: "I think that rest is the thing I need most."[21]

~ ~ ~

In October, the Republic of Turkey was established, with Angora (now Ankara) as the capital, and Mustafa Kemal as President. Between 1923 and Kemal's death in 1938, Turkey changed considerably. The caliphate was abolished, and the Ottoman dynasty exiled. Religious schools and courts were closed, dervish orders and Muslim brotherhoods were dissolved, Islam as the official religion was removed from the constitution, and "secularism" was added. New civil, criminal and commercial codes were instituted. The fez was banned, and women's rights were enshrined in society, including freedom of dress, the right to vote, and the right to be a Member of Parliament. In an attempt to modernize the country on par with Europe, Turkey adopted international numerals, weights and measures, the Latin alphabet, and the custom of using surnames.[22] Mustafa Kemal adopted the surname Atatürk, which means "father of the Turks."[23] As a result of the establishment of the Turkish Language Society "to ensure 'pure' Turkish,"[24] many place names changed: Smyrna to Izmir, Constantinople to Istanbul, and Cesarea to Kayseri, though Talas remained Talas.[25]

Many of the changes were progressive, but "when Atatürk died, Turkey was still a poor and backward country. Some four-fifths of the population lived in villages, many in primitive houses built of mud brick. . . . Muslims were gradually learning trades, but the small remaining Christian and Jewish communities were still prominent in skilled occupations. The republic Atatürk founded was run by officers and officials who had served under the sultans, as he had himself."[26] They had all served under the CUP regime, too, and were committed to the continuation of Turkification. Most Armenians and Greeks were gone. Kurds would be the next to be deported.[27] "Turkey for the Turks" was still the reigning policy.

But a new republic cannot hope to develop into a strong, healthy nation if it is rooted in evil and negativity. Therefore "a conspiracy of silence" began to grow around its recent past.[28] This phenomenon sprouted immediately after the burning of Smyrna. During Kemal's first speech before the National Assembly on November 4, 1922, where he "described in detail the events and the battles of late August and early September," he never once mentioned the great fire and "almost total destruction of the second most important city of the new nation." Izmir quickly became a "symbol of liberation rather than of destruction, gain rather than loss, joy rather than mourning."[29] In 1923 the government announced a general amnesty "for all those convicted by the Courts-Martial, as well as by civilian courts," for crimes against humanity. The Military Appeals Court overturned the verdict of the Yozgat trial of Mehmed Kemal, who had been executed in 1919. He was proclaimed a "national martyr" and a statue of him was erected in the public square of Boghazlian.[30]

In 1931 the act of selectively forgetting the past, and reconstructing it with lies and half-truths, became official. The Turkish Historical Society was founded "to produce a nationalist version of history,"[31] which was taught in schools.[32] The population was re-conceptualized "as a homogeneous group with a shared history, ethnic/religious identity and language."[33] Anatolia was identified "as the historic home of the Turks, whose earth had been coloured red by the blood of the 'martyrs' since the first Turkish conquest in 1071. . . . and old Anatolian civilizations, such as that of the Hittites, were claimed as Turkish, thus staking out a historical claim to the territory older than that of the Greeks, Armenians, Arabs or Kurds."[34] There had been no state extermination policies against Christians, and no confiscation of their properties, because if this were true, it would mean that many of Turkey's "national heroes and founding fathers were either murderers, thieves, or both."[35] The deportations of the Armenians was a result of their "rebellion . . . and their crimes."[36] It was the Greeks who burned Izmir, or maybe the Armenians.[37] And who could refute it? The state archives were "closed to most scholars,"[38] and within a generation or two, the average Turk could not read documents written in "old Turkish." This fabricated history became accepted, internalized, and calcified through the decades.[39] And Turkey's standing in the international community has suffered for it.

~ ~ ~

After the Republic of Turkey was established and acknowledged by the international community, the government relaxed its stance on deporting Christians. After all, there were hardly any left. It allowed Near East Relief to continue working in the country. The American Board had retained ownership of its properties, and began to re-open stations. The old Talas team, however, never reunited. Elsey Bristol said, "If I'm not needed, I'll go on to America—which wouldn't be altogether unpleasant."[40] She did, retiring to Madison, Wisconsin immediately after leaving Talas. Joseph and Blanche Easton delivered aid in Beirut until 1926, when they moved to the Caucasus. After delivering orphans to Beirut, Katherine Fletcher worked in Constantinople from 1924 to 1945. Genevieve and Herbert Irwin arrived in Athens in 1924, working there until 1927 when Herbert died. Genevieve and her children then returned to Canada. Lillian Cole Sewny also worked in Beirut. She spent the summer of 1926 in the United States, and then went to Salonica as Matron of the relocated Anatolia College. The college had been moved from Marsovan in 1925, thanks to the help of Carl and Ruth Compton. They taught at the college, with Carl being Dean (1925-1939), and later President (1950-1958).[41]

For six years, Albert and Elsie Dewey went wherever they were needed: Greece, Beirut and the Caucasus. In 1929 they moved to Aintab where Dr. Dewey headed the Gaziantep Hospital, staying until 1958. Theda Phelps joined the staff of the Azariah Smith Hospital in Aintab in 1924 and stayed until her retirement in 1947.

From Mersine, Clara Richmond moved to Smyrna in 1924. She took a one-year furlough in 1925, and then taught in Constantinople until 1928, retiring the next year. Stella Loughridge spent a few months in Athens, then she, too, went on furlough. In 1925 she taught in Beirut, and then moved to Scutari until her retirement in 1939. By the summer of 1923 Susan Wealthy Orvis had recovered from her illness, and decided to go back to school. She graduated with a B.A. from Oberlin College in 1924. After resting for two years, she took a teaching assignment in Adana. She remained there until her health declined again, and she was forced to retire in 1931. Only Adelaide Dwight returned to Talas. She arrived in 1924 and stayed for 17 years.[42]

~ ~ ~

Following the deportations and massacres, a young Armenian woman named Zaroohi wrote a letter of thanks to her former teacher, Dr. Nesbitt Chambers, and his wife for caring for her spiritual and moral welfare. "Expending your efforts both night and day; and not only for me, but for so many like me. Seeing the unfortunate and pitiful condition of the whole nation, you did not hesitate to put forth every endeavor for the welfare of the people. Our nation has never realized, so much as at the present time, the blessings arising from the activities of the general missionary enterprise exerted for its welfare, as well as for the progress of the race. You must ever keep in mind that that work will not be forgotten, nor will that good seed which you have sown, here and there, be lost.

"They may kill our bodies," said Zaroohi, "but our spirits will live forever, and that seed which has fallen on good ground will grow."[43] It was true. The missionaries and relief workers had saved the seeds of future generations. It was no small feat, given the madness of the times. Even so, they saw themselves as mere guardians, saving bodies and souls for some reason more important and larger than themselves.

With her characteristic understatement, Susan Wealthy Orvis reflected on her years of service. "The whole world is my neighborhood, more truly because I have had a chance to see much of it, and to take a small part in a few corners of it, trying to brighten a few lives here and there," she said. "Some had been very sad lives, and even a little sunshine goes a long way in a dark room."[44]

Glossary of Terms and Places

Abbreviations

ABCFM	American Board of Commissioners for Foreign Missions
ACASR	American Committee for Armenian and Syrian Relief
ACRNE	American Committee for Relief in the Near East
AGM	annual general meeting
Anzac	Australia and New Zealand Army Corps
CUP	Committee of Union and Progress
NER	Near East Relief
OPDA	Ottoman Public Debt Administration
SO	Special Organization
SVM	Student Volunteer Movement for Foreign Missions
WBM/WBMI	Woman's Board of Missions / of the Interior
YMCA	Young Men's Christian Association
YWCA	Young Women's Christian Association

Terms

Agha*	title of respect
Baron	title of respect, more than Effendi (Mr.)
Bey*	title of respect, like Squire
caliph	spiritual leader of Islam
caliphate	the area ruled by a caliph
Catholicos	Patriarch of the Armenian or Nestorian Church
chette	brigand, band of thugs or outlaws
Effendi*	title of respect, like Mister (Mr.)
folkmord	genocide
gavur	infidel
Grand Vizier	the chief officer of the Ottoman Empire
Gregorian	antiquated term for Armenian
hamal	porter, dock worker
Hanum*	Mrs. or Lady
hodja	Muslim teacher or scholar

idadieh	preparatory
imam	priest of a mosque or religious leader
jihad	holy war
kaimakam	governor of a kaza
kaza	county (subdivision of a sanjak)
khan	inn
konak	government office building
lavash	flat bread
Levantine	Ottoman of European descent
mudir	administrator
mutesarrif	governor of a sanjak
Pan-Turkism	movement for cultural and political unification of Turkic people
Pasha*	title of respect of a high official, like General
sandık emini	treasurer
sanjak	administrative district of a vilayet (larger than a kaza)
sheriat	Islamic law
softa	student in a religious (Muslim) school
Sublime Porte	seat of government in the Ottoman Empire
sultan	the sovereign or absolute ruler of the Ottoman Empire
vali	governor of a vilayet
vilayet	province
yerli	person native to the area

Place Names

If a place is not listed here, its name did not change. Some on this list just have a different spelling.

Then	Now
Adabazar	Adapazarı
Adrianople	Edirne
Afion Kara Hissar	Afyonkarahisar
Aidin	Aydın
Aintab	Gaziantep
Ak Hisar	Akhisar
Alexandretta	İskenderun
Alexandropol	Gyumri, Armenia

---

* Placed after the person's name

Amasia	Amasya
Angora	Ankara
Ashdarag	Ashtarak, Armenia
Askerai	Aksaray
Bardezag	Bahçecik
Batum	Batumi
Boghazlian	Boğazlıyan
Boudjah	Buca
Bozanti	Pozantı
Brousa	Bursa
Cesarea	Kayseri
Chakmak	Sırçalı
Chanak	Çanakkale
Chesme	Çeşme
Chomaklou	now part of Develi
Chukurkeuy	Çukurköy
Constantinople	Istanbul
Derevenk	now part of Talas
Derindje	Derince
Der Zor	Deir ez-Zor
Diarbekir	Diyarbakır
Dilman	suburb of Salmas, Iran
Dumlumpinar	Dumlupınar
Erevan	Yerevan, Armenia
Eregli	Erekli
Erzingan	Erzincan
Erzroom	Erzurum
Eskishehir	Eskişehir
Everek	suburb of Develi
Evkere	Gesi-Bahçeli
Hadjin	Saimbeyli
Harpoot	Elâzığ
Injesu	İncesu
Isle of Oxias	Sivriada
Julfa	Jolfa, Iran
Kaisarieh	Kayseri
Karakilisa	Vanadzor, Armenia
Konia	Konya
Malatia	Malatya

Marash	Kahramanmaraş
Marsovan	Merzifon
Mersine	Mersin
Mudros	Moudros
Nicomedia/Ismid	İzmit
Nigdeh	Niğde
Oorfa	Şanlıurfa
Oulou Kushla	Ulukışla
Persia	Iran
Petrograd	Saint Petersburg
Prinkipo	Büyükada
Salonica	Thessaloniki
Samsoun	Samsun
Sarikamish	Sarıkamış
Scutari	Üsküdar
Sharkushla	Şarkışla
Sinope	Sinop
Smyrna	Izmir
Stamboul	suburb of Istanbul
Terfurdag	Tekirdağ
Tiflis	Tbilisi
Trebizond	Trabzon
Ushak	Uşak
Zeitoon	Süleymanlı
Zinjidery	Zincidere

List of Personnel

The majority of the personnel of the American Board and Near East Relief mentioned in this book were from North American towns and cities, and all were highly educated:

Talas Personnel	Lifespan	From	Higher Education
Beach, Blanche Easton	1894-1984	Ridgewood, NJ	NYC Presbyterian NS
Beach, Joseph W. (Rev)	1889-1973	Bangor, ME	Yale
Bristol, Elsey Lois	1863-1932	Black Earth, WI	Wisconsin
Burrage, Fanny	1852-1924	Pittsfield, VT	Moody
Cushman, Emma	1863-1931	Utica, NY	Kansas State, Paterson NS
Dewey, Albert W. (MD)	1891-1980	Georgetown, CO	Denver, Pennsylvania
Dewey, Elsie Greene	1888-1940	Emporia, KS	Colorado
Dodd, Mary Carter	1863-1934	New York, NY	NY Normal
Dodd, William (MD)	1860-1928	Smyrna	Princeton, Union
Dwight, Adelaide	1878-1966	Constantinople	Smith
Fletcher, Katharine	1877-1971	Hartford, CT	Smith, Columbia
Fowle, Caroline	1854-1917	Cesarea	Mt Holyoke, Wellesley
Fowle, James (Rev)	1847-1917	Woburn, MA	Amherst, Andover
Fowle, Mary	1880-1916	Cesarea	Mt Holyoke
Gannaway, Charles (MD)	1874-1946	Guthrie, IA	Northwestern
Gannaway, Ruby Pearl Davis	1875-1957	Guthrie, IA	unknown
Holbrook, Charles H. (Rev)	1880-1913	Salem, MA	Boston, Union
Hoover, Alden (MD)	1877-1940	Muscatine, IA	Iowa State
Hoover, Esther Finger	1880-1948	Oshkosh, WI	Yankton Normal
Irwin, Genevieve duVal	1876-1952	Winnipeg, MB	Manitoba

Name	Dates	Place	School
Irwin, Herbert (Rev)	1868-1927	Port Hope, ON	Manitoba, Toronto
Loughridge, Stella	1871-1963	Lincoln, NE	Nebraska, Chicago
Martin, Edward F.	1892-1969	Peshtigo, WI	unknown
Martin, Rachel King	1893-1963	Little Britain, NY	NYC Presbyterian NS
Munro, Annette Louise	1893-1992	Newton, MA	NS
Murphy, Henry R.	1898-1963	Lawrence, MA	MIT
North, Rachel B.	1874-1927	Belfast, Ireland	Nursing School, Moody
O'Meara, John W. (MD)	1892-194+	Worcester, MA	Harvard
Orvis, Susan Wealthy	1873-1941	Dubuque, IA	Grinnell, Chicago, Oberlin
Phelps, Theda	1876-1964	Greenville, MI	Illinois Training NS
Plimpton, Barton Fiske	1894-1967	Jamaica, NY	unknown
Post, Annie Stabb	1877-1925	Brooklyn, NY	NYC Presbyterian NS
Post, Wilfred (MD)	1876-1966	Beirut	Princeton, Columbia
Richards, George L. (MD)	1863-1933	Fall River, MA	Harvard
Richards, Mary Robinson	1863-1927	Fall River, MA	unknown
Richmond, Clara Childs	1879-1966	Le Raysville, PA	Wheelock, Oberlin
Ryan, Arthur Clayton (Rev)	1879-1927	Grandview, IA	Grinnell, Oberlin
Ryan, Edith Hoover	1871-1955	Muscatine, IA	NS
Sewny, Lillian Cole	1870-1955	Tenafly, NJ	Montclair NS
Talboy, Helen Garner	1876-1941	Onawa, IA	unknown
Talboy, James H. (MD)	1863-1944	Onawa, IA	unknown
Warye, John	1890-1983	Urbana, OH	Goshen
Whitney, Raymond C. (MD)	1893-1961	New Bedford, MA	Middlebury, Harvard
Wingate, Henry K. (Rev)	1865-1944	Janesville, WI	Carleton
Wingate, Jane Smith	1865-1952	Marsovan	unknown
Wright, V.W. Murray (MD)	1897-1947	Penn Yan, NY	Buffalo

Others

Name	Dates	Place	Schools
Allen, Annie T	1868-1922	Harpoot	Wellesley, Mt Holyoke
Barton, James Levi (Rev)	1855-1936	Charlotte, VT	Middlebury C, Hartford
Birge, Anna Harlow	1887-1925	Brooklyn, NY	Wellesley
Bobb, Paul F.	1898-1983	Denver, CO	Rice
Case, Herbert E. B. (Rev)	1877-195+	Pawtucket, RI	Rhode Island, Brown, Hartford
Case, Edward P. (MD)	1888-1963	Patchogue, NY	Lafayette, Michigan
Chambers, Lawson	1883-1958	Turkey	unknown
Chambers, Wm Nesbitt (Rev)	1853-1934	Norwich, ON	Queen's, Princeton, Union
Clark, C Ernest (MD)	1875-1942	Brattleboro, VT	Dartmouth, Michigan
Cold, Edith	1879-1980	Cleveland, OH	Michigan
Compton, Carl	1891-1982	Stuart, IA	Grinnell, Oberlin
Compton, Ruth	1892-1979	Missouri Valley, IA	Grinnell
Crawford, Lyndon (Rev)	1852-1918	North Adams, MA	Williams, Hartford
Crawford, Olive	1854-1923	Plantsville, CT	unknown
Dewey, Diantha	1878-1951	Syria	Oberlin
Dewey, Seraphina	1844-1931	Medina, NY	unknown
Dunaway, John	1886-1969	Cedar County, MO	Pennsylvania
Dunaway, Rose Shayb	1893-1981	near Beirut	Colby, Mass. General NS
Elliott, Mabel Evelyn (MD)	1881-1968	England/Michigan	Rush Medical
Elmer, Theodore (Rev)	1871-1964	Bridgeton, NJ	Layfayette, Princeton
Ely, Charlotte	1839-1915	Philadelphia, PA	Mt Holyoke, Elmira
Farnsworth, Caroline F.	1825-1913	Cornwall, VT	Middlebury
Farnsworth, Wilson (Rev)	1822-1912	Greene, NY	Middlebury, Andover
Fowle, Luther	1886-1973	Talas	Williams, Union
Gage, Frances	1863-1917	Quincy, MA	Carleton

Name	Location	Dates	School
Getchell, Dana	Glencoe, MN	1870-1950	Carleton
Goodsell, Lulu S.	Ceres, CA	1881-1971	UC Berkeley
Goodsell, Fred (Rev)	Montevideo, MN	1880-1976	UC Berkeley, Hartford
Graffam, Mary	Monson, ME	1871-1921	Andover, Oberlin
Gracey, George	Belfast, Ireland	1878-1958	unknown
Greene, Phillips F. (MD)	Montclair, NJ	1892-1967	Amherst, Harvard
Greene, Olive	Crossville, NY	1883-1966	Wellesley, Hartford, Radcliffe
Harlow, Marion Stafford	Brooklyn, NY	1886-1961	Radcliffe
Harlow, S Ralph (Rev)	Grafton, MA	1885-1972	Harvard, Union, Columbia
Holeman, Jessie	Louisville, KY	1878-193+	kindergarten training
Holt, Sophie	Somerville, MA	1876-1960	Minnesota
James, Walter (Rev)	Chase, KS	1882-1937	Fairmount, Oberlin
Jennings, Asa (Rev/YMCA)	Cleveland, NY	1877-1933	Syracuse
Johnson, Frank L. (YMCA)	Newark, OH	1878-1920	Ohio
Jones, Anna B	Columbia, OH	1862-1947	Granville (Denison)
Kennedy, William A. (MD)	Hamilton, ON	1880-1963	Queen's
Kerr, Stanley E.	Darby, PA	1894-1976	Pennsylvania
Kinney, Mary	Boston, MA	1874-1930	Boston Normal
Knapp George P. (Rev)	Bitlis	1863-1915	Harvard, Hartford
Leslie, Elvestra T.	Northport, MI	1885-1979	Olivet
Leslie, Francis (Rev)	Northport, MI	1877-1915	Fargo
Lyman, James (Rev)	Dayton, WA	1880-1950	Oberlin
MacCallum, Frederick (Rev)	Warwick, ON	1863-1945	McGill, Oberlin, Yale
MacLachlan, Alexander (Rev)	Erin, ON	1858-1940	Queen's, Union
Maynard, Harrison (Rev)	Muscotah, KS	1878-1952	Washburn, Union
Maynard, Mary White	Charlottesville, IN	1883-1967	Washburn
McCallum, Emily	Warwick, ON	1858-1956	McGill, Queen's, Olivet

Name	Dates	Place	School
McLaren, Grisell	1874-1964	Glasgow, Scotland	Mt Holyoke
McNaughton, James P. (Rev)	1861-1938	Dominionville, ON	Queen's, Union
Means, Gardiner C.	1896-1988	Windham, CT	Harvard
Merrill, John (Rev)	1872-1960	Medina, NY	Minnesota, Hartford
Mills, Minnie	1872-1965	Magnolia, IA	Olivet
Morley, Bertha B.	1878-1973	Mentor, OH	Oberlin
Nilson, Paul E. (Rev)	1890-1968	Rockford, IL	Beloit, Hartford, Chicago
Parmelee, Ruth (MD)	1885-1973	Trebizond	Oberlin, Illinois, Harvard
Parsons, Edith	1880-1967	Wellesley Hills, MA	Wellesley, Columbia, Berlin
Partridge, Ernest (Rev)	1870-1955	Weybridge, VT	Andover, Oberlin
Partridge, Winona G.	1873-1961	Monson, ME	Oberlin
Peet, William W.	1851-1942	Fall River, MA	Grinnell, Williston
Perry, Henry T.	1838-1930	Ashfield, MA	Williams, Auburn
Perry, James (YMCA)	1888-1920	Camden, ME	Colby, Hartford
Putney, Ethel	1880-1967	Wellesley, MA	Wellesley, Columbia,
Raynolds, George (MD)	1839-1920	Longmeadow, MA	Williams, NY Medical
Raynolds, Martha	1839-1915	Lyme, CT	Mt Holyoke
Rice, Nina E	1878-1958	Penfield, OH	Pomona, CA Normal
Riggs, Ernest W. (Rev)	1881-1952	Marsovan	Princeton, Auburn
Riggs, Henry H. (Rev)	1875-1943	Sivas	Carleton, Auburn
Riggs, Charles T. (Rev)	1871-1953	Sivas	Princeton
Rogers, D. Miner (Rev)	1881-1909	New Britain, CT	Princeton, Hartford
Shepard, Fred D. (MD)	1855-1915	Ellenburg, NY	Cornell
Stapleton, Ida S. (MD)	1871-1946	Metamora, MI	Olivet, Women's Medical
Stapleton, Robert (Rev)	1866-1945	Saginaw, MI	Olivet, Chicago Sem.
Thom, Daniel (MD)	1844-1915	Aberdeen, Scotland	Rush Medical
Thom, Helen Dewey	1858-1915	Owatonna, MN	unknown

Name	Dates	Place	Education
Thompson, Ethel	1887-194+	Boston, MA	NYC NS
Ussher, Elizabeth B.	1873-1915	Cesarea	Baltimore
Ussher, Clarence (MD)	1870-1955	Aurora, IL	Kansas
Vaughan, Olive	1874-1936	Lansing, MI	Carleton
Vrooman, Lee (Rev)	1897-1954	Orono, ME	Maine, Hartford
Ward, Mark H. (MD)	1884-1952	Newton Center, MA	Amherst, Columbia
Washburn, George W. (Rev)	1833-1915	Middleboro, MA	Amherst, Auburn
Webb, Elizabeth	1860-1949	Bunker Hill, IL	unknown
White, George E. (Rev)	1861-1946	Marash	Grinnell, Chicago Sem.
White, Henry H.	1893-1976	East Ryegate, VT	Amherst
White, Irma	1893-1981	Paterson, NJ	unknown
Willard, Charlotte	1860-1930	Fairhaven, MA	Smith, Carleton/professor
Wirt, Loyal Lincoln (Rev)	1863-1961	Lamont, MI	Jamestown, Pacific
Woodley, Edward C. (Rev)	1878-1947	Montreal, QC	McGill
Wright, Lester J. (Rev)	1886-1922	Waukesha, WI	Wisconsin, Moody
Yarrow, Ernest (Rev)	1876-1939	Hartford, CT	Wesleyan, Connecticut, Union
Yarrow, J. Martha T.	1883-1974	Oneonta, NY	unknown

Note: Auburn = Auburn Seminary, Hartford = Hartford Seminary, Union = Union Theology Seminary, Pacific = Pacific Theological Seminary, MIT = Massachusetts Institute of Technology, NS = hospital nursing school, Normal = teacher's college, 18?? = birth date unknown, + = died after this date. SOURCES: ABH-PR, US Passport Applications, graves and memorials, university and college yearbooks, contemporary newspaper articles. If a name is not included, it is because there was little or no information available.

Endnotes

List of Abbreviations

ABCFM-AR American Board of Commissioners for Foreign
Missions, Annual Report

ABH-PR Amerikan Bord Heyeti (American Board), Personnel Record

FO British Foreign Office

HL/HU Houghton Library, Harvard University

LLW *Life and Light for Women*

MH *Missionary Herald*

MS *Missionary Studies*

NER Near East Relief

SWO Susan Wealthy Orvis

SWOP Susan Wealthy Orvis Papers

SWOTR Susan Wealthy Orvis, "Through Russia 1917"

1. A New Breed

1   Tachat Ramavarma Ravindranathan, "The Young Turk Revolution, July 1908 to April 1909: Its Immediate Effects," (master's thesis, Simon Fraser University, 1970), 64-71. Several members of the sultan's inner circle, and only a few administrative officials and army officers died.

2   James L. Barton, *Daybreak in Turkey*, 2nd ed. (Boston: Pilgrim Press, 1908), 282.

3   Anna B. Jones, "Missionary Letters: Western Turkey," *Life and Light for Woman* 38, no. 10 (1908): 458. (Hereafter, *LLW.*)

4   Harriet G. Powers, Ibid, 458-59.

5   Susan Wealthy Orvis (hereafter SWO) to Home Friends, August 8, 1908, Susan Wealthy Orvis Papers (Hereafter, SWOP).

6   George Washburn, *Fifty Years in Constantinople and Recollections of Robert College* (Boston: Houghton Mifflin, 1909), xxx.

7   Francis Wayland Orvis, *A History of the Orvis Family in America* (Hackensack, NJ: The Orvis Company, Inc., 1922), 32.

8   In 1840 the population in the United States was 17 million and the number of college graduates in that year was approximately 4,000 (US Bureau of Statistics).

9   *Handbook for Missions and Missionaries of the American Board of Commissioners for Foreign Missions* (Boston: Beacon Press, 1901), 22. The ABCFM policy on furloughs was every seven years for women and eight years for men.

10 Selim Deringil, *Conversion and Apostasy in the Late Ottoman Empire* (Cambridge, UK: Cambridge University Press, 2012), 109-10.

11 Florence A. Fensham, Mary I. Lyman, and Mrs. H. B. Humphrey, *A Modern Crusade in the Turkish Empire* (Chicago: Woman's Board of Missions of the Interior, 1908), 12. Fensham states, "The population of the Turkish Empire is estimated at 32,176,696, but this number is not easy to verify, because of the difficulty of taking a census." McCarthy puts it more bluntly: "Investigating the Muslim population of Ottoman Europe is the stuff of a demographer's nightmare." He notes most estimates were "the prejudiced guesses of nationalistic advocates" or made by travellers: Justin McCarthy, "Muslims in Ottoman Europe: Population from 1800 to 1912," *Nationalities Papers* 28, no. 1 (2000): 29-43. Accessed at tandfonline.com. DOI: 10.1080/ 00905990050002443. Fensham's lengthy description of the various ethnic groups that comprised the Muslim, Christian and Jewish populations is supported by Kieser: "The Ottoman Empire was the most religiously diverse empire in Europe and Asia . . . [and] housed large groups of Christians and a significant number of Jews; there was no clear Muslim majority." Hans-Lukas Kieser, "Minorities (Ottoman Empire/Middle East)," in *International Encyclopedia of the First World War*, ed. Ute Daniel et al. (Berlin: Freie Universität Berlin, 2014), 1. Accessed at 1914-1918-online. DOI: 10.15463/ ie1418.10512.

12 SWO to Judson Smith, February 22, 1902, Houghton Library, Harvard University, ABC 16.9.3, Microfilm A467, v34, Reel 623, 550. (Hereafter HL/ HU.)

13 American Board of Commissioners for Foreign Missions, *The Ninety-Eighth Annual Report* (Boston: Congregational House, 1908), 148. (Annual reports hereafter, ABCFM-AR.)

14 E. Alexander Powell, "The Romance of the Missionary," *Everybody's Magazine* (September 1909), quoted in American Board of Commissioners for Foreign Missions, *Missionary Herald* 105, no. 12 (1909): 553-54. (Hereafter, *MH*.)

15 Orvis, *History of the Orvis Family;* William A. Benedict and Hiram A. Tracy, *History of the Town of Sutton, Massachusetts from 1704 to 1876* (Worchester, MA: Sanford & Company, 1878), 298; Hiram Carleton, *Genealogical and Family History of the State of Vermont, Vol. II* (New York: Lewis Publishing, 1903), 227; Oliver S. Phelps and Andrew T. Servin, *The Phelps Family of America and their English Ancestors, Vol. II* (Pittsfield, MA: Eagle, 1899), 72; Ralph Stebbins Greenlee and Robert Lemuel Greenlee, *The Stebbins Genealogy, Vol. I* (Chicago: privately printed, 1904), 56; Henry R. Stiles, *The History of Ancient Windsor, Connecticut* (New York: Charles B. Norton, 1859), 66-9. Strong Family Association of America, strongfamilyofamerica.org, (1997); C.

Alice Baker, *True Stories of New England Captives Carried to Canada During the Old French and Indian Wars* (Cambridge, MA: E.A. Hall & Co., 1897), 155-192; Susan was "the daughter of the late C. F. Orvis, former paster of the Summit Congregational church here": "Miss Susan W. Orvis Missionary in Turkey, Writes Brother Here," clipping, Dubuque newspaper, n.d. (circa December 1922), SWOP.

16 Andrew Preston, *Sword of the Spirit, Shield of Faith: Religion in American War and Diplomacy* (New York: Alfred A. Knopf, 2012), 27.

17 Congregational Churches in Massachusetts, Cambridge Synod, *The Cambridge Platform of Church Discipline: 1648* (Boston: Perkins & Whipple, 1850), 78-9.

18 KJV, 1 Peter 2:5-9.

19 Patricia R. Hill, *The World Their Household: The American Woman's Foreign Mission Movement and Cultural Transformation, 1870-1920* (Ann Arbor: The University of Michigan Press, 1985), 125-7.

20 Amerikan Bord Heyeti (American Board), Istanbul, American Research Institute in Turkey, Istanbul Center Library, online in Digital Library for International Research Archive, http://www.dlir.org/archive. The ABCFM kept personnel records (individual index cards, and some memorial records) for all missionaries, noting significant dates, locations, departures and arrivals. (Hereafter, ABH-PR.)

21 Brian Johnson, *When Men and Mountains Meet: A Brief Account of Talas American School* (Istanbul: American Research Institute in Turkey, 2018), 7.

22 A Statement, n.d., SWOP.

23 Henry K. Wingate, "Triumphal Return," *MH* 99, no. 1 (1903): 25.

24 *LLW* 33, no. 2 (1903): 68-9.

25 Stella N. Loughridge, Ibid, no. 6: 281.

26 Ravindranathan, 6.

27 Barton, *Daybreak*, 256; Washburn, 101-6.

28 Ravindranathan, 18-9, 46-8.

29 Oya Gözel Durmaz, "A City Transformed: War, Demographic Change and Profiteering in Kayseri (1915-1920)," (doctoral thesis, Middle East Technical University, 2014), 53-4.

30 Henry Otis Dwight, *Constantinople and Its Problems* (London: Oliphant, Anderson & Ferrier, 1901), 38.

31 David Gaunt, *Massacres, Resistance, Protectors Muslim: Christian Relations in Eastern Anatolia during World War I* (Piscataway, NJ: Gorgias Press, 2006), 39-45.

32 Henry Morgenthau, *Ambassador Morgenthau's Story* (Garden City, NY: Doubleday, Page & Company, 1918), 283.

33 *The Orient* 3, no. 20 (1912): 5. The people called themselves *yerli*, which translates as "native." (Hereafter, *Orient*.)

34 "From the Land of Prophet Mohamet: Dubuque Lady, Missionary Among

Turks of Asia Tells of Her Life," *Dubuque Telegraph Herald,* November 1905. The newspaper article was a reprint of a letter from SWO to her brother John, and referred to the residence as being owned by "a rich American family." The land for the girls' school had been sold to ABCFM by the Gulbenkian family, a rich Armenian family, so it is probable that Susan wrote "Armenian" but her handwriting had been misread by the newspaper editor as "American."

35   Hervé Georgelin, "Armenians in Late Ottoman Rural Kesaria/Kayseri," in *Armenian Kesaria/Kayseri and Cappadocia,* ed. Richard G. Hovannisian (Costa Mesa, CA: Mazda Publishers, 2013), 237. The estimate of 15,000 is based on 3,000 households.

36   W.J. Childs, *Across Asia Minor on Foot* (Edinburgh: William Blackwood and Sons, 1917), 184.

37   Fensham, 48-52; *Orient* 4 no. 30 (1913): 1-2; Childs, 193-98.

38   Herbert M. Irwin, *MH* 115, no 12 (1919): 500.

39   *MH* 104, no 1 (1908): 22.

40   Johnson, 9.

41   ABCFM-AR 1908, 51.

42   Ibid, 53.

43   Donald Quataert, *Social Disintegration and Popular Resistance in the Ottoman Empire, 1881-1908: Reactions to European Economic Penetration* (New York: New York University Press, 1983), 80-1, 141.

44   Keith Hamilton, "Dockside Diplomacy: The Foreign Office and the Constantinople Quays Company," in *The Records of the Permanent Under-Secretary's Department: Liaison Between the Foreign Office and British Secret Intelligence, 1873-1939* (London: Foreign and Commonwealth Office, 2005), 19.

45   E. F. Knight, *The Awakening of Turkey: A History of the Turkish Revolution* (Philadelphia: J.B. Lippincott, 1909), 237-38.

46   Quataert, 84, 91-3.

47   Y. Doğan Çetinkaya, "Muslim Merchants and Working-Class in Action: Nationalism, Social Mobilization and Boycott Movement in the Ottoman Empire 1908-1914" (doctoral thesis, Leiden University, 2010), 109, 47-9.

2. In Sickness and in Health

1   James L. Barton, *Educational Missions* (New York: Student Volunteer Movement for Foreign Missions, 1913), 5.

2   Student Volunteer Movement for Foreign Missions, *Worldwide Evangelization: The Urgent Business of the Church* (addresses delivered at the 4th international convention, Toronto, 1902), 47.

3   *MH* 107, no. 4 (1911): 167-68.

4   Preston, 178.

5   Hill, 133, 137.

6   Cesarea-Talas station statistics: ABCFM-AR 1908, 60-1; Ibid, 1909, 57-8;

Orient 1, no. 2 (1910): 3; Stella Loughridge to Dr. Judson Smith, January 19, 1903, HL/HU, ABC 16.9.3, v34, Microfilm A467, Reel 623, 6-7. Like an American school: Theresa L. Huntington, *LLW* 32, no. 3 (1902): 119.

7   Loughridge to Smith, December 7, 1904," HL/HU, ABC 16.9.3, v34, Microfilm A467, Reel 623, 16-17.

8   SWO to Dr. Judson Smith, November 11, 1902, Ibid, 559.

9   Helen Barrett Montgomery, *Western Women In Eastern Lands: An Outline Study of Fifty Years of Woman's Work in Foreign Missions* (New York: Macmillan, 1910), 114-15.

10   Noriko Kawamura Ishii, *American Women Missionaries at Kobe College, 1873-1909* (New York: Routledge, 2004), 50.

11   "Salaries, Western Turkey, Cesarea, Estimates for 1911," HL/HU, ABC 16.9.3, v40, Microfilm A467, Reel 629, 178.

12   Papers of the ABCFM, Reel 667, 431, quoted in İdris Yücel, "An Overview of Religious Medicine in the Near East: Mission Hospitals of the American Board in Asia Minor (1880-1923)," in *Journal for the Study of Religions and Ideologies* 14, no. 40 (2015), 54.

13   James L. Barton, *The Medical Missionary* (Boston: American Board of Commissioners for Foreign Missions, n.d.), 21.

14   Loughridge to Smith, July 12, 1904, HL/HU, ABC 16.9.3, v34, Microfilm A467, Reel 623, 13-14.

15   Erik J. Zürcher, *Turkey: A Modern History* (New York: I.B. Tauris, 2007), 123.

16   Washburn, xviii.

17   Murat Birdal, *The Political Economy of Ottoman Public Debt: Insolvency and European Financial Control in the Late Nineteenth Century* (London: Tauris Academic Studies, 2010), 19-36.

18   Hugh E. Poynter, *The Public Debt of Turkey,* quoted in *Orient* 3, no. 7 (1912): 3-4. Actual debt was £T 111,976,915, gross revenue was £T 4,779,749, and interest payment was £T 5,195,678.

19   land of extreme poverty: Barton, *Daybreak,* 23-5; post office: Morgenthau, *Ambassador Morgenthau's Story,* 118.

20   Childs, 178.

21   Barbara W. Tuchman, *The Guns of August* (New York: Ballatine Books, reprint 1994, 1962), 137.

22   Çetinkaya, 65.

23   *MH* 105, no. 2 (1909): 53.

24   Ibid, no. 7: 303-4. The 21 pastors and preachers were named in the journal.

25   İttihad-i Muhammedi (Muhammadan Union): Zürcher, *Turkey,* 96.

26   Taner Akçam, *A Shameful Act: The Armenian Genocide and the Question of Turkish Responsibility,* trans. Paul Bessemer (New York: Henry Holt, 2006), 74.

27   "The Turkish Parliament," *The Times* [UK], March 10, 1909.

28 Ali Kemal was UK Foreign Minister Boris Johnson's great grandfather. *Who Do You Think You Are? Boris Johnson*, directed by Mary Cranitch (London: BBC, 2008), Television.

29 Zürcher, *Turkey*, 96-7.

30 William Ramsay, *The Revolution in Constantinople and Turkey* (London: Hodder & Stoughton, 1909), 201.

31 Peter Balakian, *The Burning Tigris: The Armenian Genocide and America's Response* (New York: Harper Collins, 2003), 149.

32 ABCFM-AR 1909, 67-70.

33 Ramsay, 252-53.

34 ABCFM-AR 1909, 68.

35 Washburn, xxxi.

36 Balakian, *Burning Tigris,* 153-54.

37 Zürcher, *Turkey*, 97.

38 *MH* 105, no. 8 (1909), 335-39; Gözel Durmaz, 62-4. According to Gözel Durmaz, "Cemal Paşa gave the number of dead for the Adana events as: 17,000 Armenians and 1,850 Muslims. The Armenian Patriarch claimed that the number of dead was 21,300." Other reports estimate 20,000-30,00 died in the region.

39 Balakian states that Hovagim was shot (Balakian, *Burning Tigris,* 152), whereas *MH* reports that he was stabbed (p. 338); both say that he died in Nesbitt Chambers' arms.

40 Jasper Abraham Huffman, ed., *History of the Mennonite Brethren in Christ Church* (New Carlisle, Ohio: The Bethel Publishing Company, 1920), 138.

41 *MH* 105, no. 8 (1909): 335.

42 Ibid, 336.

43 ABCFM-AR 1909, 68.

44 Herbert M. Irwin, "Private Journal" (manuscript, Armenian Library and Museum, Watertown, MA, 1903-16), 148.

45 Ramsay, 201-3.

46 Burçin Gerçek, "Turkish Rescuers" (New York: The International Raoul Wallenberg Foundation, 2015), 17; Ramsay, 201.

47 *MH* 105, no. 8 (1909): 339.

48 Ibid, no. 6: 231-32.

49 H. Irwin, 147-48.

50 Ramsay, 317.

51 Washburn, xxxi.

52 Akçam, *Shameful Act*, 69.

53 S.R. Trowbridge, *Orient* 1 no. 8 (1910): 4.

54 "Massacres In Asia Minor," *Oamaru Mail* (New Zealand) 37, no. 10247 (9 September 1909), 4.

55 Lewis Einstein, *Inside Constantinople: A Diplomatist's Diary During the Dardanelles Expedition, April–September 1915* (New York: E.P. Dutton & Company, 1918), 175.

56 Akçam, *Shameful Act,* 73-4; Garth Jenkins, *Political Islam in Turkey* (New York: Palgrave MacMillian, 2008), 73-4.

3. Squabbles, Rifts and Splits

1 Morgenthau, *Ambassador Morgenthau's Story,* 20.

2 Rouben Paul Adalian, "Talat, Mehmet," in *The Armenian Genocide: The Essential Reference Guide,* ed. Alan Whitehorn (Santa Barbara, CA: ABC-CLIO, 2015), 245.

3 Morgenthau, *Ambassador Morgenthau's Story,* 21.

4 Taner Akçam, "Review Essay: Guenter Lewy's The Armenian Massacres in Ottoman Turkey." *Genocide Studies and Prevention* 3, no. 1 (April 2008): 137.

5 Morgenthau, *Ambassador Morgenthau's Story,* 21-2.

6 Tuchman, 138.

7 Einstein, 175.

8 Morgenthau, *Ambassador Morgenthau's Story,* 23.

9 Einstein, 175.

10 Morgenthau, *Ambassador Morgenthau's Story,* 24.

11 *MH* 108, no. 1 (1912): 3.

12 Ibid, no. 2: 52.

13 Çetinkaya, 109-12.

14 Mary Mason Poynter, "The Passing Of The Dogs Of Constantinople," *The Spectator* (London), May 28, 1910.

15 "Constantinople May Be Cleared of Dogs," *San Francisco Call* 108, no. 12, June 12 1910.

16 "Constantinople's Dogs," *Wairarapa Daily Times,* September 27, 1910.

17 Zürcher, *Turkey,* 104.

18 Gözel Durmaz, 164; Akçam, *Shameful Act,* 82-4; *Orient* 3 no. 22 (1912): 5-7.

19 *Orient* 1, no. 34 (1910): 5-6.

20 Ibid, no. 31: 5.

21 Ibid, no. 30: 5.

22 *MH* 107, no. 2 (1911): 63.

23 Winston S. Churchill, *The World Crisis Volume IV 1918-1928: The Aftermath* (New York: Charles Scribner's & Sons, 1929), 374.

24 Akçam, *Shameful Act,* 74.

25 *Orient* 2, no. 12 (1911): 6.

26 William S. Dodd, ABH-PR.

27 James S. Dennis, *Christian Missions and Social Progress* (New York: Fleming H. Revell Company, 1906), 435.

28 ABCFM-AR 1903, 48.

29   Enoch F. Bell, *Your Doctor Abroad,* Envelope Series 18, no. 2 (Boston: American Board of Commissioners for Foreign Missions, 1915), 15.

30   Papers of the ABCFM, Reel 606, 25-27, quoted in Yücel, 57-8.

31   *LLW* 33, no. 12 (1903): 550; Emma D. Cushman, ABH-PR.

32   James P. McNaughton, Henry T. Perry, and George E. White to Rev. J.K. Greene, March 15, 1909, HL/HU, ABC 16.9.3, Microfilm A467, v27, Reel 616, 551.

33   *Orient* 1, no. 2 (1910): 3; Barton, *Medical Missionary,* 17, 14. Several nurses and assistants were there for a short time, such as a British nurse named Miss Mathiesen, and a Miss Tschumi. *Miss Tschumi and others at Talas*, photograph, c.1909, Missionary Church Archives, Bethel College, Mishawaka, IN.

34   Lillian F. Cole to Mr. Dodd, January 31, 1906, HL/HU, ABC 16.9.3, Microfilm A467, v27, Reel 616, 601.

35   Rachel B. North to Mr. Speers, December 31, 1905, HL/HU, ABC 16.9.3, Microfilm A467, v27, Reel 616, 591-92.

36   William S. Dodd to the Trustees of the American Christian Hospital, February 1, 1906, HL/HU, ABC 16.9.3, Microfilm A467, v27, Reel 616, 602.

37   Wilfred M. Post to Mr. Speers, February 2, 1906, HL/HU, ABC 16.9.3, Microfilm A467, v27, Reel 616, 603-4.

38   Cole to Dodd, January 31, 1906.

39   William S. Dodd to James Barton, February 8, 1906, HL/HU, ABC 16.9.3, Microfilm A467, v27, Reel 616, 620.

40   William S. Dodd to James Barton, December 24, 1908, HL/HU, ABC 16.9.3, Microfilm A467, v27, Reel 616, 696-97.

41   McNaughton, Perry and White to Greene, 551-55.

42   James L. Fowle, "Memo regarding the Talas Hospital," February 26, 1906, HL/HU, ABC 16.9.3, Microfilm A467, v27, Reel 616, 626-33.

43   Henry K. Wingate to J.K. Greene, February 26, 1906, HL/HU, ABC 16.9.3, Microfilm A467, v27, Reel 616, 660-65.

44   This should not be confused with the previously-mentioned journal *Yeni Hayat* (New Life). In the investigating committee's opinion, the New Life movement was influenced by the Keswick teachings, also known as the Higher Life movement in Britain.

45   McNaughton, Perry and White to Greene, 552.

46   Dodd to James, 620.

47   W. A. Farnsworth to Dr. Creegan, March 22, 1906, HL/HU, ABC 16.9.3, Microfilm A467, v27, Reel 616, 625.

48   Dodd to James, 620.

49   McNaughton, Perry and White to Greene, 555.

50   Ibid.

51   SWO to Mother, November 13, 1910, SWOP.

52   ABCFM-AR 1910, 111.

53   Zürcher, *Turkey,* 106.

54   *Orient* 2, no. 33 (1911): 6. Entente Libérale was also known as *Hürriyet ve İtilâf Fırkası* or Party of Freedom and Understanding.

55   *Orient* 3 no. 6 (1912): 1.

56   Ibid, no. 8: 3.

57   Hasan Kayalı, "Elections and the Electoral Process in the Ottoman Empire, 1876-1919," *International Journal of Middle East Studies 27*, no. 3 (1995): 273–74.

58   Garth Jenkins, 75.

59   *MH* 108, no. 8 (1912): 343.

60   Eliezer Tauber, *The Formation of Modern Iraq and Syria*, (London: Routledge, 1994), 1.

61   *Orient* 3 no. 31 (1912): 7; Ibid, no. 34: 7; Garth Jenkins, 75.

4. The Empire Shrinks

1   SWO to Mother, November 13, 1910, SWOP; *MH* 107, no. 10 (1911): 443; Arthur C. Ryan, ABH-PR.

2   *MH* 107, no. 6 (1911), 249; Theda Phelps and Charles Henry Holbrook, ABH-PR.

3   Phelps, *Phelps Family*, 102; SWO to John and Anna, February 15, 1923, SWOP. Their mutual ancestor was Nathaniel Phelps, a Congregational deacon and one of the earliest and youngest settlers of Northampton, Massachusetts (1656).

4   Clara Childs Richmond, ABH-PR.

5   *Orient* 3 no. 1 (1912): 7; *Orient* 2, no. 14 (1911): 3; *Orient* 3 no. 25 (1912): 3.

6   Ibid, no. 20: 1.

7   Ibid, no. 19: 7.

8   Ibid, no. 15: 2.

9   *MH* 108, no. 12 (1912): 551.

10   Ibid, 579-80.

11   *LLW* 43, no. 2 (1913): 76.

12   *Orient* 3 no. 47 (1912): 4; Ibid, no. 50: 7.

13   *Orient* 4, no. 3, (1913): 7.

14   Zürcher, *Turkey*, 107-8.

15   Morgenthau, *Ambassador Morgenthau's Story*, 15-16; *Orient* 4, no. 5 (1913): 1.

16   Ibid, no. 25: 4.

17   *Orient* 3, no. 45 (1912): 5.

18   Ibid, no. 52: 2.

19   *Orient* 4, no. 9 (1913): 7.

20   *The Wisconsin* 33, no. 9 (1932): 296; *Orient* 3, no. 45 (1912): 5.

21   Ibid, 5-6.

22   Genevieve Irwin, "Notes from the Cesarea Field," *LLW* 44, no. 8 (1914): 350.

23   *Orient* 4, no. 9 (1913): 5.

24   Simon Payaslian, "The Fateful Years: Kesaria during the Genocide," in *Armenian Kesaria/Kayseri and Cappadocia*, ed. Richard G. Hovannisian (Costa Mesa, CA: Mazda Publishers, 2013), 237.

25   *LLW* 43, no. 4 (1913): 221-23.

26   Ibid.

27   Ibid, 163.

28   *Mission Studies* 31, no. 9 (Chicago: Woman's Board of Missions of the Interior of the Congregational Church, 1913): 264. (Hereafter *MS*)

29   *LLW* 43, no. 3 (1913): 132.

30   *Orient* 4, no. 30 (1913): 6.

31   Ishaan Tharoor, "The Balkan Wars: 100 Years Later, a History of Violence," *Time*, October 8, 2012. Accessed from world.time.com.

32   *Orient* 4, no. 12 (1913): 5.

33   Arnold J. Toynbee, *The Western Question in Greece and Turkey* (London: Constable and Company, 1922), 260.

34   SWO to Mother, November 28, 1913, SWOP.

35   *Orient* 4, no. 28 (1913): 5.

36   [my italics], *Report of the International Commission to Inquire into the Causes and Conduct of the Balkan Wars* (Washington: Carnegie Endowment for International Peace, 1914), 19, 208.

37   M. Şükrü Hanioğlu, *Preparation for a Revolution: The Young Turks, 1902-1908* (Oxford: Oxford University Press, 2000), 223, quoted in Uğur Ümit Üngör, "Paramilitary Violence in the Collapsing Ottoman Empire," in *War in Peace: Paramilitary Violence in Europe after the Great War*, ed. Robert Gerwarth and John Horne (Oxford: Oxford University Press, 2012), 167.

38   Ibid.

39   Akçam, *Shameful Act*, 115.

40   Ibid, 89.

41   *MH* 109, no. 7 (1913): 322.

42   Üngör, 167.

43   Zürcher, *Turkey*, 130.

44   Akçam, *Shameful Act*, 115.

45   *MH* 109, no. 3 (1913): 101; Ibid, no. 9: 406.

46   *Orient* 3, no. 36 (1912): 1.

47   *Orient* 4, no. 34 (1913): 2; Charles Holbrook, ABH-PR.

48   *Orient* 3, no. 39 (1912): 5.

5. The Reformations

1   *Orient* 4, no. 19 (1913): 2.

2   Garth Jenkins, 74-5.

3   *Orient* 4, no. 19 (1913): 2.

4   *Orient* 5, no. 15 (1914): 145.

5   *Orient* 4, no. 37 (1913): 7.

6   *MH* 110, no. 4 (1914): 191; Gözel Durmaz, 146; Simon Payaslian, *United States Policy Toward the Armenian Question and the Armenian Genocide* (New York: Palgrave Macmillan, 2005), 3.

7   George Abel Schreiner, ed., *Entente Diplomacy and the World,* trans. B. De Siebert (New York: G.P. Putnam's Sons, 1921), 676.

8   Henry Morgenthau, *Secrets of the Bosphorus* (London: Hutchinson & Co., 1918), 32.

9   The pamphlet titles were *Müslümanlara Mahsus* (Especially for Muslims) and *Müslümanve Türklere* (To Muslim and Turks). Ahmet Nedim Servet Tör, *Nevhiz'in Günlüğü "Defter-i Hatıra,"* (İstanbul: Yapı Kredi Yayınları, 2000), quoted in Çetinkaya, 193-7.

10 Ibid, 233-34.

11 Ibid, 233, 209.

12 *Orient* 5, no. 11 (1914): 103.

13 The three medical students were Behçet Salih, Mahmut Halit and Mustafa Muzaffer. Çetinkaya, 198.

14 *Orient* 5, no. 11 (1914): 103-5; Çetinkaya, 208-10.

15 *Orient* 5, no. 13 (1914): 125; Çetinkaya, 213.

16 Ibid, 234.

17 Robert Stein, "Armenia Must Have a European Governor," *The Arena* 12 (1895), 377.

18 Joseph L. Grabill, *Protestant Diplomacy and the Near East: Missionary Influence on American Policy, 1810-1927* (Minneapolis: University of Minnesota Press, 1971), 51.

19 *MH* 109, no. 8 (1913): 345.

20 Akçam, *Shameful Act*, 97-98.

21 *MH* 109, no. 8 (1913): 345.

22 *Orient* 5, no. 16 (1914): 154.

23 SWO to Father, November 28, 1913, SWOP.

24 *Orient* 4, no. 53 (1913): 5.

25 Ibid, no. 47: 2.

26 Johnson, 10.

27 *Orient* 4, no. 47 (1913): 2.

28 Ibid.

29 SWO to Mother, November 28, 1913, SWOP.

30 *Orient* 4, no. 52 (1913): 7.

31 *LLW* 43, no. 11 (1913): 490.

32 Zürcher, *Turkey,* 110.

33 *Orient* 5, no. 1 (1914): 9.

34 Efraim Karsh, *Rethinking The Middle East* (Portland, OR: Frank Cass, 2003), 32.

35 Balakian, *Burning Tigris,* 167.

36 *Orient* 4, no. 50 (1913): 4; Jonathan A. Grant, *Rulers, Guns, and Money: The Global Arms Trade in the Age of Imperialism* (Cambridge, MA: Harvard University Press, 2007), 183.

37 *Orient* 5, no. 1 (1914): 1; Ibid, no. 4: 39.

38 "Women donated gold, and collection boxes:" This description was from the Balkan War days of Donanma Cemiyeti (Navy Society), but is applicable to 1914. N. Gülen, *Dünden Bugüne Bahriyemiz (Our Navy from the Past to the Current Day)* (Istanbul: Kastaş Yayınları, 1988), quoted in Altay Atlı, *Turkey in the First World War: Development of the Turkish Navy* (2012). Accessed at http://turkeyswar.com/navy/navy.html; "Sold hair" and "door-to-door campaigns": Morgenthau, *Secrets*, 49.

39 *Orient* 5, no. 1 (1914): 9.

40 *Orient* 4, no. 52 (1913): 1.

41 Zürcher, *Turkey*, 122.

42 Alan Whitehorn, "Armenian Reform Agreement of 1914," in *The Armenian Genocide: The Essential Reference Guide*, ed. Alan Whitehorn (Santa Barbara, CA: ABC-CLIO, 2015), 72-73.

43 Russia "spent no less than 2½ million roubles on propaganda in Eastern Anatolia alone." Ambassador Hans Baron von Wangenheim to Imperial Chancellor Bethmann Hollweg, February 24, 1913, 1913-02-24-DE-001, Wolfgang Gust, ed. *The Armenian Genocide: Evidence from the German Foreign Office Archives, 1915-1916* (New York: Berghahn, 2014), 136. (Hereafter, the date will be expressed in Gust's format: year-mo-day-DE(Deutschland)-sequence.)

44 *Orient* 5, no. 1, (1914): 1; Ibid, no. 7: 61-2; Ibid, no. 13: 123.

45 Ibid, no. 18: 178; Ibid, no. 21: 210.

46 Çetinkaya, 215-24.

47 Ibid, 230.

48 *Orient* 5, no. 25 (1914): 242.

49 Çetinkaya, 225.

50 Akçam, "Review Essay," 137.

51 Ibid.

52 Zürcher, *Turkey*, 125-26.

53 Balakian, *Burning Tigris*, 172, 163.

54 *Orient* 5, no. 29, (1914): 288.

55 *LLW* 44, no. 5 (1914): 224-25.

56 Ibid, no. 8: 351-52.

57 *Orient* 5, no. 26 (1914): 255; Ibid, no. 29: 286.

6. Mad for War

1 T. G. Otte, *July Crisis: The World's Descent into War, Summer 1914* (Cambridge: Cambridge University Press, 2014), 355.

2 *Orient* 5, no. 28 (1914): 271.

3   The actual amounts were public debt £T 139,000,000; debt servicing £T 14,983,031; and mobilization £T 5,990,000. *Orient* 5, no. 28 (1914): 271-75. The budget speech also made note of a third ship, the *Fatih*.

4   *Orient* 5, no. 31 (1914): 301-2.

5   Morgenthau, *Ambassador Morgenthau's Story*, 66.

6   Winston S. Churchill, *The World Crisis, Vol. I* (New York: Charles Scribner's Sons, 1923), 204. See FirstWorldWar.com for the ten demands of the ultimatum, which included such things as eliminating from schools all propaganda against Austria-Hungary.

7   Churchill, *Aftermath*, 378. Mikhail Nikolayevich de Griers, the Russian Ambassador at Constantinople, was also stunned by the ultimatum which was "unique in the history of international relations and aimed at implementing the dangerous principle that the enslavement of smaller states by Great Powers is permissible." Otte, 355.

8   Morgenthau, *Ambassador Morgenthau's Story*, 76.

9   *Orient* 5, no. 32 (1914): 313.

10   Mr. Beaumont to Sir Edward Grey, no. 2-3, August 3-4, 1914, *Correspondence Respecting Events Leading to the Rupture of Relations with Turkey* (Cd. 7628, Misc. no. 13), London: His Majesty's Stationery Office, 1914.

11   *Orient* 5, no. 32 (1914): 313. Interestingly, Karsh writes "The Bank of England had already refunded the Ottoman down-payment on the ships (worth some £648,000) on 7 August, and the British Government had promised due compensation for the loss of the ships upon their requisition; but these facts were concealed from the Ottoman public by their own leaders, who continued their false criticism of Britain's refusal to compensate Turkey for the ships." (Karsh, 44.) Karsh does not cite this statement in his book, and I could find no evidence of a refund nor promise of compensation in my research. Neither the Bank of England Museum nor the British Committee of Treasury minutes and the Court of Directors' minutes for that period have any record of financial compensation for the ships: Ellie Paton, Collections Assistant, Bank of England Museum, e-mail to author, May 31, 2016.

12   Grey to Beaumont, no. 4, August 4, 1914, *Correspondence* (Cd. 7628).

13   Beaumont to Grey, no. 20, August 9, 1914, *Correspondence* (Cd. 7628).

14   Churchill to Secretary A.C.L., August 8, 1914 (FO 371/2137), quoted in Ulrich Trumpener, "The Escape of the Goeben and Breslau: A Reassessment," *Canadian Journal of History* 6, no. 2 (1971): 183.

15   Tuchman, 138.

16   Churchill, *World Crisis*, 524.

17   Zürcher, *Turkey*, 111-2.

18   Tuchman, 141.

19   *LLW* 44, no.11 (1914): 501.

20   *MH* 110, no. 11 (1914): 454-55.

21   Ibid, 508-9.

22   Ibid, no. 12: 573-74.

23   Ibid, no. 11: 510.

24   Ibid, 509-10.

25   Ibid, 510-11.

26   Ibid, 508.

27   Tuchman, 141-49; Eric Grenier, "Catch Me If You Can: How a Crafty German Admiral Led the Royal Navy on a Wild Chase Across the Mediterranean and Changed the Balance of Power in the First World War," in *MHQ: The Quarterly Journal of Military History* 24, no. 3 (2012): 86-91. On board the Italian liner was the daughter of Ambassador Morgenthau, Alma Wertheim, her husband, and their three daughters, one of whom was Barbara Tuchman, author of *The Guns of August*.

28   Morgenthau, *Ambassador Morgenthau's Story*, 75-9.

29   Sir Louis Mallet to Grey, no. 39, August 26, 1914, *Correspondence* (Cd. 7628).

30   *Orient* 5, no. 38 (1914): 379.

31   Ibid, no. 50: 453.

32   SWO, Shipboard Travel Log, November 1914, SWOP.

33   Morgenthau, *Ambassador Morgenthau's Story*, 284-85.

34   *MH* 110, no. 12 (1914): 558-59.

35   Mallet to Grey, no. 134, October 16, 1914, *Correspondence* (Cd. 7628).

36   Ibid, no. 176, October 29, 1914.

37   Ibid, no. 157, October 22, 1914; Ibid, no. 162, October 23, 1914.

38   Ibid, no. 170, October 27, 1914.

39   Ibid, no. 134, October 16, 1914.

40   Ibid, no. 177, October 29, 1914.

41   *Orient* 5, no. 44-8 (1914): 437.

42   Gabriele Yonan, "Lest We Perish: A Forgotten Holocaust, The Extermination of the Christian Assyrians in Turkey and Persia," (manuscript, 1996), 84. Gabriele Yonan, "Holy War Made in Germany: New Light on the Holocaust Against the Christian Assyrians during World War I," *Nineveh On Line*, July 2, 2000. Accessed at nineveh.com.

43   SWO, Shipboard Travel Log.

7. Eve of Destruction

1   Morgenthau, *Ambassador Morgenthau's Story*, 30-2, 205; Glen W. Swanson, "Enver Pasha: The Formative Years," *Middle Eastern Studies* 16, no. 3 (Oct., 1980): 193-96; Louise Bryant, *Mirrors of Moscow* (New York: T. Seltzer, 1923), 149-56.

2   Philip Hendrick Stoddard, "The Ottoman Government and the Arabs, 1911 to 1918: A Preliminary Study of the Teşkilât-i Mahsusa" (PhD diss., Princeton University, 1963), 1-2.

3   Zürcher, *Turkey*, 109-10; Stoddard, Abstract: 1.

4   Akçam, *Shameful Act*, 95; Frank Bovenkerk and Yücel Yeşilgöz, "The Turkish Mafia and the State," in *Organized Crime in Europe: Concepts, Patterns and Control Policies in the European Union and Beyond*, eds. Cyrille Fijnaut and Letizia Paoli (Dordrecht, The Netherlands: Springer, 2004), 594.

5   Üngor, 168.

6   Akçam, "Review Essay," 131.

7   Üngor, 168.

8   Hilmi letter, September 4, 1914, quoted in Akçam, *Shameful Act*, 134.

9   Üngor, 168.

10 Ibid, 169.

11 Akçam, *Shameful Act*, 136.

12 Frederick W. MacCallum, "Constantinople and Caucasus," in *Turkish Atrocities: Statements of Armenian 12Missionaries on the Destruction of Christian Communities in Ottoman Turkey, 1915-1917*, comp. James L. Barton, ed Ara Sarafian (Ann Arbor: Gomidas Institute, 1998), 177.

13 Ramsay, 255.

14 Hannibal Travis, "'Native Christians Massacred': The Ottoman Genocide of the Assyrians during World War I," *Genocide Studies and Prevention* 1, no. 3 (2006): 342.

15 Stoddard, Introduction, 6-7.

16 Whitehorn, 73.

17 *MH* 110, no. 12 (1914): 571.

18 *MH* 111, no. 3 (1915): 104.

19 ABCFM-AR, 1915, 77.

20 Herbert Irwin, South African War, 1899-1902: Service Files, Medals and Land Applications, #9960, vol. 51, Series A1a, RG 38, microfilm reel T-2074, Library and Archives Canada.

21 *MH* 111, no. 3 (1915): 131; Ibid, no. 4: 188; Morgenthau, *Ambassador Morgenthau's Story*, 329-32.

22 *MH* 111, no. 3 (1915): 108. Yet I will send my servants unto thee tomorrow about this time, and they shall search thine house, and the houses of thy servants; and it shall be, that whatsoever is pleasant in thine eyes, they shall put it in their hand, and take it away. / And the king of Israel answered and said, Tell him, Let not him that girdeth on his harness boast himself as he that putteth it off. / And they came up into Judah, and brake into it, and carried away all the substance that was found in the king's house, and his sons also, and his wives. / Also we certify you, that touching any of the priests and Levites, singers, porters, Nethinims, or ministers of this house of God, it shall not be lawful to impose toll, tribute, or custom, upon them. / Restore, I pray you, to them, even this day, their lands, their vineyards, their oliveyards, and their houses, also the hundredth part of the money, and of the corn, the wine, and the oil, that ye exact of them. Then said they, We will restore them, and will require nothing of them; so will we do as thou sayest. Then I called the

priests, and took an oath of them, that they should do according to this promise.

23 David Fromkin, *A Peace to End All Peace: Creating the Modern Middle East* (New York: Henry Holt, 1989), 120.

24 Zürcher, *Turkey*, 113-14.

25 Üngor, 172.

26 Wangenheim to Hollweg, 1913-02-24-DE-001, Gust, 136.

27 Grabill, 49.

28 Mary Lewis Shedd, *The Measure of a Man: The Life of William Ambrose Shedd, Missionary to Persia* (New York: George H. Doran Company, 1922), 140.

29 Gaunt, 95.

30 *Orient* 5, no. 42 (1914): 419.

31 Clarence D. Ussher and Grace H. Knapp, *An American Physician in Turkey* (Boston: Houghton Mifflin, 1917), 226.

32 Balakian, *Burning Tigris*, 200-1.

33 Stoddard, 159.

34 *MH* 111, no. 3 (1915): 127.

35 William Cleveland, *A History of the Modern Middle East* (Boulder: Westview Press, 2004), 154.

36 Zürcher, *Young Turk Legacy*, 122.

37 Gerçek, 21-2.

38 Payaslian, "The Fateful Years," 293-94; Morgenthau, *Ambassador Morgenthau's Story*, 301-2; Alan Whitehorn, ed. *The Armenian Genocide: The Essential Reference Guide* (Santa Barbara, CA: ABC-CLIO, 2015), Chronology, 361. There were rare exceptions, such as the case of Captain Sarkis Torossian, a highly decorated soldier whose Turkish superior wanted to keep him in his regiment. See Sarkis Torossian, *From Dardanelles to Palestine* (Boston: Meador, 1947), 60-8, quoted in Joseph A. Kéchichian, "How the Armenian Genocide Forced a Loyal Ottoman Officer to Espouse the Arab Revolt," in *Contemporary Review of the Middle East* 1, no. 4 (December 2014): 375.

39 "Story of the Girls of the Talas Girls' School in the Year of the Deportation," n.d., HL/HU, ABC 16.9.3, v40, Microfilm A467, Reel 629, 619. Although this typed document is unsigned, it was unquestionably written by Stella N. Loughridge, who was the school's principal, and who wrote on page 3: "the 8th of August came (my mother's birthday)." Stella's mother, Julia Chandler Loughridge, was born August 8, 1832, died February 19, 1911, and is buried in Congregational Cemetery, Hancock County, Illinois.

40 Payaslian, "The Fateful Years," 294.

41 Aris Kalfaian, *Chomaklou: The History of Armenian Village*, trans. Krikor Asadourian, ed. Michael Ekizian (New York: Chomaklou Compatriotic Society, 1982), 183.

42 Payaslian, "The Fateful Years," 295.

43 Stella Loughridge, "Facts in Regard to Armenian Atrocities in the Cesarea District, Asia Minor," in *Turkish Atrocities: Statements of Armenian Missionaries on the Destruction of Christian Communities in Ottoman Turkey, 1915-1917*, comp. James L. Barton, ed. Ara Sarafian (Ann Arbor: Gomidas Institute, 1998), 116.

44 Childs, 196-97.

45 Clara Childs Richmond, "Cesarea and Talas," in *Turkish Atrocities: Statements of Armenian Missionaries on the Destruction of Christian Communities in Ottoman Turkey, 1915-1917*, comp. James L. Barton, ed. Ara Sarafian (Ann Arbor: Gomidas Institute, 1998), 121.

46 Enclosure, 1915-07-13-DE-001, Gust, 252.

47 Loughridge, "Facts in Regard to Armenian Atrocities," 116.

48 Richmond, 121.

49 Theda B. Phelps, "Story of Talas 1914-17" in *Turkish Atrocities: Statements of Armenian Missionaries on the Destruction of Christian Communities in Ottoman Turkey, 1915-1917*, comp. James L. Barton, ed. Ara Sarafian, (Ann Arbor: Gomidas Institute, 1998), 132; Richmond, 121; Loughridge, "Facts in Regard to Armenian Atrocities," 116; "Story of the Girls," 619.

50 Gözel Durmaz, 78-9.

51 Wangenheim to Hollweg, 1915-06-04-DE-001, Gust, 196-97.

52 Morgenthau, *Secrets of the Bosphorus*, 200.

53 Gözel Durmaz, 78-9; Payaslian, "The Fateful Years," 293.

54 Enclosure, 1915-07-13-DE-001, Gust, 251.

55 Theda Phelps, 132.

56 Viscount James Bryce and Arnold Toynbee, *The Treatment of Armenians in the Ottoman Empire 1915-16: Documents presented to Viscount Grey of Falloden, Secretary of State for Foreign Affairs, by Viscount Bryce* (Cd. 8325, Misc. no. 31) (London: G.P. Putnam's Sons for His Majesty's Stationery Office, 1916), 246.

57 Loughridge, "Facts in Regard to Armenian Atrocities," 116.

58 Grigoris Balakian, *Armenian Golgotha*, trans. Peter Balakian (New York: Alfred A. Knopf, 2009), 50.

59 German Consul Walter Rossler to the Imperial Chancellor Bethmann Hollweg, 1915-04-12-DE-001, Gust, 166.

60 "Armenians Fighting the Turks," *The Washington Post*, November 13, 1914.

61 Akçam, *Shameful Act*, 145-46; Gerçek, 10-11.

62 Balakian, *Golgotha*, 23-4.

63 William Dodd to William Peet, July 17, 1915, quoted in Whitehorn, *Armenian Genocide*, 328.

64 Shedd,187.

65 Grabill, 60.

66 Richard Antaramian, "Van, Siege of," in *The Armenian Genocide: The Essential Reference Guide*, ed. Alan Whitehorn (Santa Barbara, CA: ABC-CLIO, 2015), 265-66.

67   Yonan, "Holy War."

68   *Persecution of the Greeks in Turkey, 1914-1918* (Constantinople: Greek Patriarchate, 1919), 42-3.

69   Johannes Lepsius, *Le rapport secret du Dr. Johannès Lepsius* (Paris: Payot & Cie., 1918), 28-9. [my translation]

70   Payaslian, "The Fateful Years," 296.

71   Akçam, *Shameful Act,* 129-30.

72   Gözel Durmaz, 76-9.

73   Zürcher, *Turkey,* 118.

74   Ibid, 135.

75   Christopher J. Walker, "World War I and the Armenian Genocide," in *The Armenian People from Ancient to Modern Times, Volume II,* ed. Richard G. Hovannisian (New York: St. Martin's Press, 1997), 261; Simon Payaslian, "The Destruction of the Armenian Church during the Genocide," *Genocide Studies and Prevention: An International Journal* 1, no. 2 (2006): 157.

76   Gaunt, 108-9; Üngor, 172.

77   Einstein, 175-6.

8. Welcome to Hell

1   Timika Hoffman-Zoller, Office of the Registrar, University of Chicago, e-mail to author, July 14, 2015.

2   SWO to Mother, March 28, 1915, SWOP.

3   "Massacre in Armenia Has Again Begun," *The Rock Island Argus,* April 30, 1915; "Six Thousand of Armenians Slain," Ibid, May 17, 1915.

4   Whitehorn, "Chronology," *Armenian Genocide,* 362.

5   Vahakn N. Dadrian, *The History of the Armenian Genocide,* 4th rev. ed. (New York: Berghahn Books, 2004), 216.

6   Wangenheim to Hollweg, 1915-06-05-DE-001, Gust, 198.

7   Adana Consul Büge to German Embassy in Constantinople, 1915-05-18-DE-011, Gust, 183.

8   Wangenheim to Consul in Erzrum, 1915-05-19-DE-015, Gust, 183-84.

9   Stephen G. Svajian, *A Trip through Historic Armenia* (New York: Green Hill Publishing, 1983), 363, quoted in Gözel Durmaz, 106.

10   *MH* 112, no. 4 (1916): 171.

11   Gözel Durmaz, 84.

12   Ibid, 121-24.

13   *Orient* 6, no. 23 (1915): 155.

14   Dadrian, 221.

15   Gözel Durmaz, 82.

16   Wangenheim to Hollweg, 1915-06-04-DE-001, Gust, 196-97.

17   Gözel Durmaz, 81-2.

18   Theda Phelps, 132.

19 Genevieve Irwin, "Diary," June 7, 1915, (manuscript, Armenian Library and Museum, Watertown, MA, 1915-1917), 9.
20 "Story of the Girls," 1-2.
21 G. Irwin, May 1915, 8; Ibid, June 18, 1915, 9.
22 Theda Phelps, 133.
23 G. Irwin, June 16, 1915, 9.
24 "Story of the Girls," 2.
25 G. Irwin, June 16, 1915, 9; Theda Phelps, 133.
26 Richmond, 122; G. Irwin, June 18, 1915, 10.
27 G. Irwin, July 5, 1915, 11.
28 *MH* 111, no. 6 (1915): 262-63.
29 Gretchen Rasch, *The Storm of Life: A Missionary Marriage from Armenia to Appalachia* (London: Gomidas Institute, 2016), 127.
30 *MH* 111, no. 5 (1915): 234-36.
31 Marie Zenger, ABH-PR.
32 Bryce and Toynbee, 246-53.
33 G. Irwin, July 5, 1915, 11.
34 "Story of the Girls," 2.
35 Theda Phelps, 133.
36 "Story of the Girls," 2.
37 Theda Phelps, 133.
38 Gözel Durmaz, 83.
39 Enclosure, 1915-07-13-DE-001, Gust, 253.

9. In the Valley of the Shadow of Death

1 Clara Richmond stated the date was Sunday, June 13, however Genevieve Irwin's diary, the statements of Stella and Theda in *Turkish Atrocities*, and of Wedel-Jarlsberg and Elvers in *Treatment* indicate these events occurred in July.
2 Richmond, 121-22.
3 G. Irwin, July 12, 1915, 12.
4 Loughridge, "Facts in Regard to Armenian Atrocities," 116-17.
5 G. Irwin, July 12, 1915, 12.
6 Gözel Durmaz, 107.
7 G. Irwin, July 13, 1915, 11.
8 Richmond, 122; Loughridge, "Facts in Regard to Armenian Atrocities," 117; G. Irwin, 12.
9 *MH* 112, no. 2 (1916): 72.
10 G. Irwin, July 16, 1915, 9.
11 Bryce and Toynbee, 254.
12 G. Irwin, July 12, 1915, 12.
13 Theda Phelps, 133; G. Irwin, 11; *Orient* 6, no. 29 (1915):185.
14 KJV Exodus 10:4; Bryce and Toynbee, 254.
15 "Story of the Girls," 3.

16 Theda Phelps, 133.

17 "Story of the Girls," 3.

18 G. Irwin, July 16, 1915, 9.

19 Morgenthau, *Ambassador Morgenthau's Story*, 327-28.

20 Ibid, 332-37.

21 Ambassador Morgenthau to Secretary of State, July 16, 1915, telegram, US National Archives, State Dept. Record Group 59, 867.4016/76.

22 Loughridge, "Facts in Regard to Armenian Atrocities," 116.

23 G. Irwin, September 1, 1915, 16.

24 *MH* 112, no 4 (1916): 171.

25 G. Irwin, September 1, 1915, 16; Ibid, October 26, 1915, 18.

26 Ibid.

27 Ibid, November 15, 1915, 20.

28 Ibid, September 9, 1915, 16.

29 Gözel Durmaz, 83.

30 Taner Akçam, *The Young Turks' Crime against Humanity* (Princeton, NJ: Princeton University Press, 2012), 290-291.

31 [Translations for author by Kamo Mayilyan] T. Kh. Hakobyan, St. T. Melik-Bakhshyan, and H. Kh. Barseghyan, *Vocabulary of Locations in Armenia and its Surroundings,* 2nd D-K [Hayastani ev harakic shrjanneri teghanunneri bararan] (Yerevan: Yerevan University Publishing House, 1988), 41; Gerasim Aharonean, ed., *1915-1965 Memory Book about the Great Tragedy-Massacre* [Hooshamadian To Mets Yeghern] (Beirut: Zartonk/Atlas, 1965), 259; Gözel Durmaz, 35.

32 Theda Phelps, 134.

33 Richmond, 123.

34 Gerçek, 54-5.

35 Hilmar Kaiser, *The Extermination of Armenians in the Diyarbekir Region* (Istanbul: Istanbul Bilgi Üniversitesi Yayınları, 2014), 244-245, quoted in Gözel Durmaz, 85; Balakian, *Burning Tigris*, 204.

36 Richmond, 127-28; Loughridge, *Atrocities*, 117.

10. Pandemonium

1 "Story of the Girls," 4. Genevieve identified Nellie's last name: G. Irwin, 11.

2 Richmond, 123.

3 Theda Phelps, 134-35.

4 Richmond, 123.

5 "Story of the Girls," 4.

6 Theda Phelps, 134.

7 Ibid, 135; "Story of the Girls," 4.

8 Akçam, "Review Essay," 135.

9 Gözel Durmaz, 91-4.

10 "Story of the Girls," 4.

11 G. Irwin, August 12, 1915, 15.
12 Richmond, 124.
13 Theda Phelps, 135.
14 "Story of the Girls," 3.
15 Theda Phelps, 135.
16 Ibid.
17 "Story of the Girls," 4.
18 Theda Phelps, 135.
19 G. Irwin, August 12, 1915, 15.
20 "Story of the Girls," 4.
21 "Statistics of Medical Work for Cesarea Station, July 7, 1914," HL/HU, ABC
    16.9.3, v40, Microfilm A467, Reel 629, 232.
22 ABCFM AR 1915, 103.
23 *Orient* 6, no. 33 (1915): 218.
24 Jaffa Panken, "'Lest They Perish': The Armenian Genocide and the Making of
    Modern Humanitarian Media in the U.S., 1915-1925," (Doctoral dissertation,
    Paper 1396, University of Pennsylvania, 2014), 35.
25 G. Irwin, August 12, 1915, 15.
26 *Orient* 6, no. 33 (1915): 218.
27 G. Irwin, August 12, 1915, 15.
28 Ibid, September 9, 1915, 16.
29 "Story of the Girls," 2-3.
30 G. Irwin, August 29, 1915, 15.
31 "Marsovan Girls Rescued: A Thrilling Story of American Pluck," *Carleton
    College Alumni Magazine* 6, no. 4 (1916): 143-45; *LLW* 45, no. 12 (1915):
    561; *MH* 111, no. 12 (1915): 581.
32 "Story of the Girls," 2.
33 *MH* 112, no. 1 (1916), 31.
34 Akçam, "Review Essay," 137. Akçam's endnote refers to specific examples
    from Diyarbekir, Izmit and Niğde in September 1915. Niğde is very close to
    Cesarea and Talas, though in a neighbouring vilayet (Konia).
35 G. Irwin, August 12, 1915, 15.
36 Gözel Durmaz, 105-6.
37 Richmond, 125.
38 Ibid, 124.
39 "Story of the Girls," 4.
40 Ibid; Richmond, *Atrocities*, 125.
41 Theda Phelps, 136.
42 "Story of the Girls," 4.
43 *MH* 111, no. 12 (1915): 580; *Orient* 6, no. 41 (1915): 267. The *MH* reported
    the opening of the boys' school with "between fifty and sixty boys in
    attendance," but in 1914 the enrollment was 163 and in 1916 it was 170, so it
    is not realistic a hundred boys left and returned in the meantime.

44   "Story of the Girls," 4.

45   Svajian, 362, quoted in Gözel Durmaz, 106.

46   "Story of the Girls," 4.

47   Richmond, 125.

48   "Story of the Girls," 4-5.

49   Richmond, 125.

50   "Story of the Girls," 4.

51   G. Irwin, November 14, 1915, 19-20; Richmond, 125-26. This group included another young teacher, Garabed Kondahjian; the nineteen-year-old assistant druggist, Hovhannes Kitabjian; three preachers who were teaching in the school, Manook Norhadian, Vahram Tahmissian, and Meseeh; and the cook, Aris Nigogasian and his son, Bazabed. They were sent with the Catholic Bishop, two of his priests, and the sister of another priest to Mosul.

52   Rossler to Hollweg, 1916-01-31-DE-001, Gust, 539.

53   G. Irwin, December 16, 1915, 20.

54   "Story of the Girls," 5; Gözel Durmaz, 107.

55   Ibid.

56   Akçam, *Shameful Act*, 145-46; Gerçek, 10-11.

57   Ibid, 23-5.

58   Akçam, "Review Essay," 134.

59   Ussher and Knapp, 299-320.

60   *MH* 111, no. 12 (1915): 560; Ibid, no. 11: 511-12.

61   Ibid, no. 10: 444; Ibid, no. 12: 557; Ibid, 112, no. 1 (1916): 19; Ibid, 118, no. 12 (1922): 479; "A Missionary Poisoned," *The New York Times*, November 13, 1915.

11. The Need for Relief

1   Susan Wealthy Orvis, "Through Russia in 1917" (manuscript, MS Am 1544, HL/HU, Cambridge, MA, 1918-1929), 16-7. (Hereafter, SWOTR.)

2   *MS* 34, no. 1 (1916): 18; Ibid, 34, "Young People's Department," [n.d.].

3   SWO to Dr. Ernest Burton, November 22, 1915, SWOP.

4   Morgenthau, *Ambassador Morgenthau's Story*, 332.

5   Balakian, *Burning Tigris*, 290.

6   Panken, 35.

7   *MS* 34, no. 1 (1916): 18.

8   SWOTR, 17.

9   Morgenthau to Secretary of State, September 3, 1915, NA/RG59/867.4016/117, image of telegram retrieved from Abraham D. Krikorian and Eugene L. Taylor, "99 Years Ago Today: Who Knew What, When and How about 'The Massacres that Would Change the Meaning of Massacre'," *Armenian News Network* at groong.org (October 4, 2014).

10 James L. Barton, *Story of Near East Relief (1915-1930): An Interpretation* (New York: Macmillan, 1930), 8-9; Panken, 26.

11 Ibid, 27, 33.

12 *The American Committee for Relief in the Near East: Its History, Its Work and the Need for Support as Outlined by President Wilson and Others,* 1918, 11.

13 Barton, *Story of Near East Relief,* 401-3.

14 Morgenthau, *Ambassador Morgenthau's Story,* 348-50.

15 Lord Mayor's Fund (Armenian Refugees), FO 96/205, Part 1, pp2-3, First World War, The National Archives of the UK. Accessed at http://www.nationalarchives.gov.uk.

16 Ibid.

17 *Dominion* 9, no. 2854 (August 19, 1916); armeniangenocide.com.au/australiaresponse; *The Toronto Daily Star,* June 20, 1916.

18 *Orient* 6, no. 41 (1915): 266-67.

19 Gözel Durmaz, 124-25, 132-33, 146.

20 Ibid, 148-50. "Armenian sources note in particular the rapacity of [the following Talas officials] Talaslı Hacı Ahmed Effendi; Zâde Osman; Salih Mehmed; Seyeddin Evladları Ali; Mehmed; Tafiloğlu Tevfik; Alizâdeoğlu Kâzım; the president of the municipality of Talas, Ali; Mahmud, a sergeant in the gendarmerie; Hekim Balıhın Hasan; and Eli Küçük Mehmed, who were both the executioners of the Armenians of Talas and also the main beneficiaries of their elimination." Raymond Kévorkian, *The Armenian Genocide: A Complete History* (New York: I.B. Tauris, 2011), 519.

21 Morgenthau, *Ambassador Morgenthau's Story,* 21.

22 Akçam, "Review Essay," 135.

23 G. Irwin, October 2, 1915, 18.

24 "Story of the Girls," 2.

25 *MH* 112, no. 6 (1916): 253-54.

26 G. Irwin, October 2, 1915, 18.

27 Gözel Durmaz, 96-7.

28 Gerçek, 56-7.

29 Monsignor Angelo Dolci, Apostolic Delegate in Constantinople to Cardinal Gasparri, Vatican Secretary of State, December 12, 1915, Michael Hesemann, "Pius XII and the Second World War: Assumption and New Archival Evidence" (Paper, International Conference at Universitá degli Studi Guglielmo Marconi, Rome, October 2, 2014).

30 G. Irwin, October 2, 1915, 17.

31 Ibid, November 8, 1915, 18-9.

32 Ibid, 18.

33 Ibid, November 11, 1915, 19.

34 *Orient* 6, no. 50, (1915): 321; Ibid, no. 44: 285.

35 G. Irwin, December 16, 1915, 20.

36 Ibid, November 8, 1915, 18.

37 *MH* 112, no. 6 (1916): 266.

38 "Gallipoli Casualties by Country," *New Zealand History*: nzhistory.govt.nz; Liman von Sanders, *Five Years in Turkey* (Annapolis, MD: The United States Naval Institute, 1927), 4.

39 Kéchichian, 379.

40 von Sanders, 113.

41 *MH* 112, no. 6 (1916): 255.

42 von Sanders, 124-25.

43 Ibid, 113-15.

44 Vahagn Avedian, "The Armenian Genocide of 1915 from a Neutral Small State's Perspective: Sweden," *Genocide Studies and Prevention* 5, no. 3 (2010): 329.

12. More Evictions

1 *MH* 112, no. 7 (1916): 302-3.

2 G. Irwin, February 3, 1916, 21.

3 Morgenthau, *Ambassador Morgenthau's Story*, 393-94.

4 *MH* 112, no. 8 (1916): 353.

5 Ussher and Knapp, 320-21.

6 *MH* 112, no. 8 (1916): 275-76; *Fourth Report of the War Victims' Relief Committee of the Society of Friends, October 1916 to September 1917* (London: Headley Brothers Printers, 1917), 15; "Old Leightonian Notes." *The Leightonian* 3, no. 66 (1916), 90-1.

7 *MH* 112, no 4 (1916): 153.

8 Akçam, "Review Essay," 122.

9 von Sanders, 129.

10 *LLW* 46, no. 7 (1916): 337.

11 Kévorkian, 472-73.

12 *LLW* 46, no. 9 (1916): 401-2.

13 Gözel Durmaz, 97-8.

14 Avedian, 329.

15 "Story of the Girls," 5.

16 G. Irwin, March 14-28, 1916, 22. The deportation of Greeks from the Pontus region continued well into the summer: "Turks Deporting Greeks," *The New York Times*, August 21, 1916.

17 "Story of the Girls," 5.

18 Akçam, "Review Essay," 133.

19 Akçam, *Shameful Act*, 185.

20 Panken, 36.

21 Ibid.

22 *MH* 112, no. 12 (1916): 541.

23 Panken, 37-8.

24 *MH* 112, no. 8 (1916): 349-50; Ibid, no. 12: 541.

25 Fromkin, 200-3.

26   Zürcher, *Turkey*, 119.
27   *MH* 112, no 4 (1916): 153.
28   Fromkin, 188-96; Zürcher, *Turkey,* 143-44.
29   G. Irwin, May 12, 1916, 23.
30   Zürcher, *Turkey*, 119.
31   Gözel Durmaz, 107-9.
32   "Story of the Girls," 6-7; Theda S. Phelps to Keghani, June 12, 1916, SWOP; MH 113, no 4 (1917): 186.
33   Gözel Durmaz, 109.
34   "Story of the Girls," 7.
35   Wolff-Metternich to Hollweg, 1916-07-10-DE-001, Gust, 602.
36   ABCFM-AR 1916, 88-9; MH 116, no 3 (1920): 116-21.
37   *MH* 112, no. 9 (1916): 417-18.
38   Ibid, no. 11: 564.
39   G. Irwin, February 2-3, 1916, 21.
40   Loughridge, untitled letter, June 12, 1916, HL/HU, ABC 16.9.3, v43, Microfilm A467, Reel 632, 409; G. Irwin, June 8, 1916, 24.
41   *LLW* 46, no. 9 (1916): 367-68.
42   "Story of the Girls," 7-8; *LLW* 47, no. 3 (1917): 101; G. Irwin, May 16, 1916, 23-24.

13. A Door Closes

1   Loughridge, June 12, 1916, HL/HU, 409.
2   G. Irwin, July 23, 1916, 26.
3   MH 113, no. 4 (1917): 186.
4   Gözel Durmaz, 106.
5   "Story of the Girls," 8-9; *MH* 113, no. 4 (1917): 186.
6   Gözel Durmaz, 119.
7   *MH* 113, no. 6 (1917): 292.
8   Loughridge, "Facts in Regard to Armenian Atrocities," 117; Loughridge, June 12, 1916, HL/HU, 409.
9   G. Irwin, October 17, 1916, 28; "Story of the Girls," 9.
10   Ibid.
11   *MH* 113, no. 4 (1917): 186.
12   G. Irwin, October 15, 1916, 27.
13   *MH* 113, no. 4 (1917): 186.
14   Ibid, no. 3: 126-27.
15   Ibid, no. 4: 186.
16   SWOTR, 17.
17   "Missionary Tells of Life in Turkey," *Dubuque Daily Times*, 1915, [clipping, n.d.] SWOP.
18   Riksarkivet, *Utrikesdepartementet* 1149a, no. 80 (May 20, 1916), quoted in Avedian, 329.

19 About $6 million and $11.4 million respectively in today's dollar. "Latest News Concerning the Armenian and Syrian Sufferers: January 25, 1916," (New York: American Committee for Armenian and Syrian Relief, 1916), 12, quoted in Panken, 31.

20 Len Bartlotti, "A Call for a Mission Renewal Movement," *International Journal of Frontier Missions* 1, no. 1 (1984): 39-41.

21 Panken, 43-4, 47; *MH* 112, no. 6 (1916): 272.

22 *A National Test of Brotherhood* (New York: American Committee for Armenian and Syrian Relief, 1916), 28-9.

23 *LLW* 46, no. 7 (1916): 294; Lilian Cole Sewny, ABH-PR.

24 Morgenthau, *Ambassador Morgenthau's Story*, 324-325.

25 Riksarkivet, *Utrikesdepartementet* 1149a, no. 14 (14 January 1917), quoted in Avedian, 330.

26 *MH* 113, no. 4 (1917): 205.

27 G. Irwin, February 28, 1917, 31.

28 *MH* 113, no. 8 (1917): 373-74.

29 G. Irwin, March 10-26, 1917, 31.

30 *MH* 113, no. 6 (1917): 292.

31 Ibid, no. 8: 373-74.

32 Ibid, no. 6: 300-1.

33 Ibid, 291; ABCFM-AR 1917, 65.

34 "Branting might very well have been the first public figure who, decades before Raphael Lemkin, used the term *folkmord*, that is genocide, in regard to the annihilation of a nation." Avedian, 330-31.

35 *MH* 113, no. 3 (1917): 106.

36 *LLW* 47, no. 1 (1917): 5.

37 *MH* 113, no. 6 (1917): 291.

38 G. Irwin, December 17, 1916, 29.

39 von Sanders, 131; Zürcher, *Turkey*, 119; Stoddard, 112.

40 Keith Hamilton, "Chocolate for Zedzed: Basil Zaharoff and the Secret Diplomacy of the Great War," in *The Records of the Permanent Under-Secretary's Department: Liaison Between the Foreign Office and British Secret Intelligence, 1873-1939* (London: Foreign and Commonwealth Office, 2005), 29-30.

14. A Window Opens

1 *MS* 35, no. 5 (1917): 153-54.

2 SWOTR, 10.

3 SWOTR, 7-16. It was February in the old Julian calendar.

4 *MS* 35, no. 7 (1917): 214.

5 *MS* 36, no. 1 (1918): 21.

6 *MH* 113, no 7 (1917), 344; *LLW* 48, no. 4 (1918): 173.

7 *MH* 114, no. 3 (1918), 111-14.

8   Orlando Figes, *A People's Tragedy: The Russian Revolution 1891-1924* (London: Jonathan Cape, 1996), 422.

9   Ibid, 409.

10   Ibid, 421-33.

11   *MH* 114, no. 3 (1918): 115.

12   Ibid, no. 1: 22.

13   SWOTR, 7.

14   US Passport of SWO, July 17, 1917, SWOP.

15   SWOTR, 12-16.

16   *MS* 35, no. 8-9 (1917): 253.

17   SWO, *Experiences in Relief Work*, May 1923, SWOP.

18   SWOTR, 14-16.

19   Ibid, 37-43.

20   Ibid, 43-44.

21   *MH* 114, no. 1 (1918): 22.

22   SWOTR, 54.

23   Ibid, 51-2; SWO, *Experiences in Relief Work*.

24   U.S. Congress, Senate, *Bolshevik Propaganda: Hearings before a Subcommittee of the Committee on the Judiciary, February 11, 1919 to March 10, 1919 ... Pursuant to S. Res. 439 and 469*, 65th Cong., 3d sess., 163-93.

25   SWOTR, 53-5.

26   SWO to My Dear Friends, October 28, 1923, SWOP.

27   SWO, *Experiences in Relief Work*.

28   SWOTR, 57.

29   "Trans-Siberian Railway," in *The American Educator,* ed. Ellsworth D. Foster (Chicago: Ralph Durham Company, 1921), 3608-9.

30   SWOTR, 57-8.

31   Ibid, 56.

32   Ibid, 56-7

33   *MH* 114, no 4 (1918): 182.

34   SWOTR, 58.

35   SWO, *Experiences in Relief Work*.

36   Theodore A. Elmer, "T.A. Elmer's news from Moscow," November 28, 1917, SWOP.

37   SWO, *Experiences in Relief Work*.

38   In Russia, this is known as the October Revolution, because it started on October 25 of the Julian calendar (November 7 in the Gregorian calendar).

39   Sheila Fitzpatrick, *The Russian Revolution*, 3rd edition (New York: Oxford University Press, 2008), 64.

40   Fitzpatrick, 65, 68.

41   Figes, 497-98.

42   SWO, *Experiences in Relief Work*.

43   Elmer, "T.A. Elmer's news."

44   *MS* 36, no. 3 (1918): 67.

45   *MH* 114, no. 3 (1918): 129-30.

46   SWO to My Dear Friends; SWO, *Experiences in Relief Work*.

47   Woodrow Wilson, "Proclamation 1405: Thanksgiving Day, 1917," eds. John T. Woolley and Gerhard Peters, *The American Presidency Project*, http://www.presidency.ucsb.edu. For more information on the aim of creating "a new global order, grounded in Christian principles of love and brotherhood and underwritten by American leadership," see Preston, 252-54.

15. Aiding in Alexandropol

1   Lloyd E. Ambrosius, "Wilsonian Diplomacy and Armenia: The Limits of Power and Ideology," in *America and the Armenian Genocide of 1915,* ed. Jay Winter (Cambridge, UK: Cambridge University Press: 2003), 117.

2   *MH* 115, no 1 (1919): 12-4.

3   SWO, *Experiences in Relief Work*.

4   *The Leightonian* 8, no. 66 (December 1916): 90-1.

5   *Fourth Report of The War Victims' Relief Committee*, 15; Morgan Philips Price, *Dispatches from the Revolution: Russia 1915-1918*, ed. Tania Rose (Durham: Duke University Press, 1998), 26.

6   SWOTR, 59.

7   SWO, *Experiences in Relief Work*.

8   SWOTR, 60-1; SWO, *Experiences in Relief Work*.

9   SWOTR, 61-62; SWO, *Experiences in Relief Work*.

10   SWOTR, 62-63; SWO, *Experiences in Relief Work*.

11   SWOTR, 104-5.

12   Ibid, 64-73; SWO, *Experiences in Relief Work*.

13   SWOTR, 63-73.

14   Ibid, 72-63.

15   Ibid, 68-72.

16   *MH* 113, no 1 (1917): 27.

17   SWOTR, 71.

18   Ibid, 65.

19   Figes, 540-43. Troop estimates of the Czech Legion range from 30,000 to 40,000.

20   *MH* 114, no. 8 (1918): 370-71.

21   Ibid, 368-71.

22   SWOTR, 66; *MH* 114, no. 8 (1918): 373-75.

23   Preston, 27.

24   SWOTR, 65-7.

25   Mary Maynard, ABH-PR.

26   *MH* 113, no 11 (1917): 521.

27   SWO to Friends at Home, May 18, 1918, SWOP.

28 SWOTR, 82-83.

29 *MH* 115, no. 1 (1919): 14.

16. Rolling Up Their Sleeves

1   SWOTR, 85-87.

2   Ibid, 90-91.

3   Ibid, 83-5.

4   *MS* 36, no. 9 (1918): 242.

5   Fitzpatrick, 72-3.

6   Figes, 370.

7   Ibid, 529.

8   Max von Hoffmann, *War Diaries and Other Papers* 1 (London, 1929), 206-7, quoted in John W. Wheeler-Bennett, *Brest-Litovsk: The Forgotten Peace, March 1918* (London: MacMillan and Co., 1938), 245.

9   Herbert E. B. Case to Friend, February 27, 1918, SWOP.

10 SWOTR, 81.

11 *MH* 115, no. 1 (1919): 12.

12 SWOTR, 78-9.

13 *MH* 114, no. 8 (1918): 373-74.

14 *MH* 115, no. 1 (1919): 13; Williams referred to the "new Kerensky variety" of the 1000-rouble note, even though Kerensky was no longer in the government: Maynard Owen Williams, "A Forced Retreat," Maynard Owen Williams Collection, RG 77/1, Box 14, Folder 2, Kalamazoo College Archives, Kalamazoo College, Kalamazoo, Michigan, 1192.

15 *MH* 114, no. 8 (1918): 371.

16 *MH* 115, no.1 (1919): 13-4.

17 Ibid, 13; SWO to Brothers and Sisters, May 20, 1918, SWOP.

18 Figes, 543, 548.

19 Arthur I. Andrews, "Current Notes: Errors in the Ordinary Versions of the Treaty of Brest-Litovsk," *The American Journal of International Law* 13, no. 2 (April 1919): 313-17.

20 Victor M. Fic, *The Bolsheviks and the Czechoslovak Legion* (New Delhi: Abhinav, 1947), 5.

21 Figes, 547.

22 SWO, *Experiences in Relief Work*.

23 *MH* 114, no. 8 (1918): 371-73.

24 Ibid, no. 4: 160-61.

25 Fic, 164-67.

26 SWOTR, 87-8.

27 Ibid, 87-9; *MH* 114, no. 8 (1918): 371-73; SWO, *Experiences in Relief Work*.

28 *MH* 114, no. 8 (1918): 373-75.

29 Ibid, no. 10: 445; *MS* 36, no. 9 (1918): 243; SWOTR, 92.

30 *MH* 114, no. 8 (1918): 371.

31 *MH* 115, no. 1 (1919): 13.

32 *MH* 114, no. 8 (1918): 373.

33 Maynard Owen Williams, "American Relief Committee Returns," Maynard Owen Williams Collection, RG 77/1, Box 14, Folder 2, Kalamazoo College Archives, Kalamazoo College, Kalamazoo, Michigan, 1183.

34 *MH* 114, no. 8 (1918): 371.

35 Ibid.

36 Williams, "American Relief Committee Returns," 1188.

17. Eastward Ho!

1 *MH* 114, no. 8 (1918): 374.

2 SWOTR, 92; Williams, "American Relief Committee Returns," 1182. Williams erroneously called it the "Indo-Bombay Telegraph Company"; it was "European" not "Bombay." Martin Kaerner, "Pioneers of the Project Business: The Siemens Brothers and the Indo-European Telegraph Line," in *Experiencing Project Management*, eds. Elisabeth Bittner and Walter Gregorc (Erlangen, Germany: Publicis Publishing, 2010), 203.

3 *MH* 114, no. 10 (1918): 445.

4 Williams, "A Forced Retreat," 1190-91.

5 SWOTR, 105-6.

6 Williams, "American Relief Committee Returns," 1183; "A Forced Retreat," 1190.

7 SWOTR, 94.

8 Travel Certificates, March 20-22, 1918, SWOP. [Translated by Kamo Mayilyan]

9 SWOTR, 94, 107.

10 Williams, "A Forced Retreat," 1190-91.

11 Ibid, 1191.

12 *MH* 114, no. 8 (1918): 374.

13 SWO to Brothers and Sisters, May 20, 1918, SWOP.

14 SWOTR, 94-5.

15 Williams, "A Forced Retreat," 1192.

16 SWO to Brothers and Sisters, May 20, 1918, SWOP.

17 *MH* 114, no. 8 (1918): 374.

18 SWOTR, 96-7.

19 Williams, "A Forced Retreat," 1192-93.

20 Anna Stoklosa, "Chasing The Bear: William James On Sensations, Emotions And Instincts," *William James Studies* 9 (2012): 74.

21 SWOTR, 97-8.

22 Williams, "A Forced Retreat," 1192-95.

23 SWOTR, 99.

24 Williams, "A Forced Retreat," 1192.

25 *MH* 114, no. 10 (1918): 445-46.
26 Williams, "A Forced Retreat," 1192-93.
27 *MH* 114, no. 8 (1918): 374-75.
28 Williams, "A Forced Retreat," 1192-93.
29 Ibid, 1193.
30 *MS* 36, no. 8 (1918): 243.
31 Williams, "A Forced Retreat," 1194.
32 SWOTR, 107.
33 Ibid, 103.
34 Ibid, 102.
35 Ibid, 94-6.
36 Williams, "A Forced Retreat," 1192.
37 *MH* 114, no. 10 (1918): 446.
38 Williams, "A Forced Retreat," 1192; SWOTR, 101.
39 Williams, "A Forced Retreat," 1196.
40 SWOTR, 102-3.
41 *MH* 114, no. 8 (1918): 375.
42 SWOTR, 103-4; *MS* 36, no. 8 (1918): 243.
43 SWO, Signed Report, May 1923, SWOP.
44 SWOTR, 103; SWO to Friends at Home, May 18-19, 1918, SWOP.
45 SWOTR, 109-10.
46 Ibid, 110.
47 Williams, "A Forced Retreat," 1196.
48 SWOTR, 118; *MH* 114, no. 10 (1918): 445-49.
49 SWOTR, 110-13.

18. The End of the Beginning

1 *MH* 114, no. 10 (1918): 446.
2 Fic, 6-15, 23, 30, 38-9.
3 *MH* 114, no. 10 (1918): 446-47.
4 Maynard Owen Williams, "The Fighting Czechs," Maynard Owen Williams Collection, RG 77/1, Box 14, Folder 4. Kalamazoo College Archives, Kalamazoo College, Kalamazoo, Michigan, 1-2.
5 SWOTR, 113.
6 Ibid, 107.
7 Williams, "The Fighting Czechs," 5.
8 Edward A. Butler, *Our Household Insects: An Account of the Insect-Pests Found in Dwelling-houses* (London: Longmans, Green and Co., 1893), 227.
9 SWO to Friends at Home, May 18-19, 1918, SWOP.
10 Ibid.
11 SWOTR, 108.
12 Ibid.
13 Ibid, 107-9, 114; SWO to Friends at Home, May 18-19, SWOP.

14   Ibid.

15   SWOTR, 114.

16   Ibid, 115.

17   *MH* 115, no. 3 (1919): 120.

18   Jennifer Ann Polk, "Constructive Efforts: The American Red Cross and YMCA in Revolutionary and Civil War Russia, 1917-24" (Doctoral thesis, University of Toronto, 2012), 153.

19   Fic, 49.

20   SWOTR, 117.

21   Ibid, 115-16.

22   Jane Yarrow, *Ernest Yarrow Memorial*, Edward H. Hazen Memorial, quoted in Rasch, 180. Martha Yarrow's full name was Jane Martha Tuckley Yarrow.

23   Polk, 208.

24   SWOTR, 108, 115-16.

25   *MS* 36, no. 8 (1918): 226-27.

26   Aurora Mardiganian, *Ravished Armenia: The Story of Aurora Mardiganian, the Christian Girl Who Lived Through the Great Massacres,* H. L. Gates, interp. (New York: Kingfield Press, 1918), 249.

27   Anthony Slide, ed., *Ravished Armenia and the Story of Aurora Mardiganian* (Jackson, MI: University of Mississippi Press, 2014), 11.

28   James Bone, *The Curse of Beauty: The Scandalous and Tragic Life of Audrey Munson, America's First Supermodel* (New York: Regan Arts, 2016), 238.

29   Ibid, 240.

30   Slide, 12.

31   Mardiganian, 9-17.

32   Payaslian, *United States Policy*, 131-32.

33   Zürcher, *Turkey,* 144.

34   Eugene L. Taylor and Abraham D. Krikorian, "Notes and Queries Relevant to 'A Brief Assessment of the Ravished Armenia Marquee Poster' by Amber Karlins," *Armenian News Network*, December 20, 2010. Accessed at groong.org.

35   Bone, 240.

36   Slide, 10.

37   Atom Egoyan, foreword to Ravished Armenia and the Story of Aurora Mardiganian, edited by Anthony Slide (Jackson, MI: University of Mississippi Press, 2014), xii.

38   Slide, 10.

39   Both the book and movied had been renamed "Auction of Souls" for Canadian and British audiences: Aram Adjemian, "Canada's Moral Mandate for Armenia: Sparking Humanitarian and Political Interest, 1880-1923" (Master's thesis, Concordia University, 2007), 32. Though most of the film was lost, a few clips are available for viewing on YouTube.com. For more in-depth information on Canada's involvement during the period, see Aram Adjemian,

The Call from Armenia: Canada's Response to the Armenian Genocide (Lorraine, QC: Corridor Books, 2015).

40　Taylor and Krikorian.

41　*Toronto Daily Star*, August 23, 1919, quoted in Adjemian, 32.

42　Whitehorn, Chronology, *Armenian Genocide*, 365.

43　Ibid; Dadrian, 350-51.

44　Zürcher, *Turkey*, 120.

45　Hamilton, *Chocolate for Zedzed*, 33, 36-7.

46　Zürcher, *Turkey*, 121.

47　Ibid, 134.

48　ACASR *News Bulletin* 11, no. 6 (November 1918): 7.

49　SWOTR, 118-19; *MS* 114, no. 7 (1918): 323; Rasch, 180.

50　*MH* 114, no. 12 (1918): 555-56.

51　*LLW* 49, no. 6 (1919): 265.

52　*MS* 36, no. 3 (1918): 67.

53　*LLW* 48, no. 11 (1918): 447.

19. Through A Glass Darkly

1　*MH* 115, no. 2 (1919): 50-1.

2　Ibid, no. 1: 8.

3　Ibid; Ibid, no. 2: 47; Ibid, no 6: 236-37; *LLW* 49, no. 3 (1919): 110; *News Bulletin* 2, no. 6 (ACASR, 1918): 1; Ibid 3, no. 10: 11.

4　*MH* 115, no. 2 (1919): 47; Ibid, no. 1: 8.

5　SWO, "1919," (January 15, 1919), 18, SWOP.

6　SWO, *Experiences in Relief Work*.

7　The flu was first identified in Spain, hence its name; it was not determined to be a variety of swine flu until 1997. "AFIP Scientists Discover Clues to 1918 Spanish Flu," *AFIP Letter* 115, no. 2 (Washington, DC: Armed Forces Institute of Pathology, 1997), 1.

8　SWO to sister Harriet, January 25, 1919, SWOP.

9　*LLW* 49, no. 2 (1919): 50.

10　"The Lesser Belligerents," *Current History: A Monthly Magazine of The New York Times* 9, pt. 2 (January – March 1919): 419.

11　Zürcher, *Turkey*, 134.

12　Dadrian, 319.

13　Jennifer Balint, "The Ottoman State Special Military Tribunal for the Genocide of the Armenians: 'Doing Government Business'," in *The Hidden Histories of War Crimes Trials*, ed. Kevin Heller and Gerry Simpson (Oxford: Oxford University Press, 2013), 85.

14　Dadrian, 319.

15　Kévorkian, 776.

16　"The Lesser Belligerents," 419.

17 "Turkey's Surrender to the Allies," *Current History: A Monthly Magazine of The New York Times* 9, pt. 1 (October - December 1918): 399-400.

18 Zürcher, *Turkey*, 133.

19 Frank L. Polk, Acting Secretary of State to James L. Barton, telegram, January 21, 1919, HL/HU, ABC 16.9.3, v40, Microfilm A467, Reel 629, 137.

20 "The Lesser Belligerents," 419.

21 *MH* 115, no. 9 (1919): 391.

22 Bovenkerk, 594.

23 The Turkish name was *Umum Alem-i İslam* İhtilâl *Teşkilâti*. N. Bilge Criss, *Istanbul under Allied Occupation 1918-1923* (Leiden: E.J. Brill, 1999), 94-114, quoted in Zürcher, *Turkey*, 135-36.

24 Fromkin, 386-87.

25 Most of the words were from a letter by Canadian missionary Edward C. Woodley of the Marash station. *MH* 115, no. 2 (1919): 27-8.

26 Ibid, no. 4: 133; Navy Radio Message received via Washington, March 12, 1919, quoted in Abraham D. Krikorian and Eugene L. Taylor, "Ninety-Six Years Ago Today," *Armenian News Network/Groong*, February 16, 2015. Accessed at groong.usc.edu.

27 *Catalogue Number for the Sessions of 1934-1935* (Morningside Heights, NY: Columbia University, 1935), 71.

28 *MH* 115, no. 10 (1919): 421-22.

29 Ibid, no. 6: 228.

30 Ibid, no. 10: 420-21.

31 SWOTR, 124.

32 Krikorian and Taylor, "Ninety-Six Years Ago Today"; *MH* 115, no. 2 (1919): 58.

33 Ibid, no. 6: 235-37; George E. White, ACRNE Director of Personnel to Friend, April 25, 1919, SWOP.

34 *MH* 115, no. 6 (1919): 235-36.

35 *LLW* 49, no. 6 (1919): 262.

36 Ibid, 263.

37 Ibid, 263-64; *MH* 115, no. 6 (1919): 236.

38 "The Prinkipo Conference Plan," *Current History* 9, pt. 2 (1919): 407; *LLW* 49, no. 6 (1919): 263-64; SWO to Home Friends, April 27, 1919, SWOP.

39 Ibid.

40 SWO to Home Friends, March 23, 1919, SWOP; SWOTR, 124.

41 Arthur Goldschmidt, Jr. and Robert Johnson, *Historical Dictionary of Egypt*, 3rd ed. (Lanham, MD: Scarecrow Press, 2003), 424-25.

42 The relief workers did not know where they were to be located once they arrived in Turkey, though it made sense to be assigned to their old stations. SWO to Home Friends, March 23, 1919.

43 *MH* 115, no. 4 (1919): 141.

44 Ibid, no. 3: 91.

20. Making Their Way Back

1   Whitehorn, 1.

2   Estimates range from 360,000-750,000. Hannibal Travis, "On the Centenary of the Greek Genocide," *AIF Policy Journal* 8 (Spring 2017): 3-4.

3   "Chaldean Victims of the Turks," *The Times* [UK], November 22, 1919, quoted in Travis, "Native Christians Massacred," 336.

4   *LLW* 49, no. 6 (1919): 265-66.

5   *MH* 115, no. 6 (1919): 232.

6   Minnie Mills, ABH-PR.

7   *MH* 115, no. 6 (1919): 230.

8   Ibid.

9   "The Lesser Belligerents," 19-20.

10 Stanley Kerr, *The Lions of Marash: Personal Experiences with American Near East Relief, 1919-1922* (Albany: State University of New York Press, 1973), 43-8. Rose Shayb later became Mrs. John Dunaway: Kerr, 316.

11 *LLW* 49, no. 6 (1919): 265.

12 SWO to Home Friends, April 27, 1919, SWOP.

13 George L. Richards, ed., *The Medical Work of the Near East Relief* (New York: Near East Relief, 1923), 7.

14 SWO to Home Friends, April 27, 1919, SWOP.

15 Richards, 8.

16 SWO to Home Friends, April 27, 1919, SWOP.

17 *MH* 113, no. 4 (1917): 177-78; *MH* 114, no. 11 (1918): 500; *MH* 116, no. 4 (1920): 169-72.

18 *LLW* 50, no. 7-8 (1920): 333; *MH* 115, no. 6 (1919): 248.

19 *MH* 115, no. 4 (1919): 161-62; no. 6: 230.

20 Ibid, 248.

21 Karekin Dickran, "Maria Jacobsen and the Armenian Genocide," (Danish Peace Academy, 2004), 1, 3.

22 *MH* 115, no. 7 (1919): 303-4.

23 *LLW* 49, no. 7-8 (1919): 337-38.

24 Matthias Bjørnlund, "Recording Death and Survival: Karen Marie Petersen, a Missionary Witness to Genocide," *Haigazian Armenological Review* (Beirut) 32 (2012): 321.

25 *LLW* 49, no. 7-8 (1919): 337.

26 *MH* 115, no. 9 (1919): 391.

27 *LLW* 49, no. 1 (1919): 6.

28 *MH* 114, no. 4 (1918): 164.

29 *LLW* 49, no. 7-8 (1919): 327.

30 This is not to say that no one in Talas, including Susan, refrained from using generalizations. But it is an illustration of the difference in deep-seated attitudes held by those in Talas versus some other missionaries. SWO to Home Friends, March 23, 1919, SWOP.

31 The $2 million figure (ABCFM-AR, 1915, 254), was conservative because "the actual value of the property thus seized and held by the representatives of the Turkish government at Marsovan [alone] amounts to from four to five hundred thousand dollars." ABCFM-AR, 1916, 89.

32 Eric Bogosian, *Operation Nemesis: The Assassination Plot that Avenged the Armenian Genocide* (New York: Little, Brown and Company, 2015), 130.

33 The vilayet was known at various times as Smyrna, Aidin, and Smyrna-Aidin.

34 Mary A. Jenkins, "To Megali Idea—Dead or Alive?: The Domestic Determinants of Greek Foreign Policy" (Master's thesis, Naval Postgraduate School, Monterey, CA, 1994), iii.

35 Toynbee, 77.

36 "Notes of a Meeting Held at Mr. Lloyd George's Residence, 23 Rue Nitot, Paris, on Wednesday, May 7, at Noon," Papers Relating to the Foreign Relations of the United States, The Paris Peace Conference, 1919, Volume 5, Document 49, 180.03401/148 IC–181F.

37 Zürcher, *Turkey*, 146.

38 Toynbee, 77.

39 Hamilton, "Chocolate for Zedzed," 29.

40 Zürcher, *Turkey*, 146.

41 "Turkey's Surrender to the Allies," 399-400.

42 "Notes of a Meeting Held at Mr. Lloyd George's Residence."

43 George E. White, ACRNE Director of Personnel to Friends, April 25, 1919, SWOP; *LLW* 49, no. 6 (1919): 265; Richards, 14.

44 SWO to Home Friends, April 27, 1919, SWOP.

21. Suffer the Little Children

1 SWO to Sister and All the Circle, May 23, 1919, SWOP.

2 *Near East Relief* 3, no. 22 (1921), American Research Institute in Turkey and SALT Research, Records of the American Board of Commissioners for Foreign Missions, affiliates, and successor organizations: 2-3. (Hereafter, *NER*)

3 The two men were not named, and were likely not permanent members of the unit. SWO, May 23, 1919.

4 Ibid.

5 SWO to Friends at Home, June 5, 1919, SWOP.

6 Chater described the children he saw in Alexandropol a few months after Susan left the city. Melville Chater, "The Land of the Stalking Death," *The National Geographic Magazine* 36, no. 5 (1919): 407-9.

7 SWO to Sister Harriet, November 23, 1919, SWOP.

8 *MH* 115, no. 12 (1919): 500.

9 SWO to Home Folks, September 21, 1919, SWOP; Richards, 14.

10 *MH* 115, no. 12 (1919): 500.

11 SWO, June 5, 1919.

12 *MH* 115, no. 12 (1919): 500.

13 Ibid.

14 SWO, June 5, 1919; SWO, November 23, 1919, SWOP.

15 SWO, September 21, 1919.

16 SWO, June 5, 1919.

17 SWO, November 23, 1919.

18 *The Acorne* 1, no. 15 (1919), American Research Institute in Turkey and SALT Research, Records of the American Board of Commissioners for Foreign Missions, affiliates, and successor organizations: 4. (Hereafter, *Acorne*)

19 Fullerton L. Waldo, *Twilight in Armenia* (New York: Near East Relief, 1920), 12.

20 *Acorne* 1, no. 15 (1919): 4.

21 Ibid, no. 19: 2-3; Adelaide Dwight, ABH-PR.

22 *LLW* 50, no. 3 (1920): 123.

23 There are 12 stories in this collection. SWO, Stories of Children Bogilazlian Orphanage, n.d., SWOP.

24 *LLW* 50, no. 4 (1920): 177-78.

25 Richards, 14-15; *NER* 3, no. 22 (1921): 2-3.

26 Ibid; *Acorne* 1, no. 17 (1919): 2.

27 *Acorne* 2, no. 18 (1920): 3.

28 Ibid; *NER* 3, no. 22 (1921): 3.

29 SWO, September 21, 1919; *Acorne* 1, no. 15 (1919): 4.

30 There were two different totals reported in two issues of *The Acorne*: 230 vs 265 orphans in Boghazlian, and 265 vs 365 orphans in Yozgat: Ibid; *Acorne* 1, no. 17 (1919): 2.

1 *LLW* 49, no. 12 (1919): 513.

2 *LLW* 50, no. 4 (1920): 177-79.

3 Ibid, no. 1: 24-6; *LLW* 49, no. 1 (1919): 6; *MH* 116, no. 6 (1920): 265-66.

22. Order and DisOrder

1 Toynbee, 270-71.

2 Keith Jeffery, *The Secret History of MI6* (New York: Penguin Press, 2010), 125.

3 Giles Milton, *Paradise Lost: Smyrna 1922* (New York: Basic Books, 2008), 153-54.

4 Horton tallied the condemned: "three of death; four of hard labor for life; two of hard labor for a term of years; twelve of long and fifty-three of shorter terms of imprisonment. Of the seventy-four sentenced, forty-eight were Greeks; thirteen Turks; twelve were Armenians and one a Jew. The three persons executed were Greeks, one of them a soldier." George Horton, *The Blight of Asia* (Indianapolis: Bobbs-Merrill, 1926), 75-6.

5 Toynbee, 273.

6 As of 1922, none of the Allied countries released the findings. Toynbee, 78.

7 Toynbee, 269-70.

8 The Big Three were Britain, France and the United States. Toynbee, 78-79.

9   Zürcher, *Turkey*, 149-50.

10 "Turkey's Surrender to the Allies," 399.

11 Zürcher, *Turkey*, 148-49.

12 George N. Shirinian, "The 'Great Catastrophe:' The Genocide of the Greeks of Asia Minor, Pontos, and Eastern Thrace, 1912–1923," *Genocide Prevention Now* (Special, 2012): 16.

13 Zürcher, *Turkey*, 149-50.

14 Ibid.

15 *Who Do You Think You Are? Boris Johnson.*

16 Zürcher, *Turkey*, 150.

17 *Who Do You Think You Are? Boris Johnson.*

18 Zürcher, *Turkey*, 150.

19 *LLW* 49, no. 12 (1919): 513.

20 *MH* 116, no. 1 (1920): 24-5.

21 Zürcher, *Turkey*, 151.

22 Fromkin, 427.

23 Mabel E. Elliott, *Beginning Again at Ararat* (New York: Fleming H. Revell, 1924), 83-4.

24 *MH* 116, no. 1 (1920): 36.

25 Ibid, no. 2: 75.

26 *MH* 115, no. 6 (1919): 224.

27 *LLW* 49, no. 10 (1919): 420.

28 The deceased workers were Paul D. Peltier of New York, Rev. R.S.M. Emrich of Boston, and Edith Winchester of Philadelphia respectively. *Acorne* 1, no.1 (June 7, 1919): 1-2.

29 *LLW* 50, no. 5 (1920): 229.

30 *LLW* 49, no. 11 (1919): 489.

31 Edward F. Martin, US Passport Applications, January 2, 1906 - March 31, 1925 (M1490): Roll 951, October 1919, Certificate no. 127626-127999.

32 Mabell S.C. Smith, ed. "Veterans' Number: Tribute and an Appeal," *Team Work* 3, no. 6 (1924): 23.

33 Dickran, 5-6.

34 *MH* 115, no. 10 (1919): 420-21.

35 Ibid, no. 7: 303.

36 Mary Graffam, ABH-PR.

37 *MH* 115, no. 6 (1919): 230.

38 Isabella Watson, "Minnesota Workers in Foreign Missions," *Congregational Work of Minnesota 1832-1920*, ed. Warren Upham (Minneapolis: Congregational Conference of Minnesota, 1921), 135.

39 *MH* 115, no. 6 (1919): 224.

40 "Report of Women's Medical Department, Harpoot Turkey: June 1919-1920," Box 10, Folder 73, American Women's Hospital Papers, quoted in Panken, 147.

41 *MH* 117, no. 6 (1921): 218.

42 *LLW* 50, no. 4 (1920): 177-78.

43 *LLW* 49, no. 12 (1919): 525-28.

44 *MH* 115, no. 8 (1919): 331.

45 Balint, 84, 97.

46 *La Renaissance*, no. 151, May 28, 1919, quoted in Kévorkian, 775.

47 *MH* 115, no. 8 (1919): 332.

48 Ibid, 333.

49 *MH* 116, no. 2 (1920): 77.

50 *MH* 115, no. 9 (1919): 359-60. In fact, the United States never did sign it.

51 Feyaz Bey, head of the Land Registration Office in Yozgat, had also been on trial. Kévorkian, 507, 775-80.

52 Ibid, 780.

53 Ibid, 786-87.

54 Ibid, 789.

55 "Turkey Condemns Its War Leaders: Court-Martial Gives Death Sentence to Enver Pasha, Talaat Bey, and Djemal Pasha," *New York Times*, July 13, 1919. Dr. Behaeddin Şakir of the Special Organization was found guilty in a separate trial on January 13, 1920: Balint, 89.

23. On Their Own

1 *Acorne* 1, no. 19 (1919): 2.

2 SWO to Sister Harriet, November 23, 1919, SWOP.

3 *Acorne* 1, no. 19 (1919): 3.

4 *MH* 117, no. 6 (1921): 218.

5 *Acorne* 1, no. 19 (1919): 2.

6 Ibid, no. 11: 1.

7 *NER* 3, no. 22 (1921): 3.

8 SWO to Sister Harriet, April 24, 1920, SWOP.

9 Herbert and Genevieve Irwin, ABH-PR; The Irwin family lived with Genevieve's father, Frederic B. DuVal and her sister Lorraine in Winnipeg: 1921 Census of Canada, City of Winnipeg, No. 40 Winnipeg South, Manitoba (June 8, 1921), 19.

10 Katherine Fletcher, ABH-PR.

11 Henry Wingate, ABH-PR; A. H. Pearson, "Dr. A.G. Sivaslian and the Turkish Mission," Carleton College, *Voice* 6, no. 4 (1916): 141.

12 SWO, November 23, 1919.

13 Fromkin, 427-28.

14 Elliott, 126-27.

15 Ibid, 84.

16 *MH* 116, no. 4 (1920): 187-88.

17 Elliott, 94.

18 *MH* 116, no. 6 (1920): 287.

19 Elliott, 98-113.

20 *MH* 116, no. 6 (1920): 287-88.

21 Ibid.

22 Elliott, 118, 120.

23 Ibid, 135-36.

24 Fromkin, 428-29; Zürcher, *Turkey,* 151-52.

25 Fromkin, 429.

26 Edwin Carey Whittemore, *Colby College 1820-1925: An Account of Its Beginnings, Progress and Service* (Waterville, ME: Colbiana Books, 1927), 184.

27 Edwin W. Chubb, "Across The Divide," *Ohio University Bulletin* 16, no. 10 (1920), 5-6.

28 Elliott, 80-1.

29 *MH* 116, no. 9 (1920): 423.

30 Ibid, no. 3: 139.

31 Ibid, no. 10: 445-48; no. 12: 558-59.

32 Ibid, no. 7: 328-30.

33 *Acorne* 2, no. 15: 3.

34 SWO to Sister Harriet, April 24, 1920.

35 *Acorne* 2, no. 15 (1920): 4.

36 SWO, April 24, 1920.

37 *Acorne* 2, no. 15 (1920): 4.

38 Ibid, no. 8: 4.

39 Ibid, 4.

40 Fromkin, 429-30.

41 Andrew Mango, *Atatürk: The Biography of the Founder of Modern Turkey* (Woodstock, NY: Overlook Press, 2002), 310.

42 Erik J. Zürcher, *The Young Turk Legacy and Nation Building: From the Ottoman Empire to Atatürk's Turkey* (London: I.B. Tauris, 2010), 121-22.

43 Fromkin, 429.

44 *LLW* 49, no. 12 (1919): 512-13; *MH* 116, no. 6 (1920): 256; no 7: 304-5.

45 Fromkin, 430-31.

46 *LLW* 50, no. 10 (1920): 455.

47 *MH* 116, no. 10 (1920): 445-48.

48 SWO to Sister Harriet, June 17, 1920; *LLW* 50, no. 10 (1920): 456-57.

49 *Acorne* 2, no. 21 (1920): 4; "Obituary of Robertson Gannaway," *Grinnell Herald* (Grinnell, Iowa) Dec. 18, 1928.

50 SWO to Brother John, June 28, 1920.

51 Ibid.

24. No Pleasant Place To Be

1 The 433-article treaty also made provision for "a tribunal competent to deal with the said massacres" that occurred during the war years. Article 230, *The*

Treaties of Peace 1919-1923, Vol. II (New York: Carnegie Endowment for International Peace, 1924), 863.

2   Zürcher, *Turkey*, 147.

3   *MH* 116, no. 12 (1920): 539.

4   *MH* 117, no. 10 (1921): 340.

5   *MH* 116, no. 9 (1920): 396.

6   Ibid, no. 10: 474.

7   Ibid, no. 9: 396.

8   Margaret MacMillan, *History's People: Personalities and the Past* (Toronto: House of Anansi Press, 2015), 163.

9   Fromkin, 429.

10 Zürcher, *Turkey*, 147; Fromkin, 431.

11 *MH* 116, no. 12 (1920): 539-40.

12 *NER* 2, no. 42 (1920): 1.

13 Brigette C. Kamsler, Kristen Leigh Southworth and Amy Meverden, finding aid, "Near East Relief Committee Records, 1904-1950," (The Burke Library Archives, Columbia University Libraries, Union Theological Seminary, New York, 2013), 2.

14 SWO to Home Circle, July 17, 1920, SWOP.

15 *Acorne* 2, no.21 (1920): 2.

16 SWO to Brother John, September 14, 1920, SWOP.

17 Translated memorandum, Cesarea Superintendent of Education, September 7, 1920, SWOP.

18 SWO, September 14, 1920.

19 Ibid.

20 *LLW* 51, no. 6 (1921): 202.

21 SWO, September 14, 1920.

22 Travis, "On the Centenary of the Greek Genocide," 8.

23 Kâzım Karabekir, İstiklâl *Harbimiz* (Our War of Independence), 2nd edn. (Istanbul: Türkiye Yanıneve, 1969), 833, quoted in Mango, 290.

24 The border decided in 1920 is still the border today. Mango, 294.

25 Richard G. Hovannisian, "Caucasian Armenia between Imperial and Soviet Rule: The Interlude of National Independence," (Paper, Conference on "Nationalism And Social Change in Transcaucasia," Co-sponsored by Kennan Institute for Advanced Russian Studies, The Wilson Center and American Association for the Advancement of Slavic Studies, April 24-25, 1980), 33-4.

26 Fromkin, 432; Zürcher, *Turkey*, 153.

27 *MH* 116, no. 10 (1920) 441.

28 *Acorne* 2, no. 29 (1920): 3.

29 Ibid, no. 40: 3.

30 Ibid, no. 37: 2-3; *MH* 116, no. 11 (1920): 494; *NER* 3, no. 13 (1921): 3.

31 *Acorne* 2, no. 29 (1920): 2.

32 Ibid.

33 Richards, 14.

34 Ibid; *Acorne* 2, no. 40 (1920): 4.

35 *NER* 2, no. 51 (1920): 2.

36 *MH* 117, no. 3 (1921): 84-6.

37 SWO to Brothers and Sisters, November 22, 1920, SWOP.

38 *MH* 117, no. 3 (1921): 84.

39 Ibid, 105.

40 SWO to My Dear Friends, October 28, 1923, SWOP.

41 SWOTR, 99-100.

42 *MH* 117, no. 6 (1921): 216.

43 *MH* 118, no. 11 (1922): 423-25.

44 *LLW* 52, no. 11 (1922): 386-87.

45 Shenk, *America's Black Sea Fleet: The U.S. Navy Amidst War and Revolution, 1919-1923*, ebook ed. (Annapolis, MD: Naval Institute Press, 2012), Chapter 10.

46 *MH* 117, no. 6 (1921): 216.

47 The Ottoman government had been invited, but when it became clear nothing could happen without the Nationalists, representatives from the Angora government attended, too. Zürcher, *Turkey*, 154.

48 *MH* 117, no. 6 (1921): 217-18.

49 Fromkin, 540.

50 Michael Llewellyn Smith, *Ionian Vision: Greece in Asia Minor 1919-1922* (Ann Arbor, MI: University of Michigan Press, 1998), 203.

51 Zürcher, *Turkey*, 155.

52 Bogosian, 9-11.

53 Akçam, "Review Essay," 111.

54 Morgenthau, *Ambassador's Story*, 24.

55 Bryant, 158-59.

56 *LLW* 51, no. 6 (1921): 201-03; *MH* 117, no. 6 (1921): 218.

57 Ibid.

58 John H. Warye to Mrs John Cook, March 18, 1921, SWOP.

25. A Greek Tragedy

1 *NER* 3, no. 39 (1921): 4.

2 *LLW* 51, no. 10 (1921): 358-59; Ibid, no. 11: 391-92.

3 *NER* 3, no. 21 (1921): 4; Ibid, no. 43: 4; New York Passenger Arrival Lists (Ellis Island), 1892-1924: June 25, 1921.

4 *NER* 3, no. 36-37 (1921): 4; "United in Little Britain Church," *Newburgh Daily News* [NY], November 19, 1921.

5 Edward Martin, ABH-PR.

6 *MH* 117, no. 5 (1921): 160-61.

7 "The League of Nations, 1920," *Milestones: 1914–1920*, Office of the Historian, Bureau of Public Affairs, United States Department of State: history.state.gov.

8 *MH* 117, no. 5 (1921): 161.

9 Fromkin, 547-48.

10 "The Chosen Executives of America Adopt Orphans of the Near East," *The New Near East* (May 1921): 2.

11 Esther Pohl Lovejoy, *Certain Samaritans* (New York: Macmillan Company, 1927), 83, 87.

12 *LLW* 51, no. 7-8 (1921): 260.

13 Toynbee, 259-60, 262.

14 *Reports on Atrocities in the Districts of Yalova and Guemlek and in the Ismid Peninsula* (Cmd. 1478, Turkey No. 1), (London: His Majesty's Stationery Office, 1921), 4-5.

15 Fromkin, 541.

16 *MH* 117, no. 9 (1921): 310-11.

17 Fromkin, 541-43; Zürcher, *Turkey*, 155.

18 Kévorkian, 486.

19 Mango, 213.

20 Üngor, 175.

21 *MH* 118, no. 4 (1922): 146.

22 Lysimachos Oeconomos, *Martyrdom of Smyrna and Eastern Christendom* (London: George Allen & Unwin, 1922), 41.

23 newspaper clipping, n.d. (possibly Sioux City, Iowa, circa December 1921), SWOP.

24 Oeconomos, 41.

25 *NER* 3, no. 39 (1921): 2; "Appeal for Near East Relief," *Logansport Pharos-Tribune* [Indiana], April 28, 1922.

26 *NER* 3, no. 47 (1921): 2.

27 newspaper clipping, SWOP.

28 Ibid.

29 *NER* 3, no. 47 (1921): 2-3.

30 SWO to Brother John, September 13, 1921, SWOP.

31 *NER* 3, no. 39 (1921): 4.

32 *Orient* 9, no. 2 (1922): 5.

33 *MH* 118, no. 1 (1922): 22-3.

34 Ibid.

35 *Orient* 9, no. 3 (1922): 13.

36 *MH* 118, no. 3 (1922): 112-13.

26. Prelude to a Denouement

1 Bone, 239-40.

2 "Alice in Hungerland," *The New Near East* (November 1921): 4-5.

3   *Lincoln Evening Journal* [Nebraska], March 24, 1921.

4   "Lighten the Shadows of the Cross," *The New Near East* (March 1921): 10.

5   "The Chosen Executives", 2.

6   [My italics]. *Lincoln Evening Journal.*

7   "The 'Infant Phenom' Turns Philanthropist," *The New Near East* (July 1921): 8.

8   "Masonic Interest," and "Eastern Star," *The New Near East* (July 1921): 9.

9   "Radio Aids Publicity," *The New Near East* (July 1921): 9.

10   Vicken Babkenian, "Stories of International 'Goodness' During the Armenian Genocide," *Genocide Prevention Now* (Fall 2012): 7.

11   "An Ancestral Home," *The New Near East* (July 1921): 9.

12   Vicken Babkenian and Peter Stanley, *Armenia, Australia and the Great War* (Sydney: NewSouth Publishing, 2016), 195-209.

13   Vicken Babkenian, "An S.O.S. from Beyond Gallipoli: Victoria and the Armenian Relief Movement," *Victorian Historical Journal* 81, no. 2 (November 2010): 261-63.

14   *NER* 3, no. 45 (1921): 4. Obituary of Dr. V.W. M. Wright, Yates County, NY, Swan Vital Statistics, 1947.

15   *NER* 4, no. 7 (1922): 3.

16   Ibid, no. 8: 3.

17   Ibid.

18   *LLW* 52, no. 3 (1922): 111.

19   *Orient* 9, no. 7 (1922): 61.

20   *LLW* 52, no. 6 (1922): 230; Annie Allen, ABH-PR.

21   *Orient* 9, no. 1 (1922): 3; SWO to Brother John and Family, February 10, 1922, SWOP.

22   Ibid.

23   Ibid.

24   Ibid.

25   Oeconomos, 37.

26   Ibid, 38.

27   SWO to Friends, March 4, 1922, SWOP.

28   SWO to Harriet, March 5, 1922, SWOP.

29   SWO to John, March 23, 1922, SWOP; Julia Ann Orvis to author, email, February 19, 2018.

30   SWO to John, April 20 - September 13, 1922, SWOP.

31   *LLW* 52, no. 3 (1922): 187.

32   *NER* 4, no. 20 (1922): 4.

33   *Orient* 9, no. 8 (1922): 69; SWO to Harriet, August 4, 1922, SWOP.

34   NER pamphlet, n.d., SWOP.

35   *Orient* 9, no. 8 (1922): 69.

36   *NER* 4, no. 20 (1922): 4.

37   SWO to Harriet, August 4, 1922, SWOP.

38 SWO to Harriet, September 9, 1922, SWOP.
39 *MH* 118, no. 6 (1922): 210.
40 *Orient* 9, no. 8 (1922): 70.
41 Ibid.
42 Bogosian, 135-41.
43 "On 11 August 1920, the new Kemalist government in Ankara dissolved the Courts-Martial involving 'proceedings concerning the deportations' . . . On 13 January 1921, the full Courts-Martial were abolished." Balint, 98.
44 Bogosian, 244-58.

27. The Burning of Smyrna

1   Mango, 339-43, 347.
2   Extract from *Christian Science Monitor*, June 9, 1922, quoted in Oeconomos, 46.
3   Mango, 343.
4   Ibid.
5   Eleftherios Stavridis, Behind the Scenes of the KKE (Athens, 1953), 87, quoted in Llewellyn Smith, 297.
6   Dora Sakayan, *An Armenian Doctor in Turkey: Garabed Hatcherian, "My Smyrna Ordeal of 1922"* (Montreal: Arod Books, 1997), 2.
7   George Horton, *The Blight Of Asia* (Indianapolis: Bobbs-Merrill Company, 1926), 100-5.
8   Oeconomos, 6.
9   Non-Muslims were 37% Greek, 6% Armenian, 6% Jewish, and 10% Levantine. Horton claims 400,000 (Horton, 101-2), whereas Kırlı cites an 1890 census of 229,615: Biray Kolluoğlu Kırlı, "Forgetting the Smyrna Fire," *History Workshop Journal* 60 (Autumn 2005): 25.
10 Leyla Neyzi, "Remembering Smyrna/Izmir: Shared History, Shared Trauma," *History and Memory* 20, no. 2 (Fall/Winter 2008): 120-21.
11 Kırlı, 25.
12 Ibid, 42.
13 Alexander MacLachlan, "A Potpourri of Sidelights and Shadows from Turkey" (manuscript, uploaded to Google Drive by Robert Ashe, a descendant of the Blackler family, 1938), 2.
14 Llewellyn Smith, 299-300.
15 Ibid, 296.
16 MacLachlan, 2-3.
17 Sakayan, 3.
18 *LLW* 52, no. 11 (1922): 383.
19 Sakayan, 3-4.
20 Grace Williamson, "Smyrna, English Nursing Home, 1922," *Levantine Heritage Foundation*. Accessed at levantineheritage.com/note13.htm.
21 MacLachlan, 2.

22 Sakayan, 4.

23 Williamson.

24 This date is estimated; Horton had returned to Smyrna shortly after September 1. Horton, 124.

25 Ibid, 141.

26 Llewellyn Smith, 300.

27 Williamson.

28 Sakayan, 4.

29 Ibid, 5.

30 Williamson.

31 Horton, 125.

32 Robert Shenk, "Decisions at Smyrna" (speech, 91st Anniversary of the Smyrna Catastrophe, American Hellenic Institute, 2013).

33 Horton, 122.

34 Williamson.

35 MacLachlan, 4.

36 Ibid; Horton, 123; Sakayan, 6.

37 Williamson.

38 Sakayan, 6.

39 MacLachlan, 3, 7.

40 *LLW* 52, no. 11 (1922): 381-82; *MH* 118, no. 11 (1922): 428.

41 Llewellyn Smith, 298.

42 Williamson.

43 MacLachlan, 4-5.

44 Horton, 126; Llewellyn Smith, 305; MacLachlan, 5.

45 Horton, 127.

46 MacLachlan, 6.

47 Mango, 538, 558.

48 Ibid, 345; Llewellyn Smith, 307-8.

49 Horton stated that "tales vary as to the manner of Chrysostom's death," and that he was stabbed to death (Horton, 136). Others claim he was lynched (Mango, 345) or shot (Llewellyn Smith, 308). All agree on the mob and mutilation prior to death.

50 Sakayan, 24-37.

51 Horton, 137-39; MacLaughlin, 15-22; Shenk, *America's Black Sea Fleet*.

52 "Armenians, Not Turks Set Smyrna Ablaze Relief Worker Declares," *San Antonio Express*, January 22, 1923. The fire chief's name has been spelled Grescovish, Groenovish, and Gerscovich.

53 "Armenians, Not Turks Set Smyrna Ablaze".

54 Horton, 145; "Turks Set Fire, Missionary Says," *The New York Times*, September 29, 1922.

55 Horton, 145, 147; Anna Harlow Birge, ABH-PR.

56 "Armenians, Not Turks Set Smyrna Ablaze."

57 Ibid.

58 *LLW* 52, no. 11 (1922): 382.

59 Williamson.

60 *MH* 118, no. 11 (1922): 426; *LLW* 52, no. 11 (1922): 381.

61 Ibid, no. 12: 421-22. Though there was no official record of a Japanese ship, its presence was noted by several eyewitnesses: Stavros T. Stavridis, "The Japanese at Smyrna: September 1922," *The AHIF Policy Journal* (Spring 2016): 2.

62 Falih Rifki Atay, *Cankaya: Ataturk'un Dogumundan Olumune Kadar* (Istanbul, 1969), 323, quoted in Kırlı, 38-9.

63 Shenk, *America's Black Sea Fleet.*

64 Ibid; Emily McCallum, ABH-PR.

65 *Daily Mail* dispatch, 16 September 16, 1922, quoted in Oeconomos, 70-1.

66 Shenk, "Decisions at Smyrna".

67 MacLaughlin, 123.

68 Shenk, "Decisions at Smyrna".

69 MacLaughlin, 123.

70 Sakayan, 43-45.

71 Fromkin, 553.

72 Sakayan, 49.

73 SWO to Friends, October 28, 1923, SWOP.

74 Atay, *Cankaya*, 324-25, quoted in Kırlı, 39.

75 Kırlı, 27.

28. The Expulsion

1   Fromkin, 548-51.

2   Mango, 356.

3   *Orient* 9, no. 10 (October 1922): 91.

4   *MH* 118, no. 12 (1922): 518-19.

5   Ibid, no. 11: 424-25.

6   Ibid, no. 10: 379-80.

7   Carl Compton, ABH-PR.

8   *LLW* 52, no. 11 (1922): 386-87.

9   *MH* 118, no. 12 (1922): 479.

10 SWO to brother John and Anna, February 15, 1923, SWOP.

11 SWO to Friends, October 28, 1923, SWOP.

12 *The Near East: A Discussion Course for Students (New York: Student Volunteer Movement, 1923),* 22-3.

13 The Talas unit received notification on November 7, though the "invitation" was issued nationwide on November 14. *MH* 118, no. 12 (1922): 477-78.

14 Gözel Durmaz, 197; SWO to Friends, October 28, 1923, SWOP.

15 Joseph W. Beach to SWO, November 7, 1922, SWOP.

16 SWO to brother John and Anna, February 15, 1923, SWOP.

17   Beach to SWO, November 7, 1922. Joseph referred to "Mr. Nielson", but his name was Rev. Paul E. Nilson. *Orient* 9, no. 12 (1922): 112.
18   SWO 1922 clipping.
19   SWO to Friends, December 21, 1922, SWOP.
20   Susan only mentioned Dervish occasionally, but it was inconceivable she would travel alone under the dangerous conditions. SWO to NER, January 14, 1923, SWOP; SWO to Friends, December 21, 1923, SWOP.
21   *Near East: Discussion Course*, 17.
22   SWO 1922 clipping.
23   Ibid; *Near East: Discussion Course*, 17.
24   This story was reported by SWO in four different sources, citing four different dates, between November 19 and December 13. I have chosen the day of Thanksgiving, which Susan recorded in a letter to her friends: SWO to Friends, October 28, 1923, SWOP.
25   Susan kept the original permission order. It was written in Old Turkish, and kindly translated for the author by András Riedlmayer into present-day Turkish, which was translated into English by Armen Melkonyan. It reads: To the Supreme Part of the Battalion Commandership of Incesu of Kayseri Province: Accompanied by gendarmes, a group of 750 people was moving from the Nighde province to neighbouring Andaval and Misli Han. An American gentleman [gentlewoman?], who was on his way back from Nighde, noticed two miserable Christian children. He took them with him and, arriving at the police station, he could handily release those two wretched children from gendarmes and continued their way to reach to the other group. Healing and wounding the needy people, the American gentleman cares about them, and begins to deal with the needs of another big group. Waiting for your orders and instructions." SWOP.
26   Susan later found out the innkeeper had pocketed the money without feeding the women. SWO, January 14, 1923.
27   Ibid; SWO to Friends, October 28, 1923, SWOP; "Miss Orvis is the Heroine of the Near East," unnamed newspaper clipping, June 12, 1923, SWOP; *Near East: A Discussion*, 17.
28   SWO to Friends, October 28, 1923, SWOP.

29. The Exodus

1   SWO, January 14, 1923.
2   *Orient* 9, no. 11 (1922): 103.
3   *NER Discussion*, 16.
4   Dickran, 6-7.
5   Babkenian, "SOS", 264.
6   Mango, 356.
7   Ibid, 364.
8   *Orient* 9, no. 12 (1922): 111.

9   Mango, 365; *Who Do You Think You Are? Boris Johnson.*
10 *Orient* 9, no. 12 (1922): 111.
11 SWO to sister Harriet, February 18, 1923, SWOP.
12 SWO, "They Are Being Punished!" *The Near East Relief* (February 1923): 19. Courtesy Near East Relief Historical Society, Near East Foundation Collection, Rockefeller Archive Center.
13 SWO, February 18, 1923.
14 *Orient* 9, no. 12 (1922): 112.
15 I could find no reason why Elsey Bristol did not sign the resolution because she was still there at that time. Resolutions of Talas Station, December 15, 1922, SWOP.
16 SWO to Friends, December 21, 1923, SWOP.
17 Ibid.
18 Ibid.

30. The Cost

1   Clara Richmond to Stella Loughridge, March 28, 1923, SWOP.
2   Ibid.
3   Elsey Bristol to Katherine Fletcher, February 6, 1923, SWOP.
4   Richmond to Loughridge, March 28, 1923.
5   *NER Discussion*, 22-3;
6   Clara Richmond to Stella Loughridge, March 28, 1923, SWOP.
7   Ibid.
8   Kamsler, Southworth and Meverden, 2.
9   Zürcher, *Turkey*, 163.
10 There is no accurate total, though most estimates are no less than 3 million. A 1924 census showed nearly 100,000 Christians living in Stamboul alone, a suburb of Constantinople. Raoul Blanchard, "The Exchange of Populations between Greece and Turkey," *Geographical Review* 15, no. 13 (1925): 450, 455. Other estimates were 65,000 Armenians and 120,000 Greeks: Zürcher, *Turkey*, 164.
11 Taking only their portable possessions, 50,000 from Cilicia, 85,000 from the Angora area, 31,000 from the north, 18,500 from the Thrace region, and 35,000 from Constantinople arrived in Greece. Ibid, 452.
12 Ibid, 453-56.
13 Neyzi, 108.
14 A newspaper clipping stated Susan arrived on the 10th: "The Near East Heroine," —*S Journal*, February 10, 1923, SWOP. A letter to her sister referred to her arriving on the 11th: SWO to sister Harriet, February 12, 1923, SWOP.
15 Ibid.
16 Ibid.
17 SWO to brother John, February 15, 1923, SWOP.

18 SWO to John and Anna, February 15, 1923, SWOP.

19 Theda B. Phelps to Adelaide Dwight and SWO, February 11, 1923, SWOP.

20 SWO to Ernest Riggs, May 11, 1923, SWOP.

21 SWO to Sister Harriet, February 18, 1923, SWOP.

22 Mango, 559-61.

23 Ibid, 498.

24 Ibid, 560.

25 Some of the names, such as Izmir, were already in common usage by Turks.

26 Mango, 533-34.

27 David McDowall, *A Modern History of the Kurds*, 3rd ed. (London: I. B. Tauris, 2007), 184-213.

28 Neyzi, 117.

29 Kırlı, 34-5.

30 Balint, 98-9.

31 Mango, 560.

32 Kırlı, 33; Neyzi, 118.

33 Büşra Ersanlı Behar, *Iktidar ve Tarih: Türkiye'de Resmi Tarih Tezinin Oluşumu, 1929–1937* (Istanbul: Iletişim Yayınları, 2003), quoted in Neyzi, 108.

34 Erik J. Zürcher, *Young Turk Legacy*, 121.

35 Taner Akçam, "Turkey and the Armenian Ghost," *Armenian Weekly* (December 15, 2012). Accessed at armenianweekly.com.

36 Rolf Hosfeld, "The Armenian Massacre and Its Avengers," *IP Journal,* Transatlantic Edition, (Fall 2005): 60.

37 Kırlı, 35.

38 Balint, 79.

39 Akçam, "Turkey and the Armenian Ghost."

40 Elsey Bristol to Katherine Fletcher, February 6, 1923, SWOP.

41 From each person's record: ABH-PR.

42 Ibid.

43 *MH* 114, no. 6 (1918): 277.

44 SWO to Sister Harriet, November 23, 1919, SWOP.

Selected Bibliography

Periodicals and Series

More than 500 citations were used from 1,540 issues and records from the following:

The Acorne. American Committee for Armenian and Syrian Relief, 1919-1920. American Research Institute in Turkey and SALT Research, Records of the American Board of Commissioners for Foreign Missions, affiliates, and successor organizations.

Annual Reports. American Board of Commissioners for Foreign Missions, Boston, 1902-1922.

Life and Light for Woman. Woman's Board of Missions, Boston, 1902-1920.

Mission Studies. Woman's Board of Missions of the Interior of the Congregational Church, Chicago, 1902-1918.

Missionary Herald. American Board of Commissioners for Foreign Missions, Boston, 1904-1922.

Near East Relief. Near East Relief, Constantinople, 1920-1922. American Research Institute in Turkey and SALT Research, Records of the American Board of Commissioners for Foreign Missions, affiliates, and successor organizations.

The New Near East. Near East Relief, New York, 1921-1922.

News Bulletin. American Committee for Armenian and Syrian Relief, New York, 1916-1919.

The Orient. Bible House, Constantinople, 1912-1923. American Board of Commissioners for Foreign Missions. American Research Institute in Turkey, Digital Library for International Research Archive. Accessed at dlir.org/arit-periodical-collection.

Personnel Records of the American Board of Commissioners for Foreign Missions. Amerikan Bord Heyeti (American Board), Istanbul, American Research Institute in Turkey, Istanbul Center Library, online in Digital Library for International Research Archive. Accessed at http://www.dlir.org/archive.

Articles

Akçam, Taner. "Review Essay: Guenter Lewy's The Armenian Massacres in Ottoman Turkey." *Genocide Studies and Prevention* 3, no. 1 (April 2008): 111–145.

Andrews, Arthur I. "Current Notes: Errors in the Ordinary Versions of the Treaty of Brest-Litovsk." *The American Journal of International Law* 13, no. 2 (April 1919): 313-317.

Avedian, Vahagn. "The Armenian Genocide of 1915 from a Neutral Small State's Perspective: Sweden." *Genocide Studies and Prevention* 5, no. 3 (2010): 323-340.

Babkenian, Vicken. "An S.O.S. from Beyond Gallipoli: Victoria and the Armenian Relief Movement." *Victorian Historical Journal* 81, no. 2 (November 2010): 250-76.

Babkenian, Vicken. "Stories of International 'Goodness' During the Armenian Genocide." *Genocide Prevention Now* (Fall 2012): 1-11.

Bartlotti, Len. "A Call for a Mission Renewal Movement." *International Journal of Frontier Missions* 1, no. 1 (1984): 37-56.

Bjørnlund, Matthias. "Recording Death and Survival: Karen Marie Petersen, a Missionary Witness to Genocide." *Haigazian Armenological Review* (Beirut) 32 (2012): 321-340.

Blanchard, Raoul. "The Exchange of Populations between Greece and Turkey," *Geographical Review* 15, no. 13 (1925): 449-456.

Chater, Melville. "The Land of the Stalking Death." *The National Geographic Magazine* 36, no. 5 (1919): 393-419.

Chubb, Edwin W. "Across The Divide." *Ohio University Bulletin* 16, no. 10 (1920): 5-6.

Grenier, Eric. "Catch Me If You Can: How a Crafty German Admiral Led the Royal Navy on a Wild Chase Across the Mediterranean and Changed the Balance of Power in the First World War." In *MHQ: The Quarterly Journal of Military History* 24, no. 3 (2012): 84-91.

Hosfeld, Rolf. "The Armenian Massacre and Its Avengers." *IP Journal,* Transatlantic Edition, (Fall 2005): 57-61.

Kayalı, Hasan. "Elections and the Electoral Process in the Ottoman Empire, 1876-1919." *International Journal of Middle East Studies* 27, no. 3 (1995): 265-286.

Kéchichian, Joseph A. "How the Armenian Genocide Forced a Loyal Ottoman Officer to Espouse the Arab Revolt." *Contemporary Review of the Middle East* 1, no. 4 (December 2014): 371-89.

Kırlı, Biray Kolluoğlu. "Forgetting the Smyrna Fire." *History Workshop Journal* 60 (Autumn 2005): 25-44.

"The Lesser Belligerents," *Current History: A Monthly Magazine of The New York Times* 9, pt. 2 (January - March 1919): 417-424.

"Marsovan Girls Rescued: A Thrilling Story of American Pluck," *Carleton College Alumni Magazine* 6, no. 4 (1916): 143-45.

Neyzi, Leyla. "Remembering Smyrna/Izmir: Shared History, Shared Trauma." *History and Memory* 20, no. 2 (Fall/Winter 2008): 106-127.

Payaslian, Simon. "The Destruction of the Armenian Church during the Genocide." *Genocide Studies and Prevention: An International Journal* 1, no. 2 (2006): 149-171.

Pearson, A. H. "Dr. A.G. Sivaslian and the Turkish Mission." Carleton College. *Voice* 6, no. 4 (1916): 139-43.

"The Prinkipo Conference Plan," *Current History: A Monthly Magazine of The New York Times* 9, pt. 2 (January - March 1919): 407-410.

Shirinian, George N. "The 'Great Catastrophe:' The Genocide of the Greeks of Asia Minor, Pontos, and Eastern Thrace, 1912–1923." *Genocide Prevention Now* (Special, 2012): 1-24.

Smith, Mabell S.C., ed. "Veterans' Number: Tribute and an Appeal." *Team Work* 3, no. 6 (1924): 1-38.

Stavridis, Stavros T. "The Japanese at Smyrna: September 1922." *The AHIF Policy Journal* (Spring 2016): 1-5.

Stein, Robert. "Armenia Must Have a European Governor." *The Arena* 12 (1895): 368-90.

Stoklosa, Anna. "Chasing The Bear: William James On Sensations, Emotions And Instincts." *William James Studies* 9 (2012): 72-93.

Swanson, Glen W. "Enver Pasha: The Formative Years." *Middle Eastern Studies* 16, no. 3 (1980): 193-199.

Travis, Hannibal. "'Native Christians Massacred': The Ottoman Genocide of the Assyrians during World War I." *Genocide Studies and Prevention* 1, no. 3 (2006): 327-371.

Travis, Hannibal. "On the Centenary of the Greek Genocide." *AHIF Policy Journal* 8 (Spring 2017): 1-14.

"Turkey's Surrender to the Allies," *Current History: A Monthly Magazine of The New York Times* 9, pt. 1 (October - December 1918): 399-404.

Trumpener, Ulrich. "The Escape of the Goeben and Breslaus: A Reassessment." *Canadian Journal of History* 6, no. 2 (1971): 171-87.

Yücel, İdris. "An Overview of Religious Medicine in the Near East: Mission Hospitals of the American Board in Asia Minor (1880-1923)." *Journal for the Study of Religions and Ideologies* 14, no. 40 (2015): 47-71.

Papers and Manuscripts

Adjemian, Aram. "Canada's Moral Mandate for Armenia: Sparking Humanitarian and Political Interest, 1880-1923." Master's thesis, Concordia University, 2007.

Çetinkaya, Y. Doğan. "Muslim Merchants and Working-Class in Action: Nationalism, Social Mobilization and Boycott Movement in the Ottoman Empire 1908-1914." Doctoral thesis, Leiden University, 2010.

Gözel Durmaz, Oya. "A City Transformed: War, Demographic Change and Profiteering in Kayseri (1915-1920)." Doctoral thesis, Middle East Technical University, 2014.

Hesemann, Michael. "Pius XII and the Second World War: Assumption and New Archival Evidence." Paper, International Conference at Universitá degli Studi Guglielmo Marconi, Rome, October 2, 2014.

Hovannisian, Richard G. "Caucasian Armenia between Imperial and Soviet Rule: The Interlude of National Independence." Paper, Conference on "Nationalism And Social Change in Transcaucasia," Co-sponsored by Kennan Institute for Advanced Russian Studies, The Wilson Center and American Association for the Advancement of Slavic Studies, April 24-25, 1980.

Irwin, Genevieve. "Diary." Manuscript, Armenian Library and Museum, Watertown, MA, 1915-1917.

Irwin, Herbert M. "Private Journal." Manuscript, Armenian Library and Museum, Watertown, MA, 1903-1916.

Jenkins, Mary A. "To Megali Idea—Dead or Alive?: The Domestic Determinants of Greek Foreign Policy." Master's Thesis, Naval Postgraduate School, Monterey, CA, 1994.

MacLachlan, Alexander. "A Potpourri of Sidelights and Shadows from Turkey." Manuscript, uploaded to Google Drive by Robert Ashe, a descendant of the Blackler family, 1938.

Orvis, Susan Wealthy. Papers: reproductions of letters and travel documents in author's possession from a private collection, 1901-1930.

Panken, Jaffa. "'Lest They Perish': The Armenian Genocide and the Making of Modern Humanitarian Media in the U.S., 1915-1925." Doctoral dissertation, Paper 1396, University of Pennsylvania, 2014.

Polk, Jennifer Ann. "Constructive Efforts: The American Red Cross and YMCA in Revolutionary and Civil War Russia, 1917-24." Doctoral thesis, University of Toronto, 2012.

Ravindranathan, Tachat Ramavarma. "The Young Turk Revolution, July 1908 to April 1909: Its Immediate Effects." Master's thesis, Simon Fraser University, 1970.

Stoddard, Philip Hendrick. "The Ottoman Government and the Arabs, 1911 to 1918: A Preliminary Study of the Teşkilât-i Mahsusa." Doctoral dissertation, Princeton University, 1963.

Williams, Maynard Owen. "American Relief Committee Returns." Maynard Owen Williams Collection, RG 77/1, Box 14, Folder 2. Kalamazoo College Archives, Kalamazoo College, Kalamazoo, Michigan.

Williams, Maynard Owen. "The Fighting Czechs." Maynard Owen Williams Collection, RG 77/1, Box 14, Folder 4. Kalamazoo College Archives, Kalamazoo College, Kalamazoo, Michigan.

Williams, Maynard Owen. "A Forced Retreat." Maynard Owen Williams Collection, RG 77/1, Box 14, Folder 2. Kalamazoo College Archives, Kalamazoo College, Kalamazoo, Michigan.

Yonan, Gabriele. "Lest We Perish: A Forgotten Holocaust, The Extermination of the Christian Assyrians in Turkey and Persia." Manuscript, 1996.

Books

Aharonean, Gerasim, ed. *1915-1965 Memory Book about the Great Tragedy-Massacre* [Hooshamadian To Mets Yeghern]. Beirut: Zartonk/Atlas, 1965.

Akçam, Taner. *A Shameful Act: The Armenian Genocide and the Question of Turkish Responsibility*. Translated by Paul Bessemer. New York: Henry Holt, 2006.

Akçam, Taner. *The Young Turks' Crime against Humanity*. Princeton, NJ: Princeton University Press, 2012.

Babkenian, Vicken, and Peter Stanley. *Armenia, Australia and the Great War*. Sydney: NewSouth Publishing, 2016.

Balakian, Grigoris. *Armenian Golgotha*. Translated by Peter Balakian. New York: Alfred A. Knopf, 2009.

Balakian, Peter. *The Burning Tigris: The Armenian Genocide and America's Response*. New York: HarperCollins, 2003.

Barton, James L. *Daybreak in Turkey*, 2nd ed. Boston: Pilgrim Press, 1908.

Barton, James L. *Educational Missions*. New York: Student Volunteer Movement for Foreign Missions, 1913.

Barton, James L. *Story of Near East Relief (1915-1930): An Interpretation*. New York: Macmillan, 1930.

Birdal, Murat. *The Political Economy of Ottoman Public Debt: Insolvency and European Financial Control in the Late Nineteenth Century*. London: Tauris Academic Studies, 2010.

Bogosian, Eric. *Operation Nemesis: The Assassination Plot that Avenged the Armenian Genocide*. New York: Little, Brown and Company, 2015.

Bone, James. *The Curse of Beauty: The Scandalous and Tragic Life of Audrey Munson, America's First Supermodel*. New York: Regan Arts, 2016.

Bryant, Louise. *Mirrors of Moscow*. New York: T. Seltzer, 1923.

Butler, Edward A. *Our Household Insects: An Account of the Insect-Pests Found in Dwelling-houses*. London: Longmans, Green and Co., 1893.

Childs, W.J. *Across Asia Minor on Foot*. Edinburgh: William Blackwood and Sons, 1917.

Churchill, Winston S. *The World Crisis Volume I*. New York: Charles Scribner's & Sons, 1923.

Churchill, Winston S. *The World Crisis Volume IV 1918-1928: The Aftermath*. New York: Charles Scribner's & Sons, 1929.

Cleveland, William. *A History of the Modern Middle East*. Boulder: Westview Press, 2004.

Congregational Churches in Massachusetts, Cambridge Synod, *The Cambridge Platform of Church Discipline: 1648*. Boston: Perkins & Whipple, 1850.

Correspondence Respecting Events Leading to the Rupture of Relations with Turkey (Cd. 7628, Misc. no. 13), London: His Majesty's Stationery Office, 1914.

Dadrian, Vahakn N. *The History of the Armenian Genocide.* 4th rev. ed. New York: Berghahn Books, 2004.

Dennis, James S. *Christian Missions and Social Progress.* New York: Fleming H. Revell Company, 1906.

Deringil, Selim. *Conversion and Apostasy in the Late Ottoman Empire.* Cambridge, UK: Cambridge University Press, 2012.

Dwight, Henry Otis. *Constantinople and Its Problems.* London: Oliphant, Anderson & Ferrier, 1901.

Einstein, Lewis. *Inside Constantinople: A Diplomatist's Diary During the Dardanelles Expedition, April–September 1915.* New York: E.P. Dutton & Company, 1918.

Elliott, Mabel E. *Beginning Again at Ararat.* New York: Fleming H. Revell, 1924.

Fensham, Florence A., Mary I. Lyman and Mrs. H. B. Humphrey. *A Modern Crusade in the Turkish Empire.* Chicago: Woman's Board of Missions of the Interior, 1908.

Fic, Victor M. *The Bolsheviks and the Czechoslovak Legion.* New Delhi: Abhinav, 1947.

Figes, Orlando. *A People's Tragedy: The Russian Revolution 1891-1924.* London: Jonathan Cape, 1996.

Fitzpatrick, Sheila. *The Russian Revolution.* New York: Oxford University Press, 2008.

Fromkin, David. *A Peace to End All Peace: Creating the Modern Middle East.* New York: Henry Holt, 1989.

Gaunt, David. *Massacres, Resistance, Protectors Muslim: Christian Relations in Eastern Anatolia during World War I.* Piscataway, NJ: Gorgias Press, 2006.

Goldschmidt, Jr. Arthur, and Robert Johnson. *Historical Dictionary of Egypt.* 3rd ed. Lanham, MD: Scarecrow Press, 2003.

Grabill, Joseph L. *Protestant Diplomacy and the Near East: Missionary Influence on American Policy, 1810-1927.* Minneapolis: University of Minnesota Press, 1971.

Grant, Jonathan A. *Rulers, Guns, and Money: The Global Arms Trade in the Age of Imperialism.* Cambridge, MA: Harvard University Press, 2007.

Hakobyan, T. Kh., St. T. Melik-Bakhshyan and H. Kh. Barseghyan. *Vocabulary of Locations in Armenia and its Surroundings,* 2nd D-K [Hayastani ev harakic shrjanneri teghanunneri bararan]. Yerevan: Yerevan University Publishing House, 1988.

Gust, Wolfgang, ed. *The Armenian Genocide: Evidence from the German Foreign Office Archives, 1915-1916.* New York: Berghahn, 2014.

Hill, Patricia R. *The World Their Household: The American Woman's Foreign Mission Movement and Cultural Transformation, 1870-1920.* Ann Arbor: University of Michigan Press, 1985.

Horton, George. *The Blight Of Asia.* Indianapolis: Bobbs-Merrill Company, 1926.

Huffman, Jasper Abraham, ed. *History of the Mennonite Brethren in Christ Church.* New Carlisle, Ohio: The Bethel Publishing Company, 1920.

Ishii, Noriko Kawamura. *American Women Missionaries at Kobe College, 1873-1909.* New York: Routledge, 2004.

Jeffery, Keith. *The Secret History of MI6.* New York: Penguin Press, 2010.

Jenkins, Garth. *Political Islam in Turkey.* New York: Palgrave MacMillian, 2008.

Kalfaian, Aris. *Chomaklou: The History of Armenian Village.* Translated by Krikor Asadourian. Edited by Michael Ekizian. New York: Chomaklou Compatriotic Society, 1982.

Karsh, Efraim. *Rethinking The Middle East.* Portland, OR: Frank Cass, 2003.

Kerr, Stanley. *The Lions of Marash: Personal Experiences with American Near East Relief, 1919-1922.* Albany: State University of New York Press, 1973.

Kévorkian, Raymond. *The Armenian Genocide: A Complete History.* New York: I.B. Tauris, 2011.

Knight, E. F. *The Awakening of Turkey: A History of the Turkish Revolution.* Philadelphia: J.B. Lippincott, 1909.

Lepsius, Johannes. *Le rapport secret du Dr. Johannès Lepsius.* Paris: Payot, 1918.

Llewellyn Smith, Michael. *Ionian Vision: Greece in Asia Minor 1919-1922.* Ann Arbor, MI: University of Michigan Press, 1998.

Lovejoy, Esther Pohl. *Certain Samaritans.* New York: Macmillan Company, 1927.

MacMillan, Margaret. *History's People: Personalities and the Past.* Toronto: House of Anansi Press, 2015.

Mango, Andrew. *Atatürk: The Biography of the Founder of Modern Turkey.* Woodstock, NY: The Overlook Press, 2002.

Mardiganian, Aurora. *Ravished Armenia: The Story of Aurora Mardiganian, the Christian Girl Who Lived Through the Great Massacres.* Interpreted by H. L. Gates. New York: Kingfield Press, 1918.

McDowall, David. *A Modern History of the Kurds,* 3rd ed. London: I. B. Tauris, 2007.

Oeconomos, Lysimachos. *Martyrdom of Smyrna and Eastern Christendom.* London: George Allen & Unwin, 1922.

Milton, Giles. *Paradise Lost: Smyrna 1922.* New York: Basic Books, 2008.

Montgomery, Helen Barrett. *Western Women In Eastern Lands: An Outline Study of Fifty Years of Woman's Work in Foreign Missions.* New York: Macmillan, 1910.

Morgenthau, Henry. *Ambassador Morgenthau's Story.* Garden City, NY: Doubleday, Page & Company, 1918.

Morgenthau, Henry. *Secrets of the Bosphorus.* London: Hutchinson & Co., 1918.

Orvis, Francis Wayland. *A History of the Orvis Family in America.* Hackensack, NJ: The Orvis Company, 1922.

Otte, T. G. *July Crisis: The World's Descent into War, Summer 1914.* Cambridge: Cambridge University Press, 2014.

Payaslian, Simon. *United States Policy Toward the Armenian Question and the Armenian Genocide.* New York: Palgrave MacMillan, 2005.

Persecution of the Greeks in Turkey, 1914-1918. Constantinople: Greek Patriarchate, 1919.

Phelps Oliver S., and Andrew T. Servin. *The Phelps Family of America and their English Ancestors, Vol. II.* Pittsfield, MA: Eagle, 1899.

Preston, Andrew. *Sword of the Spirit, Shield of Faith: Religion in American War and Diplomacy.* New York: Alfred A. Knopf, 2012.

Price, Morgan Philips. *Dispatches from the Revolution: Russia 1915-1918.* Edited by Tania Rose. Durham, NC: Duke University Press, 1998.

Quataert, Donald. *Social Disintegration and Popular Resistance in the Ottoman Empire, 1881-1908: Reactions to European Economic Penetration.* New York: New York University Press, 1983.

Rasch, Gretchen. *The Storm of Life: A Missionary Marriage from Armenia to Appalachia.* London: Gomidas Institute, 2016.

Ramsay, William. *The Revolution in Constantinople and Turkey.* London: Hodder & Stoughton, 1909.

Reports on Atrocities in the Districts of Yalova and Guemlek and in the Ismid Peninsula (Cmd. 1478, Turkey No. 1), London: His Majesty's Stationery Office, 1921.

Richards, George L., ed. *The Medical Work of the Near East Relief.* New York: Near East Relief, 1923.

Sakayan, Dora. *An Armenian Doctor in Turkey: Garabed Hatcherian, "My Smyrna Ordeal of 1922".* Montreal: Arod Books, 1997.

Schreiner, George Abel, ed. *Entente Diplomacy and the World.* Translated by B. De Siebert. New York: G.P. Putnam's Sons, 1921.

Shedd, Mary Lewis. *The Measure of a Man: The Life of William Ambrose Shedd, Missionary to Persia.* New York: George H. Doran Company, 1922.

Shenk, Robert. *America's Black Sea Fleet: The U.S. Navy Amidst War and Revolution, 1919-1923.* ebook ed. Annapolis, MD: Naval Institute Press, 2012.

Slide, Anthony, ed. *Ravished Armenia and the Story of Aurora Mardiganian.* Jackson, MI: University of Mississippi Press, 2014.

Tauber, Eliezer. *The Formation of Modern Iraq and Syria.* London: Routledge, 1994.

Toynbee, Arnold J. *The Western Question in Greece and Turkey.* London: Constable and Company, 1922.

Treaties of Peace 1919-1923, Vol. II. New York: Carnegie Endowment for International Peace, 1924.

Bryce, Viscount James and Arnold Toynbee, *The Treatment of Armenians in the Ottoman Empire 1915-16: Documents presented to Viscount Grey of Falloden, Secretary of State for Foreign Affairs, with a Preface by Viscount Bryce* (Cd. 8325, Misc. no. 31), London: G.P. Putnam's Sons for His Majesty's Stationery Office, 1916.

Tuchman, Barbara W. *The Guns of August.* New York: Ballatine Books, 1962, reprint 1994.

Ussher, Clarence D. and Grace H. Knapp. *An American Physician in Turkey.* Boston: Houghton Mifflin, 1917.

von Sanders, Liman. *Five Years in Turkey.* Annapolis, MD: The United States Naval Institute, 1927.

Waldo, Fullerton L. *Twilight in Armenia.* New York: Near East Relief, 1920.

Walker, Christopher J. "World War I and the Armenian Genocide." In *The Armenian People from Ancient to Modern Times, Volume II*, edited by Richard G. Hovannisian, 239-273. New York: St. Martin's Press, 1997.

Washburn, George. *Fifty Years in Constantinople and Recollections of Robert College.* Boston: Houghton Mifflin, 1909.

Wheeler-Bennett, John W. *Brest-Litovsk: The Forgotten Peace, March 1918.* London: MacMillan and Co., 1938.

Whitehorn, Alan, ed. *The Armenian Genocide: The Essential Reference Guide.* Santa Barbara, CA: ABC-CLIO, 2015.

Whittemore, Edwin Carey. *Colby College 1820-1925: An Account of Its Beginnings, Progress and Service.* Waterville, ME: Colbiana Books, 1927.

Zürcher, Erik J. *Turkey: A Modern History.* London: I.B. Tauris, 2007.

Zürcher, Erik J. *The Young Turk Legacy and Nation Building: From the Ottoman Empire to Atatürk's Turkey.* London: I.B. Tauris, 2010.

Chapters, Sections and Forewords

Adalian, Rouben Paul. "Talaat, Mehmet." In *The Armenian Genocide: The Essential Reference Guide*, edited by Alan Whitehorn, 245-46. Santa Barbara, CA: ABC-CLIO, 2015.

Ambrosius, Lloyd E. "Wilsonian Diplomacy and Armenia: The Limits of Power and Ideology." In *America and the Armenian Genocide of 1915*, edited by Jay Winter, 113-145. New York: Cambridge University Press, 2004.

Antaramian, Richard. "Van, Siege of." In *The Armenian Genocide: The Essential Reference Guide*, edited by Alan Whitehorn, 265-66. Santa Barbara, CA: ABC-CLIO, 2015.

Balint, Jennifer. "The Ottoman State Special Military Tribunal for the Genocide of the Armenians: 'Doing Government Business'." In *The Hidden Histories of War Crimes Trials*, edited by Kevin Heller and Gerry Simpson, 77-100. Oxford: Oxford University Press, 2013.

Bovenkerk, Frank, and Yücel Yeşilgöz. "The Turkish Mafia and the State." In *Organized Crime in Europe: Concepts, Patterns and Control Policies in the European Union and Beyond*, edited by Cyrille Fijnaut and Letizia Paoli, 585-601. Dordrecht, The Netherlands: Springer, 2004.

Egoyan, Atom. Foreword to *Ravished Armenia and the Story of Aurora Mardiganian*, edited by Anthony Slide, i-xii. Jackson, MI: University of Mississippi Press, 2014.

Georgelin, Hervé. "Armenians in Late Ottoman Rural Kesaria/Kayseri." In *Armenian Kesaria/Kayseri and Cappadocia*, edited by Richard G. Hovannisian, 231-64. Costa Mesa, CA: Mazda Publishers, 2013.

Hamilton, Keith. "Chocolate for Zedzed: Basil Zaharoff and the Secret Diplomacy of the Great War." In *The Records of the Permanent Under-Secretary's Department: Liaison Between the Foreign Office and British Secret Intelligence, 1873-1939*. London: Foreign and Commonwealth Office, 2005.

Hamilton, Keith. "Dockside Diplomacy: The Foreign Office and the Constantinople Quays Company." In *The Records of the Permanent Under-Secretary's Department: Liaison Between the Foreign Office and British Secret Intelligence, 1873-1939*. London: Foreign and Commonwealth Office, 2005.

Kaerner, Martin. "Pioneers of the Project Business: The Siemens Brothers and the Indo-European Telegraph Line." In *Experiencing Project Management*, edited by Elisabeth Bittner and Walter Gregorc, 193-208. Erlangen, Germany: Publicis Publishing, 2010.

Loughridge, Stella. "Facts in Regard to Armenian Atrocities in the Cesarea District, Asia Minor." In *Turkish Atrocities: Statements of Armenian Missionaries on the Destruction of Christian Communities in Ottoman Turkey, 1915-1917*, compiled by James L. Barton, edited by Ara Sarafian, 115-17. Ann Arbor: Gomidas Institute, 1998.

MacCallum, Frederick W. "Constantinople and Caucasus." In *Turkish Atrocities: Statements of Armenian Missionaries on the Destruction of Christian Communities in Ottoman Turkey, 1915-1917*, compiled by James L. Barton, edited by Ara Sarafian, 175-78. Ann Arbor: Gomidas Institute, 1998.

Payaslian, Simon. "The Fateful Years: Kesaria during the Genocide." In *Armenian Kesaria/Kayseri and Cappadocia*, edited by Richard G. Hovannisian, 283-312. Costa Mesa, CA: Mazda Publishers, 2013.

Phelps, Theda B. "Story of Talas 1914-17." In *Turkish Atrocities: Statements of Armenian Missionaries on the Destruction of Christian Communities in Ottoman Turkey, 1915-1917*, compiled by James L. Barton, edited by Ara Sarafian, 130-42. Ann Arbor: Gomidas Institute, 1998.

Richmond, Clara Childs. "Cesarea and Talas." In *Turkish Atrocities: Statements of Armenian Missionaries on the Destruction of Christian Communities in Ottoman Turkey, 1915-1917*, compiled by James L. Barton, edited by Ara Sarafian, 119-28. Ann Arbor: Gomidas Institute, 1998.

"Trans-Siberian Railway." In *The American Educator*, edited by Ellsworth D. Foster, 3608-3609. Chicago: Ralph Durham Company, 1921.

Üngör, Uğur Ümit. "Paramilitary Violence in the Collapsing Ottoman Empire." In *War in Peace: Paramilitary Violence in Europe after the Great War*, edited by Robert Gerwarth and John Horne, 164-83. Oxford: Oxford University Press, 2012.

Watson, Isabella. "Minnesota Workers in Foreign Missions." In *Congregational Work of Minnesota 1832-1920*, edited by Warren Upham, 115-47. Minneapolis: Congregational Conference of Minnesota, 1921.

Whitehorn, Alan. "Armenian Reform Agreement of 1914." In *The Armenian Genocide: The Essential Reference Guide*, edited by Alan Whitehorn, 72-73. Santa Barbara, CA: ABC-CLIO, 2015.

Online Access

Accessed April 1915 to July 2018:

Akçam, Taner. "Turkey and the Armenian Ghost." *Armenian Weekly*, December 15, 2012. Accessed at armenianweekly.com.

Amerikan Bord Heyeti (American Board), Istanbul, "Personnel Records 1890-1922.," American Research Institute in Turkey, Istanbul Center Library, Digital Library for International Research Archive. Accessed at dlir.org/archive/items.

Atlı, Altay. *Turkey in the First World War: Development of the Turkish Navy,* 2012. Accessed at http://turkeyswar.com/navy/navy.html.

Dickran, Karekin. "Maria Jacobsen and the Armenian Genocide." *Danish Peace Academy*, 2004. Accessed at fredsakademiet.dk/library/karekin.

Gerçek, Burçin. "Turkish Rescuers." *The International Raoul Wallenberg Foundation*, 2015. Accessed at raoulwallenberg.net.

Kieser, Hans-Lukas. "Minorities (Ottoman Empire/Middle East)." In *International Encyclopedia of the First World War*, edited by Ute Daniel, Peter Gatrell, Oliver Janz, Heather Jones, Jennifer Keene, Alan Kramer and Bill Nasson, 1-14. Berlin: Freie Universität Berlin, 2014. Accessed at 1914-1918-online.

Krikorian, Abraham D. and Eugene L. Taylor. "99 Years Ago Today: Who Knew What, When and How about 'The Massacres that Would Change the Meaning of Massacre'." *Armenian News Network,* October 4, 2014. Accessed at groong.org.

Krikorian, Abraham D. and Eugene L. Taylor. "Ninety-Six Years Ago Today." *Armenian News Network,* February 16, 2015. Accessed at groong.org.

Lord Mayor's Fund (Armenian Refugees), FO 96/205, Part 1, pp2-3, First World War, The National Archives of the UK. Accessed at nationalarchives.gov.uk.

McCarthy, Justin. "Muslims in Ottoman Europe: Population from 1800 to 1912." *Nationalities Papers* 28, no. 1 (2000): 29-43. Accessed at tandfonline.com.

Taylor, Eugene L. and Abraham D. Krikorian. "Notes and Queries Relevant to 'A Brief Assessment of the Ravished Armenia Marquee Poster' by Amber Karlins." *Armenian News Network,* December 20, 2010. Accessed at groong.org.

Tharoor, Ishaan. "The Balkan Wars: 100 Years Later, a History of Violence." *Time,* October 8, 2012. Accessed at world.time.com.

Williamson, Grace. "Smyrna, English Nursing Home, 1922." *Levantine Heritage Foundation.* Accessed at levantineheritage.com/note13.htm.

Wilson, Woodrow. "Proclamation 1405: Thanksgiving Day, 1917." edited by John T. Woolley and Gerhard Peters. *The American Presidency Project.* http://www.presidency.ucsb.edu.

Yonan, Gabriele. "Holy War Made in Germany: New Light on the Holocaust Against the Christian Assyrians during World War I." *Nineveh On Line,* July 2, 2000. Accessed at nineveh.com.

Pamphlets and Reports

AFIP Letter. Washington, DC: Armed Forces Institute of Pathology, 1997.

Armerican Committee for Relief in the Near East: Its History, Its Work and the Need for Support as Outlined by President Wilson and Others, 1918.

Barton, James L. *The Medical Missionary.* Boston: American Board of Commissioners for Foreign Missions, n.d.

Bell, Enoch F. *Your Doctor Abroad.* Envelope Series 18, no. 2. Boston: American Board of Commissioners for Foreign Missions, 1915.

Catalogue Number for the Sessions of 1934-1935. Morningside Heights, NY: Columbia University, 1935.

Cranitch, Mary, dir. *Who Do You Think You Are? Boris Johnson.* London: BBC, 2008. Television.

Fourth Report of the War Victims' Relief Committee of the Society of Friends, October 1916 to September 1917. London: Headley Brothers Printers, 1917.

Handbook for Missions and Missionaries of the American Board of Commissioners for Foreign Missions. Boston: Beacon Press, 1901.

Johnson, Brian. *When Men and Mountains Meet: A Brief Account of Talas American School.* Istanbul: American Research Institute in Turkey, 2018.

Kamsler, Brigette C., Kristen Leigh Southworth and Amy Meverden. Finding aid, "Near East Relief Committee Records, 1904-1950." The Burke Library Archives, Columbia University Libraries, Union Theological Seminary, New York, 2013.

Reader's Guide

Discussion Questions

1. Why would missionary work be an attractive profession to Susan, Stella, Clara, Adelaide and other women of their generation?

2. After the trauma of the deportations, massacres and subsequent religious conflicts, why would missionaries return to Turkey?

3. Genocide is defined in Article 2 of the United Nation's Convention on the Prevention and Punishment of the Crime of Genocide (1948) as "any of the following acts committed with intent to destroy, in whole or in part, a national, ethnical, racial or religious group, as such: killing members of the group; causing serious bodily or mental harm to members of the group; deliberately inflicting on the group conditions of life calculated to bring about its physical destruction in whole or in part; imposing measures intended to prevent births within the group; (and) forcibly transferring children of the group to another group." Although more than 20 countries have acknowledged that genocide occurred against Armenians in the late Ottoman Empire, and some countries acknowledge genocide against Assyrians and Greeks, the official position of the Republic of Turkey is that genocide did not occur. The United States of America has never acknowledged the genocides, though most of its individual states have. Was there genocide in Turkey in 1915-1922? What would happen if Turkey acknowledged it? Why does the USA not acknowledge it, and what would be required for the American government to do so?

4. After the Holocaust of World War II, Germany accepted responsibility for it, apologized, and over the following decades made more than €66 billion in reparation. The subject is mandatory study in German schools. Germans today do not feel responsible for the actions of their ancestors, but believe it is their responsibility to prevent a recurrence. Germany is now one of the most respected countries in the world. It has been more than 100 years since the genocides of the late Ottoman Empire. Is it possible for Turkey to reconcile with the descendants of the victims after so long? What would be required to do so?

5.   Dr. Gregory H. Stanton of Genocide Watch has defined ten non-linear stages of genocide: classification, symbolization, discrimination, dehumanization, organization, polarization, preparation, persecution, extermination, denial. At each stage, preventive measures can stop it. What examples of these stages can you cite from this book. Are there parallels with events occurring today?

6.   What were the steps that led the Ottoman Empire from the euphoria of the 1908 revolution to its inevitable demise in 1922? Could any of the steps been avoided, and if so, how?

7.   The Near East Relief and its predecessors, the American Board of Commissioners for Foreign Missions, and especially the Woman's Board of Missions were sophisticated fundraising organizations, rivalling any today. What methods did they use, which were the most successful, and why?

8.   The Dodds, Posts, and Emma Cushman left Talas for Konia in 1911 over a serious disagreement in religious perspectives. The doctors' families left Konia when the United States entered the war in 1917, but Emma stayed. During the war she became "Acting Consul of the Allies and Neutral Nations," administering relief funds to prisoners of war. In 1919 she joined Near East Relief and cared for 1,000 orphans. After the exodus of 1922 she ran an orphanage in Greece for 5,500 children. Her obituary noted that in the latter part of her life, she lost her faith. Given her strong spiritual beliefs in 1911, what kind of internal struggle might she have gone through?

9.   Many North Americans have the belief that mass atrocities or genocide "would never happen here." How valid is this attitude?

10. During the deportations and massacres of Assyrians, Armenians and Greeks at various times between 1914 and 1922, the international community did not prevent them from happening. How and at what points could they have acted differently?

11. People are reluctant to interfere in another person's family life. On the international stage, governments are reluctant to interfere in another country's sovereignty. Though there is always a hue and cry when genocide occurs, countries are slow to act to prevent it or end it. Can this be changed? If so, how?

12. The four parts of the book are entitled A Time to Plant, A Time to Mourn, A Time to Mend, and A Time to Uproot. The inspiration for the titles was a popular 1965 rendition by The Byrds of Pete Seeger's 1962 song, *Turn, Turn, Turn*, which in turn (forgive the pun) was inspired by Ecclesiastes 3:1-8. The Bible verses begin, "To everything there is a season." Is this true? Why does this cycle of human behaviour have to include war, atrocities and genocide?

13. Susan Wealthy Orvis was amazed to see the "bird men" and "flying machines" at the aerodrome in Baku, Azerbijan. Do you remember your first experience with an amazing new technology?

14. American exceptionalism is the loosely-defined belief that the United States is unique among nations because of its history, democracy, personal freedoms, and mission to transform the world, and therefore should be treated differently. What examples of this were demonstrated in the book? What do you think of this belief? Does it still exist?

15. The British managed to keep the Ottoman ships when the Great War broke out, without paying compensation. How was this possible? In war, who makes the rules? How much power does the United Nations have today?

16. There were many examples of Turks and Kurds helping Armenians, Greeks and Assyrians, but it became a dangerous activity after the order was issued that anyone caught helping them would have their house burned down, and their families and themselves killed. Although we never really know how we would react in a similar situation until we're faced with it, how do you think you would have reacted in their place?

17. The relief effort that started in 1915 and continued to the late 1920s was a massive new phenomenon. Has humanitarianism changed since then, and if so, how?

18. There were many examples in the book of the power of rumour, fake news, censorship, and political deception. In addition to the press, today we have television, radio, and social media. What are the similarities and differences between then and now, truth and lies, trust in institutions, and the path to social destruction?

19. Which part of the book did you find most unsettling, and why?

20. How do the motives and decisions of the main perpetrators of the genocides, such as Talat and Enver, compare to world leaders today? Are there any disturbing trends?

Suggestions for Further Engagement:

*   Volunteer at your local organization for immigrant or refugee settlement to understand the circumstances and decisions of these people to leave their homelands.

*   Volunteer to write letters on behalf of your country's branch of Amnesty International. Visit the website for more information on the letter-writing campaign.

*   Record the oral history of immigrants and refugees, and citizens' opinions of the national immigration policies. There is a growing recognition among historians of the important contribution of oral history to historiography.

*   Visit museums to learn more: e.g., American Indian Genocide Museum (Houston), Anne Frank House (Amsterdam), Armenian Genocide Museum (Yerevan), Auschwitz Concentration Camp (Oświęcim, Poland), Canadian Museum for Human Rights (Winnipeg), Ellis Island Immigration Museum (New York), Imperial War Museum (London), Lower East Side Tenement Museum (New York), the Matenadaran (Mesrop Mashtots Institute of Ancient Manuscripts, Yerevan), Museum of Occupations and Freedom Fights (Vilnius), Simon Wiesenthal Center (Los Angeles).

*   When you see a law or policy you disagree with, write your elected representative, and encourage or organize like-minded people to do so, too. Representatives act when enough constituents complain.

*   When you listen to or read the news, listen with a critical ear, read with a critical eye. Ask yourself who is reporting it, what kind of bias might the reporter or agency have, could there be a political agenda or propaganda attached to the story, and how truthful is it? How do you know you can trust the source to report the facts? The source may not even be human. There is a growing trend for automation ("bots" in the digital world) to manipulate data, so it is important to scrutinize the source of the information.

*   Donate to humanitarian organizations, such as the International Red Cross/Red Crescent, Doctors Without Borders/Médecins Sans Frontières, and similar "without borders" groups, such as engineers.

*   Speak up. After WWII, German Lutheran pastor Martin Niemöller wrote several versions of a poem about the Nazi purge of target groups. One version includes, "First they came for the Socialists, and I did not speak out because I was not a Socialist. Then they came for the Trade Unionists, and I did not speak out because I was not a Trade Unionist. Then they came for the Jews, and I did not speak out because I was not a Jew. Then they came for me—and there was no one left to speak for me." It's important to speak out.

Index

Royal Irish Fusiliers 116
Royal Newfoundland Regiment 116
Rugova 47
Russia 7, 9, 54, 57, 58, 63, 64, 67, 72,
74, 80, 84, 107, 109, 111, 117,
121, 131, 135, 136, 139–141,
147, 151, 156, 160, 161, 164,
165, 170, 174, 176, 179, 241,
248, 272
Ryan, Arthur C. 39, 40, 60
Ryan, Edith 40

S

Sabri Bey, Ali 78, 91, 96, 105, 112–
114
Sahabeddin, Colonel 100, 113
Saibalian Effendi 91
Said Halim Pasha 42, 62, 274
Saint Petersburg (Petrograd) 142
Salonica 9, 27, 29, 198, 199, 210, 311
Samara 142, 176–181, 183
Samimi Bey, Ahmet (editor of *Sada-yi
Millet*) 32
Samsoun 6, 195, 225, 228, 241, 246,
252, 254, 255, 259, 260, 270
San Francisco 136, 139
Sanders, Liman von 57, 78, 116, 118,
122, 134
Sarajevo 60
Saratov 179, 180
Sardinia 66, 67
Sarikamish 74, 80, 170, 248
Schaefer, Miss 249
Scutari 64, 203, 311
Sea of Marmora 30, 67
Semenoff, Grigori 183
Serbia 7, 41, 62, 132
Servet Bey, Edib 53
Servet Tor, Ahmet Nedim 53
Sewny, Levon 35, 87
Shakir, Bahaeddin 48, 71, 187, 188
Sharif Huseyn 121
Sharkushla 103

Shayb, Rose 202
Shedd, Mary 78
Shehabeddin Bey, Dr. Cemal 229
Shepard, Fred 75
Shevket Bey, Mehmet 277
Shevket Pasha, Mahmut 38, 42
Shikoku, Japan 141
Singer Sewing Machine Company 52,
112
Sinope 120
Sis 39
Sivas 6, 22, 35, 43, 47, 49, 54, 55, 73,
87–90, 92, 93, 99, 103, 106, 118,
120, 124, 129, 131, 133, 139,
195, 205, 210, 211, 221, 225,
227, 228, 242, 255, 260, 262,
267–270
Smith, Dan 186, 187
SMS *Breslau* 66
SMS *Goeben* 66, 69
Smyrna (Izmir) 32, 35, 53, 57, 58, 67,
86, 195, 201, 209–211, 223, 225,
230, 233, 242, 245, 252, 264,
275–283, 285, 286, 289, 295,
301, 306, 309, 310, 311
Society of Progress and Union 8, 9
Soma 58
Souchon, Wilhelm 57, 65, 67, 69
South Africa 62, 289
Special Organization (SO) 71, 72, 75,
79, 84, 85, 88, 95, 106, 119, 187,
194, 232, 259
SS *Acropolis* 255
SS *Critic* 67, 68, 70
SS *Leviathan* 197, 199, 211
SS *Porthos* 192
SS *Umbria* 304
Stalin, Josef 179
Standard Oil Company of New York
52
Stapleton, Elinor 87
Stapleton, Ida 87, 115
Stapleton, Robert 87, 157, 169, 172,
182, 188

Acknowledgments

There are many people to thank for their help with this book, but first and foremost is Susan Wealthy Orvis for understanding the importance of eyewitness accounts, and asking her family to save her letters and photographs. Her family passed her trunk of documents down through the generations to Julia Ann Orvis who made it available to me. I'm exceedingly grateful for Julie's trust in me to handle Susan's information however I saw fit, and for sending me some of her photographs to reproduce, including the photo on the front cover. Julie has generously donated Susan's archives to the Matenadaran, a repository of ancient and recent manuscripts in Yerevan, for future scholars to have access to them.

Kamo Mayilyan described the origins of the book in the Foreword and his "relentless insistence" that I write it, but that only hints at his driving passion to see the information made public. He helped with the early phase of research, and for three years was a sounding board for me when I was confused, saddened or elated by my discoveries. He was the first reader of this book, and will undoubtedly be its most enthusiastic promoter.

In addition to Kamo, Nancy Johnson, Linda Mitchell and Sheilagh Scanlon provided me with excellent feedback and careful proofreading. I appreciate their considerable time, honest scrutiny, and unending support more than I can possibly say.

Wendy Jacobson and Vicken Babkenian were extremely helpful in accessing for me research documents that I could not easily obtain myself, and often gave me much-needed words of guidance and encouragement.

I also want to thank Inessa Hakobanyan and Vahram Chilingaryan for their generous hospitality on my research trip to Boston and Watertown, and Isla Horvath for reminding me that I was writing the book I wanted to read. Thanks also to Rubina Arakelyan, Lilia Asatryan, Jean Christie, Aileen Csermak, Mary Hovhannisyan, Jane Johnson, Vivian Moutafian, Jean Rose and Aldeana Ryckman for being occasional but timely cheerleaders. There are more than fifteen hundred other people who have stuck by me during the past year of writing this book, through my mailing list and on Facebook and Twitter—too many to name but whose support is so appreciated.

Many thanks to the countless custodians who safeguard information and make it publicly accessible, whether in libraries or through the invaluable Internet Archives. For personal assistance I want to thank Kevin Blowers, Curator, Missionary Church Archives, Bethel College; Heather H. Georghiou, Librarian, Newburgh (NY) Free Library; Susan Gilroy, Librarian, Lamont Library, Harvard University; Heather Home, Private Records Archivist, Queen's University; Brian Johnson, Librarian, American Research Institute in Turkey; Gary Lind-Sinanian, Librarian, Armenian Library and Museum of America; and Lisa Murphy, Archivist, and Kaspar Hudak, Intern, Kalamazoo College.

A special thanks goes to Victor Ostapchuk, Near and Middle Eastern Civilizations, University of Toronto, for the introduction to bibliographer András Riedlmayer of Aga Khan Program for Islamic Architecture, Fine Arts Library, Harvard University, who kindly translated the Old Turkish text to modern Turkish, and to Armen Melkonyan for translating the modern Turkish text into English.

Jean Christie, Marcy Gerstein, Vahan Kololian, Andrea Mann, and Mark Stiles were instrumental in connecting me with the people who have endorsed this book, and I sincerely thank them for their help. I am exceedingly grateful to Terry Brown, Kumru Bilici, Atom Egoyan, George Weber and Alan Whitehorn for taking the time to read the manuscript and writing such a positive endorsement. An additional thanks goes to Alan for suggesting a few clarifying adjectives and verbs that made a significant difference in a few key paragraphs.

Finally, and by no means least, my enormous thanks to Ara Sarafian of Gomidas Institute who agreed to publish the book on the strength of an outline and two chapters. Without his commitment as publisher and meticulous efforts as editor, it would not be in your hands now.